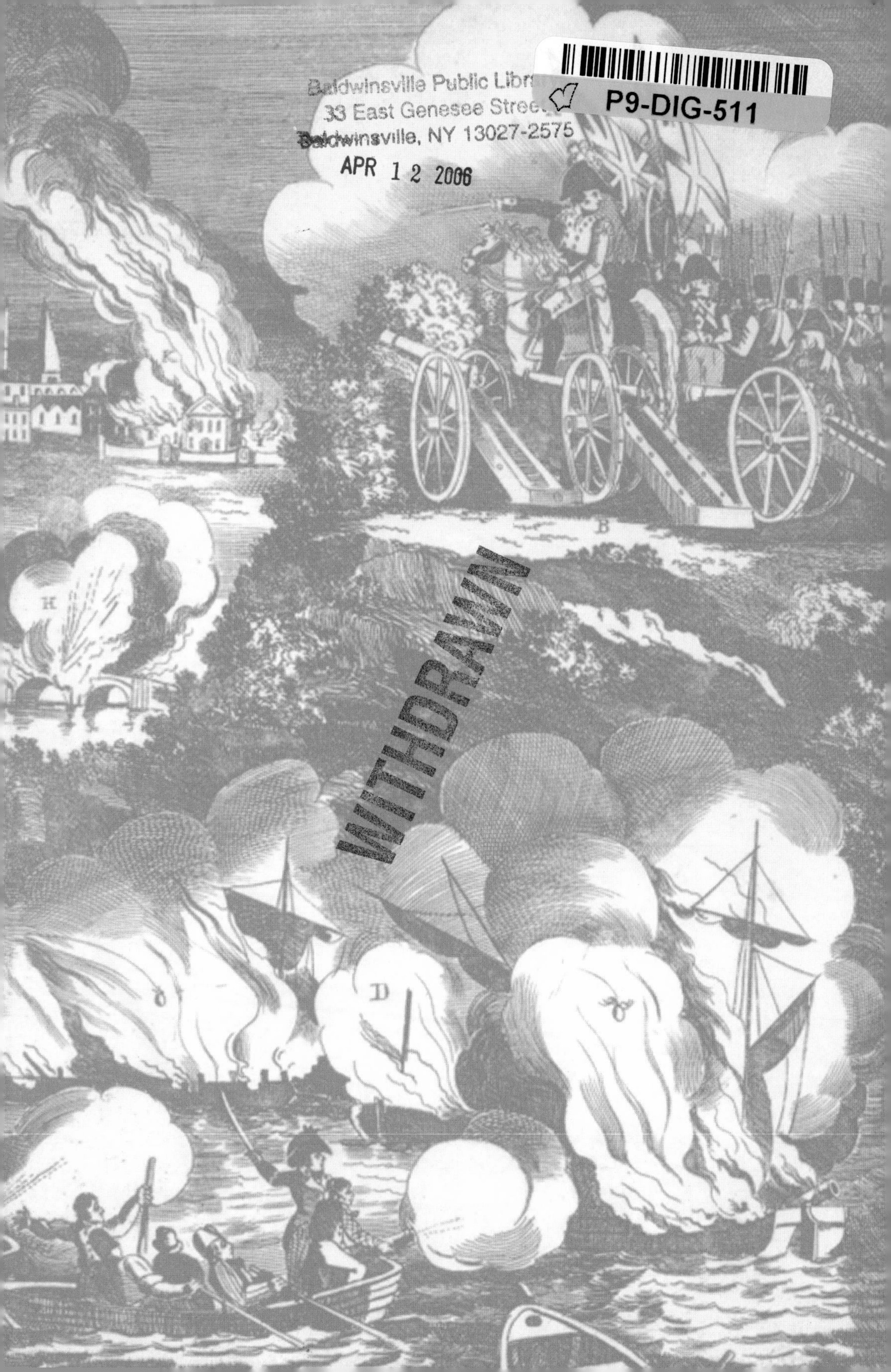
H
B
D

A
PERFECT
UNION

A
PERFECT
UNION

Dolley Madison and the Creation
of the American Nation

Catherine Allgor

Henry Holt and Company
New York

Henry Holt and Company, LLC
Publishers since 1866
175 Fifth Avenue
New York, New York 10010
www.henryholt.com

Henry Holt® and 🄷® *are registered trademarks of Henry Holt and Company, LLC.*

Part of chapter 11 previously appeared in *Establishing Congress: The Removal to Washington, D. C.,
and the Election of 1800*, ed. Kenneth R. Bowling and Donald R. Kennon (Athens: Ohio University
Press, 2005) and is used here with the kind permission of the editors.

Distributed in Canada by H. B. Fenn and Company Ltd.

Library of Congress Cataloging-in-Publication Data
Allgor, Catherine, [date]
  A perfect union : Dolley Madison and the creation of the American nation / Catherine
Allgor.—1st ed.
     p.   cm.
  Includes bibliographical references.
  ISBN-13: 978-0-8050-7327-0
  ISBN-10: 0-8050-7327-2
  1. Madison, Dolley, 1768–1849.   2. Madison, Dolley, 1768–1849—Political and social
views.   3. Presidents' spouses—United States—Biography.   4. United States—Politics and
government—1783–1865.   I. Title.

E342.1.M2A45   2006
973.5'1092—dc22
[B]   2005055127

*Henry Holt books are available for special promotions and premiums.
For details contact: Director, Special Markets.*

First Edition 2006

Designed by Meryl Sussman Levavi

Printed in the United States of America

1 3 5 7 9 10 8 6 4 2

To Gianna C. Gifford and Sarah K. Hagan,
women who made history on June 13, 2004

Contents

A Note on Names

Some readers will notice that I have not observed the convention of referring to my subject primarily by her last name. At any given point in the narrative, Dolley Madison could be a "Payne," a "Todd," or a "Madison," therefore "Dolley" is the choice for the leading lady of this story. To refer to James Madison as "Madison" replicates outdated biographical forms in which men are given the respect of last names and women are relegated to informal designations.

The final choice here is a blend of the old and the new. When a man stands alone in the text, he is referred to by his full name or his last. Likewise, a woman who appears on her own will be identified by her full name, e.g. Margaret Bayard Smith, at least at first mention. When discussing men and women in political partnerships, both will be referred to by first names; hence, the Madisons will be "James" and "Dolley." If this seems excessively familiar to modern readers, at least both women and men will suffer any diminishment equally.

A
PERFECT
UNION

Prologue

On Wednesday, August 24, 1814, Dolley Madison stood at the window of the White House and watched thousands of Washingtonians, rich and poor, white and black, pouring down Pennsylvania Avenue. News and rumors of the approach of British troops had thrown the city into confusion, and the population had been evacuating for days. Vehicles were at a premium, and any conveyance with wheels was pressed into service by the fleeing throngs. It had not rained for three weeks, and the clouds of dust raised by the people, horses, carriages, and carts lingered ominously on the horizon.[1]

With chaos at her door, Dolley sat down at her desk to continue a letter to her sister Lucy, which she had begun the previous day. "My husband left me yesterday morng to join General Winder," Dolley had written on Tuesday. "He enquired anxiously whether I had courage, or firmness to remain in the President's house until his return, on the morrow, or succeeding day, and on my assurance that I had no fear but for him and the success of our army, he left me, beseeching me to take care of myself, and of the cabinet papers, public and private."[2] James had gone to review the troops stationed in nearby Maryland, hoping to discern, if he could, the intentions of a small force of British soldiers who had landed on the banks of the Patuxent River in June. He had sent Dolley two messages, framing the confusion as comfort: "The reports as to the enemy have varied every hour. The last & probably truest information is that they are not very strong, and are without cavilry and artillery, and of course that they are not in a condition to strike at Washington." But, James had to admit, "it is possible, however they may have a greater force or expect one, than has been represented or that their timerity may be greater than their strength." His second letter was "alarming," Dolley admitted, "because he desires I should be ready at a moment's warning to enter my carriage and leave the city."[3]

By midday on Wednesday, Dolley had packed, "press[ing] as many cabinet papers into trunks as to fill one carriage; our private property must be sacrificed," but she was also determined to wait for her husband. From time to time, she went onto the roof of the executive mansion, anxiously casting her spyglass in every direction. By this point, 90 percent of the populace had fled, even the men guarding the city. The mayor of Washington, James H. Blake, came twice to plead with her to evacuate, but Dolley would not leave until James returned.[4]

This disastrous state of affairs—the capital city under threat and the president in physical jeopardy—had taken Americans by surprise. Though there certainly had been signs that the British were targeting Washington, the country had for the most part denied the danger. As recently as early August, Dolley had assured her own son that "the British on our shore's are stealing & destroying private property, rarely comeing to battle but when they do, are allways beaten," yet the truth was far less rosy. Over the course of the two-year war with Great Britain, victories on the American side had been few, and the losses significant and frustrating. American troops had repeatedly tried to invade Canada, across the Niagara frontier, from Lake Champlain toward

Montreal, and from Detroit into upper Canada. Though American forces had won two decisive battles in 1813—led by Oliver Hazard Perry at the battle of Lake Erie, and under William Henry Harrison's command at the battle of the Thames—Canada remained under British control. And despite several widely heralded victories by the American ships *Constitution* and *United States,* the powerful British navy blockaded the east coast, leaving coastal towns from the Penobscot River in Maine to the Chesapeake Bay vulnerable to hit-and-run raids. Now the papers and commanders could deny it no longer: the British had landed at Benedict, Maryland, and were heading, four thousand men strong, for the capital of the United States.[5]

Dolley feared not only marauding British soldiers but also nearer enemies. "Mr. Madison's War," as his detractors dubbed it, had divided the country, inflaming an already combustible political climate. Treachery filled the air, and on the eve of invasion Dolley had American foes in mind when she darkly hinted to her sister: "Disaffection stalks around us." Indeed, she wanted to leave the city with James as much for his safety as her own: "I hear of much hostility towards him."

Even as she was deciding whether she should wait for the president, Dolley was overseeing the preparations for that day's dinner party, supervising the table setting for forty guests, ordering the wines, ale, and cider to be brought from the cellar. This occasion was one of many she had hosted in the past months, designed to reassure government officials and local gentry alike that all was well.[6] By three o'clock, however, she received word of a devastating rout near Bladensburg, Maryland, during which the Americans turned tail and ran so quickly that the episode would come to be known as the Bladensburg Races.

Now "within sound of the cannon," Dolley "lived a lifetime," waiting for her husband to return, but "Mr. Madison comes not; may God protect him!" She was in an "agony" of fear that the British would take James prisoner. Urged on by friends, she organized herself and her slaves to leave the house. Charles Carroll, a wealthy Maryland landowner and Madison supporter "has come to hasten my departure, and is in a very bad humor with me because I insist on waiting until the large picture of Gen. Washington is secured." The full-length portrait of the beloved Washington hung in the presidential portrait gallery in the state dining room. Unfortunately, there was no time to unscrew the frame from the wall. "I have ordered the frame to be broken, and the canvass taken out," Dolley related to Lucy, "it is done." She entrusted the precious painting to "two gentlemen of New York" for safe passage.[7]

Dolley's departure could not be much longer delayed. James Smith, a free black man who had accompanied the president to Bladensburg, came galloping down the street, warning Dolley and the remaining capital residents to flee, as the American forces were in retreat. Clearly, James would not come now; if Dolley lingered any longer, she risked capture as a political prisoner or death as a casualty of war. It was time to end her missive. "And now, dear sister, I must leave this house, or the retreating army will make me a prisoner in it, by filling up the road I am directed to take. When I shall again write you, or where I shall be tomorrow, I cannot tell!!"

That day the British did indeed invade Washington City. They looted and burned only the public buildings, taking particular relish in consigning the "president's palace" to the flames. Before they did so, however, they sat down and enjoyed the elegant meal that had been set out.[8] Given the effort Dolley Madison had put into establishing her White House as the capital's social and political center, it seems fitting that a dinner party, even one attended by uninvited guests, occupied the last moments of the executive mansion.

⁂

This is how most Americans know Dolley Madison, as the heroine who saved the portrait of George Washington. In fact, next to the tale of Fort McHenry and the writing of "The Star-Spangled Banner," the story of Dolley and the White House is the only one Americans typically associate with the ill-fated War of 1812. To be sure, very few have the story right—for instance, many believe Dolley saved the Declaration of Independence. This is not true, though she did save crucial government documents. One version of the legend holds that Dolley herself cut the portrait out of its frame with a butcher knife; some later illustrations even depict

Dolley fleeing the burning White House, the canvas flapping behind her as she runs through the street.

The truth is more sobering, more complicated, and more interesting. Black hands tried to unscrew the picture, and when that failed, enslaved Americans wrestled the "Father of Liberty" out of his frame. The portrait, a copy of the famous Gilbert Stuart painting, was not even particularly valuable. But this event is remembered as pivotal for precisely the reason that Dolley intended. She knew the picture was only a copy, nonetheless, she insisted: "Save that picture! Save that picture, if possible; if not possible, destroy it."[9] She recognized that it would have been disastrous for any image of the venerated Washington to fall into British hands, to be burned with the house, or even worse, to be paraded through London streets as a prize of war. Dolley understood how fragile the country's sense of identity was. Even her famous letter to her sister stands as testament to her political savvy: producing the document decades later, she may well have edited or sharpened the text to present a more overtly patriotic account.[10]

However, Dolley Madison's fame is not restricted to this single incident—nor to the packaged pastries and ice cream that bear her (misspelled) name—and did not take hold years after her death. In an age before the modern cult of celebrity, when people nonetheless lionized the living, Dolley Madison was *famous*. During her tenure as the president's wife and for decades after, she was one of the best-known people in the United States. Travelers, diplomats, private citizens, and government officials alike raved about her charismatic charm and gracious presence, her legendary parties, and her impressive wardrobe. Even the occasional criticism centered on the excess of these qualities—she was *too* charming, *too* regal, *too* popular. In a time when no respectable woman ever had her name in the newspapers, stories about Dolley, both laudatory and slanderous, periodically appeared in the press.

After her husband's death in 1836, when she returned to Washington on her own, Washingtonians official and unofficial lined up to pay homage. The House of Representatives granted her free lifetime postal franking, a perquisite of congressmen during their terms and a privilege previously granted only to former presidents and the widow of the revered Washington. They also presented her with her own seat on the floor of the House (along with appointed escorts), an honor unprecedented for a man, let alone a woman. And when she died in 1849, at age eighty-one, Washington City honored her with a state funeral, the largest one the capital had yet seen. Along with President Zachary Taylor and his cabinet, both houses of Congress adjourned to march in the procession, escorting, one last time, the woman who had come to be known as "America's Queen."

Why was Dolley Madison so famous? In a culture that had no place for a woman in the political spotlight, and in which the only "public women" were prostitutes, Dolley was undeniably a public woman. She became a national figure when the United States was barely a nation and only men such as George Washington occupied a place in the pantheon above party politics. And, most inexplicable of all, Dolley proved herself a powerful political player in an age when women were excluded from politics. Married women had no independent legal identities; they were legally "covered" by their husbands, lacking the right to vote, make contracts, or own property, even the clothes on their backs. Dolley's fame derived from sources other than her association with James Madison; how else to explain her position as Washington City's social leader and political consultant in the years after James's death in 1836? And while one might assume her influence to be greatest during her time as the president's wife, how then to explain the many honors bestowed on her, and favors beseeched, decades after she had been the "Presidentess"? Such public attention and acknowledgments of respect are hard to reconcile with a woman who, in our time, is almost exclusively associated with Raspberry Zingers and Gem Donuts.

Dolley Payne Todd Madison was famous for precisely the same reason as her male counterparts: power. She possessed considerable political capital, which, under the veil of her culturally appointed roles of wife and hostess, she used to further her own and her family's political aims. Paradoxically, while her sex prevented her from openly playing politics, those very bonds of womanhood allowed her the scope in which she accomplished her greatest political successes—granting political favors, constructing a modern ruling style that emphasized cooperation over coercion, and achieving her husband's political aims. Within the conventional bounds of "ladyhood," Dolley legitimized her husband's administration to the nation and the world and went a long way to establishing Washington City as a capital (and to retaining it after the British burned it in 1814). Using parties, social calls, and correspondence, she built the structures of government that the new United States needed, and she presented political models of bipartisan cooperation—building bridges instead of bunkers—that would prove crucial to democratic rule. Perhaps most important, she used the persona of a lady motivated solely by feminine love and patriotism to create a sense of nationality and unity for the new Americans. In spite of a disastrous war and domestic unrest, her husband's presidency was universally acclaimed; after the smoke cleared in 1817, former president John Adams noted that, "notwithstand[ing] a thousand Faults and blunders," James Madison's administration "has acquired more glory, and established more Union, than all his three Predecessors . . . put together."[11] Other political observers, no doubt giddy with relief, concurred. Their judgment reflected the triumph of Dolley's efforts at least as much as—perhaps even more than—her husband's.

Had she lived a century earlier, Dolley would probably have passed her life in contented obscurity as a Virginia gentry woman. However, the American Revolution changed her destiny as surely as it did the country's. The challenge of the generation after the founders lay in creating a working republic. The enterprise needed not only great leaders and great thinkers but also skilled politicians able to translate revolutionary ideas and ideals into living, breathing reality. Dolley brought considerable personal gifts—including unsurpassed conciliatory skills—to the political arena.

As is true of all good politicians, the public and private sides of Dolley did not quite match up. The popular image of a sunny, gracious, serene hostess who gained fame and prominence with apparent ease obscures the real woman, a person as driven by passion for country and by demons as any founding father. She worked hard at constructing a persona that masked her darker side. Ironically, the public Dolley won the admiration of the world by seeming natural and unaffected. In cultivating this image, Dolley did indeed draw on genuine parts of herself, including her capacity to cultivate love and her authentic generosity of spirit. She had been a cheerful, charming child and a captivating young woman; these qualities she carried into adulthood and into politics. From earliest childhood, however, her character and her view of the world had been shaped by adversity and difficulties.

Like many extraordinary people, Dolley cannot entirely be explained by her origins. If leaders are born as well as made, Dolley seems to have been born a leader, full of ambition and the desire to be the center of attention and activity. But she was also born a girl, and so was taught from the first the cardinal virtues of meekness and femininity; her early life experiences only underscored her sense of helplessness. And she was raised in Quaker culture, which prized passivity and retirement from the world. Yet even as the Quakers themselves used their passivity as a catalyst for radical action, Dolley turned compliance into an art, transforming female submissiveness into a political tool. She employed conciliation to disarm and defuse a violent political culture, while winning friends and supporters for her husband. And, in repudiation of her Quaker upbringing, she did so while becoming the most famous, most visible woman in the United States.

⁂

It was no accident that Americans seized upon the image of the heroic Dolley saving the George Washington portrait as their predominant memory of the first invasion of American soil. August 1814 was a fragile moment in the country's history. In the 1780s, the former colonists, flush with their victory over what was then the world's greatest superpower, and with the ratification of a brand-new constitution, had watched with dismay as vicious partisan bickering threatened the untried political system, reaching its peak (or depth) with the first real presidential contest, the election of 1796. In the wake of a campaign filled with gossip, slander, backroom "tampering," and accusations of treachery all around, John Adams won narrowly, and the nation remained polarized.[12] From the new Americans' point of view, it boded ill that the infighting disintegrated into the establishment of two proto-parties—the Federalists, represented by John Adams, and the Republicans, led by Thomas Jefferson and James Madison. The Republicans had their revenge, however, when John Adams proved a one-term president, and the election that Jefferson would call "the revolution of 1800" swept them into power.

The establishment of a new capital in the southern wilderness, holding as much risk as promise, added to the national sense of uncertainty. The only official guide that the founders had was the untried Constitution and the discouraging history of past short-lived republics. It was one thing to plan a new order founded on liberty, quite another to realize it. To Americans and to outsiders, it was not clear at all that the republican experiment was going to last, let alone thrive.

Into this atmosphere of uncertainty entered Dolley Madison. Her unofficial status as a "Lady" of a political family allowed her to supply the informal politicking sorely needed by the official men who were trying to build a government. In an era in which overtly monarchical behavior was to be avoided at all costs, Dolley's institutionalized, ritualized social events compensated for the lack of bureaucratic and governing structures, which were deliberately neglected by the Constitution. Her person and personality—feminine, attractive, charming—fostered collaboration, and she brought together the government, the capital city, and the nation. She was quick to grasp the lessons of the political world in which she found herself, acting in ways that neither James nor any man could.

And although in many ways a conventional eighteenth-century woman, Dolley was an innovator as a politician. With her emphasis on civility, she offered Americans an alternative to older, coercive models of governing, a modern form of politics, one that would prove crucial to the developing government in ordinary times and would hold the capital city and nation together in a time of crisis. These models helped to create the first modern democracy and young nation-state; the recognition of the inevitability of bipartisanship and the need for compromise and power sharing would prove the foundation of a democratic government. Cooperation and negotiation with one's enemy may have seemed inconceivable to most of the founding men, for whom verbal and physical violence were political tools of the trade, but not to Dolley, who built coalitions and connections every week in her drawing room.

Filling the role that would come to be known as "First Lady" did not necessarily guarantee either visibility or power. Devoted wife Martha Washington approached the job doubtfully, albeit dutifully. An intellectual at heart, Abigail Adams was her husband's partner in the realm of political theory and public policy (she co-created the infamous Alien and Sedition Acts), but she was not interested in inhabiting the role of official hostess offered by her husband's elevation to the presidency. Indeed, she spent much of his term at home in Braintree, Massachusetts. In contrast, Dolley took the opportunity to transform the president's wife into a figure of national importance, expanding the role into an office. The position would remain unchanged until the twentieth century; even to the present, certain key aspects of the job that she invented still stand.[13]

When Dolley Madison died, the newspapers rightly called upon "all of our own country and thousands in other lands" to mourn her passing.[14] While she never traveled beyond the United States' borders, she was a figure of and, thanks to her diplomatic work, for the world. Dolley's life unfolded within several historically significant American landscapes, including Virginia and Philadelphia. But her proper milieu was, and always would be, the brand-new capital of the new United States, Washington City. It was her creation, her playground, the scene of her greatest triumphs and best work. Though Dolley became a politician's wife when she married James in 1794, her own political life began in 1801, when the Madison carriage turned onto Pennsylvania Avenue.

Mrs. Madison Goes
to Washington

For anyone in Washington City taking the air on that sunny spring morning of May 1, 1801, the carriage that bumped along the rutted and muddy streets of the newly minted capital made for an arresting sight: James and Dolley Madison in their elegant attire, seated alongside Dolley's sister and young son and their slaves, had arrived. The Madisons had left their family seat, Montpelier, in Orange, Virginia, nearly five days earlier. They followed the travel recommendations of a family friend, the new president of the United States, Thomas Jefferson, who had preceded them that week: the ninety-mile trip took them over roads so rough that farmers had to haul the carriage over Bull Run Hill, one of many "bad hills" calculated to give the horses "a great deal of vexation," but finally, the party was headed for the executive mansion.[1]

It had been four years since James had laid eyes on the wilderness capital; the view from the carriage revealed progress. Two white edifices on either end of Pennsylvania Avenue—the president's house and the Capitol building—dominated the scene. Newly rebuilt after a recent fire, the impressive brick treasury building and combined offices of the State and War Departments flanked the executive mansion in a cluster called the Six Buildings. (Another nearby grouping was, unimaginatively, "the Seven Buildings.") The grounds around the president's "palace," however, resembled a construction site, littered with bricks, planks, kilns, and workmen's sheds. The Capitol, which one new resident disparagingly called "a large, square, ungraceful white building," had just one wing; a stone box set on bare ground, it looked more like an ancient ruin than a new construction.[2]

It was a rough ride for the Madisons on the city's main road. "Pennsylvania Avenue" was a grand appellation for the slash of mud that proved almost impossible for any vehicle to navigate. A "tolerably good footway," made of chips and gravel, ran parallel to the thoroughfare, allowing for pedestrian traffic. James and Dolley saw no sign of the majestic avenues featured in the grandiose city plan, save for the leftover tree stumps that served as markers.[3]

James Madison was already famous for his role in the Constitutional Convention and the co-author of the 1800 electoral revolution that had brought Thomas Jefferson to the presidency. He carried these substantial achievements, however, on an insubstantial frame. Dressed in a black suit, as was his custom, James sported the style of the revolutionary generation—short breeches, buckled at the knee, with black silk stockings. He wore his powdered hair pulled back, carefully arranged to cover his ears and to disguise his incipient baldness. With blue eyes so pale that some described them as gray, James possessed a "tawny" complexion, which contemporaries attributed to a life of study. At five feet six inches tall, he was just under medium height, but he weighed only 140 pounds and so gave the appearance of a much smaller man.[4] At the sight of this frail fifty-year-old, a passerby might understandably wonder whether such an unimpressive figure was indeed the renowned James Madison.

In contrast, the woman by his side would have warranted a closer look. Approaching her thirty-third birthday, Dolley Payne Todd Madison outshone her husband in every way. The effect was not only an equation of blue eyes, curls so dark that they looked black, rosy complexion, and tall, curvaceous figure, but also an arresting combination of confidence and vulnerability that drew every eye to her. Her "engaging countenance" attracted them, "not so much from mere symmetry or complexion as from expression."[5]

The Madisons had intended to arrive months earlier, but had been delayed in setting off by the illness and then death of James's father. James had suddenly found himself the head of the Madison family and the master of Montpelier. On the heels of his ascension to the status of paterfamilias and a recent bout of rheumatism that even "temperance and flannels" could not cure, James harbored a fresh sense of his own mortality.[6] He could not have known this as the carriage made its way down Pennsylvania Avenue, passing the small, sluggish stream pretentiously called Tiber Creek, but, politically speaking, his greatest accomplishments were behind him. James Madison resided most comfortably in the theoretical realm, happiest when composing or untangling complex political theories. His talents were perfectly suited to creating the Constitution and to constructing a rudimentary political party, as he had done with Jefferson before the last election. Though he would prove an able secretary of state, he would find himself in over his head eight years later as president. Over the course of his two terms, almost everything that could go wrong almost did: he would come close to losing the war with Britain, the capital city, and the union itself.

Dolley, on the other hand, was poised to fulfill her enormous political potential. She had suffered significant personal trials in her past, trials that had solidified her character, and she approached the challenge of political life at the nation's center with optimism, determination, and a certain wariness born of experience.

❧❧❧

If 1801 marked a new stage of life for the Madisons, it was also an auspicious year in the nation's development. The United States of America had a new seat of federal power in a new city, though the metaphorical road to Washington City's capitalhood had been as rough going as Pennsylvania Avenue. It was always understood that the previous capitals, New York and Philadelphia, were temporary. Throughout the 1780s, the discussion surrounding the capital's permanent location had been far-reaching and, geographically speaking, wide-ranging; politically, it had been positively fraught. Members of government and commentators alike agreed that the federal seat should be "central," but disagreed on how to determine the center of the country. Should it be judged by population, which would result in a capital based in the Northeast? Northerners and easterners thought so. Or, as spokesmen from southern states and western territories urged, should the United States look to the future and place the capital in the geographic center of the country? That would locate the federal government within the untapped potential of the western frontier. Accessibility to the West and to the Atlantic Ocean was also at issue, along with innumerable other considerations, from the availability of natural resources to quality of the scenery. Before 1790, more than thirty sites, including Kingston, New York, Pittsburgh, Pennsylvania, and various locales along the Ohio and Susquehanna Rivers, were proposed and bitterly fought over.[7]

The decision to seat the capital on the Potomac had been sealed at a dinner party held by Thomas Jefferson on June 20, 1790. The guests numbered two: Congressman James Madison and Secretary of Treasury Alexander Hamilton; the goal was clear: to undo a congressional roadblock around Hamilton's plan to settle Revolutionary War debt and to establish the public credit of the United States. Southern legislators opposed one particular aspect of the plan—the federal government's assumption of Revolutionary War debts incurred by the states, primarily those in the Northeast. Already questioning the nationalistic vision that he had fostered through the Constitution and *The Federalist*, essays in support of ratification, James Madison was also worried about the implications of the federal government's economic policy trumping the states'. Over the course of the meal, Hamilton consented to vote for the Potomac legislation in exchange for James's support. For James to vote for Hamilton's program would amount to political suicide, but he agreed not to organize a "strenuous" opposition. Accordingly, on July 9, the House passed the Residence Bill, establishing the capital's new location while keeping the government in Philadelphia for another ten years in order to allow the new city to be built. And on July 26, the Assumption Bill passed in the House. The congruence of events did not pass unnoticed. One newspaper remarked dryly that the Potomac capital had been purchased for "twenty-one and one-half million dollars," the exact amount of the assumed debts.[8]

This proved only the beginning of a long and arduous struggle, of course. Developers had a mere ten years to turn "ten miles square" of southern countryside into a city that would house a functioning and growing federal government as well as serve as a symbol to the new nation's citizens and to the world. The process of designing, financing, and building the capital was so filled with frustration, corruption (or at least loud accusations of it), and delay that when the government, under President John Adams, officially relocated in November 1800, Washington City still sorely lacked many of the things that define either a capital or a city—from roads and amenities to a stable population.[9]

Another woman might have been daunted by the prospect of starting a new life in a strange city, but Dolley Madison was an old hand at moving and starting over. Indeed, she was born during a family relocation. Dolley liked to say that she was a Virginian born and bred, and it is true that when her parents, John Payne and Mary Coles, married in 1761, it marked the union of two of the state's oldest white families. The Coleses may have had a slightly higher standing than the Paynes, but certainly they would not have entrusted their beloved daughter to a social inferior. Hindsight probably accounts for the later implications that the Payne side of the family was not quite *quite*. Throughout the nineteenth century, the Coleses would continue their climb up the social ladder, while the Paynes occupied lesser, though still respectable, rungs. The whiff of instability and failure left on the historical record by John Payne and his male descendants may have also have influenced the impression that he had married above himself. At the time that John and Mary married, however, the Paynes nearly matched the Coleses in the three areas important to the Virginia gentry: lineage, land, and the

ownership of enslaved people. And if there were differences in rank between John Payne and Mary Coles Payne upon their marriage, they
were nothing that could not be overcome by that American combination of hard work and luck. This was a new country after all, and many
a landed family began with some good family connections, a bit of capital, and a hardworking and ambitious young couple.[10]

One thing that did set Dolley's maternal relations apart from the
majority of their Virginia neighbors was their religion: the Coleses
were members of the Society of Friends. This offshoot of the Protestant Reformation began in England in the mid-seventeenth century
with the vision of a twenty-three-year-old artisan and religious re-
former, George Fox. The Friends, as the group's members called themselves, believed that each person possessed the potential for God's
grace, expressed as a "Light" or a "Seed," and that Christ spoke directly
to the individual through immediate revelation, without priestly intermediaries or the trappings of ritual. Like the more famous Puritans,
the "Children of the Light" infused all aspects of life with religion, in
the Old World and the New.[11]

From the Friends' simple but profound philosophy, many precepts
followed, including pacifism and the refusal to swear oaths. Under the
rubric of "equality, simplicity, and peace," the Friends refused to engage
in outward signs of social superiority; they did not use titles of address,
men did not remove their hats or bow, and women did not curtsey or
nod in greeting. They eschewed the new custom of using forms of
"you" to denote superiority, retaining the "plain" forms of "thou." Along
the way, the Society of Friends acquired an official nickname: "Quakers." It began as a scornful appellation referring to their physical response to God, but the Friends adopted it and made it their own.[12]

For their principles, Friends suffered oppression, even in the New
World; Quaker missionaries in the 1650s experienced deportation,
imprisonment, and, in Massachusetts, branding and mutilation. Massachusetts even enacted a death penalty for banished Friends who returned
to the colony, and, in 1660, hanged four Quakers on Boston Common.
By the time Dolley's parents were wed, however, persecution had given
way to toleration. In Virginia, they remained a bit of an anomaly on a

largely (if laxly) Anglican landscape. Quakers did not permit intermarriage with "strangers"; accordingly, three years after the wedding, John Payne applied for membership in the society. For neither side was this a hasty, pro forma conversion; John's successful admission to the Cedar Creek Meeting in 1765 took eight months. Perhaps it was the zeal of the convert that led him, six months after his admission, to apply for a certificate of removal to the New Garden Meeting, located in what is now Guilford County, North Carolina. North Carolina was the southern frontier, offering uncultivated, inexpensive land to the intrepid. For the Quakers who joined the steady stream of emigrants south and west, it also promised a place where they truly could live apart from "the world." Within a year of John's conversion, the couple packed up their belongings and their newborn son, Walter, and, along with ten other Cedar Creek families, traveled almost two hundred miles to the western wilderness of North Carolina to establish a new Quaker community.[13]

As befitted its name, New Garden, the North Carolina location seemed truly Edenic. With its lush green hills and rich lowlands, the landscape was described by some as "bewitching." There Mary Payne gave birth to her second son, William Temple, in 1766. May 20, 1768, saw the birth of the Paynes' third child. She was a girl, and they named her Dolley. Like many famous Americans, she was born in that traditional symbol of mobility and pluck, a log cabin.[14]

The Paynes certainly intended to settle. Leaving family and friends behind was a serious step; more significantly, John had sold his Virginia land to buy property in North Carolina. Once in North Carolina, he identified himself as a merchant, though it is not clear what he sold. But like a more famous couple before them, John and Mary Payne found their tenure in Eden ending abruptly: they moved back to Virginia after only a year. Possibly the adult Paynes discovered that concentrated Quakerism was too much for them, or perhaps Mary missed her extensive and extended family, especially as hers began to grow. Maybe the expanding Regulator movement in North Carolina, where backcountry protestors (or vigilantes, depending on one's point of view) disrupted colonial government, made it hard for the Paynes to live as peaceful landowners. Or did John Payne simply fail as a farmer and a merchant? The bald facts of the case suggest some kind of painful break: John was so eager to leave that he essentially dumped his land-holdings, disposing of them at a loss even before Dolley's birth. The way Dolley handled the issue as an adult also hints at failure: she simply rewrote the record. She was a Virginian, Dolley insisted, although born "on a visit of one year, to an Uncle" in North Carolina.[15]

Back in Virginia, the family continued their peripatetic pattern, moving within the Cedar Creek neighborhood at least twice in Dolley's first four years. She would claim memories of a local estate called Scotchtown—"I can just remember the mantel pieces, they were of black marble supported by white figures. There were twenty rooms on a floor, every one had marble hearths and mantels"—but it is likely that she remembered these details from later visits.[16]

Regardless of their literal address, the Paynes were at home in the familiar neighborhood of Quaker community and family; the North Carolina sojourn, if it was mentioned at all, must have seemed an aberration. They rejoined the Cedar Creek Meeting, and devoted themselves to farming and to raising their expanding family. Dolley grew up within the loving embrace of kin from both sides of the family. A younger brother, Isaac, was the only new sibling to arrive in her early years, but at age eight, Dolley became a big sister, a role she relished all her life. Lucy was born in 1777, followed two years later by Anne, and in two more years, the last of the girls, Mary Coles. The baby of the family was a boy, John Coles.[17]

Dolley was eight years old when news of the Declaration of Independence reached Cedar Creek. The Revolution apparently made little impression on her: because of the Quaker commitment to pacifism, John Payne took no part in the hostilities. In 1783, however, their lives changed abruptly when he decided to free his slaves. (Though the refusal to own human beings seems an obvious choice for a Quaker, slave emancipation was not yet a condition of membership at the time. Laws forbidding manumission complicated the situation; only when the legislature made it legally possible in 1782 could Virginia Quakers free their slaves.)

Unable to work land without slave labor, John had to make other drastic changes, which would require uprooting his family once again; he settled on Philadelphia, the unofficial headquarters of the American Society of Friends. The "City of Brotherly Love" was also the most cosmopolitan city in the new United States—indeed, when the colonies were still under English rule, Philadelphia had been, next to London, the most glittering urban jewel in the empire's crown. Beautifully planned and executed, Philadelphia had paved streets and gracious English-style houses. Its streets were named for the trees that lined them: Chestnut, Walnut, Spruce, and Poplar. In a city of close to twenty thousand people, the upper class of what Gilbert Stuart called the Athens of America aspired to be the social and intellectual leaders of the new nation.[18]

The family settled into this unfamiliar environment of an eastern seaboard city, making their eventual home at 57 North Third Street. The house also probably housed John Payne's struggling starch manufactory. Life in Philadelphia was hard on the Paynes. A baby daughter, born after the move and christened "Philadelphia" in celebration of the family's new venture, did not survive infancy. Within a year of the move, Dolley's oldest brother, Walter, also died, presumably at sea.[19]

✦

Dolley was fifteen years old when the family moved to Philadelphia, and the beautiful young girl made an indelible impression upon its inhabitants. Her lifelong friend and fellow Quaker Anthony Morris remembered how "she came upon our comparatively cold hearts in Philadelphia, suddenly and unexpectedly . . . with all the delightful influences of a summer sun, from the Sweet South . . . bringing with her all the warm feelings and flowing fancies of her Native State." No wonder, that, with a "complexion . . . from Scotland," "soft blue Eyes from Saxony," "a stately step, and [a] sweet engaging Smile," "she soon raised the mercury there in the thermometers of the Heart to fever heat."[20] Nearby Haddonfield, New Jersey, boasted one of the oldest Quaker communities in the region, and Dolley visited there for weeks at a time with family friends, the Creightons. Locals remembered her as "possessing a delicately oval face, a nose tilted like a flower, jet-black hair, and blue eyes of wondrous sweetness. Those beautiful eyes, with their power to scintillate with playfulness or mellow with sympathy, wrought great havoc with the hearts of the Quaker lads of Haddonfield."[21]

In Philadelphia, she met a sister Quaker, Eliza Collins, to whom she would be close all her life. Virginia friends, such as Deborah Pleasants and Elizabeth Brooke, also visited. Dolley's educational experience—both in Virginia and Philadelphia—remains unknown. The Friends set great store by education for women, and though Philadelphia had some of the fledgling country's best schools for girls, Quaker and otherwise, it is not clear where Dolley learned to read and write.[22] Judging from her correspondence, it is safe to say, however, that she received a better education than most Americans, male or female.

Philadelphia offered Dolley her first taste of institutionalized Quakerism. Always a dutiful daughter, she was an obedient member of the Meeting, though evidently Quakerism in its purest form did not take. Never one to fade into the background in any situation, she made a strong impression on the local Friends. Decades later, "strict Female friends" described young Dolley Payne "as inclined . . . for the gayeties of this world." She had "often given offense" by her caps, "the cut of her gown and the shape of her shoes." One Quaker matron, strongly disapproving of the "dashing tendency of her character," declared that had it not been for Dolley's mother, she would have had the girl "excluded from Our Society." (The lady in question, a "Mrs. W.," was probably disgruntled because she used to lecture Dolley often, and during one of these admonishments, "she at first smiled, and afterwards fell asleep.")[23]

Home provided no respite from the complexities and rigidity of the Friends. Quaker tradition offered numerous stories of strong-minded and courageous women who took leading roles alongside men. But for Dolley, feminine examples paled beside familial models. If John Payne had gone into the wilderness seeking an unadulterated atmosphere of Quakerism, ironically, he found it on the busy streets and within the densely woven networks of Philadelphia. He soon became a leading figure in the Philadelphia Meeting.

Mary Coles Payne had been the original Quaker in the family; however, her character, rather than her religion, was the source of her daughter's admiration and love. Dolley's feelings for Mary Payne were unambiguous—she adored her mother, to whom she felt that she could express her emotional vulnerability and needs without reservation. According to Dolley's niece, Mary Cutts, Dolley's father, on the other hand, was not just a Quaker but a "strict" member of the Society of Friends. His Virginia neighbors thought him "a fanatic," a label that on the evidence not only reflected the dramatic decision to free his slaves but also remarked on a general flintiness of character. He had chosen to relocate his family in an alien city because he had "seemingly . . . one aim, the maintenance of his religious belief." Even in that ultra-Quaker atmosphere—one group of fathers reportedly went so far as to send the "ruthless hands" of "a deputation" to a Philadelphia home in order to strip a clock of its "ornamental work"—John Payne stood out. He became an elder, and "spoke in the meetings and was called a 'Quaker Preacher.'"[24] "Strict," "single-minded," "exact"—all words that appear in Dolley's recollections of her father and Quakerism.

If John Payne enjoyed success as a "Quaker preacher," however, he was less successful in the business world. Having floundered for years, his starch business finally went under in 1789; the final humiliation came when his industrious fellow members, who equated business failure with weak character, read him out of the Pine Street Meeting. Like many people whose strength lies in rigidity, John Payne broke rather than bent in the face of adversity. Apparently overwhelmed by depression, John Payne took to his bed, "never raising his head" or leaving his room until he died almost three years later.[25]

Controlling to the last, however, he managed to impose his wishes on his oldest daughter from his premature "deathbed." At twenty-two, Dolley had "gr[own] in grace and beauty," with many beaux. Beauty was a commodity in the marriage game, allowing Dolley her choice of suitors, but Payne bypassed his daughter's say in the matter, insisting on her immediate marriage to twenty-seven-year-old John Todd. Tall, red-headed, and handsome, Todd was a rising young lawyer, who was also a member of the Society of Friends.[26]

One of Dolley's girlfriends, Sarah Parker, wrote frankly to a mutual acquaintance of the match: "Dolly Payne is likely to unite herself to a young man named J. Todd, who has been so solicitous to gain her favor many years, but disappointment for some time seem'd to assail his most sanguine expectations." Sarah approved of John, both because he had been "a Constant Lover indeed" and because he had not withdrawn his suit when "her father's misfortunes might have been an excuse for his leaving her."[27] Apparently, Dolley had known John Todd and refused him previously. John Payne may have wanted Dolley to marry for the best of reasons—security for her, one less mouth to feed for his future widow—but a deathbed promise is manipulation all the same.

The wedding took place on January 7, 1790, at the Pine Street Meeting house. According to family lore, Eliza Collins was the bridesmaid and Anthony Morris performed the office of best man.[28] Regardless of John Payne's status, this was an important alliance for the community of Friends, and the cream of Quaker society signed their names to the Todds' wedding certificate.

The Todds and eleven-year-old Anne Payne, now called Anna, settled in a modest but elegant brick Georgian house on the corner of Fourth and Walnut Streets. A stone's throw from Congress Hall, and with the houses of a university professor and an Episcopal bishop as neighbors, the Todd house stood in one of Philadelphia's finest neighborhoods. John and Dolley Todd lived the life of "gay" Quakers, indulging in luxury items such as mahogany chairs, silver plate, fine china, and looking glasses. They even purchased a new kind of furniture—a sideboard.[29] Dolley hardly missed her family as they were only blocks away, and younger siblings came to live with her at different times.

Unlike her husband, Mary Payne rose to the challenge of keeping her family together. A sheltered woman, trained to run a rural home, who found herself in a precarious financial situation in a strange city, might well have followed her husband's lead and taken to her room as well. Instead, in 1791, Mary opened the Payne house to boarders, catering to the congressmen and government officials who had moved that year from New York. Philadelphia had just become the nation's temporary capital, and Mary Payne soon became well known in government circles for running a good house. By the time the reclusive John Payne finally died on October 24, 1792, his wife had a thriving business.[30]

John Payne Todd, bearing his father's and grandfather's names, was born to Dolley on February 29, 1792. Whatever reservations Dolley had had about John Todd, the couple seemed to have settled into a loving, happy partnership. John Todd offered Dolley a sense of security that she had yet to experience in her adult life. Moreover, he clearly adored his wife and young family. Even in a short note written on a business trip his playful affection shines through: "I hope my dear [D]olley is well & my sweet little Payne can lisp *Mama* in a stronger Voice than when his Papa left him—I wish he was here to run after Mrs. Withy's Ducks he would have fine sport—." Dolley was also his helpmate, seeing to the "Boys," John's law apprentices, while he was away. "I have no Doubt of my Dear Dolleys Assistance when necessary. Thine forever."[31]

❧

The summer of 1793 marked the arrival of a second son, named William Temple Todd for Dolley's brother. It also marked the arrival of yellow fever. The illness had appeared in late July and by August had reached epidemic proportions, sweeping through Philadelphia; ultimately it would claim the lives of five thousand people, nearly one fifth of the city's population. Uncertainty bred panic. No one knew a cure or an effective preventative for yellow fever, and they could only speculate as to its origins. Some blamed it on rotting coffee down by the docks; others insisted that foreigners brought it. In one respect, the latter group was correct: the disease is transmitted by mosquitoes, which in this case may have arrived on a ship from the West Indies. The symptoms were horrific, death agonizing and sudden, and the transmission rate high. Fever, chills, headache, muscle aches, lethargy, and black vomit signaled the onset of the disease. A brief period of recovery might bring false hope, for the infection only rebounded with greater virulence. Kidney and liver failure could send the patient into shock; the resulting jaundice yellowed the skin and eyes and gave the disease its name. Death could occur within a day.

The one thing that everyone "knew" about yellow fever was false: it was *not* contagious. Tragically, not only were families broken up and children orphaned by death but the panic over contagion led people to isolate and even abandon their loved ones. The federal, state, and city governments shut down as officials from President Washington on down fled. Though other eastern cities tried to exercise quarantine, forbidding Philadelphia residents to cross their borders, almost half the population deserted the city. The empty streets made the death toll seem even more dire.[32]

In August, Dolley was recovering from the birth of William; John Todd, alarmed at the outbreak's spread, sent the family to Gray's Ferry, south of the city on the Schuylkill River, and, he hoped, beyond infection's reach. Dolley was transported there on a litter; Mary Payne went along to tend her. After delivering his wife and children to safety, John Payne returned to the city to take care of business and his parents; along with the general population, lawyers had fled or died, and with inhabitants perishing at terrifying rates, someone had to ensure the orderly transmission of property.

In October, Dolley sent off a hasty note to her brother-in-law, James, safe in Darby, Pennsylvania, about eight miles southwest of the city: "Oh my dear Brother what a dread prospect has thy last Letter presented to me!" Dolley's "reveared Father[-in-law]" lay "in the Jaws of Death"; her "Love'd Husband in perpetual danger." She had "repeatedly Entreated John to leave home . . . but alass he cannot leave his Father." Thwarted by her enforced "banishment," Dolley longed to do something. "Is it two late for their removal? or can no interfearance of their Earthly friends rescue them from the two general fate?" Part of the reason for her frustration—"I wish much to see you"—as well as her "distress & apprihension" lay at home. "I have no way of geting to you," she fretted, because "my Child is sick." In Philadelphia, John witnessed the deaths of both his parents, and nursed his clerk, Isaac Heston, who also perished. When he visited Dolley at Gray's Ferry a few days later, she begged him to stay. John proposed a compromise, promising that after closing his office "he would never again leave her."

John returned to Gray's Ferry, sequestering himself in a different part of the house, in case he had brought the infection from the city. Within a few days, he felt "the fever in [his] veins"; since he had gone out hunting in the marshes the evening before and early that morning, he may, ironically, have caught the city plague from local mosquitoes. In order to protect Dolley and his family, John Todd returned to his brother's house in Philadelphia, where he died, on October 14, 1794, the same day his son William succumbed to the fever.[33]

By late autumn, with a grieving Dolley fully recovered from her own bout of illness (whether she contracted yellow fever is unclear; certainly a woman weakened from childbirth must have been susceptible) and the epidemic subsiding, the family left Gray's Ferry. This in itself presented difficulties. From Gray's Ferry, Mary Payne wrote to Dolley's former nurse, "Mother Amey," in Philadelphia asking whether John Todd had left money with her: "O my Dear Dear Nurse How shall I express my feelings. . . . My poor Dear Dolley, what does she & will she suffer . . . the same day Consined her Dear husband & her little babe to the silent grave." Mary went on to relate that Dolley had only nineteen dollars to her name but owed money for the burial of little William and had other debts to pay before she could return home. She asked Mother Amey to send any money along as soon as possible, presenting her daughter as "amonge strangers & frenless."[34]

Back in Philadelphia, Mary Payne gave up her boarders, sold the Payne house, and headed down to Virginia to live with Lucy, who, shortly after Dolley's wedding, had married George Steptoe Washington, nephew of the president. Dolley, Payne, and Anna moved back to the Todd house.[35]

As for Dolley, she found herself starting over once again, this time in a devastated city as a widow and a bereaved mother. The general desolation, grief, and loss that accompany a major catastrophe only compounded and magnified her private anguish. And she was responsible for her surviving child, eighteen-month-old John Payne Todd. Even now that she was back in Philadelphia, money was a pressing issue. Food prices were unconscionably high, for farmers, fearing infection, would not bring their produce into the city.[36] The unexpected deaths of the senior Paynes and then her husband left Dolley embroiled in a tangle of legal affairs, with a lack of ready cash. The legal disabilities attached to her sex only complicated her position. Thousands of other families were in the same position, and the courts struggled with heavy caseloads. Dolley's in-laws might have been a source of help, but she found herself quite abandoned by them. John's brother, James, a bank clerk, proved reluctant to part with the money John had left to the "Dear Wife of my Bosom and first and only Woman upon whom my all and only affections were placed." It would not have been unusual at that time for a husband to assign trustees and guardians for a widow with children, but, aside from naming two colleagues as advisors, John Todd had designated his "amiable and affectionate wife" as his ex-ecutrix, entrusting her with all of his worldly goods and the welfare and education of his offspring. In addition, since John's parents had prede-ceased him, Dolley was to receive his portion of their estates.[37]

She requested copies of both wills along with John's papers and ef-fects from brother James, but to no avail. When James suggested that she sell those parts of the estate in her possession, Dolley replied with sorrow and some asperity: "I was hurt My dear Jamy that the Idea of his Lib[r]ary should occur as a proper source for raising money. Book's from which he wished his Child improved, shall remain sacred, & I would feel the pinching hand of Poverty before I disposed of them."

Dolley became quite insistent as the weeks passed, indignantly protesting the "unnecessary Detention of my part of my Mother in Law's property and of the Receipt Book and papers of my late Hus-band." She gave James one last chance—"I am constrained once more to request—and if a request is not sufficient—to *demand* that they may be delivered this day." She would not be put off any longer: "I cannot wait . . . without material Injury to my Affairs," she wrote, adding frostily, "The bearer waits for thy answer."[38] James Todd finally settled out of court after Dolley engaged a lawyer, William W. Wilkins, to act on her behalf. Dolley emerged from the confrontation a wealthy woman, albeit wiser in the base ways of the world.

Meeting Madison

etween the congressmen who stayed at Mrs. Payne's boardinghouse and the advisors she had engaged in her legal woes, Dolley was well acquainted with the most prominent men, Quaker and otherwise, in town. William Wilkins was one of Philadelphia's leading citizens; Aaron Burr, the senator from New York, was a former boarder and also a friend. Not that Dolley wanted for male attention: not only was she now a wealthy widow but also she had grown from a pretty girl to a beautiful woman. At five foot seven and three quarters, "well proportioned" with an ample bust and slim waist, and a "mouth which was beautiful in shape and expression," she had male Philadelphia "in the Pouts." Men stationed themselves in the street in order to catch a glimpse of the Widow Todd. Passing her, they turned back to look, leading her friend Eliza to gently chide: "Really, Dolley, thou must hide thy face—there are so many men staring at thee."[1]

Among her admirers was the congressman from Virginia, James Madison. Already celebrated for his contributions to the new nation—most notably, his role in framing the Constitution and drafting the Bill of Rights—at forty-three, he was seventeen years older than the young widow, and a lifelong bachelor when, in the spring of 1794, he asked his friend and fellow Princeton classmate Aaron Burr for an introduction. Apparently, he had also seen Dolley on the street, walking with one of her innumerable Coles kinsmen. As Dolley later reported to her niece Mary Cutts, she turned to Eliza Collins for help: "Thou must come to me, Aaron Burr says that the great little Madison has asked him to bring him to see me this evening."[2]

Family legend has Dolley receiving the "great little Madison" in a mulberry-colored satin gown; regardless of what she actually wore, she undoubtedly captivated the shy, bookish James Madison. James was reserved in many situations; the presence of women only exacerbated his awkwardness. His voluntary bachelorhood stood out in a culture that viewed marriage as a pragmatic necessity; love was scarcely a requirement. But the coolly rational, intellectual Madison was a romantic. He would not marry except for love and, over the years, at least twice disappointed, he had withdrawn from the marriage market. At thirty-two, he had fallen in love with fifteen-year-old Catherine Floyd, daughter of William Floyd, New York delegate to the Continental Congress. "Kitty" Floyd accepted his proposal in April 1783, but then changed her mind, spurning James for a young medical student, William Clarkson. In July, James received a letter with Kitty's "expression of indifference" (as he confided in Thomas Jefferson), the letter, according to Floyd family tradition, sealed with rye dough to show that her affections had soured.[3]

Eight years later, James became "fascinated" with a celebrated salonnière and hostess, Mrs. Henrietta Maria Colden, "who was so noted for her masculine understanding and activity, as well as for feminine graces and accomplishments."[4] It was presumably on her account that James lingered in New York City for months, even though President Washington and Thomas Jefferson importuned his return to

Philadelphia. (Perhaps Mrs. Colden's Federalist tendencies squelched the romance.)

Like most romantics, once James fell, he fell hard, and when he finally met twenty-five-year-old Dolley, he was smitten. He was also taking no chances, embarking upon a campaign worthy of a master political strategist. As he had done with Aaron Burr, James enlisted Dolley's relative Catharine Coles to write on his behalf. Catharine gleefully reported: "He told me I might say what I pleas'd to you about him," and went on to relay the information that "he thinks so much of you in the day that he has Lost his Tongue, at Night he Dreames of you & Starts in his Sleep a Calling on you to relieve his Flame for he Burns." And, she added, "he has Consented to every thing that I have wrote about him with Sparkling Eyes."[5]

In spite of the age difference, the couple had a great deal in common. Two southerners exiled in a chilly northern city, they came from the same world of slaveholding Virginia. But their respective genders meant that they experienced that world very differently. Dolley had been raised to be a dependent from cradle to grave, "covered" by the legal status of, first, her father, second, her husband. As a white male, James was destined to be lord and master of all he surveyed. He had been born on March 16, 1751, to one of the first white families of Virginia, the eldest son of the wealthiest landowner in the region. The "Maddisons" had been farming Albemarle County, Virginia, since 1653, and while subsequent generations lost a "d" in their surname, they also had gained considerable wealth and prominence.

James seemed slated for great political success as well. Along with his friend and colleague Thomas Jefferson, James had embarked upon an experiment in government never before attempted in the modern world. With the rebellion against Great Britain successful, the revolutionary generation set out to build a nation founded on a political theory that had its roots in the ancient Roman republic—"republicanism." A distrust of centralized power, such as an absolute monarchy, lay at the heart of republican theory, along with a fear of all monarchical trappings—courtiers, hereditary privilege, luxury, patronage, a complicated court bureaucracy that concealed the abuse of power. Modern republicanism was not just a form of government; it extended to include all parts of life. It offered a utopian vision of a simple world of rustic virtue, in direct contrast to the corruption of city and court.

Though a republican government had been the Revolution's goal, history was not terribly reassuring about the outcome of this experiment. The only successful modern republics—the Netherlands and certain city-states in Italy and Switzerland—were small, with homogeneous populations. They were also fragile, since the power to govern rested not in a sovereign, but in the people. Consequently, "the people," meaning property-owning men, had to be virtuous, capable of putting the public good ahead of their own interests; the rulers of an independent people should be even more unselfish and civic-minded. A monarchy could depend on armies, churches, and practices like patronage for stability. The only source for stability in a republic lay in the hearts of men—that is, in the characters and judgment of "the people."

Republicanism was not democracy. In the late eighteenth century, "democracy" had negative connotations; in the 1790s, the bloody example of mob rule furnished by the French Revolution would stand as a demonstration of its perils. But republicanism, with its promotion of the idea of "equality," contained the seeds of modern democracy. Of course, "equality" did not extend to women or people of color; nor did it signify the absence of rank distinctions among men. Republican "equality" meant that, unfettered by birth, family, or wealth, white men of talent and merit would rise to the top.[6] Republicanism drove the rhetoric of revolution, and served as the foundation for the Constitution, which James had largely written and defended. And so in 1794, currently serving as a representative from Virginia, he was more than a mere congressman. Depending on one's ideological bent, it was James or Alexander Hamilton who stood second to President Washington in the public mind, an object of either veneration or ignominy. James was a close consultant to the president, advising him on issues as diverse as foreign policy and etiquette. Along with Hamilton, he even had a hand in drafting Washington's Farewell Address.

Dolley was surely aware of her beau's stature and prospects. In the unlikely event she was not, Martha Washington, perhaps also under

James's hand, allegedly informed her of the wisdom of making this match.[7] Understandably, Dolley seems to have been more accepting than rapturous. This would be the second marriage in her short life, and although remarriage was universal among the widowed in early America, John Todd had been dead for less than a year. Such a hasty recoupling would shock many and was contrary to Quaker practice, which dictates at least a year of widowhood before remarriage. In addition, an alliance with James would cut significant ties with her past. Dolley was still a Quaker; James shared the Anglican (later Episcopalian) religion of the southern gentry. (As the Virginian saying went, anyone could be a Christian but only a gentleman could be an Anglican.)[8] For marrying a "stranger," Dolley would almost surely be "read out" of Meeting.

Also, by marrying James, Dolley would be returning to the world of chattel slaveholding, from which she had been absent for over ten years, and about which she doubtless had mixed feelings. This was the world that her father had utterly rejected, and in so complete a way as to change Dolley's life forever. With all the tragedy that followed the move to Philadelphia—the deaths of his sons and his own financial ruin and demise—John Payne, it could be said, had paid for his scruples with his life. But it was not only his life. His repudiation of slavery tore young Dolley out of the only home she had ever known, forcing her to cope with increasingly traumatic circumstances, including a marriage not of her own choosing and young widowhood. Dolley watched her mother, too, pay the price for her husband's conscience. Perhaps rather than cementing any nascent abolitionist views that a younger, more devout Dolley might have shared with her father, the disastrous Philadelphia sojourn, with its intensified contact with other Quakers, made Dolley long to rejoin the world of her childhood, one that, in her memories, had always offered her safety and security.

On a more personal level, she was a young, sexually charismatic woman yoking herself to an older man who boasted a sterling character, but not, perhaps, sexual charisma. (Famously frail, James suffered lifelong—and perhaps hypochondriacal—illness.) However, as an eighteenth-century woman, she no doubt took a more practical view of marriage, one in which romance played a very small part. She was nobody unless she was married. If she married James, she would acquire financial security, a legal protector, and a social position.

In the summer of 1794, Dolley rented out her house in Philadelphia and traveled to Virginia to visit relatives. James had learned from experience; Kitty Floyd had broken their engagement during such a summer separation, and he continued to press his suit. In mid-August, Dolley sent him word from Fredericksburg that she would be his wife. Words failed the usually articulate James Madison: "I can not express, but hope you will conceive the joy it gave me." Not only was the news felicitous, but the "welcome event was [e]ndeared to me by the *stile* in which it was conveyed."9

On September 15, 1794, the wedding anniversary of James's parents, Dolley and James were married by a Madison cousin, the Reverend Alexander Balmain, at Harewood, the Virginia estate of Dolley's sister Lucy and her husband, George Steptoe Washington. It was a quiet affair, with only Dolley's immediate family, James's sister, and a small group of friends in attendance. Preparing for the afternoon nuptials, Dolley "stole from the family to commune [by letter] with" Eliza Collins, now married herself to another Virginia congressman, Richard Bland Lee. Dolley wrote of the impending event cheerfully enough, noting her respect for James and saying that she expected her marriage would bring her "every thing that is soothing and greatful in prospect—& my little Payne will have a generous & tender protector." She did not speak of love, but instead discussed the financial arrangements she had made for her son. That afternoon, she signed the letter to Eliza "Dolley Payne Todd." In the evening, following the short ceremony, she amended that, signing underneath "Dolley Madison! Alass!" In perhaps another sign of ambivalence, she first dated this letter "September 16," then corrected it.10

In December 1794, Dolley was indeed read out of Meeting as her sister Lucy had been when she married the Anglican Washington.11 But on the face of it, both Dolley and James had made a good match. She had allied herself with a rich, powerful man of good family; he had acquired a beautiful young wife of his own class. Friends and observers alike acknowledged that Dolley's gracious high spirits would go a long way to compensating for James's retiring manner and social diffidence. Beyond worldly considerations, however, and despite the obvious contrast in their public personas, Dolley and James enjoyed a compatibility of character, a match in personal style.

James was an extraordinarily considerate, even-tempered, and conciliatory man. In his private interactions, he proved unfailingly attentive to the needs of others and never used his intellect to intimidate, instead adjusting the level of his conversation to his audience. For the most part, he carried that style into his public life. In an excessively heated, even violent, political culture, James's colleagues marveled at his character; it was generally agreed that he was "the most virtuous, calm, and amiable, of men, possessed of one of the purest hearts, and best tempers with which man was ever blessed." Even his valet, Paul Jennings, proclaimed his master "one of the best men that ever lived."[12] For Dolley, a woman who detested conflict and who would become celebrated for her pacifying effects on others, it was a perfect fit.

⟡

Back in Philadelphia after their wedding tour, her husband quickly proved himself the "tender protector" Dolley had hoped for. James Todd had still not completely fulfilled the settlement to his former sister-in-law; a firm demand from Congressman Madison brought results. Dolley's family difficulties were far from over—her brothers William Temple and Isaac would meet sudden ends in 1795—but they were easier to withstand with her new husband by her side.[13]

In her new incarnation as a legislator's wife, Dolley moved in the highest circles, where her natural gifts and good spirits quickly established her, and by extension, James, as assets to the scene. From her front-row seat in the theater of government, she witnessed an ongoing debate about the place that women—especially ruling-class women— would have in the new government. During the Revolution, American women of all classes had been called upon to expand their traditional roles, managing not just homes but farms and stores, and even in some cases taking up arms. With little government bureaucracy to support troops, women's labor made it possible for the former colonists to conduct a war with a full-time army. Without their work, men could have only fought as militia in short, local battles. The Revolution also required women's work in other ways. Urged by their leaders in print and from pulpits, women boycotted British goods, substituting American-made homespun for imported cloth and drinking herbal brews instead of English tea. While such actions had economic impact, they also had profound psychological and political uses that were more important. If anyone, at home or in the Mother Country, questioned the rightness of the Patriot cause, or whether a motley group of far-flung colonies could possibly unite enough to resist, wives and mothers from Massachusetts to North Carolina presented an image of solidarity.

Once the war was over, however, the rules and roles were not so clear. After a major conflict, the barriers between the genders are usually strengthened, perhaps in a backlash against expanded freedom for women. But this war was somewhat different: the American Revolution had been fought for liberty, grounded in natural rights conferred upon every human being at birth. Change—or, rather, the potential for change—was in the air. There was even an uneasy, short-lived discussion about giving women the vote, though this was quickly quashed. (For a brief period, property-owning women voted in New Jersey, though they lost that privilege in 1807, as the Republicans gained power across the country. It turned out that the ladies voted by class and tended to be Federalists.)

The "woman question" was, of course, only one of those facing the post-Revolutionary age. Having successfully rebelled *against* their oppressor, the founders and the generation that followed had to decide what the new nation stood *for*. In the face of so much radical change, the leading men could not seriously consider political equality for women. Revolutionaries such as Thomas Paine and Thomas Jefferson had always used "nature" in their arguments for revolution; John Locke's "state of nature" gave credence to the idea of natural liberty. To let women vote or hold office seemed to fly directly in the face of nature: the favored simile was "the world turned upside down."

Instead, the rhetoric of the new republican government offered white women the chance to transform society—as wives and mothers. This notion, sometimes called "republican motherhood," raised traditional female roles to new levels of importance. It was a consolation prize, substituting rhetorical and indirect influence for real power, but it was a seductive one. It even took the most feared characteristic of "woman" and gave it a virtuous twist: a good republican woman, for instance, could use the sexuality that had always threatened government to "entice" her husband to republican virtue. According to the theorists of the time, "the ladies" could use their sexual power not only to quell men's "licentious manners" and to "confirm . . . virtuous habits," but also to "excite his perseverance in the paths of rectitude." Later, as mothers, they would inculcate their sons in republican ways. According to some theorists, the doctrine of maternal influence could pave the way for a modern liberal state.[14]

As republican mothers, women could even overcome the challenges of modern politics and a growing capitalistic nation. According to the Scottish Enlightenment writers favored by James, by buying and using new goods and technologies, women would civilize modern nations increasingly reliant on market forces. As the teachers of children and the queens of society, they could also create sets of behaviors and standards of interaction calculated to bring out the best and control the worst in human beings, thus allowing them to live together in large national groups. For political thinkers such as David Hume and Lord Kames, *manners*—not government—provided the basis of civilization. Like Adam Smith's invisible hand in the marketplace, manners constituted a kind of natural law, more deeply woven into a culture and therefore longer-lasting and more powerful than the mere creations of legislators. The stabilizing function of manners was especially appealing to new governments, such as the United States, with only untried systems of law standing between anarchy and order.[15]

The hostesses who presided over the Philadelphia and New Jersey parties, balls, and calling circles consciously saw themselves as engaged in the process of originating a national style of American manners and culture. American salonnières, such as Anne Willing Bingham, the leading hostess of the Philadelphia capital, experimented with European models, crafting a social network that would bind together leading families across the country, and so stabilize the union.[16] At the center of capital society, Dolley was ideally placed to observe their efforts; that education would serve her well when she became the head of national society.

Not that she had any expectation of that eventuality. She may have become a political wife when she married James, but it was not clear, in the climate of the middle and late 1790s, that he would be able to continue his career. Even under the reign of the universally beloved George Washington, political unity was rapidly disintegrating. The members of Washington's cabinet fought amongst themselves, and old friendships and alliances broke down over clashing political ambitions and ideological differences. In 1787–88, united in their mission to ratify the Constitution, James had collaborated successfully with Alexander Hamilton on essays compiled as *The Federalist*. By 1796, they were declared enemies. Thomas Jefferson and John Adams had been brothers in revolution, even serving together on the committee to draft the Declaration of Independence. But postwar tensions led to polarized positions, until by 1800 they were no longer speaking.

The cause and effect of all this animosity was the emergence of two political parties, which, though they would assume different labels over the years, articulated the ideas and conflicts that would become the hallmark of the United States' bipartisan system. The leading party, the Federalists, identified itself with long-cherished English political traditions, and claimed George Washington, Alexander Hamilton, and John Adams. They saw themselves as men of national vision, espousing federal power over states' rights. To them, the American Revolution was just the latest installment in a saga that began with the Magna Carta. Elitist in political and personal style and always looking back to a nostalgic past, Federalists opposed democratic reforms that would expand suffrage and give more voice to the ruled. Champions of industry and commerce, they tended to come from the North and East.

Less organized than the Federalists, the opposition lacked even a name in the 1790s, though eventually they would call themselves the Republicans and, later still, the Democratic-Republicans. Personified and led by James Madison and Thomas Jefferson, they mistrusted the Federalists as an aristocratic party. Always aware of the link between power and luxury, the Republicans obsessively monitored the dress, manners, and style of the ruling Federalists, watching for signs of encroaching monarchy. Though James had championed the federalizing document, the Constitution, by 1796 he and Jefferson feared that Hamilton and the Federalists had taken centralization too far. The two men also identified with ancient political traditions, but they emphasized liberty over power. Always focusing on the future, they regarded the Revolution as the dawn of a new day of freedom for the world. Republican followers tended to be from the South and West, and they emphasized agrarian interests and states' rights. They had a more expansive view of "the people," which, though it did not include women or people of color, did encompass white men of modest means. Pure republican ideology did not brook the idea of a responsible dissent, a loyal or legitimate opposition; it presumed only one, clear common good, and viewed any opposition as treacherous.

For all his mild manner, James found the tumultuous political climate stimulating; as when he seized the debate at the Constitutional Convention, he saw opportunity in chaos. Thomas Jefferson reacted differently. He harbored an almost pathological revulsion against conflict, and he experienced his political wounds personally and deeply. Retreat was his strategy: in 1794, after serving as George Washington's secretary of state, Jefferson had decided to retire.

Even as Jefferson maintained his distance at Monticello, though, James had kept his colleague connected with political life. It is easy to see tall, handsome, charismatic Thomas Jefferson as the leader of the Madison-Jefferson partnership, but James was no mere functionary or hatchet man. The combination of the two men exceeded the sum of their various and multifaceted parts; as John Quincy Adams would later say, "The mutual influence of these two mighty minds upon each other is a phenomenon, like the invisible and mysterious movements of the magnet in the physical world." In some ways, James knew more about Jefferson than Jefferson did; he even anticipated Jefferson's return to politics before Jefferson himself. Thomas Jefferson could not stay out of the fray: in 1796, he allowed himself to be put forth as a presidential candidate against his old friend, John Adams. These were the days before the candidates campaigned directly to voters, so Jefferson could "run" for office, while still maintaining a pose of magisterial indifference.

The election of 1796 was the first true presidential contest; George Washington had served the two previous terms almost by acclamation and would have probably won a third with similar unanimity. In contrast, this election was fierce and dirty. Jefferson supporters openly denounced the Federalists as tools of the British monarchy; for their part, the Federalists assailed the new "Republicans" as "Jacobins," the violent and bloody revolutionaries who wrought so much havoc during the French Revolution. When it came to the actual voting, however, other considerations played their part. Electors from each state decided presidential contests. Only in Pennsylvania and Maryland did the people vote for electors; in the other fourteen states, the legislatures chose them. Neither side could count on "party" (such as it was) loyalty among the state electors: a man might vote according to regional loyalty, local interests, or even personal honor. In the end, John Adams won the presidency, with 71 electors to Jefferson's 68, and, according to the rules of the time, acquired his rival, Thomas Jefferson, for a vice president.[17]

Such a situation might have seemed ripe for conflict, but direct confrontation was not the elliptical Jefferson's style. Quite on its own, John Adams's administration proved fractious and fractured. Jefferson spent as much of his vice presidency as he could on his Virginia mountaintop and let the Adams administration collapse upon itself. John Adams was not being unreasonably suspicious or cynical when he remarked to Abigail upon Jefferson's earlier "retirement": "It seems the Mode of becoming great is to retire. It is marvelous how political Plants grow in the shade." Once again, Jefferson was simply biding his time. Upon John Adams's election, James had "retired" as well, taking Dolley, Payne, and Anna back to join his parents at the family home, Montpelier, in Orange, Virginia. Using a mix of slave and free labor, his father had built the simple rectangular building, the second largest brick dwelling in Orange County, when James was a little boy, and he had grown up there with his six brothers and sisters.

The estate's name, which James and Dolley spelled in the old way, "Montpellier," meant "Mount of the Pilgrim," and was the name of a small French town, a center of learning and health. As the oldest son, the house and grounds were his patrimony, and since his marriage, James had set about a making a home for both his families, marital and natal. He built a thirty-foot extension so that each family could live in relative privacy and added windows, staircases, and more improvements both structural and decorative. He also transformed the Virginia country house into a neo-classical Federalist mansion by attaching an elegant portico with pillars. (Later, during his first presidential term, he would add two one-story wings on each side.) The result was a beautiful, graceful house in a stunning setting, where one could sit on the front porch and gaze out over the gently rolling lawn to the Blue Ridge Mountains far in the distance. For the next four years, Dolley, Payne, and Anna lived at Montpelier, easing into the role of southern gentry. If life in busy, cosmopolitan Philadelphia had presented Dolley with the latest word in everything from fashions to ideas about women, the conservative, rural countryside had its own part to play in her education. Reentering the world of her childhood put Dolley back into direct contact with chattel slavery. She left no written reaction to the change, but the transition may have been eased by her own subordinate position. She did not have to be the slave mistress; Nelly Conway Madison was still firmly at the plantation's helm.

While women, such as Anne Willing Bingham, and men, like Dolley's own husband, were working out the construction of a postrevolutionary social and political order, Dolley was learning the older ways of gentry life in the area around Orange, Virginia. The visits and parties that incorporated much political and economic business, the dense networks of family obligation, the sense of self that came from material possessions—these, too, would be part of Dolley's political arsenal, should the time come.

And indeed, even as Dolley and James settled into the life of country squires, James continued to work for his friends. While Jefferson led a life seemingly cut off from politics, Dolley entertained neighbors and political supporters of the new Republican party, with James securing loyalties and party bonds behind the scenes.[18]

The two men set their sights on the next election, a replay of Jefferson against Adams, with Aaron Burr as Jefferson's choice for first runner-up and so vice president. Only decades later would Jefferson describe the election as "the revolution of 1800," but it was revolutionary, though not in the way that he meant. Jefferson's inauguration represented the nation's first peaceful transfer of power from one party to another. After such a contentious political season, the country was ready for reconciliation, but how that was to come about was not evident. As President Jefferson welcomed his newly appointed secretary of state and his family into the executive mansion in May 1801, it was clear to the two men that this was a chance to put the country on the right track, to begin afresh after a false, Federalist start. And they had a new capital in which to start over.[19]

THREE

Lady About Town

our months before the Madisons' arrival, the New York congressman Albert Gallatin arrived in Washington City to assume his legislative duties. In those first years, when Washington had few real dwellings and with the business of government a seasonal affair, running from autumn to spring, most officials chose to live in temporary lodgings, usually boardinghouses. Housing shortages in the capital made it necessary for congressmen to double up, so Albert and Joseph Varnum, the representative from Massachusetts, decided to "mess together" at Conrad and McMunn's boardinghouse. They agreed to pay $15 a week each for "attendance, wood, candles and liquors." Writing home to his wife, Hannah Nicholson Gallatin, Albert judged "our local situation" as "far from pleasant," and listed the scanty selection of services around the Capitol: "Seven or eight boardinghouses, one tailor, one shoemaker, one printer, a washingwoman, a grocery shop, a pamphlets and stationery shop, a small dry-goods shop and an oyster house." Like a college freshman, he complained of having to share his room and of the food: "We have hardly any vegetables, the people being obliged to resort to Alexandria for supplies, our beef is not very good, mutton and poultry good: the price of provisions and wood about the same as in Philadelphia."

The greatest hardship, however, was not the lack of the amenities usually found in cities, but the dearth of social opportunities ordinarily available in even the smallest town. Albert found the "mess" congenial, "but it is always the same, and unless in my own family, I had rather now and then see some other persons." While such proximity might bring intimacy, it also brought conflict. Albert confided to Hannah, "You may suppose that being all thrown together in a few boarding-houses, without hardly any other society than ourselves, we are not likely to be either very moderate politically or to think of anything but politics." Though some men might drink or gamble, "the majority drink naught but politics." When these men met others of "different or more moderate sentiments, they inflame each other."

One reason for the unsocial atmosphere stemmed from the lack of women. During those early days, few male officials brought wives or other female relatives to the capital. To be sure, for Albert, there was no substitute for his beloved Hannah and growing family, but a female so-cial circle would doubtless have helped relieve the tedium and loneli-ness. Instead, he sighed, "I believe, we are from twenty-four to thirty [at the dinner table] and was it not for the presence of Mrs. Bailey and Mrs. Brown, would look like a refectory of monks."[1]

In his first days at the federal seat, Albert experienced, in micro-cosm, many of the characteristic experiences of life in early Washing-ton. Years passed before the capital had adequate commercial and city services. Boardinghouse life would for decades remain a staple for con-gressmen and other members of the government, including Supreme Court justices, and while in some cases this led to solidarity among small groups of officials, generally speaking the cramped quarters fostered deep-seated discord through the institution of government as a whole.

Rough living conditions, physical, psychological, and political isolation, diverse populations, and an amorphous sense of impermanence—in a new nation with an untried government and an uncertain future, these factors posed greater threats than they would to a more established union. The presence of ladies and society was required to temper and disperse the tension of a situation where men ate, drank, and slept politics. Fortunately for Albert, and for Washington City, Dolley Madison would pave the way for a governmental culture that, paradoxically, not only offered a respite from politics, but also created alternative ways for power to flow.

During their first three weeks in town, Dolley, James, Anna, and Payne stayed with the president in quarters that may not have been as tight as the congressmen's but were certainly far from grand. Given the leaking roof, unfurnished rooms, few servants, and lack of even the most basic comforts, it was no wonder Thomas Jefferson quipped that he and his private secretary, Meriwether Lewis, rattled about the drafty, barrackslike building like two mice in church.[2] Jefferson would have been just as happy for the Madisons to live permanently with him; they had other offers as well. Even before they had left Montpelier, Dr. William Thornton, the designer of the Capitol, and his wife, Anna Maria, had invited them to stay at their house on F Street, near the president's house. But James and Dolley wanted their own home. Thomas Law, an Englishman and early city investor and developer, pleaded with James to buy one of his houses, inconveniently located on Capitol Hill. Instead, they chose to live "over the store," in the Six Buildings at Pennsylvania Avenue and Twenty-second Street that also temporarily housed the Department of State.[3]

Even after moving out, however, Dolley served as the president's occasional hostess. As a widower, Jefferson had no easy way to include women in events at the president's house. Consequently, he expressed gratitude to Dolley for initiating "an acquaintance with the ladies of the place," lamenting that his own "ladies," his daughters, Martha and Maria, stayed home at Monticello.[4] While under the executive roof, Dolley began making contact with her future collaborators, colleagues, and allies—the women of Washington.

It was at a Jefferson dinner that Dolley made the acquaintance of a woman who would become one of her closest friends and confidantes, Margaret Bayard Smith, who had come to town with her journalist husband from Philadelphia only the year before. Margaret, a recent convert to Republicanism, expressed herself "highly pleased" with Dolley: "She has good humour and sprightliness, united to the most affable and agreeable manners." She also admired the "simplicity and mildness" of James's manners, noting "a smile [that] has so much benevolence in it, that it cannot fail of inspiring good will and esteem." Within days of this first meeting, Margaret confessed to her sister that, though she had only known Dolley and Anna a short time, she had already formed a close attachment to the sisters. The two women apparently invited such instant intimacy: "Indeed it is impossible for an acquaintance with them to be different."[5]

The Madisons stayed in the Six Buildings for only two months. After an attack of bilious fever (or perhaps just a good dose of Washington summer), James opted for the more salubrious air of the Virginia countryside, and the Madison household took their leave in July, making plans to return to Washington City in the fall when the legislative season resumed. Before he left, James asked William Thornton to arrange for a permanent home for his family. Dr. Thornton borrowed money on James's behalf and arranged for "Mr. Voss's house" at 1333 F Street—right next door to his own house and two blocks east of the president's—to be renovated. The Madisons' new home had four bedrooms on the third floor and a cellar divided into wine and coal rooms; the roof boasted a cupola. The residence proper was finished by the time James and Dolley returned to town in mid-October, with plans for a coach house and stabling for four horses. The rent was six hundred dollars a year.[6]

Upon her arrival back in Washington, Dolley began in earnest to create a new home, and a new life. She and James would spend the congressional "season"—roughly from October to April or May—in the capital, and summers at Montpelier. Dolley took care of the myriad mundane details—deciding which furniture to bring from the country, and what she needed to buy in town; helping settle her husband and

nine-year-old Payne into their routines. And there were more significant logistical decisions to be made as well. Some enslaved people came
up from Montpelier, including Paul Jennings, James's valet; Sukey, Dolley's personal maid; and Joe Bolen, a coachman. Dolley also hired slaves
from local families to meet the Madisons' needs.

It was all an improvisational affair. Washington City offered Dolley,
and its other new residents, a unique opportunity. The long-established
cities of Philadelphia and New York possessed entrenched social structures and hierarchies, to which the federal government had to adapt
during each city's tenure as capital. Washington City lacked such existing configurations or customs and so invited innovation. Society, in all
its forms, could be—in fact, had to be—created from the ground up, a
necessity that held a great deal of interest not only to those eager for
the benefits of social interactions but also to the capital's politicians.
However, the very novelty and nature of the capital city presented its
residents with several formidable obstacles to realizing their dream of a
"new Rome" on the Potomac.

⁂

To paraphrase a famous jibe, Washington was a town of houses with no
streets and streets with no houses. In 1801, and for years to come, the
city existed primarily on paper. From a political point of view, Washington City's very blankness constituted one of its greatest assets. Largely
rural, removed from older, more "corrupt" eastern seaboard cities, the
new capital provided the Republican founders with a fresh slate.

The scattered nature of the built landscape was not merely a matter
of lagging development. Most towns and cities grew more organically,
outward from a unified, central location, such as a market square or a
waterfront. In contrast, the city planners Peter Charles L'Enfant and
Andrew Ellicott, along with George Washington and Thomas Jefferson, had laid out Washington City all at once; with only the most crucial buildings constructed, it would take a while to fill in the huge
stretches of space between them. Designed along republican principles,
the city plan stressed separation and spatial grandeur. The Constitution
may have been the official blueprint for the new government, but the

streets and buildings of the federal seat were the living embodiment of it, the first attempt of the founding men to translate republican ideals into reality. The capital city was as much a product of political theory as of architectural engineering.

Just as the Constitution eschewed a central, consolidating power, Washington lacked a city center. The distance between the executive and legislative branches reflected the decreed separation of powers. The Capitol, high on the hill, was intended to house both branches of Congress, suggesting the collective nature of their work. In contrast, the president's mansion was home to only the chief executive, but comprised both living and working spaces. A web of intersecting avenues connected the buildings to one another and to the rest of the city, out to its borders. As befitted its independent position, the judiciary had no easy access to either of the other branches or to the outside world. The most visible of the city's boulevards was, of course, Pennsylvania Avenue. Anyone traveling between the executive and legislative branches would be observed on the avenue, this openness and visibility again embodying the republican ideal of transparent power. In some distant day, the finished capital would not only inspire awe with its visual beauty, but also serve as the physical manifestation of the "noiseless machine" of the Constitution, dispensing power, law, and justice, quietly and efficiently.[7]

Faced with the actual site, however, most travelers and new residents saw only its barren present and not its future promise. L'Enfant and Washington had dreamed of magnificent buildings lining the streets, but when the officials of the federal government moved to the city during the spring of 1800, all they found were "magnificent distances." One hundred and six representatives and thirty-two senators, along with other federal employees and officers, joined 2,464 white people, 623 slaves, and 123 free blacks already living inside Washington proper. By comparison, the two former capitals, Philadelphia and New York, boasted populations between forty thousand and sixty thousand.

It was a good thing that the federal city had a small population, because there was nowhere for them to live. Only 109 "habitable" brick houses existed, along with 263 wooden ones. This total building count did not include the many shacks and hovels that dotted the landscape—some no more substantial than a booth at a country fair.[8] With respect to many of these structures, "habitable" meant one or two rooms, with an overhead loft, housing no fewer than six or eight people. Architecturally speaking, the first houses in the capital of the United States resembled the crude shanties built by the English emigrants right off the *Mayflower* in 1620. The new capital resembled less a city than a series of small villages sprouting up around the public buildings. Only the Madisons' F Street neighborhood, near the president's house, resembled a town; the Capitol was surrounded by congressional boardinghouses, with the judiciary equidistant between it and the executive mansion. A small settlement had sprung up on the shores of the Anacostia River, south of the city center; the closest real town was Georgetown, across Rock Creek. The unfinished roads made everyday errands a laborious and treacherous undertaking. The few byways actually laid out quickly turned to mud when it rained (and it often rained), miring carriage wheels and foolhardy pedestrians. A simple trip between the president's house and Capitol Hill proved a trial; "mud, bushes, thorns, briers" barred the way.[9]

Not surprisingly, many travelers and government officials reacted with shock and dismay to the raw conditions, and especially to the idea that they would be expected to live here. Most did not hesitate to express their opinion of the enterprise's folly, but they had to tread cautiously. After all, George Washington himself had chosen the spot. In life, Washington had achieved godlike status; Americans were still reeling from his death two years earlier, a death that fixed his star even more solidly in the firmament. People carefully separated their distaste for Washington City from the regard in which they held "the Father of His Country." Ebenezer Mattoon, representative from New Hampshire, spoke for many when he declared Washington City "secluded from every delightful and pleasing thing—except the *name* of the place, which to be sure I reverence." Albert Gallatin, always careful with words, ventured that George Washington's choice of the capital's location was the only instance of defective judgment Gallatin had ever known him to show.[10]

Making jokes about the backward capital became a local sport, one that would continue for many decades. Humorous stories abounded—some apocryphal and some not—about sophisticated Europeans, standing in forests or hip-deep in mud, asking directions to the city, only to be informed that they were in it. Indeed, Europeans proved particularly acerbic—"Washington would be a beautiful city if it were built," sniffed the English traveler Lady Wortley, "but as it is not, I cannot say much about it." Even patriotic Americans, however, did not hold back. Thirty years later, after several building booms, Job Pierson, a congressional representative from New York, could still tease his daughter, Sarah, "This City is what you Yankees would call a darn'd little City on a tarnation large scale."[11]

Underneath the humor and mock horror lay real anxiety. After all, this "swamp," this "desert," was supposed to be not only a capital city, but also the "permanent seat of empire" of a great nation. The people of the age put a great deal of stock in the symbolism of architecture; they constantly fell back on building as a metaphor for understanding government and society. When the Constitution was presented to the states for ratification, newspapers often referred to it as "the Grand Federal Edifice" and the process of ratification as building "a Temple of Liberty." What metaphorical meaning, then, would the public read in Washington's impassable roads and isolated buildings? If the built environment was to reflect the soaring majesty of republican ideals, what did the scattering of shacks around the president's house signify? No wonder many Americans who first laid eyes on Washington City worried about the future of the union and their republican experiment: the contrast between "the grandeur and magnificence" of the planned city and rough reality "render[ed] the conception no better than a dream."[12]

But even as some new Washingtonians expressed their anxiety about their wild, unbuilt capital, the opportunity of creating a city and a government from scratch energized others. Generally speaking, Washington City's unfinished state appalled northerners and Europeans more than it did southerners. This was owing partly to their preconceptions: people who came to Washington expecting to encounter a European or northeastern cityscape obviously expressed more surprise than local people. Southern cities and towns, such as Charleston, South Carolina, might be sophisticated, but many smaller state capitals and county seats were quite rustic. Southerners like the Madisons and Thomas Jefferson accepted more easily the abrupt juxtapositions of aspiring refinement and downright crudeness that struck others as an absurdity peculiar to Washington. White members of southern families were accustomed to sitting down to a table set with fine linen and silver, while being waited on by a half-naked, unwashed slave who might well be a mixed-blood relation.

Visitors could not fail to notice the active role of slaves in the city's construction, including the Capitol and the White House, nor could they miss the coffles of human beings chained together or held in pens as they awaited transportation South.[13] Urban and rural styles of slavery differed greatly, and in spite of the southern setting, slavery in Washington City more closely resembled that of Philadelphia than plantation slavery. The city was home to both slave and free blacks, sometimes slave and free in the same family. Enslaved laborers enjoyed more freedom of movement than their plantation counterparts, and some slaves could, with their masters' permission, hire themselves out or take on a side business in order to earn money for their freedom. Slavery was on the landscape in other ways as well; many of the new town houses were bought with the proceeds of distant slave plantations.

Of course, individual reaction to the infant city could also depend on personality. Sometimes opinion divided along generations, even within families. Abigail Adams, as the first presidential wife to live in Washington, complained in great detail about the primitive conditions of the city and the executive residence.[14] In contrast, her daughter-in-law Louisa Catherine Johnson Adams responded with optimism. Louisa Catherine had lived in European cities and capitals, and though she conceded the usual drawbacks, she pronounced herself "delighted with the situation of this place" to her husband, future congressman John Quincy Adams, adding, "I think should it ever be finished it will be one of the most beautiful spots in the world."[15]

Fortunately, like Louisa Catherine, Dolley was a "glass half full" personality. Unlike the famous carpers, she left no written defense of the city, but her actions make clear her faith in the enterprise. She did not dwell on the theoretical implications of the scenery; her concerns were practical. The sturdy, optimistic side of her nature enthusiastically embraced the challenges of life in the new capital. And these challenges were daunting, beyond logistical inconvenience. Dolley's impulse was always toward unity, which was precisely what the city, the government, and the country needed. But she would have to contend with a sense of isolation that extended beyond the far-flung buildings. Dolley began by establishing her family's presence on the landscape, both literally and otherwise.

❧

With Jefferson and Vice President Aaron Burr both widowers, the Madisons were the leading family in the nation's capital, and it was up to the lady of that family to create society for the city. The universal opinion seemed to be that "there was never a woman better calculated for the task." Even as she presided occasionally at Jefferson's table, Dolley set about making her own house, in the words of John Quincy Adams, "one of the social centers of the city." The presence of Anna Payne—young, pretty, outgoing, and accomplished—drew many youthful visitors to the Madisons'. Middle sister Lucy, with and without her husband, often stayed with them on F Street. The three attractive women brought a vibrancy that leading Washingtonians appreciated, dubbing them "the Merry Wives of Windsor."[16] Dolley did not wait for Washington to come to her, however. Society dictated that "calls"— short, ceremonial visits—opened relations between families, and Dolley proceeded to call with a vengeance.

Setting a precedent that she followed when she became the president's wife and that guided all subsequent First Ladies, Dolley called on everyone, new arrivals and established residents. Her dark-green "chariot" (bought secondhand by James in Philadelphia for $594), with a silver monogram on each door and sporting venetian blinds, cut glass, and candles, soon became a regular sight on the city streets; so familiar a figure was she in her pelisse and matching hat that when

Martha Jefferson Randolph borrowed these garments, Washingtonians mistook her for Dolley.[17]

Dolley's calling focused on three distinct and disparate segments of the population: local gentry families, many of them not connected to the federal government; the "official" families, who came to the seat of power through officeholding; and the few but significant foreign visitors and officials.[18] Each of these groups had a different investment in Washington City, and each was linked with its various enterprises. The local gentry, both long-term residents and new arrivals, were tied to the place itself, and they strove to profit by retaining and developing it as the nation's capital. The official families worked toward the success and stability of the federal government. The diplomatic corps, along with influential European visitors and observers, represented the main business of the U.S. government—foreign relations. In a day of slow communication, these foreign emissaries embodied the great nation-states of Europe, each with the potential to be a powerful friend or a dangerous enemy. All three sets of residents intersected and overlapped with one another.[19] In her quest to create an ideal capital society, Dolley had to find ways not only to reach each group individually, but to blend and connect all three.

Dolley had begun her Washington "campaign" by making friends with the local families, including those of long standing within the ten-mile square and in the nearby cities of Georgetown and Alexandria. Unlike the residents of other cities, these families did not think of themselves as necessarily linked until the Washington City planners placed them on a map and gave them a regional designation—"the Federal District." Other families had moved to the Maryland and Virginia countryside upon the capital city's founding, attracted by the opportunities promised by its promoters and the chance to be in on the ground floor of a magnificent enterprise. The results were mixed at best, though local entrepreneurs constantly tried to entice wealthy families to relocate.

In most cities, members of the local upper classes ruled economic, social, and political life. If Washington City gentry hoped that this would happen in the new capital, they were disappointed. It rapidly became clear that the pageant of government—starring officials from outside the area—would remain the only show in town. Contrary even to the expectations of the venerated George Washington, no industry or successful capital-intensive ventures developed. Once Congress was seated, the locals did not even control their own town governance. They no longer lived in a state, but in a District, within which they had no local voting rights, ironically (for a revolutionary generation) experiencing true taxation without representation.[20] After a few abortive attempts to create independent industry, such as a canal system for commercial transport, the Washington City locals realized that they had hitched their wagon to a political star and that their best bet lay in developing the city around the federal government. Even so, "a capricious Congress" often refused to implement city improvements, such as paving the notoriously bad roads, and stymied their efforts.[21]

The leading local family were the Van Nesses, in themselves a "mixed marriage" between an established local resident and a newcomer. Marcia Burnes Van Ness's father achieved immortality when George Washington pronounced him "The Obstinate Mr. Burns," one of the last holdouts against efforts to secure the land for Washington City's ten miles square. When Davy Burnes died, he willed his enormous estate of $1.5 million—$14 million in present-day value—to his daughter upon his wife's death. Attractive, accomplished, and wealthy, twenty-year-old Marcia Burnes chose as her husband Representative John Peter Van Ness of the Seventh Congress, a member of a distinguished New York family, whom she may have met through Dolley. The couple would play leading public roles in virtually every major political, economic, and cultural venture in Washington, and Dolley and Marcia would prove particularly close and effective collaborators.[22]

Dr. William Thornton and Anna Maria Brodeau Thornton, Federalist transplants from Philadelphia, were among those who had moved to Washington to seek their fortune. Dr. Thornton had won the contest to design the Capitol building, and the Thorntons arrived in the 1790s to oversee the implementation of the doctor's design. They quickly found themselves at the center of both local and official society. A Renaissance man who dabbled in everything but medicine, Dr. Thornton served as a federal commissioner of the city and later superintendent of patents. (Some of Dr. Thornton's "amateur" activities included writing novels, breeding merino sheep, inventing a language for the deaf, designing buildings, drawing and painting, organizing a fire insurance company, a market, and other businesses, serving as magistrate and in the militia, and inventing many gadgets and machines, most notably a steamboat.) Anna Maria Brodeau Thornton rendered drawings, sketches, and blueprints for her husband's schemes and, as a well-educated Frenchwoman, entertained diplomats, officials, and travelers at the Thorntons' houses in town and in the nearby countryside.[23]

Next-door neighbors, the Thorntons and the Madisons became fast friends. Though the two couples differed politically, the attraction of the well-educated and creative Thorntons proved hard to resist. Dolley Madison and William Thornton shared a Quaker background. The men's mutual love of horseflesh induced them to buy a racehorse together, which, considering the nature of capital city enterprise, they aptly named Wild Medley.[24] Drawn together by their mutual love for French fashion and taste—and, no doubt, by the frontier experience of life in Washington—Dolley and Anna Maria soon developed a whole world of shared interests.

In those first years, they exchanged news of friends, swapped books, and visited constantly. Not long into their acquaintance, Anna Maria felt that she could confide in Dolley "with freedom & carelessness, expecting that none but the partial eye of my dear Mrs. M. will see what I write." Anna Maria passed on news of all kinds; it was from her that Dolley learned that the celebrated portrait painter Gilbert Stuart "denies most pointedly having painted the picture [of George Washington] in the President's house, and says he told Genl: Lee that he did not paint it—but he had bargained for it."[25]

Both women had married brilliant, visionary men, and both approached life and politics more pragmatically than did their husbands. In addition, Dolley and Anna Maria had another important commonality.

Anna Maria was childless, and though Dolley had Payne, he became a young man during the Washington years, passing out of his mother's world, while no little brothers or sisters followed to fill the gap. Certainly, Dolley and James expected that they would have children. Dolley had produced two children within three years of her marriage to John Todd; James came from a startlingly fecund family, where broods of eight or more were not uncommon. Birth control was unreliable at best and pregnancy was expected soon after a wedding; but eighteen months after the Madisons wed, Aaron Burr reported to James Monroe not only that "Madison still childless," but also "I fear like to continue so." (Some evidence exists that Dolley might have had one or more miscarriages. Jefferson's comment to a Republican colleague, Benjamin Hawkins, that James was "not yet a father" eleven years into the marriage suggests that there may have been pregnancies, even if they came to nothing.)[26] In any case whatever losses the two women mourned in private, freed from the unrelenting round of pregnancy, childbirth, lactation, and child care that ruled most adult women's lives, Anna Maria and Dolley had the time to develop their own potentials—artistic in one case, political in the other.

Margaret Bayard Smith and her husband, Samuel Harrison Smith, also belonged to and influenced both the local and the official communities. The Smiths had been on the scene from the start, having moved to Washington City from Philadelphia in 1800 as newlyweds. First cousins Samuel and Margaret had been ardent Federalists, but Jefferson made Republican converts of them. When he wanted his own editor, the newly elected Jefferson brought Smith down to head *The Daily Intelligencer.* The city's first newspaper, as well as the organ of the administration, the *Intelligencer* posted all government notices and recorded all official business, including congressional debates, thus serving as a prototype of the *Congressional Record.* Under her own name and under pseudonyms, Margaret was herself a prolific journalist as well as a popular novelist; she published her account of James Madison's inauguration in the *Ladies' Magazine and Literary Gazette* and made Dolley an exemplary figure in her Washington fiction. Her most significant writing, however, was the huge body of letters she wrote to her sisters and sisters-in-law over four decades.[27]

Certainly Dolley cultivated Margaret because she was the wife of Jefferson's own newspaper editor. (When Samuel sold the paper to Joseph Gales and William Seaton in 1810, Sarah Gales Seaton, sister of one and wife of the other, found herself part of Dolley's charmed circle for the same reason.) Both Sarah and Margaret had unerring instincts for what would become "public relations," especially the early nineteenth-century equivalent of the "photo op"; Dolley profoundly influenced their ideas about the new government, ideas that both Samuel and Margaret transmitted to the American reading public, and that Sarah conveyed in her own correspondence.

Margaret also involved herself in female charity projects spear-headed by the Van Nesses and the Thorntons. These investments were risky; with Congress entertaining periodical proposals to remove the government to Philadelphia, the locals often felt that their investment in the city was under threat and that they could do little about it. But in fact, their contribution to creating the capital far outweighed what seemed to them their relative helplessness.[28] Government families con-stituted a "floating society," since they had permanent homes elsewhere and came to Washington City for only part of the year, and for set terms, completely at the whim of the electorate. In contrast, the afflu-ent Van Nesses, the aristocratic Thorntons, the resolutely Republican Smiths—these three families, brought together by Dolley, along with the Tayloe, Custis, Nourse, Brent, and Carroll clans (among others) supplied the social matrix, which, although fragile, held the young city together.[29] By interacting with these local families and participating in civic activities, Dolley brought the federal government into the life of the city. It worked the other way as well. Dolley sought opportunities to weave the prominent locals into government business.

In 1803, when Thomas Jefferson commissioned Meriwether Lewis and William Clark to explore the lands west of the Mississippi, he soon found that the mission's expenses fell beyond the funding purview of the minimalist government. Jefferson arranged for a secret appropria-tion of federal funds, but he still fell short. Dolley and her friends stepped in to fill the gap, and the expeditionaries "were fitted up with Camp equipage and every thing thought to be suitable for them."

Lewis and Clark showed their appreciation three years later, bringing back souvenirs and curiosities for the ladies, and Dolley even received some of their silver cooking utensils.[30]

⁓

Cultivating the Thorntons and the Smiths was easy for Dolley. Both she and the local gentry had a stake in making their relationship work, and local families also included female members, with whom she could connect. Much more difficult was building a social relationship with the men of the official government, many of whom lived in Washington without their families and, moreover, spent much of each working day opposing her husband.

In many ways, Washington City mitigated against cohesion of any sort. For Dolley, the biggest challenge lay not in the city's rural setting or in the inconvenience of shopping and travel—she could entertain mightily in spite of that. Rather, these surface troubles reflected and exacerbated a deeper psychological isolation in the city and the new government.

No established town threw up so many impediments to the development of an integrated society, not to mention a working government and bureaucracy. The city had been designed to affirm constitutional ideas of checks and balances, not built to accommodate human beings: there existed no single place that could hold all the members of government, let alone their families. The people who came to Washington found themselves following the city's intent. The separation of persons followed the separation of powers, with officials from each branch living around "their" buildings and generally associating only with colleagues. Some government personnel took rooms in Georgetown, which was connected to the Capitol district by what passed for a major road; some boarded near the executive mansion; but most crowded into the eight boarding-houses near the Capitol.[31] Congressmen would usually "mess together" by region: men from the same state or area often occupied a single boardinghouse, and such men tended to be more alike politically than different.

The famously bad roads aggravated the segregation of the branches.

In inclement weather, "every turn of your wagon wheel . . . is attended with danger." Even on a fine day, since few legislators and other part-time residents brought carriages to Washington, many depended on a hackney coach or a scheduled stage that went through Georgetown, stopping at Capitol Hill and the president's house. The total round trip took three hours.[32]

The problem of isolation was not just a matter of bad roads or structural considerations. The very philosophy that drove the nation's founding also laid the most serious obstacles to cohesion and the construction of a working government. Republicanism demanded that lawmakers possess "virtue"—the ability to put aside one's personal interest for the common good. Such a lofty, uplifting view of human nature appealed to Jefferson and James Madison. Unfortunately, the ideal was so high as to be inhuman. It did not acknowledge that there might be more than one obvious "common good." Nor did it take into account that human beings do not operate as separate cogs in a perfect machine, but rather are motivated by a variety of interests and identifications.

Still, at least for the first years of the federal government, politicians strove to embody the ideal. In order for a politician to appear virtuous, then, he had to adopt the pose of the outsider. To be seen "accommodating" anyone would call down accusations of weakness and even treason upon his head. His fellow legislators remained alert to any sign of collaboration, conciliation, or cooperation, especially with "the enemy." Despite the clear evidence of the election of 1800, politicians still believed that there should only be one party in American politics. Unfortunately, two different camps believed this. To each one—the Federalists and the Republicans—the other party was a "faction," a source of danger and disorder and a very personal as well as national threat. In such an atmosphere, legislators did not even tolerate a discussion that included difference. In fact, if one did not shout down an opposition argument fast enough, one's colleagues might read a sinister motive into such softness. The government of Washington City, officially at least, emerged as one of lone gunmen, all irascible—hence virtuous—outsiders. Ironically, this group culture produced, through peer pressure, a uniformity of individualism. The fractious legislators were not operating in a vacuum. Their vociferousness reflected the larger American distrust of power and a view of politics as evil. Members of government, then, vied for public approbation—and buttressed their own sense of worth—by trying to distance themselves from the very job that had brought them to Washington City.[33]

This was a perilous condition for a government trying to get on its feet and to get something done. As Thomas Dwight, representative from Massachusetts, complained to his wife, Hannah, "Six long weeks have passed since my arrival in this place yet very little has been done in Congress, of public importance."[34]

The legislators in Washington felt themselves isolated at many levels. Not only did their political philosophy work against collaborative effort, they found themselves stuck in a country capital, lacking in civilized amenities and cut off from the rest of the nation. Women could alleviate some of this isolation; luckily, only a year or so into Jefferson's first administration, some members of Congress and federal bureaucrats brought along a wife or daughter. Soon, the "messes" boasted significant populations of women, as budding politicians realized they needed female relatives for political as well as personal reasons.

Among those early arrivals, Dolley made a particular friend and future ally in cabinet wife Hannah Nicholson Gallatin. Like Dolley, Hannah was a superb political wife, and she brought considerable intellectual discernment to the position. Raised in a prominent political family, she spent evenings by the fireside listening to Thomas Paine, Aaron Burr, and various members of the Livingston clan, which ruled New York; famously, her father talked politics with her. Doubtless prompted by her husband's lonely longings, among other considerations, Hannah joined him two weeks after the Madisons arrived, on May 13, 1801.

Hannah and Albert lived next door to the Six Buildings, the Madisons' first, temporary house. Again, the frontier atmosphere brought the two women closer together than life in a more cultivated and structured city might have done. Not physically compelling or obviously charming, Hannah was a less public, less visible kind of political wife than Dolley. Polite Washingtonians differentiated between the two by dubbing

Hannah "more domestic," faint praise in a capital where society and politics inextricably intertwined.[35] Even as the Madisons settled on F Street and the Gallatins moved to Capitol Hill, the families remained close.

⚜

As the wife of the secretary of state, Dolley had more than foreign relations in mind as she made efforts to keep members of the diplomatic corps close. In this era, foreign emissaries unabashedly involved themselves in domestic affairs, lobbying for tariff legislation, courting senators and representatives, and sponsoring propaganda that encouraged division between the Federalists and Republicans.[36]

During James's tenure as secretary of state, both France and Great Britain replaced their chargés d'affaires, Louis-André Pichon and Edward Thornton, respectively, with full ministers. Great Britain sent Anthony Merry in January 1803; Louis-Marie Turreau de Garambouville arrived in November 1804. Denmark also sent representatives, first Minister Peder Blicherolsen and then Chargé d'Affaires Peder Pedersen. Russia as well had a "presence" in the new United States and soon sent its first chargé, Andrei Dashkov.

Augustus John Foster, secretary of the British legation, was on the Washington scene, as was the Spanish minister, Carlos Fernando Martínez de Yrujo, who had married the lively Sally McKean, an old friend from Dolley's Philadelphia days. Though the foreign population was never large (and though some diplomats lived part-time in Philadelphia), it remained always highly visible and influential, adding glamour and dash to Washington City. The Tunisian ambassador, the exotic Sidi Suleiman Melli Melli, made the president gifts of horses, and the French ambassador danced quadrilles with naked women, thus guaranteeing Washington residents sizable doses of foreign ways.[37]

To more anxious republicans, such as Thomas Jefferson, the presence of courtly foreigners, infusing the capital with luxury goods and European ideas, proved worrisome. The small size of Washington society, however, forced a certain cosmopolitanism, as reflected in this report by Margaret Bayard Smith: "Mrs. Madison, Meredith and Gallatin . . . [and] Mrs. Law ha[ve] been here, and we dined there [at Dolley's house] in company with the Swedish minister, a Danish colonel and other gentlemen."[38]

Diplomats recognized and appreciated Dolley's efforts to incorporate them into city and government life. Augustus John Foster noted that she was "so perfectly good tempered and good humoured that she rendered her husband's house as far as depended on her agreeable to all parties." Peder Blicherolsen acknowledged the importance of an "agreeable house" and gave Dolley credit for his diplomatic success, as he thought he would have been "poisoned" in his experience of Washington "without Mrs. Madisons Generosity." He gallantly added: "If it was not too old fashioned, I should here have a fine opportunity to drop a few words, about Nectar, Divinities, Goddesses, etc."[39]

No doubt the wife of the Spanish minister, Sally McKean Martínez de Yrujo, who matched Dolley in outgoing charm, paved her way with the other diplomatic spouses. Marie-Angélique Lequesne Ronsin Turreau, the wife of the French minister, also became a particular friend. Dolley praised Marie-Angélique as "good natured & inteligent generous plain & curious." Together, the women rode and walked through the Washington town and countryside and when in Marie-Angélique's chambers, "sans cerimoni," Dolley said, "I crack my sides a laughing."

As well as providing company, Marie-Angélique played a part in "finishing" Dolley. Dolley said that Marie-Angélique spoke "no english but we understand each other well." Marie-Angélique Turreau was teaching Dolley French, and, as Dolley reported to Anna, "You would be surprized to hear my improvement in the language." An encouraging mentor, Marie-Angélique "allways understands me" as Dolley worked at French conversation. Thanks to Marie-Angélique and Anna Maria, Dolley became proficient in the official language of diplomacy and government and thus able to communicate with any foreign emissary—not to mention that knowledge of French marked her as a polished and accomplished lady.

Madame Turreau also taught Dolley how to dress: "She decorates herself according to the french Ideas & wishes me do so two—." Generously, "she shews me every thing she has, & would fain give me of *every thing*." But Marie-Angélique Turreau was no conventional fashion plate, nor was she a conventional political wife. Reputedly, she came from a common background; her husband had married her out of gratitude, since she helped him to escape imprisonment during the French Revolution. Dolley appreciated this exceptional person: "In short I love the woman for her singularitys which are [s]carcely known to others." Following Marie-Angélique's example, Dolley was beginning to develop a public persona for the political world, while retaining an individuality "scarcely known to others."[40]

Surrounded by women of the world, Dolley was acquiring an education beyond the sartorial. Dolley did not like Marie-Angélique's husband, the French minister, Louis-Marie Turreau. In fact, he appalled her. Even in a culture that allowed husbands to "correct" their wives, Turreau shocked Dolley—indeed, he shocked Washington: "He whiped his wife & abused her before all his servants." Though Dolley expressed sympathy for her friend—"I pity her sincearly"—in the interest of politics, she bade her sister Anna (then in Philadelphia), "dont breath it in your country as it will make them all [the French] so odious as *he* deserves to be."[41]

At times, Dolley and her colleagues took more active roles in specific situations. In 1804, fallout from the Louisiana Purchase led to a tense exchange between Spain and the United States. Martínez de Yrujo signaled his displeasure by leaving Washington for Philadelphia without calling on James Madison. This breach of diplomatic etiquette could have been unforgivable, but because the women enjoyed a personal relationship, Sally mended fences by calling on Dolley before she left town.

Dolley wasn't leaving anything to chance. Even with the Martínezes in Philadelphia she worked to keep the channels of communication open, bidding young Anna: "Remember me to McKeans & to Sally say a great deal for I feel a tenderness for her & her husband independent of circumstances." The women's efforts did not stem the deteriorating relationship between Spain's official representative and the

U.S. government; indeed, Jefferson would spend the next two years trying to force Martínez de Yrujo out without completely rupturing relations with Spain. But the bonds between Dolley and Sally helped to
ease the tension, ensuring that diplomatic channels could remain open.[42]

⁂

Like a metaphor for the republican experiment that it housed, Washington City faced many obstacles to its future. Even before the Revolution had ended, the women and men of the founding generation had
worried about "union"—whether the states and the American people
could unify around the abstractions of nationhood. The years that followed, with their fierce and divisive politics, offered little reassurance.
From in its first days, life in the capital city suggested that unification
did not lie in the political realm; indeed, the very configuration of government and of the government's city militated against it. Only in the
social sphere could Washingtonians—Federalist and Republican, official and unofficial, local and foreign—begin to come together. Dolley
was more than up to the role of the city's social leader, but one more
obstacle had to be overcome, or at least circumvented. The immediate
impediment to the city's amalgamation, and America's, lay in the mind
of the man in the executive mansion.

Social Work

*W*hen Jefferson arrived in Washington in 1801, he had resolved to rein in the nascent American elite that had taken root in Philadelphia and New York during the Washington and Adams administrations. His predecessors had instituted several kinds of events, including the large receptions that enemies sneeringly labeled "levées," a term that carried the monarchical taint of the foreign and the foppish. More ominously, such large gatherings, where women and nonofficial men could politick, smacked of corrupt Old World courts. Jefferson immediately did away with them, opening the president's house to the public only twice a year, on New Year's Day and the Fourth of July. But the ladies of Washington would have none of it, and in their own genteel, indirect way, they tried to undermine him. Society, after all, was their area of expertise, and, from the moment the government arrived in the capital, according to Abigail Adams, "the ladies [we]re impatient for a drawing room."

As a nineteenth-century historian quaintly put it, "they mustered in force," arriving at the executive mansion, in their most fashionable attire, determined to have a grand levée in spite of their president. Jefferson was out riding; upon his return, he understood immediately that a coup of sorts was in progress. He decided to pretend that his visitors were mere callers, serendipitously arriving at the same time. Clad in spurs and dusty riding clothes, he greeted each guest with delight and surprise, marveling at the "happy coincidence" of the ladies' mass arrival: "Never had he been seen so cordial and attentive." The ladies went along with his scenario, and dutifully took their leave after the quarter-hour customary for visits, even as Jefferson drove his point home by urging his visitors to stay longer. Apparently, they accepted the joke graciously, "laughing heartily at the result of their experiment," as they retreated from the field.[1] This was hardly the last time that politics and society would collide in Washington.

❧❧❧

Partisan politics had reached a new low during John Adams's administration, with the enactment of the Alien and Sedition Acts in 1798. Ostensibly a measure to restrict subversive activity from abroad, yet directly aimed at his political enemies, the four acts targeted foreigners, especially French immigrants, all of whom were more likely to be Republicans. The acts rendered the citizenship process longer and more complicated, and granted the government the power to deport foreigners without due process. More seriously, they curtailed the right of assembly for American citizens, if for the purpose of protesting the government, and encroached on the freedom of the press, making it a crime to "print, utter, or publish . . . false, scandalous, and malicious writing" against the government.

Such latitude in the language destined the acts to be abused, as they were, most notably in the prosecutions of journalist Thomas Cooper and the Republican congressman from Vermont, Matthew Lyon. All across the country, Republicans and Americans who had yet to affiliate with a party protested, correctly understanding the acts as an assault on liberty.

In an extreme form, the Alien and Sedition Acts reflected significant currents in American politics. On one hand, they originated from a very personal impulse, that combustible mixture of personality, personal honor, and ideology characteristic of American politics of the day. John and Abigail Adams, shocked at the ingratitude of their critics, were determined to quell and even forestall what they saw as treasonous speech and action. Yet support for the acts also had an institutional basis, and the Republicans played this angle for all it was worth, revealing the Federalists' distaste for and distrust of ordinary people. It was not hard to make the case for Federalist arrogance, which Jefferson and James did, spearheading a pamphlet war against what they called "the reign of witches."[2]

The nation was still reeling from the impact and implications of this first assault on citizens' civil rights when the campaign for the 1800 presidential election began. Fear and uncertainty characterized the proceedings. Everyone knew the mettle of the man currently in the executive mansion. No one knew for sure what electing Thomas Jefferson would mean, and Jefferson's failure to specify his views only added to the anxiety. Detractors associated his emphasis on "pure republicanism" with the bloody and radical French Revolution; Jefferson's years in Paris as a diplomat only seemed to confirm that he had fallen under a Jacobin spell. Religious leaders feared a government headed by a godless "infidel," using Jefferson's statements on religious tolerance as proof of his atheism. They forecast a leader who would "destroy religion, introduce immortality, and loosen all the bonds of society." A few votes cast the wrong way would result in "*Civil War*... [where] Murder, robbery, rape, adultery, and incest will all be openly taught and practiced, the air will be rent with the cries of distress, the soil will be soaked with blood, and the nation black with crimes."[3]

In spite of such dire predictions, the election had itself been a relatively peaceful affair; only when it came to the House did the tension mount. Jefferson was elected after nineteen identical tie ballots. The general relief at his inauguration, as power was peacefully transferred from one ruler to another, was palpable. No wonder that at Jefferson's inaugural address, Americans seized upon one line—"we are all republicans—we are all federalists"—as a hopeful sign for the future. Since the printed version of the address capitalized the two designations, most happily viewed the statement as Jefferson's attempt at reconciliation, a call for unity between the two proto-parties. In Jefferson's handwritten version, however, the two words were in lowercase; his statement was less about bringing two parties together and more about affirming the "first principles" upon which all Americans could agree: a republican form of government, with states held together by a federal bond.[4]

That the new Americans wanted to interpret Jefferson's platitudes as an attempt to repair a partisan breach demonstrated their eagerness for a national reconciliation, but Jefferson was not the man to give it to them. As it was for the Adamses, politics was always personal for Jefferson, and he did not just oppose the opposition: he hated them, and in his hatred could only see them as larger-than-life political bogeymen. Jefferson had no intention of reconciling with the enemy; rather, he aimed at extermination. In the future, he expected that those Federalists capable of redemption would convert to Republicanism, and voters would cast out the rest, cursing, into the darkness.[5]

A man who "loved to dream, eyes open," Jefferson did not focus on the reality of the election's wreckage, but rather on his own utopian plan. He envisioned a nation where everyone from independent yeoman farmers to the highest rulers would embody in their persons and lives the republican ideals of simplicity, transparency, and virtue. The United States of America would be a new kind of society and government, one never before seen in human history, the precursor to a worldwide movement toward liberty and light.[6] To change not only the politics, but also the hearts and minds, of men, then, required that republicanism be applied to every aspect of life, especially to collective public and semi-public enterprises, such as "society."

Eighteenth-century society in the western world was not about leisure or fun, nor did it center on family and "togetherness." The social realm was part public, part private; ostensibly separate from the worlds of politics and business, it was also less intimate than the family circle. Ideally, "social circles of the best sort" allowed elite social equals to come together in a setting of beauty and refinement. Nothing was ordinary or everyday; the luxurious food and music, light and fabrics, were used to create a heightened experience, which, so the theory went, would inspire the participants to be their best selves, with the resulting conversation and interactions elevating the company to a pinnacle of sensibility and refinement. The reality, of course, was a bit baser. Society involved power struggles. All the elements of refinement supposedly intended to improve individuals also offered opportunities to assert superiority.[7]

From the beginning of the republican experiment, the founders understood that the survival of a republic depended on the "right" kinds of society, appropriate for each class of people. Since in republican theory "the people" could enjoy liberty only when ruled wisely and well, government socializing came in for particular scrutiny. Accordingly, after his inauguration, safely ensconced in the executive mansion, Jefferson began his plan for a New World by reforming high society at the seat of power.

Jefferson recognized the importance of society for "softening" and civilizing; a captivating and entertaining man, he delighted in social activities. But in his view, society needed to be restricted to the home, far from the taint of politics, to ensure it stayed pure and free of political corruption.[8] If politics could taint society, the reverse was even more true, and more grave. In Europe, social events had always formed part of the political process, being an integral component of rule. In royal courts, the business of state unfolded within a network of social events. National observances, religious holidays, even royal family members' birthdays provided contexts for courtly entertaining and the attendant personal politicking, as did the balls, pageants, and calls woven into the fabric of everyday court life.

In the Jeffersonian model, this kind of business as usual had no place in a republic. History had demonstrated that lavish social events at court, with their luxury and covert politics, signaled a nation's eventual slide into dissipation and tyranny. Jefferson's commitment to the separation of society and politics was no mere ideological stance; he feared that if left unsupervised, American politics would stray from the path of republican virtue, down the dark and twisted way of monarchies. Indeed, he thought that under John Adams and the Federalists this disaster had almost happened. Someone had to guard the gates—and Jefferson could vouch for no one's republican purity but his own. Nothing in

Washington, he determined, would happen in secret, that is, without his knowledge. After all, one of the advantages of the unbuilt condition of the federal city was that it literally lacked the halls of power, the back rooms and secret closets of corrupt Old World courts.[9] Similarly, Jefferson wanted to eliminate what he called "unofficial characters," people accountable to no one, by whom he meant courtiers and women.

In the court tradition, only the slightest division between "public" and "private" existed; there was no "behind the scenes." Everywhere politics happened was center stage—in the bedroom and in the throne room, while people were eating, bathing, or dressing. Within this kind of political society, women played a large part. Obviously, their exclusion (for the most part) from the openly official sphere limited the kinds of activities they undertook. But with politicking a crucial part of social events—and indeed of daily life—in traditional monarchical systems, there was no "sphere" that did not offer some kind of political opportunity for women.

In contrast, only men had a political place in Jefferson's America; after all, there were neither female yeoman farmers nor female rulers. This state of affairs not only reflected republican theory, which had shunted women into the corner of republican motherhood and wifehood, but also fit with older political traditions. Lacking legal identity, women had few ways to wield official power. Still, women's very exclusion made them dangerous. Falling outside of male categories such as "citizen" or "individual," women could be political wild cards, sowing disruption and disorder; lacking legal power, women could draw on natural and sexual resources. Even within the court setting, which depended on female political activity, the most feared creature of all was a highly sexed and highly placed character such as Madame Pompadour.[10]

Samuel Johnson's aphorism "Nature has given women so much power that the law has very wisely given them little" was the conventional wisdom of the day. In her famous "Remember the Ladies" letter of 1776, Abigail Adams asked John to amend the laws of coverture that controlled women's bodies and property, allowing men "to use us with cruelty and indignity with impunity," when he was reforming the legal system of the new nation. John's humorous reply acknowledged what

seemed self-evident to all. The "Masculine systems" of law and government were "little more than Theory. We dare not Exert our Power . . .
in Practice you know We are the Subjects." The source of her power,
John pointed out, was "the Despotism of the Peticoat," or, more accurately, what was underneath.[11]

The unregulatedness of women was certainly no joking matter to
Jefferson, and he spent a lot of time worrying about the female exercise
of "unnatural" power in unofficial, often social, settings. As ambassador
to France during the French Revolution, he had ample opportunity to
see women acting politically, from peasant women taking up lances in
the street to aristocratic salonnières influencing government officials.
Such sights evoked in Jefferson animus to the point of unbalance. He
blamed the whole French Revolution on the queen. To George Washington, he wrote despairingly that the reforms sought by revolutionaries would come to naught, unless the men controlled "a kind of
influence . . . I mean the influence of women in the government." Jefferson did not approve of women who "mix promiscuously in the gatherings of men," whether in streets or in drawing rooms. Most threatening
were the women who "visit[ed], alone" men in their offices, for the purpose of patronage.[12] It is hard to know what disgusted him more,
women employing their natural sexuality for nefarious purposes, or
women using their intellects at all.

Jefferson hoped to check any similar aspirations on the part of
American women. Using appropriately martial imagery, he opined
that only keeping women "behind the domestic line" could save
America from a "desperate state." From France, Jefferson had written:
"Our good ladies, I trust, have been too wise to wrinkle their fore-
heads with politics. They are contented to soothe and calm the minds
of their husbands returning ruffled from political debate. They have
the good sense to value domestic happiness above all."[13] As demonstrated by his encounter with the ladies who wanted a levée, Jefferson
had a knack for using denial to avoid confrontation while nevertheless
sending his message. The recipient of that definitive statement on
women and politics was America's most noted salonnière, Anne Willing Bingham.

Like many issues in the political climate of the early republic, the inter-play of society and politics in Washington City was fraught with tensions and contradictions. On one hand, Jefferson believed in confining society to the hearthside, while keeping politics "pure" and infused with republi-can simplicity. On the other, like all republican theorists, he had long rec-ognized that politics could not exist in a vacuum—that "republicanism" was more than just a political arrangement; it was a way of life. Jefferson knew he had a chance, in his almost-rural test tube of a capital city, to forge a society in his own image, to set a new style, simple, frugal, "Amer-ican," that matched his vision of a republican political dreamworld.[14]

The contradictions abounded in Jefferson's famously compartmen-talized mind, which allowed him to rail about the "promiscuous mix-ing" of men and women and the pollution of politics by social forms, while simultaneously using his position to his own advantage. Again, underdeveloped Washington City provided unparalleled opportunities. In place of larger entertainments, Jefferson instituted a round of small dinner parties, at which he introduced a series of practices ostensibly designed to foster intimacy and open communication. Guests sat at round tables, eliminating the head; Jefferson had a dumbwaiter system installed and served his guests himself, so as to eliminate eavesdropping servants and slaves. With the best cuisine in Washington, a genial and gracious host, and freely flowing wine, his parties were praised by his guests as the height of hospitality.[15]

However delightful, these affairs served a serious purpose. Canny as any French hostess, Jefferson used his dinner parties both to achieve spe-cific political ends and to curb the power of those he feared. He was not above manipulating the social world to make statements, issue rebukes, and mete out punishment to troublemakers, as when, during the 1805–1806 congressional season he banished the Federalist congressmen from his table. Over food and drink, the president kept track of the en-emy, rallied the troops, and even went so far as to keep some guests for a nightcap in order to pass on his legislative wishes. In a little journal he called his "Anas" (*anas* is a Latin word meaning a collection of random information), Jefferson revealed his political plans, logging in his dinner parties, the guest lists, the subjects discussed, and the eventual legislative outcomes. The most telling clue that Jefferson considered these "social dinners" as political events lay in the fact that he rarely invited women.

While on their face his dinners reflected the simpler, more easygoing American style he was cultivating, Jefferson was a man who needed to control his world, and the configuration of his dinner parties reflected that need. A limited number of small events in a town with few social venues meant that, indeed, no extrapolitical activities could take place beyond his eyesight or behind his back. Jefferson generally invited men of only one party or the other to a dinner, reflecting his famous distaste for contention as well as his desire for domination. He also tended to entertain congressional and cabinet guests separately. The small number of guests, and their close clustering at a round table, invited intimacy but also foreclosed the ability to converse out of Jefferson's hearing. The lack of slaves or servants waiting on table not only eliminated eavesdropping and below-stairs gossip but also made it easier to trace leaks.[16]

Given society's power to reconcile and to create binding ties, Jefferson could have implemented a social program that would foster the interparty reconciliation that the nation, and certainly the government, needed. But he did not; instead, his brand of society had quite the opposite effect. For instance, when the Federalists realized that they were not being invited to dinner, they were furious, and escalated the hostilities by boycotting the annual New Year's reception. Ironically, by sidestepping direct political conflict with his rule of inviting members of only one party at a time, Jefferson's dinners only increased partisan feeling among the Federalists and Republicans. Some thought that Jefferson erred in not inviting members of both parties to the same table, noting that "an interchange of sentiments tends to correct ones own errors and lead us to think more favorably of others." Representative William Plumer of New Hampshire correctly surmised that "under the necessity of being civil to each other" at Jefferson's table in the evening, Federalists and Republicans would "treat each other with more decency and respect" during the day in Congress. "The more men of good hearts associate," opined Plumer, "the better they think of each other, notwithstanding their differences of opinion."[17] But Jefferson saw no benefit to learning to work with his enemies, nor did he care to nurture bipartisan cooperation.

This was no way to run a government. Not interested in developing political structures among his legislators, Jefferson firmly suppressed any sign of coalition or party-building activity within Congress. This worked for a while, mostly because Jefferson's powerful and charismatic personality inspired supporters to blindly follow and opponents to shut up. Conflating personality with polity, however, "restrain[ed] the freedom of debate in Congress," Plumer worried. This effect seemed "highly improper" to congressmen desperately trying to work together, demonstrating "a littleness of mind unworthy of the President of the United States." As a result, no single individual, besides Jefferson himself, rose from the ranks to a leadership position. In his quest for a perfect and pure republic, completely under his control, Jefferson actively worked against the development of a multi-party, democratic system.[18]

❧

It was a testimony to Dolley's diplomatic skills that she did not attract the ire of the vigilant Jefferson. In fact, Jefferson, who disliked and distrusted almost everyone, evinced great affection for Dolley, even though she stole a bit of his thunder every New Year's Day. New Year's was one of the two annual occasions when Jefferson opened the president's house to the world; during his first term, word quickly got out that the good times were on F Street. It became a Washington custom, after one's obligatory appearance at the "official" function, to call at the Madisons'.

Dolley succeeded in operating under Jefferson's republican eye by adopting a simpler style than would distinguish her eight years later. Her events were not marked by an abundance of money spent, but rather "it was only in hospitality and charity that her profusion was unchecked." Guests noted that the Madison house was furnished simply and that though Dolley wore "expensive and fashionable" gowns, she also wore a modest Quaker cap and shielded her bosom with a kerchief.[19] Dolley was no political theorist, but her social intelligence and practical knowledge had taught her the value of socializing and its role in establishing a ruling class.

If Americans across the country hoped that the two warring parties were reconciling in Jefferson's Washington, the only venue where that took place was Dolley's table. She did her best to bring everyone in the capital—locals, officials, and visitors—together under her roof. In contrast to Jefferson's carefully calibrated events, the Madisons invited men of both parties to the house on F Street. A congressman, who might receive an invitation to dine at the president's house only once or twice a season, could attend the Madisons' dinners and various entertainments every week. Away from the homogenous, hothouse atmosphere of his boardinghouse, he discovered how to discuss politics without "inflaming" his colleagues.

The Madisons' dinner parties also mixed men and women. By their very presence, women softened the tone of political rhetoric, while paradoxically forwarding the opportunities for political wheeling and dealing. At one of Jefferson's stag dinners, John Quincy Adams found the conversation "desultory," though he wryly noted that Jefferson's "itch for telling prodigies [tall tales] was unabated." At the Madisons', John Quincy found himself amongst "a company of about seventy persons of both sexes," in a stark contrast to Jefferson's ten or twelve male guests. In the midst of the gay throng, he and James Madison had "considerable conversation . . . on the subjects now most important to the public."[20] A not unimportant development, this, for John Quincy Adams was a Federalist. At Dolley's house, men from both parties, along with their womenfolk, came together, learned about each other, and began to construct a political culture.

Dolley's willingness to entertain did her husband much political good. Uncomfortable in large groups and at public events, at dinner James Madison became a charming companion. Writing to his wife, Samuel Harrison Smith related that he had "rarely spent more agreeable hours" than at a recent dinner party with the Madisons. On this particular occasion, the champagne made everyone giddy, leading James to observe that "it was the most delightful wine when drank in moderation, but that more than a few glasses always produced a headache the next day." In a spirit of Enlightenment inebriation, he proposed that the party discover exactly how much champagne it took to induce a hangover, "as the next day being Sunday would allow time for a recovery from its effects." "Bottle after bottle" came in; but Samuel assured Margaret: "Its only effects were animated good humor and uninterrupted conversation."[21]

Flying under the radar of Jefferson's disapproval of elaborate events, Dolley confined herself to formal dinners and more informal types of entertaining. In what would be a characteristic dynamic, Dolley mixed her inclusive southern hospitality and her easy manners with sophisticated cuisine and wine. At one "excellent dinner" at the F Street house, the Reverend Manasseh Cutler, a Federalist, did not recognize a dish "called *Bouilli*," a boiled round of beef in a rich gravy, infused with garlic, spices, and "something of the sweet herb." A familiar main dish followed, a "large ham" surrounded by mashed cabbage. However, Cutler found himself stumped by one of the desserts. Among the array of delicacies were "two dishes which appeared like Apple pie, in the form of the half of a Musk-melon, the flat side down, tops creased deep, and the color a dark brown." The Reverend Cutler, congressman from Connecticut, may not have been able to name all the dishes, but he ate them, and he enjoyed himself. Dolley, he wrote, was "very amiable, and exceedingly pleasant and sensible in conversation."[22]

Even a Madison tea party (an evening event in Dolley's Washington) could be luxurious. Guests partook of coffee as well as tea, along with ice cream, cordials, punch, jelly, cake, and fruit. Small baskets were passed among the guests, containing raisins, almonds, and pieces of candied sugar wrapped in white paper printed with verses. Hot chocolate rounded out the treats.

Tea and coffee were not the only available stimulants. Dolley and her set also indulged in the aristocratic practice of gambling, though at a much lower level than real aristocrats; the card tables came out as soon as tea was over.[23] Generally, the gentleman played brag while ladies played loo, a game that resembled both poker and bridge, combining complicated card sequences with rapidly rising stakes. According to the rules of refinement, how one played the game was as important as winning or losing. Some men found the sight of ladies gambling oddly alluring. According to one admirer, when ladies lost, they dubbed themselves "looed," "pronounc[ing] the word in a very mincing manner." (The first time Samuel Harrison Smith played loo, he won two dollars from Dolley and another lady: "I confess I felt some mortification at putting [their] money . . . into my pocket.")[24] Dolley lost more than she won, and ran up gambling debts. She also sometimes chose not to play, not for reasons of economy but because gaming interfered with the atmosphere she endeavored to create in her home. She wrote to Anna in 1804 that "I have scarsly played since you left us—I find it disagreeable unless the partys are pleasant." Above all, Dolley valued harmony.

Gambling was not the only aristocratic practice in which Dolley indulged. She also used snuff, a habit some deplored, but her snuff-taking was not the "chaw" indulged by country farm wives but rather the "dipping" affected by upper-class women in England and on the Continent. But it was addicting, as Dolley confessed to Anna: "I'm glad you take no more snuf—but I must."[25]

American social circumstances demanded more sangfroid than ever imagined by any European courtesy book. As the wife of the secretary of state, Dolley entertained the dignitaries of foreign nations, including Native American tribal leaders. After one such event, Dolley was preparing for bed when she saw reflected in the mirror "the face of a wild Indian." She quickly surmised that her guest had left the festivities by "ascending instead of descending from the drawing room." Always sensitive to anyone's social gaffes, Dolley pretended not to see her uninvited guest and went into the next room, summoning one of her slaves to escort him down.[26]

What attracted people to the Madisons' house were "the frank and cordial manners of its mistress." To characterize the social scene at the Madisons' house on F Street as "in opposition" to Jefferson's executive dinner tables, however, goes against the very nature of the process. If Jefferson seemed almost feminine in his hatred of contention and in his ability to manipulate his way through sticky situations, he was more than matched by Dolley, who had been trained by her culture always to take the ladylike path of least conflict.[27] She did not challenge Jefferson's "plan" for Washington society as a man would have, in a pamphlet or by letter, nor with a direct assault, like the ladies who tried to force a levée; significantly, Dolley does not appear in that story of social miscalculation.

Instead, her actions demonstrated a clear plan to gently, subtly, make the Madison home the center of Washington life. And in a town built on, by, and for politics, that meant a center of political activity for government officials, locals, and the diplomatic corps. Jefferson had not chosen the path of reconciliation, though his fractured government and new nation sorely needed healing. Reconciliation in Washington City took place at the Madisons' house, under the "partial eye" of the lady of the house and during "the sweet simplicity of Mrs. Madison's conversation."[28]

⚜

A good republican wife, Dolley understood the theories behind republicanism's social goals. But she also brought to Washington her own ideas and experiences of society, based on models of southern hospitality. Like Jefferson, like most Americans, Dolley would have shuddered at the thought of "petticoat politicians." Nevertheless, like many women excluded from direct political power, she set a great deal of store in the power of society to create economic, personal, and political bonds.

Of course, she was not fostering social relations for purely altruistic reasons or out of an abstract commitment to republicanism. Even in 1801, Dolley and James had every reason to expect that he would be the next Republican candidate for the presidency. No two political collaborators were closer than James Madison and Jefferson, and because foreign relations—most notably, the American responses to the course of the European wars—dominated the business of the federal government, the post of secretary of state was popularly regarded as a stepping-stone to the presidency. Everyone assumed that Jefferson would serve two terms and then designate James as his successor. This is, of course, exactly what happened. With their eyes on the future, the budding power brokers of Washington City were more than ready for James and Dolley to lead them, even early in Jefferson's reign.

So the ladies of Washington got their levées, or something like them, but at the house of the secretary of state rather than at the executive mansion. Presiding over the dinner table on F Street, Dolley acted within a long European tradition of political women, from the salonnières of France who made political connections in their parlors to the women of the English country gentry, who treated an electoral borough as a family possession, caring for their husbands' parliamentary careers and constituents. To be sure, Dolley exhibited extraordinary skills as a traditional political wife. Other American women dutifully fulfilled such obligations but had no particular charm or special taste for sociability; Dolley brought an inimitable presence to any room. She fully inhabited the role of political wife, filling it up to the very brim, as she began to construct a public persona for herself.

In spite of Jefferson's efforts to limit social life (except for his own ends), Dolley had only been in town eighteen months when she remarked complacently to Eliza Collins Lee that "we have many agreable strangers here, & every body seems disposed to keep up that hospitable intercourse which forms the best trait in the character of any place." Her set supplied so many "rational amusements" that even a confirmed bon vivant (and committed Federalist), Massachusetts senator Harrison Gray Otis, expressed fatigue after a few weeks of the "incessant" socializing.[29] But he kept attending the events because he recognized, as everyone did, that politics required many kinds of parties.

Two years into Jefferson's administration, the question of the relationship between society and politics remained in abeyance. The house on the hill—the executive mansion—stood for the stern republican rejection of older, courtly European ways. As a quiet counterpoint, the Madisons' house on F Street accommodated inextricably linked political and social needs but in ways designed to soothe rather than inflame. Dolley operated her Washington version of a salon discreetly. In their different ways, Dolley and Jefferson valued harmony above all, though Dolley's vision emerged as the more optimistic, not to mention less controlling, of the two. Jefferson monitored all activity for signs of deviation from his party line; in contrast, Dolley's strategy included as many people as possible, gave them the freedom to mix and mingle, and trusted that matters would all work out for the best.

FIVE

The Merry Affair

On November 4, 1803, a bedraggled and weary pair of travelers disembarked from the frigate *Phaeton* in Norfolk, Virginia. Forty-seven-year-old Anthony Merry, newly appointed as His Britannic Majesty's envoy extraordinary and minister plenipotentiary, and Anthony's new bride, the former widow Elizabeth Leathes Merry, of Suffolk, had left Portsmouth, England, on September 28. The transatlantic crossing was rough, alleviated for Elizabeth only by the charming company of a fellow traveler, the Irish poet Thomas Moore. Relieved as the Merrys were to reach land, their travails were not over. Delayed in Norfolk for two weeks by lack of transportation and by illness (Elizabeth contracted a fever, apparently from Norfolk mosquitoes), the Merrys had to board another ship to Alexandria, Virginia. Poor winds and poorer navigation dragged out the short journey to six days. The last leg was overland; escorted by Edward Thornton, secretary of the British legation, the Merrys set out for Washington City in an unfamiliar contraption called a coachie. The poor roads, the bone-chilling cold, and the unstable ride caused Anthony "quiet astonishment and inward groaning."

Like others before them, the pair expressed shock at the primitive city. With no house even remotely suitable, the Merrys put together two "mere shells of houses, with bare walls and without fixtures of any kind." They even had to have their own well dug. Though they had brought a large staff and a great stock of personal possessions and furnishings (so many that Washingtonians suspected the pair of smuggling) they discovered that they had to send to Baltimore and Philadelphia for vegetables and butter, as well as for the special comestibles needed to supply a diplomatic household.[1]

This rough start presaged what would prove to be a difficult diplomatic assignment for the Merrys. Even as they found their footing on this new continent, the couple continued on unfamiliar terrain.

❧

In his dealings with the Merrys, Jefferson took his use of social events as political statements to a new level, using the realm of foreign relations. Tensions between Great Britain and the United States around Jay's Treaty were still running high almost a decade after the fact. In 1795, the Americans had entered negotiations asking for the withdrawal of the remaining British troops from U.S. soil, for trade concessions with British possessions, and for reparations for, among other things, runaway slaves. The finished treaty, however, provided only modest trade concessions, while they also insisted that Americans honor pre-Revolutionary debts to British merchants. Most ominously, the treaty acquiesced to the British position that the merchant ships of a neutral nation could not trade with warring countries.

The Senate ratified the treaty, and it was reluctantly signed by then-President Washington, who wished to avoid embroiling the nation in another dispute with the European superpower. Nonetheless, many Americans perceived the treaty as an international humiliation and a betrayal of their own leadership. John Jay, the diplomat who had negotiated the despised document, ruefully noted that every evening his burning effigies lit up the eastern seaboard, turning night into day. In an era rich with political controversy, the contention over Jay's Treaty, more than any other single event, contributed to the schism between those who would be Federalists and the future Republicans.

Great Britain was not the only European nation to present diplomatic difficulties. France had been the rebellious colonists' warmest ally and greatest help during the American Revolution; in 1793, after its own revolution, relations between the two nations cooled. Initially, the Americans had greeted the French upheaval with enthusiasm: this revolt against an absolute monarch was clearly the next phase in a global fight for liberty that had started in their own country. But unlike the American rebellion, the French Revolution disintegrated into bloody chaos, and many Americans reacted with horror. Though some in the government still supported the French, officially the United States would neither aid nor endorse the revolutionary government.

Struggling to establish itself, the new French rulers distrusted any preference or concession given to Great Britain by their former allies. They, too, saw Jay's Treaty as treacherous, as some of the clauses directly refuted shipping agreements that America had negotiated separately with France. In 1797, when the French foreign minister, Charles Talleyrand, refused to receive the new U.S. minister to France, Charles Cotesworth Pinckney, President John Adams sent a special mission to Paris to defuse the situation. But relations only deteriorated when Talleyrand, through agents designated in the diplomatic dispatches as X, Y, and Z, demanded a bribe of the American commission. The pro-English Federalists exulted at this news, while pro-French Americans accused Adams of deliberately trying to provoke public opinion to support a war with France. Two years of "Quasi War" followed, which took the form of French depredations on American ships, until the Treaty of Morfontaine, signed by both nations in 1800, brought an uneasy peace.

The most worrying development in European affairs was the emergence of Napoleon Bonaparte, the ruthless Corsican military man who had risen to be a leading general in the French army. From the Americans' point of view, Napoleon was the dark side of power; if Jefferson and James saw themselves as the saviors of republicanism, they viewed Napoleon as the antichrist. As good republicans, James and Jefferson might struggle with issues such as how to control political dissension while maintaining a properly weak central power or how to reconcile their own ambitions with the ideal of the common good. Napoleon harbored no such compunctions. An aggressive, ambitious, charismatic leader, he seized power through force.

This diminutive figure loomed large over America's foreign policy for several reasons. During both the Jefferson and the Madison administrations, Napoleon would fight almost every country and state in Europe, eventually controlling or influencing most of western and central mainland Europe, but his ambitions were not limited to the military realm. In 1799, he took over the Directory, France's postrevolutionary executive power, becoming first consul, and then consul for life. In 1804 he declared himself emperor and, in imperial fashion, secured his dominance in Europe by replacing the king of Spain in 1806 with his brother, Joseph Bonaparte.

Though he battled his way across the continent, Napoleon's primary focus lay in crushing the powerful Great Britain. With England defeated, not only could he take over its lucrative shipping trade, but no nation could stop him from being the emperor of all he surveyed. Napoleon first tried to subdue the English in Egypt in 1798; his 1805 defeat by Lord Nelson at Trafalgar did not dim his commitment to domination. Instead, he increasingly employed economic strategies, aiming to limit England's ability to conduct war by cutting its shipping revenues. Accordingly, Napoleon instituted his "Continental System," which forced the countries under his control to stop trading with Great Britain. With countries not under his direct control, Napoleon had ways of ensuring compliance. While the United States was never more than an ancillary component in Napoleon's game of manipulation, the new nation could not help but feel threatened by the French emperor.

Thomas Jefferson had long been an ideological ally of France, even sanctioning some of the excesses of the Revolution. Ironically, when he

became president, it was France that drove him to consider the unthinkable: alliance with Great Britain and repudiation of the very
ideals of both revolutions. When in 1802, First Consul Napoleon Bonaparte regained the Louisiana territory from Spain, threatening to seize
control of the Mississippi River and challenging the United States' sovereignty over the continent, Jefferson actually contemplated joining
forces with the hated British. And when in 1804, the slaves of a French
possession, Saint Domingue, inspired by the rhetoric and ideas of the
American Revolution, rebelled against their oppressor, Jefferson could
have pledged the support of the United States. Ultimately, his fear of
domestic slave rebellion held him back.

In May 1803, Great Britain and France declared war on each other,
and European nations, notably Spain, scrambled to both protect themselves and take advantage of the situation. As the hostilities intensified
and alliances shifted, the European nations looked to the United States
as either a tool or a weapon.

For years, the Royal Navy had been kidnapping American seamen,
claiming that they were deserters and impressing them into His
Majesty's service. This arrogance rankled the new Americans. The resumption of European hostilities in 1803 brought fresh outrages, this
time by both England and France; the latter, though never as aggressively as Great Britain, had been picking off American ships even before
the Quasi War. Though American shippers tried to trade as neutrals,
both nations treated U.S. vessels as adversaries. French privateers
turned up in American ports, and British warships trawled American
waters with impunity. Great Britain and France used American ships as
pawns, seizing them right and left as prizes of war.[2]

Even as the encroachments of the English and French seemed increasingly threatening, however, another occurrence in 1803 provided a
psychological boost. Jefferson's refusal to help the freedom fighters in
Saint Domingue, soon to be called Haiti, yielded a surprising dividend.
The renewed war with Great Britain, coupled with the Caribbean drain
on resources, forced Napoleon to dump some of France's foreign
possessions. To keep his North American holdings from falling into the
hands of the British, Napoleon struck a deal to sell most of the land

between the Mississippi River and the Rocky Mountains to the United States for $15 million. The Louisiana Purchase created complex boundary issues with Great Britain and France, but also made both nations seem less relevant to the United States' destiny. With the French in such desperate straits, America would not need to ally itself with Britain in order to resist French infringements in New Orleans. And certainly the acquisition of such an impressive amount of real estate should give Great Britain pause. The year 1803, then, may have seemed the perfect time to challenge the former mother country on maritime, trade, and boundary issues, as well as to establish the former colony as a nation in its own right.

It was a mark of the new country's rising status in the world that the Court of St. James had now sent its first full minister to the United States since Robert Liston left in 1800. The appointment of Anthony Merry, and the fact that he brought with him a wife, provided a chance to mend fences between the two nations, as well as to create new bonds. Even the pro-French Philadelphia newspaper *Aurora* heralded the Merrys' arrival as a rare opportunity, declaring that a period "more favorable to amiable and generous views" had never existed.[3]

But Jefferson was not in a mood to be either amiable or generous and he had no more intention of reconciling with these former enemies than with the Federalists. Jefferson's antipathy toward the British predated the Revolutionary War, when he found himself deeply in debt to English merchants. When British forces invaded Virginia in 1781, then-governor Jefferson fled, prompting accusations of cowardice that marred his public career. That General Cornwallis, while occupying Jefferson's Elk Hill plantation, destroyed stock, horses, buildings, and crops, and stole thirty slaves, only added fuel to his fire. In addition, when at the Court of St. James as an ambassador, Jefferson was treated shabbily by King George and his court, an experience that no doubt produced his bitter characterization of "diplomacy as the pest of the peace of the world, as the workshop in which nearly all the wars of Europe are manufactured."[4]

With the Merrys in his capital city, Jefferson saw a chance to put Great Britain in its place while asserting the United States' unique, superior identity. The episode that would come to be known (ironically, given its distinctly un-merry aspects) as the Merry Affair allowed Jefferson to take several stands at once, regarding diplomacy, foreign affairs, Great Britain, and the place of women in his republic. Not only did he not avail himself of this opportunity for reconciliation, but also he turned to the social sphere in order to send blatant and aggressive anti-British statements, using his version of an American social style to initiate the hapless Merrys into the New World.

⁂

The first salvo in the etiquette war was fired in December 1801, during an official event, the all-important "presentation," a ceremony in which the diplomat of one country presents his credentials to the ruler of the host country, signaling the opening of relations between two nations. At the very least, this was a time and place for the parties to convey their mutual respect and honor. At best, it could serve as the beginning of an enriching friendship between two people and thus two nations.

Jefferson decided that this particular presentation had a different purpose. Formality signaled respect; accordingly, Anthony Merry, escorted by James Madison, appeared for the ceremony "bespeckled with the spangles of [the] gaudiest court dress." In contrast, Jefferson's clothes were downright shabby, and his air deliberately casual: the president led the two men from room to room, and at one point even dangled his slipper from his toe. The Englishman was shocked. He quite rightly interpreted Jefferson's "actually studied" style as his way of denigrating the representative of Great Britain, and hence the King of England himself.

The rest of the etiquette war took place in the social sphere. James was always more than Jefferson's loyal lieutenant, but in this case he was the follower, not the initiator, of the plan. After the rocky presentation, James informed Anthony that, contrary to all precedent and to the rules of diplomatic etiquette, the ceremony of the "first call" upon the official men of the government, a gesture that paid honor, would be his. Anthony quite correctly protested this as contrary to even previous American usage, but James countered that Jefferson did not feel bound by Federalist precedent, then used Dolley to soften the blow, promising that she, as leading cabinet wife, would pay the first call on Elizabeth Merry.[5]

The full declaration of war came three days later. Once again, the scene took place at the president's house, this time at a dinner supposedly held to honor the Merrys. Rules of precedence strictly governed which gentleman would escort and seat which lady; the guests of honor were given the best seats at the dinner table. Instead of escorting the lady guest of honor—Elizabeth Merry—and seating her to his right, however, Jefferson gave his arm to Dolley.

Startled, because Jefferson surely knew better, Dolley whispered, "Take Mrs. Merry." But Jefferson insisted. The other guests shared Dolley's chagrin; Sally McKean Martínez de Yrugo exclaimed, "This will be the cause of war!" James Madison followed with Elizabeth Merry, leaving Anthony to fend for himself. Flexibility and improvisation were not his strong suits, and a shocked Anthony Merry, having no idea which lady he was supposed to escort, entered the dining room alone. Attempting to salvage the situation, he moved to seat himself next to Sally, which, since she was the wife of the Spanish minister, would have been a place still suitable for a diplomat of his rank. But an eager congressman pushed Anthony aside, and he had to make his way down the table, hunting for a chair.[6]

Jefferson ignored the plight of his guest of honor, a sure sign that the usually courteous president was consciously trying to make a point. This diplomatic slapstick, however, was not the only appalling display. The presence of the French chargé d'affaires, Louis-André Pichon, sounded an even more worrying note. Not only did Pichon (a chargé rather than a minister) hold inferior rank but also a rigid rule of diplomacy forbade inviting the representatives of warring countries to the same social gathering. This was an unforgivable affront, especially at this event, the Merrys' first official introduction to Washington society. As soon as the meal ended, the Merrys called for their carriage and left.

Had these insults been merely personal, the Merrys could have swallowed them and proceeded professionally. But such slights, and in particular the presence of Pichon at the table, could only be interpreted as a matter of state. After all, it was only by chance that England had not been seated next to France. Insult was later added to injury when Anthony Merry learned that Jefferson had asked the French chargé to make a special effort to attend, to the point of cutting short his business in Baltimore.[7]

To what extent Jefferson and James discussed or planned these episodes or what followed is unclear; the women's responses suggest that they, in any case, had not been prepared. But the scene was repeated a few days later at the Madisons' house in F Street. Open confrontation and pointed rudeness were not either Madison's style, but James evidently decided to emulate his chief, and Dolley followed James's lead without public demur. At the announcement of dinner, James bypassed Elizabeth Merry and escorted Hannah Nicholson Gallatin to the table. This time, however, no man gave his arm to Elizabeth Merry. According to reports in the Federalist newspapers, the rest of the party entered the dining room, parading directly past the Merrys. This left Anthony to escort his own wife into dinner, a circumstance that would have been outrageous even in the modest social circle of the smallest town, let alone by the standards of diplomatic etiquette. Upon entering the room, Anthony brought his wife to the head of the table, where Hannah ceded her place to Elizabeth Merry.[8] The dinner proceeded civilly enough, but the Merrys left the F Street house determined to fight these attempts to belittle them and Great Britain.

To be sure, the Merrys were not the most sympathetic characters (Elizabeth took Hannah's proffered place without a word of thanks) but they were correct in assuming that this new, ostentatiously casual American style had everything to do with their arrival, and that it expressed hostility toward England. The day of the Madisons' dinner party, Anthony Merry wrote to the British Foreign Office to complain of his treatment; the day after, he requested instructions on how to proceed. In the worst-case scenario, the king might have recalled the Merrys, breaking off relations between the two countries.

Anthony suspected that James Madison had never before followed this extraordinary usage, and he was correct. The British secretary Augustus John Foster concurred, adding that "Mr. Jefferson and Mr. Madison were too much of the gentleman not to feel ashamed of what they were doing, and consequently did it awkwardly, as people must do who affect bad manners for a particular object."[9]

However, any reply from the British government would take weeks, so Anthony Merry made an interim decision. Anthony instituted the equivalent of a "work to rule" policy: he would attend official functions, and only official functions. Because he refused to expose Elizabeth to further insult, she stayed at home. This was not the best solution for either side, as Anthony was deprived of one half of the diplomatic team, and Washingtonians who wished to connect with the official representative of the Crown lost half their opportunities. Besides, when Anthony pointedly socialized without Elizabeth, most notably at the New Year's Day levée, which all of Washington attended, he reminded everyone that the administration had blundered and that the issue was unresolved.

The difficulties continued, and five weeks after the Merrys' Washington City debut, the highest social circles in Washington had come to a standstill. The couple steadfastly refused most invitations (and all presidential dinner invitations) that winter and through the spring of 1804. Anthony insisted that he took his stand not merely in the name of Great Britain, but for the sake of all foreign diplomats and the nations they represented. He even persuaded the Spanish minister to join him and Elizabeth in their social boycott.[10] Unfortunately, diplomacy and politics do not work to rule. Without Elizabeth Merry, without social intercourse, the business between Great Britain and the United States stalled. Moved solely by personal pique and ideological purity, Jefferson had chosen to insult Great Britain through the persons of the Merrys. By doing this within the realm of diplomacy—where personal relations dictated policy—Jefferson had ensured that his message was received all too well. In order to repair the damage, he would have to reciprocate in kind, with a personal apology. But that was not Jefferson's way, and it was up to the people around him to explore other options.

⟨⟩

It was the characteristic dynamic of their collaboration that Jefferson made sweeping statements and lofty, impractical (and often impolitic) pronouncements, which James Madison would ameliorate or temper. Extreme positions were Jefferson's specialty, whether with respect to the Bill of Rights (he took both the pro and con positions), to the use of "a little rebellion now and then," or to the radical idea that laws made by one generation were not binding to the next. Sometimes Jefferson's ideological zeal made him seem downright bloodthirsty, most notably as regards his willingness to see "half the earth desolated" in the pursuit of liberty and to water "the tree of liberty" with the "blood of patriots." In these matters, and others, James was the one who talked Jefferson down from his rhetorical aeries. As James himself tactfully phrased it, "allowances ought to be made for a habit in Mr. Jefferson as in others of great genius in expressing in strong and round terms, impressions of the moment." A less charitable interpretation was that Jefferson could be hasty in his words, giving little thought to the consequences.[11]

In speaking of the party at his own home, James later confessed that he would have led Elizabeth Merry in, but that, being loath to contradict the president, he followed Jefferson's example. He feared, however, that by doing so he was abandoning his own role as the voice of reason. Always meticulous and precise, he decided to research his position and gather facts. On December 18, only a few weeks after the Merrys' arrival, James wrote for advice to the former American minister, Rufus King, recently returned from London. Confessing that he was "mortified at troubling you," James touched precisely upon the points of the current dispute: the rules about the "first visit," the orders of precedence, and the role of women, whether in "scenes of public ceremony" or those of "ordinary hospitalities."[12]

Backing Jefferson and defending the substitution of "pell mell" for more traditional forms, James affirmed their common aim "to unfetter social intercourse as well as public business, as much as possible from ceremonious clogs." But he also worried about the consequences of such radical informality, both at home and abroad, "as it is proper that we should not be behind other nations either in civility or self-respect." "It is well," he wrote King, "to know the manner in which other nations respect both us & themselves." Rufus King's reply was lengthy and elaborate, but also confusing, presenting a wide variety of circumstances and exceptions: for instance, foreign ministers at the British court had to pay the first visit to the royal ministers, but preceded them into the king's bedroom. The overall picture was complicated, and James took that complexity as a justification for the "anything goes" style of American simplicity.[13]

Though this interpretation of King's letter gave the president and his secretary of state some confidence in their new program, they also knew that they had gone too far. Their response, an early republican version of damage control, spoke to both the seriousness of the situation and the contradictions they had created for themselves. Belatedly, Jefferson decided to give his rather fanciful plan some official legitimacy, and on January 12, 1804, the Merrys received a copy of his "Cannons of Etiquette," complete with martial misspelling. Simply put, the "Cannons" declared equality the basic principle governing personal relations. While conceding that by custom residents paid the first calls on visitors, "Cannons" articulated an exception for foreign legates, who were expected to play the subordinate role and pay the first call on official families. At social events, no consideration of rank or degree would dictate events. In arriving at this policy, Jefferson and James adapted a court practice called *pêle-mêle*, a French verb meaning to tumble. Within the varied and arcane rules of court etiquette, on a few very specific occasions, such as a large party, the "company" might be allowed total freedom of movement, or pell-mell. Ignoring the larger, more elaborate structure that allowed for such disorder, the "Cannons" declared that the rule of *pêle-mêle* (with official French spelling) should be followed, even in the private homes of public officials.

The only concession to "ancient usage" would be the "gentlemen in mass giving precedence to the ladies in mass," when moving between rooms. Anthony Merry restrained himself from commenting on these drastic departures from long-established custom, only pointing out that he should have been given these instructions upon arrival.[14] Of course, Jefferson and James had no reply, given that the instructions were a recent improvisation.

Without actually apologizing, the two men tried to negotiate a compromise, suggesting, for instance, that Anthony attend dinners at the president's house without his wife. Anthony's reply that he would have to seek counsel on the matter prompted Jefferson's own exasperated retort: "I shall be highly honored when the king of England is good enough to let Mr. Merry come and eat my soup."[15]

But Anthony Merry's response was legitimate: he had to await instructions. Not only were women and wives essential to the social component of government business but also their function in political matters extended to the symbolic realm. Nations had long been represented by female figures—America was "Columbia," for example—and, conversely, real women often stood as representations of the nation in its "purest" form. Besides depriving Elizabeth of her practical role in her husband's mission, Jefferson's refusal to accommodate her might be read as a rejection of Britannia's womanhood. The exclusion of Elizabeth was so novel that Anthony Merry and his government had to consider it from every angle.

The situation deteriorated still further, when Anthony Merry learned that Jefferson had given precedence to a visiting lady, the former Betsy Patterson of Baltimore. Because she had married Jérôme Bonaparte, Napoleon's brother, Anthony interpreted Jefferson's decision to conduct her in to dinner as a very public pro-French (and thus anti-English) statement.[16]

By the winter of 1804, affairs were in a tangled mess. In trying to deny that the social sphere "meant" anything, while at the same time using it to send a political message, the president and secretary of state left themselves dangling from their own petard. It had taken only one failed presentation and two disastrous dinners to damage foreign relations seriously. In a letter accounting for the situation to James Monroe, minister to England, James apologized for having to take such a frivolity so seriously as to write "so much trash." But even as he called the matter "nausious," he admitted: "Questions of this sort were known to have been sources of the most serious and scandalous consequences." In spite of his efforts to downplay "a foolish circumstance of etiquette," he went on at great length, justifying and explaining the hash they had made of Anglo-American relations.[17]

James actually wrote twice to Monroe. The first letter, dated January

19, 1804, outlined the situation and defended his actions. A month later, on February 16, he went more deeply into the subject, now so sensitive that much of the letter was in code. The etiquette war was, in his view, no less than a battle of "the right of the *government here to fix its rules of intercourse* and the sentiments and *manners of* the country." Behind all the fuss about diplomatic precedence, he suspected, lay Anthony Merry's belief that in every situation all foreign diplomats should be elevated over all Americans. Though James did not make the connection, Dolley Madison and Hannah Gallatin, whom Anthony described as "a Set of beings as little without the manners as without the appearance of Gentlewomen," exemplified America.[18]

With manners as a proxy for laws, and "sentiment" signifying the heart of the nation, what was going on was a power struggle over the United States' legitimacy. Like Jefferson, Anthony Merry was using the social world to send his message and using the women as stand-ins for their respective nations. Anthony's insistence that his wife be elevated over the wives of the highest American officials reflected his assumption that, while the United States was free to dabble in republican fancies all it wanted, it should always give precedence to Europe. No wonder James firmly advised James Monroe: "To apply an *antidote to this poison* will require *your vigilant and prudent attention.*"

James was writing for Jefferson as well: "The President wishes you to *lose no opportunity and* to *spare* no *pains* that may be necessary to *satisfy the British* Administration . . . and to *prevent or efface* any *different impressions* which may be transmitted from hence." James even relayed a presidential concession, admitting that Jefferson had stopped favoring the cabinet wives by escorting them to the table, leaving all the dinner seating to *pêle-mêle.* The dispute over the Merrys only made James Monroe's job more difficult, as he nervously looked for fallout in the British court, and was sure that he had found it when Queen Charlotte ignored him at a court function.[19]

Dolley left no written account of these events, but she undoubtedly learned much. In Philadelphia, she had observed "leading women" Martha Custis Washington and Abigail Smith Adams struggle to create society and ceremony that provided the pomp and reassurance of royalty without offending republican sense and sensibility. From the sidelines, Dolley also had witnessed the efforts of nongovernmental women to create a salon culture that could form the foundation for a set of national manners. Neither example proved wholly satisfactory; the previous presidential receptions were too stiff for sociability and the unofficial entertainments suffered from an excess of aristocracy, as when Anne Willing Bingham adopted the affectation of having a butler announce guests.[20]

If the choices made by the ladies in Philadelphia were too formal, too pseudo-monarchical, it was obvious that Jefferson's self-consciously egalitarian style would not do either. But as the Merry Affair continued to wreak havoc on the capital, Dolley also had occasion to learn another lesson that was more to the point: the role of an aristocratic woman in a republic.

Perhaps the Merry Affair would have not come to such a drastic pass if Anthony Merry had more grace and humor, but he was a man of little imagination or charm, a dutiful, methodical, slightly fussy professional. But, in important ways, it was the personality of his wife that seemed to strike the deepest chords of anxiety and spite. In contrast to her husband, Elizabeth Leathes Merry cut a charismatic figure. She was known as a good hostess and even as something of a scholar, with an interest in botany.[21] Intelligent, gregarious, physically striking, she possessed the qualities of a traditional political wife. Indeed, had she been a man, Elizabeth might have been the better minister.

No doubt she was a force to be reckoned with. Elizabeth's portrait reveals the kind of woman called handsome; the always observant Margaret Bayard Smith described her as a "large, tall, well-made woman, rather masculine, very free and affable in her manners, but easy without being graceful." The adjective "masculine" signified, as Margaret went on to elaborate, that "she is said to be a woman of fine understanding, and she is so entirely the talker and actor in all companies, that her good husband passes quite unnoticed; he is plain in his appearance and called rather inferior in understanding."[22] So Elizabeth Merry brought excellent qualifications of intelligence, tact, experience, and charm to her husband's new post in Washington City.

Elizabeth Merry ensured that the British mission would not go unnoticed. Even in the thick of the Merry Affair, she did attend a few large events, though none at the presidential mansion. At a "large and splendid ball" given by Secretary of the Navy Robert Smith, she stood out in a white satin dress with a long train, draped with "dark blue crape" and "white crape down to her knees and . . . so thickly cover'd with silver spangles that it appear'd to be a brilliant silver tissue." Instead of wearing her matching shawl around her shoulders, she wrapped it around her head. In this "brilliant and fantastic" ensemble, lavish in décolletage and bedecked with diamonds, Elizabeth Merry was dressed for a royal court.[23]

Unfortunately for Elizabeth, she embodied two things Jefferson detested: the English and political, intellectual women. Perhaps her chief crime was that she outshone her husband in public. With her elaborate dress, her conversational skills, even her "fine understanding," she was the personification of the very court culture that Jefferson hoped to eradicate from the United States. She knew how to politick like a professional, like an aristocrat, and that was all Jefferson needed to set him off. Elizabeth was the first such European woman to enter official society on his watch, and he did his best to make an example of her.

In his own letter to James Monroe in England, Jefferson began his assessment of Anthony with ritual niceties—"Mr. Merry is with us, and we believe him to be personally as desirable a character as could have been sent to us"—before detailing Anthony's "troublemaking" insistence on following rules of etiquette and diplomacy. Jefferson also acknowledged the impact of Elizabeth's defection from society on Anthony's work: "He will lose half of his usefulness to the nation, that derived from a perfectly familiar and private intercourse with the secretaries and myself."

But though Jefferson had specific complaints only about Anthony— and these were shaky enough—he placed the blame for all at Elizabeth's door. On his own, Jefferson implied, Anthony would have been fine, "but he is unluckily associated with one of an opposite character in every point. She has already disturbed our harmony extremely." After this sweeping indictment, the president did not go into specifics, doubling back to decrying "the offense that Mr. Merry took" at his wife's treatment. Nonetheless, he regretfully reported "the consequence is that Mr. and Mrs. Merry will put themselves into Coventry." He went on to indulge in name-calling (Elizabeth Merry was "a virago") and cattiness ("in the short course of a few weeks [she] had established a degree of dislike among all classes which one would have thought impossible in so short a time"). In his coded messages to James Monroe, James agreed: "The *manners* of *Mistress Merry disgust* both *sexes* and all *parties*."[24]

While women could stand for the best of a nation—for pure womanhood and sacred motherhood—they could also represent the worst. And they could serve as lightning rods in political disagreements. At the most basic level, opponents could attack the comparatively powerless woman as a way to express dislike of the male members of her family.[25] Indeed, Jefferson and James knew better than to insult Anthony Merry directly. After all, he was the one they had to work with. By following complaints about *his* actions with remarks about *her* personality, they deflected their objections to Anthony onto the hapless Elizabeth.

Outside the executive circle, the real issues raised by the treatment of the Merrys were almost lost in the propaganda feast that ensued. In person and in print, enemies used Jefferson's boorish behavior and foolish obstinacy to portray him as an unfit leader who endangered foreign relations out of "pride, whim, weakness and malignant revenge." On the other side, his fellow Republicans lauded their chief's "bravery" in standing up to English pretensions and championing "Americanness." Enemies and friends alike used women to make their points; the French minister even tried to blame all women, not just the principals, for paralyzing the capital: "Washington society is turned upside down; all the women are to the last degree exasperated with Mrs. Merry."[26]

At a Georgetown party given to celebrate the Louisiana Purchase, Jefferson's followers, taking their cue from the president, insulted Elizabeth Merry, trod on her dress, and refused her admittance until she removed the "undemocratic diamonds" that she wore to honor America. More than once, the British secretary, Augustus John Foster, saw

Elizabeth Merry reduced to tears by their treatment of her. Though he was usually appreciative of America in general and Washington City in particular, the cruelty toward Elizabeth so disturbed Foster that he exclaimed: "It is indeed a country not fit for a dog."[27]

The newspapers seized upon the story. Respect for the private nature and modesty of "the sex" debarred any discussion of white women of the elite and middle classes in print; a woman's name would not appear in a newspaper except in announcements of her birth, marriage, and death. But all gloves were off when politics required it. Both Federalist and Republican publications gleefully reported on the war on women that raged in Washington, jeering at the hapless cabinet wives, including Dolley, as "a pretty set" used by Jefferson for his nefarious ends.[28]

The mudslinging by Federalist papers grew so intense that on February 13, 1804, the president himself had to step in, defending himself in the Philadelphia newspaper, *Aurora,* albeit anonymously. "His" women did not have that option. Jefferson expressed relief that his daughters were not part of the social scene, for they would surely have been "butchered . . . bloodily" by partisan journalists. "The brunt of the battle now falls on the Secretary's ladies, who are dragged in the dirt of every federal paper." And indeed, Dolley and Anna had become substitute targets for criticism of Jefferson and James Madison; charges were made that the sisters felt keenly for years after, though the stories were ridiculous on their face.[29] The Federalists claimed that Dolley had an affair with Thomas Jefferson, and that James (his lack of offspring being evidence of impotence) facilitated it. For proof, they pointed to the three weeks during which Dolley and James stayed in the president's house when they first arrived in Washington.

In addition, newspapers and gossips held that Jefferson pimped the Payne sisters to foreign visitors and officials (a gross misinterpretation of Dolley's social connections with the *corps diplomatique*) and that the two women prostituted themselves for votes.[30] Their harmless sobriquet, "the Merry Wives of Windsor," now took on an unsavory cast, as people recalled that the characters in Shakespeare's comedy were venal men and sexually manipulative wives.

Small comfort to Dolley and the unmarried Anna that such

charges had a long and dishonorable history in politics, and that they constituted a backhanded acknowledgment of the ladies' power. (In 1784, English critics had hoped to derail the political support that Georgiana, Duchess of Devonshire, had amassed during a campaign for Charles James Fox by accusing her and her sister of, at the least, kissing men for their votes. Georgiana admitted that she had kissed some prospective voters on the cheek, but pointed out quite rightly that male candidates kissed women, men, children, and even animals when on the campaign trail.)[31]

The political fallout continued. The incident colored the Merrys' view of almost everything American and also gave some Americans ideas of their own. Anyone who was plotting against the United States or who a held grudge against Jefferson came to the Merrys first, including Aaron Burr, with his scheme to set up a kingdom in the West, and Federalists Timothy Pickering and Roger Griswold, who had a plan for New England to secede from the Union.[32] Anthony Merry's refusal to pledge British support for any of these schemes demonstrated his good diplomatic judgment and forbearance, since he could easily have taken revenge on Jefferson. However, Anthony used knowledge of them only to advise the British government on policy. He had read loudly and clearly Jefferson's intention to humble Great Britain at every turn, and he became hypersensitive to insult, convinced that the "unfriendly . . . executive" always picked fights for conflict's sake. Accordingly, in all discussions of the boundary and maritime issues that set the stage for the War of 1812, Anthony advised that the British government stand firm against American "pretensions," consciously or unconsciously echoing Jefferson's own vocabulary of complaint about him.[33]

Diplomats from other nations jockeyed to use the breach to their own advantage. The Napoleonic wars had recast Europe as a giant chess game, and with just the right move, a nation-player could reap rich rewards. The affair brought together strange bedfellows; though Anthony Merry had come to the United States suspicious of Carlos Martínez de Yrujo, their alliance against Jefferson soon made them true allies.[34]

In Jefferson's zeal to humble Great Britain, he had overplayed the new nation's attachment to the French, conflating his partiality with the

American government's official position. Not only did the British now expect that the Americans would actively side with the French during the hostilities between the two countries, but they would remain wholly skeptical of future American gestures toward reconciliation, including some made under President Madison.[35]

"This foolish circumstance of etiquette" had also stirred up the hornet's nest of party rancor that had barely died down at Jefferson's inauguration. The fierce newspaper war, the various plots that came his way, the obvious popularity (at least among Republicans) of the pro-French president, and the actual abuse suffered by his wife all convinced Anthony Merry that the union's inherent instability and the divisiveness would soon rip it apart.[36]

The factors Merrys observed were mostly limited to elite urban political circles. But as they rarely traveled beyond that milieu, the actual stability of the union, the ballast of the everyday life of ordinary Americans, was not apparent to them. Rather, they saw contention and rivalry at every turn. Convinced that the republic would soon be divided against itself, Anthony Merry counseled the British government not to accede to U.S. demands concerning boundaries in the Northeast and Northwest and the impressment of sailors. When disunion came, and with it an almost inevitable takeover attempt by France or Spain, it would be better for England not to have given away too much to what history would see as an illegitimate and temporary regime.[37]

Anthony's assumption had a certain logic; unfortunately, it also had legs. When the United States finally declared war in 1812, the British, believing that they could ultimately negotiate a separate peace with the New England Federalists, decided it was in their best interest to prolong the conflict. The Merry Affair did not cause the war of 1812, as some contemporaries believed, but it laid the groundwork for the outbreak of hostilities and prepared the course that the British would take.

❦

When stories about the Merry Affair began to appear in the papers, Dolley, Anna, and Hannah found themselves in an untenable position. Lacking an official station, they had no platform from which to protest or exert any influence. At the same time, their participation in the various events in the affair was required, as the presence of women had signaled the "non-political" nature of the political message Jefferson sent. On the surface, the women seemed mere passive participants, literally waiting to be escorted, forced to follow their menfolk in whatever political dance the latter chose. Any power they seemed to possess was purely symbolic—as, from Anthony's point of view, representatives of the American government that had to be humbled—and certainly not their own to wield.

But they were more than political pawns. Like good housewives, they had to clean up the mess their men had made. And Dolley and Sally did speak up, though Dolley only whispered. When they could act, they did. While the men attempted to repair the damage through official channels, Dolley employed social means to make amends. Jefferson never apologized, and the Merrys never dined at the president's house during their two years in Washington. Accordingly, the Madisons' house became a surrogate. Since they expected an apology only from the chief executive, the Merrys felt they could dine with James: moreover, diplomatic protocol distinguished between private and official events, and a dinner at the private house of the secretary of state, presided over by a visibly gracious Dolley, could certainly seem "private."

Dolley did not particularly like Elizabeth Merry. Their relationship had not begun auspiciously. Early in their stay in the capital, according to a story that made the Washington rounds, Elizabeth remarked that Dolley's table resembled more a "harvest home" (a peasant's feast) than a state dinner. Dolley replied that "she thought abundance was preferable to elegance; that circumstances formed customs, and customs formed taste; and as the profusion, so repugnant to foreign customs, arose from the happy circumstance of the super-abundance and prosperity of our country, she did not hesitate to sacrifice the delicacy of European taste, for the less elegant, but more liberal fashion of Virginia."[38] Like Jefferson, Dolley stood up for "Americanness," but the way she rebuked Elizabeth also left room to maneuver. Apparently, Elizabeth Merry did not reply, but relations between the women continued.

Unlike Jefferson, who used diplomacy to vent personal biases,

Dolley did not exclusively cultivate relationships with people that she liked. She never warmed to the wife of the British minister—the gregarious, outgoing Virginian found Elizabeth's aloofness off-putting—but she persevered. After months in Washington, Dolley confided to Anna that she regarded Elizabeth as "still the same strange [lasse?]" and as (perhaps understandably) distant: "she hardly associates with any one—allways rideing on Horse back."[39] Nevertheless, Dolley repaired the diplomatic wounds as much as she could. Hearing from the secretary of the British legation that Elizabeth wished for a certain perfume, Dolley relinquished her own Essence of Roses. By 1805, Dolley characterized their relations as "unusially intimate," though she still found "[her] airs" amusing. Elizabeth could be volatile—"You know when she chuses she can get angry with persons as well as *circumstances*"—yet the two were sufficiently close that when Dolley fell ill, Elizabeth Merry declared herself Dolley's nurse. And diplomacy with Great Britain, possibly the most threatening enemy and potentially the most powerful ally to the new United States, transpired at Dolley's dinner table, minus the president.[40]

Clearly, politics and society could not be separated in the new capital; not coincidentally, it took a diplomatic contretemps to drive this lesson home. Traditionally, diplomacy took place at social events and in home settings, where people who might have little in common, or even antithetical interests, could form bonds. Diplomats had always consciously used the home to create feelings of intimacy and trust; not surprisingly, when the Merrys did not go to Jefferson's "house," foreign relations had broken down.[41] In order for politics to work, it needs two arenas of action. The official sphere includes the documents of government such as treaties, legislation, and meeting minutes, as well as events like cabinet meetings, congressional debates, and public speeches. Though the structures of government have their own processes—by which a bill may become a law, for instance—the official sphere is about the final product of politics.

The "unofficial" sphere concerns the *process* of politics. The "life and soul" of politics unfolds in the spaces between the official actions of "policy declarations, open debate, and polished legislation." This realm allows for "informal" politicking, which includes proposals, negotiations, the sharing of information, and patronage. Social events and social spaces are important parts, though not the only parts, of the unofficial sphere. At a party or diplomatic dinner, face to face and side by side, official men could discuss issues without repercussions, using the elements of the events—the music, food, wine, and dancing—to entertain a good suggestion or to deflect and dismiss a bad one. In the flickering candlelight of the unofficial sphere, diplomatic families could exchange sensitive information or send *sub rosa* messages that could never have been articulated in the glare of the official spotlight.[42] The power of the unofficial sphere lies in its ability to "cover" politics with a veil of sociability. Indeed, in the best cases, the boundaries between the spheres blur beyond recognition.

As Dolley did at Jefferson's table and at her own, women deflected, softened, and obscured political purposes.[43] The very femininity that made such obscurity possible, however, also allowed detractors to dismiss social activities as "merely" female, thus superficial, trivial, and even silly—"so much trash." Jefferson and James could dismiss the etiquette war as silly, even as they thought they could manipulate it and even as its political implications and consequences spun out of their control.

⁂

The Constitution, with its stress on separation of powers rather than coalition, provided no official channels through which to network. Republicanism be damned—no government needed the unofficial and social sphere more than Washington City. As a result, the social and personal avenues that Dolley set in place at the Madisons' house became even more necessary to the young capital and nation. Washington was a company town; its only products were power and politics. It did not take long before politics subsumed all other goals of society.

The utility of the unofficial sphere is precisely matched by the damage that can ensue if poorly used. After Jefferson's disastrous experiment, the model set by the house on F Street clearly prevailed in the capital. Following Dolley's example, the strategy focused on bringing people together and fostering politicking, rather than trying to control and contain it.

As the sole guardian of republican purity, Jefferson had approached politics with a single focus, using his dinner table to bend all to his will. In contrast, though obviously Dolley and James had their own goals, Dolley's unofficial sphere accommodated, even encouraged, the expression of everyone's political needs and visions. In capitalist terms, Jefferson's political economy suffered from the protective tariffs of his own ideology, while Dolley offered a free market of political options.

After the initial explosion, the "Cannons" were never heard from again. By the end of the Merrys' stay, Jefferson was receiving diplomatic personnel in more formal garb and setting, and the style of the capital was tending toward the conventional and established norms. Washingtonians had had enough of *pêle-mêle*. They recognized that they needed to innovate a style all their own, one that was properly American, but that also borrowed the best from court practices. A lighter touch than Jefferson's was needed, however, one more in tune with people's needs and the subtle turns of power.

Like others in Washington City, Dolley learned a great deal from the Merry Affair. Though she would not have recognized the language of modern political science, she knew quite well the uses and dangers of the unofficial sphere. The capital city setting only raised the pitch and the stakes. In particular, she observed the struggle of Elizabeth Merry, a most aristocratic (or, more accurately, aristocratic acting) woman in the most rural and republican of capitals. The relish and entitlement with which she assumed the spotlight, her social domination of her husband, her "brilliant and fantastic" dress, all conspired to earn Elizabeth Merry near universal loathing. Dolley saw firsthand that stepping too far onto the political center stage could be dangerous for a woman, and for female bystanders. As she was preparing to take the leading role in Washington City, she resolved that she would not make the same mistakes.

Portrait of a Lady

In the summer of 1803, the celebrated painter Gilbert Stuart moved to Washington. The most popular artist of his day, hailed by all as the Father of American Portraiture, Stuart was American born and European trained. After a sojourn in London and Dublin from 1775 to 1793, he returned to the new United States with the express intention of capturing the likenesses of the revolutionary generation, primarily that of George Washington. In painting these portraits, Stuart would not only assure his place in history but could also make a significant contribution to the nation's future. The people of the time took face-reading seriously, believing that the lineaments of a person's visage would reveal his or her character, whether it was one of heroic strength or of secret depravity. Portraits provided ordinary people with their only chance to study the faces of those leading them into the next stage of the country's young life.

Following a brief stay in New York, where he painted the infamous John Jay, Stuart moved to the then capital, Philadelphia. Thanks to the connection with Jay, Stuart got his sitting with President Washington, and so began his famous series of portraits. Sittings with John and Abigail Adams, Thomas Jefferson, and "the American Sappho," Sarah Wentworth Apthorp, soon followed.

By 1803, it only made sense for Stuart to take up residence in the newest power center. He stayed in Washington City for eighteen months, and was "all the rage, he is almost worked to death." Everyone wanted to be painted by him; and he was enormously productive. The ladies of Washington, he wrote, expressing concern about his pace, bade him to take a long rest—after he finished *their* portraits, of course. These were times to try an artist's temperament. When importuned by a husband to paint his wife a third time, making her prettier, Stuart allegedly exclaimed in exasperation, "You bring [a painter] a potato and expect he will paint you a peach."

Stuart specialized in paired portraits of married couples, immortalizing many of the Madisons' friends this way: the Marqués Martínez de Yrujo and Sally McKean Martínez de Yrujo; William and Anna Maria Brodeau Thornton; and prominent locals, such as John and Ann Ogle Tayloe of Octagon House. Of course, Dolley and James were on Stuart's painterly itinerary. In May 1804, Dolley reported to Anna that "Steward has taken an admirable picture of Mr. Madison—his & mine are finished." Mischievously, she offered her review: "Quite pritty he has made us."[1] Artistic convention determined several prominent elements of Stuart's portrait of Dolley, from the classic three-quarter pose to the sweeping drapery and glimpse of sky in the background. Dolley adhered to another set of conventions as well. According to contemporary courtesy books, a firmly closed mouth differentiated the truly refined from the slack-jawed uncouth. Like Stuart's most famous subject, George Washington, Dolley faces the viewer with a beautifully composed, compressed mouth.

Stuart's fame lay not just in his skill as a copyist or his ability to please patrons, but also in his talent for distilling the essence of his subjects. To keep his sitters alert during the tedious business of posing, Stuart engaged them in conversation, a technique that also had the effect of eliciting more of the subject's true nature. This ploy paid off in Stuart's painting of Dolley, and not just because in his vocabulary of vegetation, she was indubitably a peach and not a potato. Despite the constraints of artistic and social convention, her vitality springs forth, her eyes crackling with intelligence and humor, her cheeks burning with high color; her body, while properly erect, conveys ease and comfort in its soft curves. Dolley seems at once relaxed and vibrant; a shawl falls from her shoulders, as though she is about to rise. Hers is a picture of health, vigor, and optimism.

Dolley is not framed by a backdrop of books, as James is, nor does she appear in a domestic scene as female subjects often did. It is a blue sky for Dolley, where the white fluffy clouds only add piquancy and variety; touched by a sunbeam, the clouds echo the warm glow of her dress and skin. Her sunny strength seems blessed and reflected by nature herself.[2]

This was precisely the image that Dolley wished to show the world, and that would become increasingly important through the Madisons' political career. As James entered his second term as secretary of state, he and Dolley readied themselves for the challenge of achieving the presidency. Dolley began crafting a persona for political purposes, drawing upon these optimistic aspects of her character. In and of itself, this was quite in line with the values of her culture. People of the upper classes, and those who aspired to them, consciously strove to present their "better selves" in public. These "selves" were not phony; rather, as the phrase implies, they were considered to represent an individual's highest, most refined traits. Ideally, the effort of striving to appear at one's best could effect lasting moral, mental, and psychological improvement.[3] What differentiated Dolley from other society women and men was the political use to which she put this process—and the extraordinary success she achieved.

As the result of the election of 1804 was a foregone conclusion, the preceding presidential campaign season had passed almost unnoticed.

Along with the Louisiana Purchase, the reduction of the federal deficit and the repeal of the excise tax on whiskey boosted Jefferson's popularity. The Federalists did not help their cause by refusing to identify a candidate until just before the election. With George Clinton as his running mate, Jefferson trounced the Federalists Charles Cotesworth Pinckney and Rufus King in a 162–14 electoral vote.

Because the immortal Washington had served two terms, it was widely assumed that Jefferson would step down in four years, leaving the presidential field to his closest colleague and friend, James Madison. Of course, people had been making this assumption as early as 1801, but after the Republicans' overwhelming 1804 victory, James's position as heir apparent seemed assured.

Dolley and James shared the general expectation, and Dolley may have altered her behavior to reflect her future standing. As early as 1803, Margaret Bayard Smith noted a change in Dolley's demeanor: "Mrs. Madison appears to more than usual advantage this winter." Margaret noted approvingly that "her manners are just what they ought to be." The Dolley presented to Margaret primly and "entirely renounced cards," and indeed the two conversed on the evils of cardplaying. Dolley, who nonetheless continued to use gambling and card games to attract and please guests, was playing to her audience; Margaret exclaimed that she "was delighted with the sentiments she avowed, they seemed sincere as well as wise." "She is realy a lovely woman," Margaret pronounced.[4]

❦

In March 1804, twenty-five-year-old Anna Payne married Richard Cutts, a congressman from a prominent Massachusetts family. (The Cuttses' part of the state would, in 1820, become Maine.) In an era that offered females no worldly accomplishment but marriage, Anna Payne had unquestionably done well. Though she would live part of the year with her husband's family at Cutts Island, in Saco, Richard Cutts also served in Washington, so the marriage did not entail a complete separation from Dolley and her sisters and mother living in Virginia, as a wedding outside political circles would have done.

Anna and Richard married in a church at the Navy Yard, attended by the government and local elite, except for those foreign diplomats who were Catholic. Eugenia Osipovna Dashkov, the wife of the Russian chargé d'affaires, sent the couple a traditional Russian gift of salt and bread—signifying the essence and the staff of life—presented in two wine coolers. In a time before elaborate wedding presents, all of Washington sent "tokens of affection," handmade offerings of pincushions, embroidery, and paintings, as well as celebratory verses written for the occasion.[5]

Dolley participated fully in the wedding festivities, exhibiting the gracious generosity for which she was endlessly celebrated, but privately she was devastated. She often referred to Anna as her "daughter-sister" or "sister-child," writing of herself to Anna as "a sister who has ever loved you like her own child!"[6] When people commented favorably on Anna and her new husband, Dolley responded as she would for her own child: "If Payne was a Man Married & gone from me I could not feel more sensibly every thing that regarded him than I do."[7] That she equated her pride and love for Anna to that which she felt for her twelve-year-old son showed that her feelings for her "daughter-sister" ran deeper than even the bond of shared childhood. Since Anna's birth, the two sisters had never been separated. Anna had been a loving presence during the sad events of 1793 and had assumed her place in the Washington City household with ease. The fact that Anna waited until her mid-twenties to marry testifies to her happiness in the Madison family circle. Dolley had never known adult life without her little sister, and now Anna had gone.

Perhaps if more children had followed Payne, the attachment to Anna would have been less fierce; but, after years of childlessness with James, Dolley knew Anna was probably the only daughter she would ever have. In many ways, a substitute daughter could be closer to a woman than her own son. Sons, after all, were expected to separate from their mothers at a young age; on the other hand, since their adult lives mirrored their mothers', daughters were supposed to grow closer to their mothers as they neared womanhood.[8]

Immediately after Anna and Richard embarked on wedding visits to family and friends in Philadelphia, New York, and Boston, Dolley fell into a deep depression. As she described to Anna: "I shut myself up from the Morg [morning] you entered the stage, & wrote Mama P. & Lucy until Saturday 3 oClock when we went in the rain to dine." The letters Anna wrote during her travels gave Dolley her "greatest pleasure," if for a most pathetic reason: "to find that even there [in Philadelphia], you can recollect with affection the solatary being you have left behind . . ." That, at least, "reflects a ray of brightness on my *sombre prospect*."[9]

With her mother and Lucy at Harewood, with Mary Payne Jackson married in Clarksburg, Virginia, and with "the Publick business" keeping Dolley and James in Washington City, Dolley felt her isolation keenly. In a series of letters to the new bride, she gave full, if veiled, vent to her sadness and resentment, alternately seeking reassurance of Anna's love and wielding guilt like the most experienced mother. She framed Anna's marriage as "your . . . leaving me," and she mourned, "Oh my dear sister that I was with you who was allways accustomed to accompany you where ever you went—but tis in vain that I wish & sigh!"—She was restless even in her own home, fretting "as this place seems not natural or scarsly agreable without you—." The least that Anna could do was to write—"I am absolutely crying to hear from you again"—but in Dolley's view, her sister did not write soon or often enough after departing for her honeymoon: "Tho few, are the Days, passed since you left me my dearest Anna they have been spent in anxious impatience to hear from you."[10]

The theme of reproach and regret continued. Dolley sighed in another letter: "You dont speak of the long letter I wrote you—but still I hope you have it, nothing has occured since I wrote worth your knowing—I continue to miss you both, & to lament a separation from you, who could have made my happiness—but when I read your letters & see you in those charming places enjoying yourself, & every advantage, I reflect on my own selfishness & strive to be reconciled—." And it *was* a struggle; even as Dolley acknowledged that "tis natural all these things happen & in reality I wish you to be happier now than ever you ware," she could not resist adding "& that you should derive all your pleasures independent of poor me."[11]

To the young bride, Dolley also imparted the dark news of the death of Thomas Jefferson's younger daughter, Maria Jefferson Eppes, who, like Anna, was in her mid-twenties and, like Anna, had married a good Republican congressman. Maria Eppes died of complications after giving birth, a circumstance ordinary enough to worry a woman just embarked on the married state. Dolley reflected gloomily on "the consequent Misery it has occation'd them all—this is among the many proofs my dr. Sister of the uncertainty of life! A girl so young, so lovely—all the efforts of her Father docters & friends availed nothing—." She ended this account with a melancholy non sequitur: "I have locked up your little Trunk in the Store room."[12]

Dolley became reconciled to Anna's married state, but by the following summer, she had problems of her own. In June 1805, she had developed an ulcer on her knee that would not heal. She wrote to Anna, now pregnant with her first child, from her bed "to which I have been confined for Ten days with a sad knee." The Madisons called in doctors when the sore became painful; caustic substances were applied in order to burn it out. The medical attention gave Dolley hope of an eventual recovery, "but heaven knows when as it promises to be Tedious."[13]

A month later, she was still in bed, ill enough that it was decided she could not make the usual trip home to Montpelier. Fed up with "confinement and calomil," she felt "reduced & weak."[14] Things became so serious that by the end of July, Dolley and James traveled to Philadelphia to undergo treatment with the fortuitously named Philip Syng Physick, one of America's leading doctors, as well as a professor of surgery at the University of Pennsylvania. Settled in rented lodgings, Dolley remained under Dr. Physick's treatment until November. James stayed with her for as long as possible, returning to his duties in Washington City only in October.

Dolley was not alone in Philadelphia; before and after James left, she had many visitors, and several people stayed with her, including her childhood nurse and former slave, Amey. Even confined to bed or a chair, she was the most popular woman in town—she compared her "attendance" to that of "a New Play"—but she missed her home and family. For much of the time, she suffered from physical pain and immobility. As soon as she arrived, Dr. Physick splinted her knee so thoroughly that she could not even sit up. His treatment consisted of immobility, bed rest, the occasional application of caustics, and at least one "little incission."[15] It was not clear whether she would ever recover or even walk again. Had the wound become infected, she might have even lost her leg.

To Anna, suffering through the last stages of pregnancy in Maine, Dolley poured out her heart. During her first consultation in July 1805, with James at her side, Dr. Physick was optimistic: "[he] says he will cure me in a month." She knew this news should "comfort me—but Anna, if I was not affraid of death I could give way to most immoderate greaf, I feel as if my heart was bursting." Once again, Dolley had been left behind. She felt abandoned by her female support system— "No Mother no Sister"—even as she castigated herself as a "fool," since after all she was attended by her "beloved Husband siting anxiously by me & who is my unremiting Nurse."[16]

But James was not enough. In fact, his own uncertain health remained a source of worry to Dolley. Though at present she was the patient, Dolley felt deprived of protection, forced to rely on a man she described as "delicate . . . I tremble for him." Indeed, on the initial trip to Philadelphia, James was "taken very ill with his old bilious complaint." Herself thoroughly incapacitated, Dolley "thought all was over with me, I could not fly to him & aid him as I used to do."[17] Not surprisingly, given the summer season, she also worried that James would catch yellow fever; while none was reported in the city, she nervously monitored every rumor. Though Anna had her own health problems, Dolley leaned on her as a strong and comforting presence. Whether young Anna would have been a better nurse than James matters little; Dolley projected the qualities she needed onto her.

In mid-August, she rallied sufficiently to greet the news of Anna's safe delivery of her first child, named James Madison Cutts. Dolley fondly dubbed him "our little tinker," casting the baby as a lovable scamp, but even at that celebratory moment, she admitted to being "lowspiritted" in spite of Dr. Physick's encouraging prognosis. She was not finding the return to her former home city easy. Philadelphia was still the cradle of the American Society of Friends. Philadelphians Nancy Mifflin and Sally Zane paid bedside visits and "remonstrated with" her for having so much company: "they said that it was reported that half the City of Phila had made me visits." Dolley confessed to Anna that this "lecture made me recollect the times when *our Society* [of Friends] used to controle me entirely & debar me from so many advantages & pleasures."

Being forced to endure a "lecture" while trapped by her immobility— it must have seemed a sad parody of Dolley's earlier experiences. For all her stature as a grown, married woman, read out of Meeting many years earlier and thus "so entirely from their clutches," when she was faced with the censorious Quaker ladies in 1804, Dolley "really felt my ancient terror of them revive to disiagreable degree." Again, Anna understood better than anyone what she meant. For good or ill, Dolley was the center of an admiring crowd, but she longed for her sister: "I had a thousand times rather be in your Chamber with . . . babe & self."[18]

Coming back to Philadelphia was a shock to Dolley's psyche. The memories of the epidemic, as well as the uneasy associations with her tumultuous childhood, were to remain vivid throughout her life; how much sharper must they have been as she lay confined to her bed, alone with her own thoughts. On their way to Dr. Physick's, the Madisons had spent the night at Gray's Ferry, where young Dolley Todd had been overwhelmed, physically weak, and frustrated by her own helplessness. Twelve years later, Dolley found herself once more frightened by her own physical condition and powerless to do anything about it. "Unavoidably Banished" was Dolley's phrase in 1793; it also described her state in 1805.

In spite of Dr. Physick's initial optimism, Dolley was not cured in a month; in early October, her recovery was still dragging on, and James returned to Washington City. This was one of the first times that the couple lived apart, and Dolley found it difficult. She had surrounded herself with substitutes for her cherished Anna—including young, spirited Betsy Pemberton, who slept by her side and flirted with James via postscripts to Dolley's letters—but there was no substitute for James. When Betsy donned a hat that he had left behind and imitated James in hopes of making Dolley laugh, Dolley could not even look at her.[19]

Mail between Washington and Philadelphia took about four days, and the letters between James and Dolley flew, sometimes two a day. Dolley's letters were quite romantic, full of love, longing, and reassurance about her health. Generally, the only uncheerful sentiment she conveyed to James was her longing for him, though on occasion, she felt so desperate, that in a departure from her usual mode, she confessed the "oppression of my mind," alluding to a certain melancholy day and sleepless night. Still, she could only express her fears and anxiety to her husband by deflecting them onto concerns about him. She focused on his journey home—"detention cold and accident seemed to menace thee!" In a culture that prized selflessness in wives, such redirected fretting offered one of the few ways Dolley could complain. Only to Anna could she reveal her real fears and vulnerabilities—her dread of death and the "sad" feeling engendered by the treatments.[20]

Though Dolley's protective instincts may have made her reluctant to share her fears with her husband, the couple freely expressed their great affection and tenderness for each other. Dolley had come a long way from the bride who wrote "Alass!" on the evening of her wedding. She regarded her communication with her husband as precious, assuring him that she cherished "speaking to you in this *only* way," and getting letters "from one who is all to me." In an age when husbands and wives often addressed each other as "Mr." and "Mrs." Dolley signed her letters "Your Dolley" and "D.," sometimes with a romantic "adieu, my beloved." Both Dolley and James ended their letters with "ever affectionate."[21]

James signed more formally, using his full name or initials. But he addressed "his Dolley" as "my dearest" and teased her with the light-hearted flirtation with young Betsy Pemberton. "I repeat my kisses to Miss P.," he wrote a few weeks after he left; "I wish I could give her more substantial ones than can be put on paper." But, he added, only "after I have sett the example on those of another person whose name

I flatter myself you will not find it difficult to guess." He ended this playful letter reassuringly: "with unalterable love I remain yrs." As Dolley knew, "our hearts understand each other."[22]

In her letters to most people, including her sisters, Dolley used the second-person form "you." In contrast, she sprinkled the "thee"s and "thy"s of Quaker usage throughout her letters to James, as she did in her correspondence with her mother. Though she was not consistent—"I am so impatient to be restored to you," she wrote—at intimate moments she often reverted to her first language, the one of love and childhood: "Think of thy wife! who thinks and dreams of thee!"[23]

James and Dolley each made the other the center of concern. Even from a distance, Dolley gave wifely advice, bidding her workaholic husband to "take as much relaxation, & pleasure as you can." Too much business "will not agree with you," she declared, threatening to come home sooner than she should "unless you amuse yourself." James expressed love with practical care, and he lavished time, attention, and money on Dolley, begging her to tell him if she needed funds: "Let me know without reserve, and I will do all I can in that as in all cases, to evince the happiness I feel in giving proofs of my unlimited affection & confidence."[24]

James also cared for thirteen-year-old Payne Todd, whom he called "our son" and Dolley called "our child." He reported that "Payne is well, and I am endeavoring to keep him in some sort of attention to his books." It proved a struggle to keep his young charge "in the path of the Student," for James confessed that "the close employment of my time, at this juncture leaves much to his own disposition." Leaving Payne to "his own disposition" was not a good idea; the young man was already showing signs of fecklessness. In 1805, James obtained a place for Payne at St. Mary's College, a school for both Roman Catholic and Protestant boys in Baltimore. No doubt the discipline of such an institution appealed to the Madisons. Dolley rejoiced: "I am very greatful for the prospect you have opened for our child, & shall now look forward to his Manhood, when he will bless—and do honor to his guardians."[25]

As always, politics remained a constant in the Madisons' partnership, and their correspondence was filled with news from both Washington and Philadelphia. Dolley's sickroom became a place for prominent Philadelphians to meet and, more important, to make connections with the seemingly remote federal government. From the beginning, the founders had worried about how to connect the isolated capital to the rest of the country. For a short time, Dolley *was* the capital, and canny Philadelphians were not prepared to pass up this unexpected opportunity.

Over her four-month stay, Dolley's letters to James regularly reported on visits from diplomatic families—such as the Martínez de Yrujos and General Turreau—as well as important citizens. Visitors boasting such illustrious Philadelphia names as Dallas, Donaldson, Steward, Butler, and Logan paid their respects. Women in European and American cities had begun to use such calls to further their families' political, economic, and social positions; a visit to Dolley's chamber allowed Philadelphia women to do so at the level of federal politics. Political men visited with women and on their own as well, though after the whispers in Washington during the Merry Affair, Dolley was wary. One evening, alone upstairs, she did not receive General Turreau and "two or three frenchmen," as "I resolved not to admit a gentleman, into my room unless entitled by age and long acquaintance."[26]

As Dolley's health improved in late October and early November, she began using the crowds for her own brand of politicking. Both patronage requests and pension "lobbying" from constituents had long been the province of the women of political families, but Dolley was unusually adept as an influence peddler. She was just beginning a long and successful career staffing the federal government with friends and supporters, but even then she felt comfortable asking James to "speak a word to General Dearborn in favor of poor Mrs. Jackson." Mrs. Jackson may have come to Dolley with a request for a military post for a male relation, or she might have been asking for intervention with a pension for her husband's Revolutionary War service. She was, Dolley reminded James, "the Doctor's widow who used to supply so well the soldiers."[27]

James was not above a nudge here or there: "I hope you have not been unmindful of the civilities recd. from your friends, and among them the particular attentions of Mrs. Leiper [the wife of a prominent Philadelphia tobacco merchant]." Dolley dutifully reported that in the case of Mrs. Leiper "I have been careful to make every return she expected" for her "civilitys." Indeed, when she was mobile, "I have call'd at the doors generally of those who visited me—they all seem satisfied with my . . . acknowledgments."[28]

Along with affection and family news, James sent newspaper reports of political happenings. He kept Dolley apprised of the comings and goings of public figures, especially the diplomatic corps: "that Col. Hawkins [the U.S. Indian agent] with his Indians is about leaving us, that Mr. Skipwith is just arrived from France, and that the Tunisian Ambassador is expected soon from Norfolk."[29] Not surprisingly, given James's position, much of the news exchanged between the two concerned foreign relations. In an age of slow communication and less than reliable journalism, having a trustworthy reporter on the scene proved crucial. In November, Dolley informed James that contrary to the newspaper reports that he might see in Washington, Spain had not declared war on the United States. During a soirée in Dolley's sickroom, Gilbert Stuart's wife, Charlotte Coates Stuart, had obtained a denial from the Spanish minister.[30]

Dolley again bridged the distance between remote Washington City and major metropolitan centers when she reported that General Turreau, the French minister, had not impressed the Philadelphians. No wonder that "he says, that the Americans hate him."[31] In the delicate balance of public opinion, especially in "Frenchified" Philadelphia, such information was key to future policy decisions. Turreau was a frequent visitor, and Dolley worked toward ameliorating the enmity between him and her other callers.

She saw herself, quite rightly, as James's pupil in political matters; if she demurred at sharing her emotional vulnerabilities, she felt free to ask him questions about political business. During her last month of convalescence, after joyfully informing James that her knee had mended enough that she might ride in a few days, Dolley asked: "I wish you would indulge me with some information respecting the war with

Spain and the disagreement with England, as it is so generally expected here that I am at a loss what to surmise." She went on, teasing James and deprecating herself: "You know I am not much of a politician but I am extremely anxious to hear (as far as you may think proper) what is going forward in the Cabinet."[32]

Connecting Dolley's request for information with her possible reappearance in public, James responded, "Your question as to our situation in regard to Spain & England is puzzling," referring to the nature of the question, not to the fact that she had posed it. He went on to hypothesize that "if a general war takes place in Europe[,] Spain will probably be less disposed to insult us; and England less sparing of her insults." It was also possible that one of the powers would change its attitude toward the United States solely in reaction to the other. While there was no telling, he continued, whether war would be "forced by either . . . it certainly will not if they consult their interest."

The letter took a practical turn. "The power however of deciding questions of war and providing measures that will make or meet it, lies with Congress, and that is always our answer to newsmongers." He and Dolley both understood that newspaper writers would query her on political issues and that she needed to be armed with the early republican version of a sound bite.[33]

Dolley's discussions of politics with her husband did not overstep the bounds thought appropriate for a lady from a political family. In fact, "family concerns" allowed her to think, write, and act politically. James knew his wife had his best interests at heart when he gave her "our answer." Like many politically engaged women who existed within a culture deeply anxious about female politicking, Dolley expressed her concerns with a mix of the self-deprecatory and assertive, always conscious that her letters might fall into unfriendly hands. (In the early republic, even "private" letters were considered public property if they contained political information. At times, if a postmaster spread the word that a letter from an important person had arrived, groups would gather at a post office, demanding the recipient read the missive aloud. Not surprisingly, politicians, their supporters, and their detractors began to "leak" or compose letters with this in mind.)[34]

Dolley's disingenuous statements—"You know I am not much of a politician"—are typical of those found in the correspondence of political women, who often offered disclaimers before talking politics. And her disavowal seems quite compatible with the lighthearted, loving tone of other letters to her beloved James. But a warier disclaimer that appears in the same letter seems intended to ensure that her actions would not be misinterpreted by an unfriendly political public: "I beleive you would not desire your wife the active partizan, such as her neighbor Mrs. L., nor will there be the slightest danger whilst she is conscious of her want of talents, and her diffidence in expressing her opinions always imperfectly understood by her sex."[35]

Finally, by November's end, Dolley's knee was much recovered and, to her delight, Anna and her husband came to fetch her home. They arrived in the evening, and "so pleased and agitated" Dolley that she "could not sleep." The party did not leave town right away, but Dolley's tone to James became quite cheerful. To be sure, her health seemed quite restored and she could look forward to an imminent departure, after which she would be "safely lodged" in her husband's arms, but the renewal of her spirits was partly due to the presence of Anna.[36]

After almost four months away from home and two months separated from her husband, Dolley returned to James and to Washington City. The experience of separation and loneliness, the physical suffering and limitations had all affected her. For too many weeks, her little room in Philadelphia had been her only world. Freed from the routines of her busy Washington City life, she had turned deep within herself. In this liminal time and place, she had faced her most painful memories, both traumatic and chronic. She returned to Washington City, stronger in some ways, but also more vulnerable.

⚜

Dolley was not characterologically given to depression, though at times her seemingly forced cheer hinted at a tendency to melancholy, and her public face sometimes masked a palpable anxiety. In addition, her will often failed in the face of adversity, and she would collapse. Over the course of the next few years, the experience of loss drove her to her darkest places. In 1806, her sister Mary lost her two little girls, Dolley and Lucy, aged five and three, in quick succession. "Dolley Lucy, both gone!" Dolley wrote to her mother. "[T]hey are now angels!" She had taken to her bed after "the first letter from my dear afflicted Mary" that broke the news of one daughter's death; the next letter "makes me think I shall never feel as I have done, so deep is the sorrow which takes possession of my mind."[37]

Only a year later, in the teeth of the fierce electioneering that led up to the election of 1808, Dolley suffered two more devastating losses, which she felt so keenly that she almost lost the will to live. In October, her mother died, probably of a stroke, while nursing Dolley's bereaved sister in Virginia. For weeks after, Dolley could not pick up her pen, let alone cope with ordinary business. Later, in a letter to a financial agent, she apologized: "Deep affliction my dear friend has for some time past arrested my pen! My beloved & tender Mother left us forever . . . she died, without suffering or regret."[38]

Mary Coles Payne's cousin and brother-in-law, Isaac Winston III, reached out to his grieving niece: "A Day has not passed for some Time, in which I have not thought with great Tenderness and Affection of my ever dear Dolley." He understood the depth of her loss of such "a tender, affectionate, and most excellent Parent." More than just a source of love or a moral exemplar, in bequeathing her daughter a demonstration of the power of practical actions over mere words, Mary had also "left you with an example of inestimable Value." She "never for a Moment lost sight of your best and dearest Interests," Isaac wrote, even in the face of financial hardship and the defection of her husband. Though given her sex she could do little to help her sons, Mary completely fulfilled her duties toward her daughters. She trained them for marriage and ensured that all of the girls married well. Indeed, each of her daughters married into ruling families. Her resilience and ability to cope with life's adversity—"conformity to All the Duties of her station in life"—was indeed an example to value.[39]

In February 1808, sister Mary herself succumbed to the tuberculosis she had battled for two years, leaving her husband, John G. Jackson, and her remaining daughter, also Mary, to carry on. To her oldest friend in the world, Eliza Lee, Dolley gave full vent to her feelings, asking her to grieve for her who had lost her mother and now "whose heart is bursting with grief whilst she tells you that the grave of her beloved Polly [Mary] is within the same inclosure!" Struggling to make sense of her "deep affliction," Dolley invoked the conventional religious view of resignation and acceptance: "Oh God! We must bow our heads to thy decrees however awful—we cannot change or avert them."

But resigning oneself to the will of God can be cold comfort, and in the next sentence Dolley gave way: "Eliza, I cannot write—tho I wish to communicate every thing to you; when I trace the sad events that have occured to me, I feel as if I should die two." In her despair, Dolley called upon all her resources, "exerted all my fortitude, all my religion in order to live for [my husband] & my son." Grief now tried Dolley beyond her own imagining. She wondered to Eliza: "Alass! my friend, I used to think that I could not survive the loss of my Mother & my sisters yet I am still here; & in all the bitterness of mourning striveing to reconcile my heart to the greatest misfortune."[40]

A broken heart still beats, and Dolley went on with the presidential campaign, entertaining and swaying the congressmen who would elect her husband president. She kept her feelings shuttered from the world, while everyone she saw socially described her carefree and charming presence. But insecurity and dread of loss would never leave her.[41]

Even as she struggled to present her "best self " to the world, the stress of grief took its toll. In June 1808, she suffered a bout of what she believed to be inflammatory rheumatism. Writing to Anna, she made the connection between her physical and psychological state: her mother-in-law and other Madison kinswomen kindly nursed her with "great attention & kindness," but as far as Dolley was concerned, they were "strangers . . . for what in this world can compensate for the sympathy & confidence of a Mother & a sister." The answer was clear: "nothing but that tye that binds us to a good Husband—such as ours, & we aught to be satisfied." As loss piled on loss, Dolley clung increasingly to James. Dolley's reluctance to share her vulnerabilities notwithstanding, he had long been the primary focus of her emotional life; now he became her main support.

Dolley understood the joint or back pain (as well as a pain in her arm she complained of at this time) that she suffered as "rumatism," but these conditions may have been manifestations of the mind-body connection. (Modern research has shown that joint pain and back ailments, as well as skin conditions such as shingles, are commonly associated with stress and fatigue.) During this time, Dolley also began to have recurring "pains" in her face, which may have been erysipelas, a strep infection that affects the skin and is particularly exacerbated by stress.[42]

In their shared loss, Dolley, Anna, and Lucy drew even closer together, and Dolley's need for family, for love and comfort, increased. As the sisters mourned Mary Payne Jackson's death in their separate households, Dolley dreamed that Anna "return'd" to her, "dress'd in beautiful & shineing Blue." Where others might have withdrawn, Dolley responded by reaching out, strengthening family bonds and creating them among friends and the children of friends as she needed and wanted. Still, anxiety and fear infused her letters. No wonder that when the news came in 1808 of Anna's safe delivery of her third son, a baby with "promising health," that "we all claped our hands in triumph."[43] Dolley must have feared that she would lose this most precious connection.

Dolley's letters had always tended to jump back and forth among topics and bits of news, often returning to one subject that worried her. After her mother and sister died, the topic of death, unsurprisingly, appeared over and over. One letter to Anna, filled with news, gossip, and politics, was also sprinkled throughout with accounts of various illnesses of family and friends, including her remaining niece, little motherless Mary: "I fear the prediction of her Father, who thinks she will not live to be a woman." John G. Jackson's anxiety was understandable, since he had lost his two other daughters and his wife in such a short time: "He writes me often but all in his old stile of melancholy." In the same letter, Dolley mentioned to Anna that "Unkle's family have been two sick" to visit, and "Patsy and Eleck have been at the point of death." She moved on to complain of the slowness of the post, but since she could not send the letter for three days, she promised to add "whatever seems to interest us." That included the news that "Mrs. F's little girl is threatened with another riseing on her side which I fear will be its death." Even the news of Martha Jefferson Randolph's safe delivery of a son sounded a gloomy note: "[She] hopes tis her last."[44]

The sisters had only one remaining brother, John C. Payne, the youngest of the Payne children. Far from being a comfort or support, John was a separate source of worry. In 1806, when James Madison assigned him a post as secretary to George Davis, the American consul in Tripoli, twenty-four-year-old John was already a full-blown alcoholic and gambler. Sending an undisciplined dissolute to an exotic locale, far from home and accountability, was not a good decision. John C. Payne began deteriorating almost immediately and, never a good correspondent, stopped writing his sister altogether. Dolley could not even tell him of the deaths of his mother and sister until 1809, when she received her first letter from him in a year.

⁂

To a close observer, the Dolley of Gilbert Stuart's painting stood not contradicted but complicated. To the public, especially the political public, Dolley continued to exude energy and charm. What the viewer saw was true, but the viewer did not see everything, as Dolley's averted face signaled. That firm mouth in Stuart's painting was not just a matter of fashion; Dolley kept her own secrets. As she began to campaign for James's presidency in earnest, she would need and use both the positive image that she and Stuart had created, and the discretion and discipline that grief had taught her.

SEVEN

Sex, Lies, and
the Election of 1808

1807–1808

*S*amuel Latham Mitchill, representative from New York, was widely acknowledged as the most intelligent and wisest man in Congress. Trained in medicine and law, holding professorships in chemistry, natural history, botany, agriculture, and *materia medica* at Columbia and the New York College of Physicians and Surgeons, Dr. Mitchill also possessed a "varied and intimate acquaintance with classical literature, both ancient and modern," "attainments in history and political science," as well as a "practical acquaintance with public affairs." No wonder his fellow congressmen affectionately dubbed him the "Stalking Library."[1]

The most incontrovertible evidence of his wisdom may have been his marriage to a sister intellectual, Catharine Akerly Cocks, who shared his interests, especially regarding the political life of the new capital. Dr. Mitchill served several terms in the House and the Senate, and, with no children to keep her at home, Catharine often accompanied him to Washington City. She stayed at his boardinghouse, socializing with all, and joining the other ladies in attending legislative and Supreme Court sessions. When Catharine stayed behind in New York, her husband kept her apprised of political news and events through regular correspondence.

By November 1807, Senator Mitchill considered the presidential election season open; he offered his assessment of the process, as well as a prediction. After passing along best wishes to Catharine from Dolley and Anna, he added: "The former of these ladies has the prospect of being *Lady President*." According to Mitchill, Thomas Jefferson was already shipping his belongings back to Virginia, and everyone knew that James Madison and Vice President George Clinton were the contenders for the Republican candidacy. Mitchill went on to compare their campaigns: "The former gives dinners and makes generous display to the members. The latter lives snug at his lodgings, and keeps aloof from such captivating exhibitions." The crucial factor? "The Secretary of State has a wife to aid in his pretensions. The Vice-President has nothing of female succor on his side. And in these two respects Mr. M. is going greatly ahead of him."[2]

Though in this matter, as in many others, the Stalking Library was precisely right on all points, the election of 1808 was not by any means a foregone conclusion. In December 1807, Thomas Jefferson responded to continuing assaults by England and France on American shipping by launching the Embargo Act into the stormy seas of international trade. The embargo forbade ships to depart with cargo from American ports. This not only saved ships, goods, and men, but also put a stop to the humiliating seizure of American ships before the world's gaze. It also, however, had dramatic economic effects. Not only were Americans unable to export their own goods and raw materials, but the import trade was shut down as well. Though ships from other nations could legally bring goods into an American port, they would have to leave empty.[3]

Embargoes and other means of financial coercion had long been James's pet strategy. The boycotts during the American Revolution had been extraordinarily successful, not merely in their effect on the British but also in rallying the colonists to rebellion. The exhilaration of the revolutionary moment, along with a sense of wartime emergency, accounted for much of that success. The situation had changed by the early 1800s, however, and Americans would not be shamed or bullied into a boycott or an embargo by their own government. Smuggling and other forms of resistance began almost immediately. "The President & M[adison]" have been greatly perplexed at the remonstrances from so many Towns to remove the Embargo," Dolley observed in a letter to Anna. The contention the measure caused in Congress and the ordinary people "evading it" was "a terrible thing."[4]

Though the embargo quickly showed itself both a practical and a public relations failure—Albert Gallatin wrote that he would rather have gone to war than continue it—the president and his secretary of state refused to recognize reality. From their point of view, the embargo *should* have worked, by God, and when smuggling and other means of dodging the shipping restrictions increased, their efforts to enforce the failing embargo made John Adams's implementation of the Alien and Sedition Acts look moderate. The supplemental Enforcement Act of 1809 expanded the government's powers, especially to stop and detain ships on mere suspicion. The lowest point in the process came when Jefferson authorized the use of military force to coerce Americans into compliance.[5]

Of course, shippers bore the brunt of the punitive measures. The Federalist stronghold of New England was hit especially hard, and the anguish and anger of New England voters breathed new life into the Republicans' opponents. The Republican "revolution of 1800" had almost crippled the Federalist Party, but it remained viable. Many of the nation's moneyed elite were Federalists, and they enjoyed strong, albeit regionally lopsided, support. Now they had an issue they could exploit.

No doubt Federalist legislators in Washington City and all across the country opposed Jefferson out of sincere outrage and in defense of their economic interests, but they also seized on the chance to attack Jefferson personally and take down their opponents' leader. The Federalists were losing national power, and "nothing in their term of office so ill became them as their leaving it." Even as they accused Republican Party leaders of stirring up Jacobin-like passions, the Federalists employed rumor, gossip, and scandalmongering of all kinds to discredit personalities and policies. Personal attacks in newspapers were de rigueur during this time, but Federalist denunciations outnumbered Republican attacks three to one.[6] For both camps, utter confidence in the righteousness of their cause justified the use of any available means.

It didn't help that each of the proto-parties of the day identified with one of the European belligerents, the Federalists with England and the Republicans with France. These European affinities played a role in each party's self-conception, while providing the opposing group with a negative image against which to identify itself. The members of each party took developments in England and France not merely at face value but as a reflection and refraction of their own politics. Theorists and party operatives on both sides frantically probed for meanings, sure that each development in European affairs contained a code for the domestic political opposition. Because American men of both parties could not unite against both Great Britain and France at once, the European situation wreaked havoc in the federal government years before the United States involved itself in actual hostilities.

⁂

The last half of Jefferson's second administration had passed in a kind of malaise, perhaps owing to the death of his daughter Maria, or perhaps to one of the bouts of personal and political paralysis to which he was prone. Unfortunately, when the administration stirred itself to action—as with the passage of the Embargo Act—it produced disastrous results. It was telling that, as Senator Mitchill had noted, Jefferson began moving out of the president's house almost eighteen months before his term officially ended.

The collapse of Jefferson's second term seemed even more dramatic in contrast to his successful first. When European hostilities had begun escalating in 1803, they provided America with a boon in the form of the Louisiana Purchase. But as the European wars intensified, American shipping increasingly suffered, and with an almost nonexistent navy, the United States could not even use the threat of physical force in its bargaining with the two European rivals. Jefferson announced his retirement the same month that Congress passed the Embargo Act—December 1807—and essentially dropped out of the presidency, leaving the ship of state in the hands of James Madison and Albert Gallatin, the secretary of the treasury. Jefferson's behavior gave rise to comparisons with Pontius Pilate, even among Republicans, and the old story resurfaced of Governor Jefferson's retreat from the oncoming British during the Revolution.[7]

In some ways, it made sense for Jefferson to cede the reins of power to his secretary of state. The Napoleonic Wars were the cause of most of the United States' woes, and, after all, foreign affairs was James's bailiwick. Jefferson may have seen his defection as providing a kind of on-the-job training. In choosing his secretary of state, Jefferson had assumed he was also picking his successor; however, it was not at all clear, thanks to the contentious and unsuccessful embargo, that his choice would prevail.[8]

Federalist opposition was not the only problem. The Republicans were hardly a united party. When Catharine Akerly Mitchill asked her husband, "What is the matter with the Republicans . . . that they quarrel so?," she spoke for many. Samuel Latham Mitchill stated the case bluntly: "The principal Cause is that the majority is too great. The minority [the Federalists] is too inconsiderable to keep them in order." Such was the nature of men, Samuel supposed; they were "disputing animals," and his fellow Republicans were no exception. Having triumphed over "their old opponents the federalists, they have nobody but their own side to contend with."[9]

As a result, when Jefferson announced that he would not run again, the power struggle was not merely between the two parties. Dissenting Republicans saw a chance to take over a political machine that, while riven with conflict, continued to grow in power, and several candidates emerged to challenge James's succession to the presidency. As Dr. Mitchill had predicted the month before Jefferson's official announcement, the New York wing of the Republican Party wanted one of their own in the highest office and put forward a man from the state's preeminent political family—Jefferson's own vice president, George Clinton. A Virginian faction, led by the brilliant and erratic John Randolph, preferred James Monroe, then minister to Great Britain.

With the Republican Party thus split, James would have to prevail over both these powerful candidates. Region constituted an important element of self-definition, often transcending even party loyalties; though one of the Madisons' strongest supporters, Senator Mitchill leaned toward fellow New Yorker Clinton "as the man of my preference." And of course, there was the strong chance that the Federalist candidate, Charles C. Pinckney, could take advantage of Republican divisions and return the Federalists to power. Accordingly, the Federalists not only ran their own candidate, but also nurtured the Republicans' internal disruption. Maria Beckley, whose husband was the clerk of the House and the librarian of Congress, predicted that with the embargo "Federalizing all the eastern states . . . Clinton will get all the Federalist interest."[10]

Even national politics had local roots. In the first decades of the U.S. government, Congress played a major role in presidential elections, down to determining the candidates. The state legislatures that chose the presidential candidates were filled not with ordinary voters, but with the family members and colleagues of government officials, including congressmen. Beginning in 1800, Republican congressmen had formed a caucus to decide the nominees for president and vice president. The first caucus met secretly; by 1804, it was openly acknowledged and part of the public discussion. In an age with little existing party machinery, the caucus was an extremely powerful mechanism. Indeed, it was so successful that until 1824, those nominated by the congressional caucus proved, to a man, the victors. And congressional influence was not limited to the powerful caucus. In the early national period, elections had more than a fair chance of being decided in the House of Representatives, giving congressmen direct control over the outcome.[11]

With no party system, no formal electoral machine in place, the house on F Street became James's campaign headquarters, and Dolley, in essence, became his manager. No matter the quality of the entertainment at their home, the Madisons had little chance of winning over diehard Federalists. However, they certainly could rally the Republican troops—not only those securely in their camp but also potential defectors. Indeed, if they were convinced that James was a power to contend with, these apostate Republicans might be reluctant either to split the party, allowing Federalist Charles C. Pinckney to triumph, or (possibly worse) to find themselves on the wrong side of a Madison win.

This was not a quid pro quo situation; Dolley did not trade dinner invitations for votes. The dynamic operated more subtly; much election activity operates on the psychological and symbolic levels. Because no politician would debase himself by open electioneering, James could not even run for office overtly; he had to appear uninterested and disinterested in the political process. To show one's ambition on the stump, making promises to constituents or Congress, would demonstrate a candidate's essential unfitness for the public trust. The model of the compleat politician was Cincinnatus, the noble Roman, reluctantly relinquishing his plow only when called by the people to take up the reins of state. The people could depend on such a man not to abuse power.[12]

Of course, politicians craved office, then as now, but they had to keep their ambitions well hidden, stifled, or channeled. Political men noted approvingly that James was so scrupulous about not campaigning that he did not even go to dinner with members of Congress for fear of seeming corrupt. But he did not have to go out to dinner. With Dolley doing his politicking for him, dinner was at his house. Dolley gave the dinners and the parties, and she invited the congressmen who not only would endorse James in the congressional caucus and influence state electors but might also be voting for or against him in the House. A woman could court favor; correspondingly, congressman and their families, whose own republican virtue prevented open endorsement of candidates, could respond, signaling their allegiance by attending. As in other issues, what was standard practice in European political contexts—the use of social and family channels to muster support—had to be kept hidden in Washington City.

Within the western ruling classes, possessors of personal sociability could make claims to power. In the face of institutional weakness, people used character, cordiality, and personality as indicators of the "people's choice."[13] The theory of republicanism, however, was uneasy with charisma, since its possessor could use his gifts for power-seeking purposes. In Washington City, then, a republican man had to walk a fine line between effortlessly attracting support as a consequence of obvious virtue, and currying favor. Like other political couples Dolley and James solved the problem by ceding to men the high road of unsocial virtue, while wives on the ground, in essence, won friends and influenced people.

In her own ladylike way, Dolley "stood in" for her candidate. Her gracious hospitality and social skills drew supporters into the Madison camp. Her refined persona and the easy, elegant nature of her social events assured the incipient ruling class that a family of superior breeding was leading them along the right path. As one of the chief architects of the U.S. government, James might strike twenty-first-century Americans as the natural choice for president. Apparently being the Father of the Constitution was not a sufficient credential, however. In Dolley's presentation, they found the reassurance they needed that the republican experiment was a flesh-and-blood reality and not a set of abstractions. If the republican ideal of equality promised that the cream would rise to the top, Dolley Madison fulfilled that promise.

Did Dolley have motivations of her own? Certainly, she did not covet the position of "First Lady," as the office was so new that it did not even have a name or a public function. Nor would Dolley have regarded the question of her own desires as relevant, except to deny them. Ambition of any sort, particularly political ambition, was outside the province of ladies. Still, the prospect carried attractive options. For all intents and purposes, Dolley's life was in Washington City, admittedly a more exciting place than Orange, Virginia. As the president's lady she would not only remain in the capital but also play a leading role in society. Like it or not, Dolley was growing as a political animal, developing an instinct for political situations and possibilities, and was being rewarded for her acumen by the praise of legislators and diplomats. Like her competent and self-motivated mother, Dolley was good at her job, and given the evident zest with which she threw herself into it, it is clear that, ladylike disclaimers aside, she had her own ambitions, albeit carefully controlled ones.

Dolley also carried her own message, one that contrasted with the Federalists'. She could not challenge them on policy issues, but on questions of style and manners, she reigned as expert. Margaret Bayard Smith adroitly analyzed Dolley's message and the role her personality played in transmitting it: "In these trying times, Mrs. Madison appeared to peculiar advantage, her husband was assailed with all the violence of political animosity, and calumnies invented where facts were wanting. Amid this cruel warfare of conflicting parties, so calculated to excite angry feelings, Mrs. Madison . . . met these political assailants with a mildness, which disarmed their hostility of its individual rancor, and sometimes even converted political enemies into personal friends." Where that was not possible, Dolley "still oftener succeed[ed] in neutralizing the bitterness of opposition."[14]

In 1807, Dolley mused to her aunt, "Public business perhaps was never thicker"—an understatement indeed.[15] The situation in the capital had changed in focus and intensity since Dolley's first days there. Though the political scene had proven stormy during Jefferson's first administration, Dolley had been relatively sheltered by the focus on the president. Newspaper attacks notwithstanding, people did not assail Dolley as they had Elizabeth Merry. She was, in effect, free to be everyone's darling. But as the question of the presidential succession grew, Dolley would find herself a target and an issue, and correspondingly, would assume a more active part in her husband's politics.

✺

Margaret Bayard Smith's minute dissections of Dolley's character and actions reflected the importance of personality in an age of face-to-face politics. In the absence of a more impersonal party system or a professional politician class, a man's personality constituted his greatest political capital. The public viewed the other elements of a successful political career—money, family, popular support—only in relation to a candidate's fundamental character, as assessed by other men of character, of course. Character was an internal state; for it to count in politics, it must be expressed publicly. It was not enough for a man to know himself; he needed a reputation to precede him. Character plus personal reputation constituted a man's "honor." A deep national anxiety underlay this obsession with personal reputation. The new Americans had little trust in the untried theories of the Constitution and the newborn institutional structures of the government, and by design the government lacked a powerful bureaucracy. The stability of the nation depended on character, on men of honor and trustworthiness.

With so much at stake, a man's reputation was what qualified him for political participation and so it was worth guarding—with a strong defense and also, at times, with a vicious offense. This was the era of Congress behaving badly, with regular exhibitions of high-flown denunciations, personal insults, and even flying glassware. When a political man denounced another's politics, he to some degree denounced the man himself—his honor—while augmenting his own honor at the same time. No wonder verbal attacks flew not only in the Capitol and other public venues but in personal letters and papers. This was not a matter of empty rhetoric. In the "honor culture" of masculine violence that defined the new government, all the shouting and hitting on the floors of Congress, and even an event such as the Burr-Hamilton duel, made sense. The legislature seemed one big playground, where all the participants tried to be King of the Mountain. The game could have only one winner, while the losers were not merely defeated but crushed beneath the victor's feet.

Though the national spotlight rendered the congressional stories more noteworthy, men all across the country participated in the elaborate "grammar of political combat" that dictated exchanges. Reputation was so crucial, and at the same time so intangible and mutable, that even the most outlandish charges would force a man to defend his honor, even to the death. Though relatively few politicians did die for their honor, the political duel constituted the final means to settle disputes. Not only was the personal political, to borrow a modern phrase, but the political was deeply personal.[16]

Dissension, distrust, and a certain suspiciousness characterized the culture. To be sure, the stakes were high—the very fate of the nation seemed to hang on the outcome of each decision—but other factors also contributed to this atmosphere of "passion." As a political theory, republicanism cautioned against ever-present conspiracies. It also presupposed that only one side could ever be right, so that politics was by definition an all-or-nothing matter. Because politicians could not conceive of a two-party system, the "other side" was always seen as a dissenting, even treasonous, faction. Republican virtue demanded that such factions should be denounced loudly and with certainty, so members of both houses of Congress regularly framed their political positions in radical and bloodthirsty terms. Such was the state of partisanship that it was almost impossible to administer the government and keep the union together.[17]

Ironically, this honor culture did not engender highly moral behavior; rather, since one man could accrue honor by attacking another's, it gave rise to malice. In the face of the increasingly contentious and unpopular Embargo Act, even Jefferson's own cabinet members disassociated themselves from the administration and worse. As Dolley's widowed brother-in-law, John G. Jackson, wrote to her from Virginia in 1808, issues of "political warmth" dominated the scene; specifically, Secretary of the Navy Robert Smith had declared that Jefferson and James had "urged the embargo" notwithstanding "the opposition of his cabinet." The Federalists seized upon the story for political gain. Jackson also corresponded with James, but he particularly wanted to share his outrage with his confidante. It was all about jealousy, according to Jackson: "Depend upon it those little great men are filled with venom & Gall at the idea of M[adison] being taken from among them to preside over them."[18]

Political nastiness took many forms, and sexuality remained a weapon enemies could wield. In the absence of any accounts of sexual peccadilloes by James, political whisperers compared his diminutive stature and frailty with the physical presence and virility of James Monroe. More than once in his career, Madison was called a "pygmy" or "pigmian majesty." In politics, size mattered, and James's enemies used his slight stature and his intellectual "coldness" as signs of impotence and infertility. His lack of issue seemed to confirm this, especially since he was married to a woman who had given birth by a previous husband (though the revered "Father of his Country" had been in exactly that situation, as far as the public was concerned, James Madison was no George Washington). Federalist newspapers compared him to an anchovy, a tortoise, and a "dead head" in his cold-blooded, sterile "lack of amorous passion."[19] Power connected sexual aspersions to political ones. Only a real man—a man capable of fighting and procreating—could lead the United States. No one could conceive of power along anything other than a masculine, physically powerful (and violent) spectrum.

The honor culture and the conflation of personal and political reputation belonged, of course, to the province of men. But when a woman found herself in the public arena (whether by happenstance or by choice), her reputation also became an issue. Unfortunately, in this aspect of the campaign, Dolley also stood in for her husband. If James was too "cold," in the lexicon of slander, Dolley, in contrast, was too "hot." Following traditional medical models, excessive sexual appetite, or "heat," was the possession of men, and it was so contrary to the law of nature for a woman to evince heat that it could turn the world upside down, rendering both her and her husband sterile. Too much female lust, and sex would lose its procreative capacity. As Samuel Mitchill wrote to Catharine, "Your friend Mrs. Madison is shockingly and unfeelingly traduced in the Virginia papers," which took as their topic not politics, but sex.[20]

This was not the first time, of course, that Dolley found herself the target of slander. The newspaper stories alleging that Jefferson had pimped Dolley and Anna to foreign visitors still stung. In fact, they had never really died: cropping up at tense political moments, the rumors appeared in constantly evolving forms. The Madisons dismissed them and ignored them, figuring, as Jefferson did, that refutation only drew attention. Consequently, Dolley and James had been exasperated when, in 1804, Postmaster Gideon Granger decided wrongheadedly to defend Dolley's honor. By offering to duel New Hampshire congressman Samuel Hunt over the slurs, Granger inadvertently (or so it seemed) spread them further.

Now, as the Madisons geared up for the campaign, the slander took on a new life thanks to James Monroe's chief supporter, the vituperative and mentally unstable John Randolph, who endorsed his fellow Virginian for reasons of spite as well as politics (Randolph hated all things Jefferson, including his protégé). In fact, it was he who had pushed Monroe into the presidential ring. In a letter that attempted to discredit James Madison, he alluded to the old rumors. He had nothing new or definitive to add (specifics, after all, could be refuted), but that did not stop him. "You, my dear Sir," wrote John Randolph to Monroe, who was serving as minister to England, "cannot be ignorant . . . how deeply the respectability of any character may be impaired by an unfortunate matrimonial connexion—I can pursue this subject no farther. It is at once too delicate and too mortifying."[21]

The newspapers could not resist entering the fray. The Georgetown *Federal Republican* ran an "advertisement" for a pretended volume about "a new system of moral and political law." One of the chapters, titled in French with the English translation "Love and Smoke Cannot Be Hidden," dealt with the sex lives of a thinly disguised political couple—the oversexed and adulterous wife of an impotent man.

Some things were too much, even for the ever tactful Dolley. Senator John Quincy Adams reported in his diary that "Mr. Bayard told me he had last evening some conversation with Mrs. Madison upon the presidential electioneering now so warmly carried on, in which she spoke very slightingly of Mr. Monroe."[22] Given her own standards of diplomacy, this public outburst suggests how strongly Dolley felt about her reputation and her husband's political career. Later in her own career, she would guard more effectively against such open expressions of feeling.

As ridiculous as the stories of a sexually insatiable Dolley appear now, some took them seriously. Reports were that Randolph knew the truth and would not hesitate to tell it. As one gossip gushed, "Jack says he will make the hairs of congress stand [as] erect" as porcupine quills with his "evidence" of Dolley's indiscretions. Dolley and James fought these slanders within the unofficial sphere. During the flare-ups of the old rumors, they demonstrated their utter innocence by publicly inviting Samuel Hunt, one of Dolley's supposed lovers, to dine *"en famille."*[23]

One anonymous writer, feeling that he had to explain and defend Dolley abroad, addressed a chronicle of her travails to Mrs. George Hammond, whose husband was the British under secretary negotiating impressment issues with the United States. Dolley's champion noted that "her frankness, and patriotism, her loveliness, and sincerity have long excited the suspicions, alarms and apprehensions of the factious partisans of France" and other distasteful groups, including what he called "democrats," meaning radical American supporters of the French Revolution. Dolley's defender had a pro-British agenda, and he indignantly related that no sooner did James seem to side with Great Britain, than Dolley's "influence was proclaimed, her character assailed and her reputation bespattered" in newspapers, usually headed by "Irish rebels in French pay." Dolley was "called a British Tory, and an American Federalist," and she was attacked for "her political creed as well as her conjugal management."

Her visibility unleashed the democratic, pro-France hounds, who proceeded to scour every part of her life. Neither "the delicacy due to her sex," nor sympathy for her parents' "misfortunes," nor her own personal and domestic virtues could stop them. According to this observer, the attackers of Madame Pompadour were less nasty and more gallant than the democratic dogs in "republican America," who lacked only the guillotine.

The slander campaign was not restricted to sex; other allegations touched Dolley's personal life more deeply. Causing particular pain, the papers dug up the story of John Todd's death from yellow fever, seizing upon the fact that John had left her and his family at the Gray's Ferry lodgings, rather than dying in his wife's arms. Some accounts accused Dolley of banishing her husband to die, if not for the intervention of a compassionate farmer, "in the open air." Indeed, they intimated, the "unfeeling treatment" he had received at the hands of what the gossips sarcastically called his "so affectionate wife" probably hastened John Todd's end. Just as James's sexual capability seemed an indicator of his political performance, so the Madisons' enemies wondered, "Can a woman, who thus acted with a worthy husband, love her country, be a republican and know anything about patriotism?" (Dolley's defender excused her for not being there to "shut his dying eye," by explaining that "contagious fevers" were much more virulent in the New World than in England and that family members routinely adopted similar strategies for "self preservation.") Astutely, the anonymous observer concluded that in the American political press, if a man is "of their party . . . he is . . . the best of men; if a political opponent,—the worst of all created beings."[24]

In these contentious times, party feelings began to divide friends and family. When the Madisons first came to Washington, Dolley and the Federalist Anna Maria Thornton became close so quickly that Anna wrote with "freedom & carelessness" to her "dear Mrs. M." Eight years later, Anna Maria chose her words more tentatively: "I fear my letter may be an intrusion, & indeed not having had any encouragement, verbal or written to address you I do not know whether I ought to take the liberty to do so, but I feel loth to relinquish all my ancient privileges and pleasures."[25]

Before the Madisons left for their usual summer sojourn in Montpelier in 1808, Dolley once again stood in for James in a very visible way. On July 4, she reviewed a cavalry troop that passed before the Madison house, presenting them with "an elegant standard" along with "a patriotic address." Once at home in Orange, Dolley carried on her campaign, entertaining "a continuel round of company," while keeping abreast of the political news as carried by visitors and conveyed by newspapers and letters. In reply to some political gossip sent by Anna's husband from Boston, the heart of Federalism, she joked that it "frighten'd" her, then volunteered that "we hope from the public prints that we shall not be quite *out done* by the Feds. this time." Entertaining at Montpelier was a crucial part of the unofficial campaign, since Dolley could court any Federalist who happened to be in the neighborhood and any Virginians who were thinking of shifting their alliances to the Monroe camp. Even when Dolley was too sick to "quit her bed," the Madisons still hosted between fifteen and twenty for dinner.[26]

Significantly, though the Madisons traveled to Monticello to see Jefferson, they did not visit their neighbor James Monroe. The Madisons also pulled family strings in order to deprive John Randolph of his strongest supporter, Joseph Nicholson, the Republican representative from Maryland. A relative of Hannah Nicholson Gallatin, he received a patronage post—a federal judgeship—and soon all of Randolph's congressional support faded away. Wisely, James Monroe had never committed himself to Randolph but merely bided his time.

Back in Washington for the congressional season, Dolley took up the practical task of winning her husband supporters and presented her family, and by extension James, as a force of political power—in the parlance of the time, a "leading family." The French minister, Turreau, certainly got the message. Six months before the election, he decided that "it is necessary to act from now on as if [Madison] were President," a circumstance that he traced not to an overt show of power, but a "secret but well assured and very constant influence."[27]

Since coming to Washington City, Dolley had worked on cultivating a flexible, accommodating social sphere; ironically, she did such a good job that her rivals co-opted it. The Federalists understood the power of society well and wasted no time using the unofficial sphere to make political statements. At times, they refused as a body to dine at the president's house or attend a levée. No stronger argument that social attendance meant political allegiance exists than the Federalists' use of social events to make negative statements. Dolley responded to such churlishness with her message of open kindness and a lofty disdain of such vulgar pettiness. She remained gracious, charming, and, her own passions notwithstanding, bipartisan. By welcoming all and making her house the place to see and be seen, Dolley also upped the social ante, making society even more necessary to politics in the capital city. With the Federalists and Dolley contending for control of the unofficial sphere, as the sage Samuel Latham Mitchill noted, the spoiler Republican, George Clinton, made the unwise choice not to compete in that arena.

By election time, in spite of his preference for his fellow New Yorker, Mitchill had shifted his allegiance back to James. He was too savvy to hitch his wagon to a falling star: "But really there does not appear the re-motest probability of his [Clinton's] success as President." In a demon-stration of the power of the personal, Samuel confessed to Catharine: "I like Mr. Madison too well to come forward and make a noise about it."[28]

Dolley's role in the victory proved paramount. Though the psycho-logical effect is hard to quantify, no election can be won without it. Al-ways a person who put on a good public face, Dolley took her skill to a new level during the election season. With so much at stake, she sub-merged her true feelings, presenting a serene and gracious persona to the outside world. The work of political campaigning—the weekly parties, the daily visits, and the constant entertaining—paid off. By the time of the 1808 election, support for the Republican splinter candi-dates had declined; Monroe received only a few scattered votes, for vice president. James won the election, with 122 electoral votes, over Charles Cotesworth Pinckney, who garnered a mere 47. James's erstwhile chal-lenger George Clinton became vice president once again (he received only 6 presidential electoral votes from New York, his home state) with 113 votes over Rufus King's 47.

Winners might write history, but losers often have a clearer sense of events. Clinton had so few votes that his candidacy was not the de-ciding factor in the resounding loss by the Federalist Charles Pinckney. No, Pinckney admitted, he "was beaten by Mr. and Mrs. Madison. I might have had a better chance had I faced Mr. Madison alone."[29]

It would become a pattern among presidents' wives that the women enjoyed their greatest political influence in the period just before their husbands' ascension to the presidency—as the wives of congressmen, cabinet members, or governors, or as campaign managers. Often, far from their local bases of power and under the increasingly relentless glare of the White House spotlight, First Ladies found themselves isolated—"prisoner" was a favorite metaphor—and frustrated. This was not the case for Dolley. She would fulfill her potential as an innovator during her years as the president's wife.

Still, because Dolley not only would go on to be the best-known First Lady for decades, but, indeed, would set the pattern for the job, her pres-idential success often eclipses her earlier work. The most far-reaching effect that Dolley had as the political partner of James Madison during Jefferson's administration lay in elevating and enhancing the power of the office of secretary of state. Arguably, that position was second only to the presidency (and at times outranked the presidency) in the world of international relations. Dolley's work in the unofficial sphere made the position a central one within the federal government and on the domestic policy scene as well. In a town that needed a structural core, she made the home of the secretary of state a center of political power for the capital. With Jefferson deliberately restricting access to the executive mansion, the Madisons' home had become not an alternative political space but a primary one.[30] With James's election, Dolley acquired a new home and an increasingly complicated set of challenges that would call on all the skills that she had honed on F Street.

EIGHT

Lady Presidentess

n December 1808, with almost all the votes in and the election's outcome virtually assured, Catharine Akerly Mitchill reported to her sister back home in New York on how the Madisons were handling James's ascension to high office. She was pleased to see that Dolley did not let her change in fortune go to her head. "On the eve of becoming Lady Presidentess," Catharine found Dolley to be "as agreeable . . . as she was three years ago, when if she anticipated these honors, there was no certainty of success." Dolley was always smiling, according to Catharine, "and she attaches you to her person by her sociability and friendly attentions."

There were some changes, though, from the Dolley whom Catharine had first met as the wife of the secretary of state. "I think she is more than usually dignified in her deportment. She visits less, & indulges less in her favorite amusement of cards." Approvingly, Catharine noted that "this is certainly the most correct course to pursue when her husband is about to be exalted to the highest and most honorable station in the gift of our government."

But if Dolley made fewer visits, she received more visitors. When Catharine called one morning, she found Dolley's parlor crowded with ladies and gentlemen. They "were making their obeisance to her by dozens," and Dolley received their attentions "with all the grace imaginable." Catharine shrewdly assessed the throngs of callers to the Madisons' home on F Street: "They are all now worshipping the rising Sun."[1]

A rising sun indeed. Spring had come to Washington City by March 4, 1809, bringing enough real sun that people from all over the country and the countryside turned out to see James Madison elevated to "the highest and most honorable station." Inauguration day began with guns fired in a dawn salute at the Navy Yard and nearby Fort Warburton. With daybreak, local militias were assembling, ready for escort duty; by mid-morning, crowds on foot and in carriages began a loose procession toward the Capitol, where James would make the inaugural address in the Hall of Representatives, which could hold more spectators than the Senate chamber. The hall was, of course, also one of the grandest spaces in the city, though, like other Washington City structures, it was better on paper than in execution. It was lucky that the weather was fine; the hall's glass-domed ceiling leaked so badly that a heavy rain would leave pools of water on the House floor. It was also fortunate that inaugurations were not held in high summer. As it was, the combination of the sun beating through the glass roof and the heat rising from the furnaces installed beneath the floors led some representatives to faint and others to feel like baked oysters.

James traveled from the house on F Street in his carriage, escorted by the cavalries from Washington and Georgetown. His party moved slowly down Pennsylvania Avenue, where thousands lined the street, toward the Capitol. There another ten thousand citizens waited to greet him. The legislative building cast a more graceful silhouette on the landscape than it had upon the Madisons' arrival eight years earlier. Gone were the two desolate boxes; the sections had been finished and joined. James reached the Capitol at about noon, just after President Jefferson. The two men entered the hall, accompanied by James's cabinet, including Secretary of the Treasury Albert Gallatin, Secretary of State Robert Smith, and Jefferson's private secretary, Isaac A. Coles, who happened to be Dolley's cousin.

The interior of the Hall of Representatives had also been improved since Jefferson's inauguration (Jefferson had taken his oath in the Senate chamber, the only part of the Capitol that was finished in 1801). The architect Benjamin Henry Latrobe had overseen the elaborate interior decoration of the hall, importing stone carvers from Carrara, Italy. Everyone noted approvingly the slender, fluted columns, topped not with the acanthus leaves of classical Greek architecture, but with the agricultural emblem of North America: corn tassels. Radical republicans might grumble about the abundance of English imports used in the construction and decoration, including the goatskin chairs and the mahogany wood throughout the building, but the effect was undeniably impressive.[2]

Margaret Bayard Smith had a place in the crowd as both an observer and a reporter. Margaret had been present for Jefferson's inaugurations and was in a comparative mood: "In eight years how was the scene changed—the city rapidly—almost miraculously increased—so had the republican party." James Madison was the perfect choice for president; not only was he the protégé and "beloved son" of Margaret's adored Jefferson, he was not "personally, as obnoxious to the federal party as Mr. Jefferson." And of course he had Dolley, who entertained "the chiefs of both parties" with "cordial attentions" and "undistinguished politeness." No wonder "men of all parties willingly united to do honor to the choice of the people" by supporting James.[3]

While the principals took their places, the public awaited admittance. Though "punctilious regard to etiquette" dictated the seating—president in the Speaker's chair, senators and cabinet members on the right, justices of the Supreme Court on the left, ladies on elevated seating, ordinary people in the galleries—the crush at the chamber door made this impossible. "Females of all classes, from the highest to the lowest," pushed open the doors, "eagerly taking possession of the appropriated seats."[4]

Dressed in an American-made suit, fashioned from the wool of New York merino sheep, President-elect James Madison was escorted by congressmen to the front of the chamber. He delivered his address immediately, reading it rather than speaking to the crowd. Worried observers in the crush noted how pale the little man looked: "he seemed scarcely able to stand." James began his inaugural address with a voice so trembling that only the people closest to him could hear. He gained confidence as he spoke, "but his voice continued too low and feeble to reach the opposite side of the house." To Sarah Ridg, a young lady in the crowd, the head of state looked "embarrassed."[5]

After taking the oath of office, James proceeded with guns and militias to the house on F Street, joining Dolley in greeting "the numerous company." Guests noted with approval Dolley's clothes and manner. In her ensemble, she mixed simplicity and luxury, wearing a fine linen cambric gown and an elaborate bonnet, made of purple velvet and white satin and sporting white plumes. To the enthusiastic guests, "the sparkling radiance of her countenance" more than made up for her lack of elaborate trimmings. She moved through the crowd, blending a "frank and affable . . . republican equality" with an almost royal mien. To Margaret Bayard Smith, "she was all dignity, grace and affability"; to a visiting foreigner who had been at European courts, "she looked and moved a Queen."[6]

Later that evening, the citizens of Washington City gave an inaugural ball for the Madisons at Long's Hotel on Capitol Hill. Four hundred invitations had been issued, but a newspaper announcement of the event indicated that anyone who bought a ticket could attend. The dancing began promptly at seven. Balls and parties had been held for George Washington and John Adams, but none on inauguration night. Since Thomas Jefferson had discouraged such displays, the Madisons enjoyed the first inaugural ball in the new capital. The directors of the Dancing Assembly, which sponsored the event, included the Madisons' good friend Captain Thomas Tingey, head of the Navy Yard; Dolley's cousin Isaac A. Coles; and many of the local families that Dolley had wooed over the last eight years—the Van Nesses, the Carrolls, the Tayloes, and Thomas Law. As the band struck up "Madison's March,"

Captain Tingey led in Dolley, followed by Anna and James. Dolley again invited royal comparisons in a velvet gown with a very long train, topped off with a matching velvet and white satin turban, trimmed with bird-of-paradise feathers from Paris. But the gown was cut simply and of a neutral buff color, without excessive trimming. Even Dolley's jewelry—pearl necklace, earrings, and bracelets—evoked modesty and simple elegance. Though the plumes made her taller than the new president, they were "extremely becoming." Once again, Dolley earned a rave review from Margaret: "It would be absolutely impossible for anyone to behave with more perfect propriety than she did. Unassuming dignity, sweetness, grace." She added what was no doubt her fervent wish in that heated political atmosphere: "It seems to me that such manners would disarm envy itself, and conciliate even enemies."[7]

Captain Tingey presented Dolley with the first dance in order to open the ball. Dolley refused the offer, using her Quaker background as an excuse: "But what shall I do with it? I do not dance." Captain Tingey suggested that she give it to another lady. Wisely, Dolley refused to engage in a display of public favoritism. "Oh no," she demurred, "that would look like partiality." Margaret Bayard Smith applauded such politesse: "I really admired this in Mrs. M.," adding mysteriously, "Ah, why does she not in all things act with propriety?" Margaret did not explain but went on to dismiss her cavil: "She would be too much beloved if she added all the virtues to all the graces."[8]

The new president, "pale and spiritless—absolutely exhausted," did not make much of an impression. It was Dolley's night; the spotlight followed her, and she did not make a wrong move. Not only was she "affable to all," she engaged in a bit of what observant guests understood as diplomatic maneuvering. Always sensitive to the delicate foreign situation, Dolley charmed the representatives of France and England equally, sitting between them at supper.[9]

Margaret Bayard Smith's assessment—"She really in manners and presence answered all my ideas of royalty"—only presaged what would be a national reaction. The people loved Dolley, almost "press[ing] her to death" in their zeal to connect with her. Indeed, she drew so much attention that windows had to be broken to relieve the suffocation caused by the crowd. Her "title" was already in the people's vocabulary; the inaugural edition of the *National Intelligencer* called Dolley the "Presidentess."[10]

These two pictures of Dolley on the eve of her greatest accomplishments—the discreet lady seen by Catharine Akerly Mitchill and the flamboyant "queen" depicted by Margaret Bayard Smith— captured the genius of Dolley's political strategy. Her connection to the local community and her strength in diplomatic relations, her blending of democracy and aristocracy to invent an American political style, her creation of a persona larger than life and in contrast to her husband— all formed the foundation for her work as the figure who would become known as First Lady. Significantly, in both Catharine's and Margaret's descriptions, Dolley was the center of the scene.

Catharine and Margaret were not the only Washingtonians to subject Dolley to such positive analyses. Scores of admirers over the next eight years would join them in singing her praises. The effusions may be partly attributed to the flatterers' wish to please, but some of the extravagance stemmed from the need to reassure themselves of the unquestioned supe- riority of the woman (and, by proxy, her husband) in the executive man- sion. As Margaret's aside—"Ah, why does she not in all things act with propriety?"—reveals, the analyses offered by supporters and detractors had little to do with neutral information. There was no room for shades of gray in these black-and-white characterizations, not even, in the posi- tive reviews, for a moment of constructive critique. In early republican politics, as Dolley's defender had decided, "A person is with them in everything or nothing!"—those of one's own party being "the best of men," of the opposite party "the worst of all created beings."[11]

Even as Dolley would continue to politick in practical ways, be- cause she operated at the national level, and since the nation had many needs (and would soon come to crisis), her work would also function symbolically. People would project their needs for stability, reassurance, and the ineffable imprimatur of legitimacy onto Dolley Madison; her audience would anxiously probe her words, actions, and her very being for clues and signs of the republic's fate.[12] The measure of Dolley's suc- cess would be how well she met these needs.

❧

By the time that James took office as the president, the Madisons had been married for fifteen years. James and Dolley did not have a relationship that moderns would recognize as egalitarian (an almost unimaginable option in a hierarchical and patriarchal world) but neither felt that as a lack. The adventure and anguish of the presidency would bring them even closer. During the White House years, Dolley was so attached to her "darling husband" that she rarely left his side, describing herself as his "shadow." In turn, James was openly tender and respectful; in an era when husbands and wives addressed each other with the honorific, though Dolley was properly respectful in referring to her "Mr. M.," she was "Dolley."[13]

James Madison had always treated his wife seriously as a political partner. As early as 1794, she served as his secretary; she went on doing so through James's presidency, as he dictated letter drafts to her and conducted presidential business freely with her when his official secretary was ill. The extent and quality of their collaboration had strengthened since the 1805 correspondence while Dolley was ill in Philadelphia. In almost all of their exchanges from the presidential years, James and Dolley discussed what they called the "public business" more substantively.[14]

In mid-July of the summer after the inauguration, the Madisons left Washington City for Montpelier. But the press of presidential business shortened their stay: less than a month later, James "came ahead" to the city, with seventeen-year-old Payne in tow. James sat down to write Dolley immediately upon arrival. He had not even a chance to peruse the latest information brought by messenger from France. "You may guess therefore the volumes of papers before us. I am just but dipping into them." As was their style, he mixed sentiment—"Every thing around and within reminds me that you are absent, and makes me anxious to quit the solitude"—with information: "In my next I hope I shall be able to say . . . something of the intelligence just brought us." As a substitute, he sent along a newspaper "which has something on the subject."[15]

Almost half of a short note sent two days later to assure Dolley that he and young Payne were well was devoted to politics. James alerted Dolley to the latest developments in the press, while offering his own analysis. "I send you all the foreign news in the inclosed papers. That from France has a better complexion than preceding acc[oun]ts of her temper towards the U. S.," he told her. "The tone of Cannings speech also is a little different from the arrogance of his instructions to Mr. Erskine." Always the cautious politician, James added, "Payne writes. I must refer to his letter for what I am prevented from adding, relative to Capt. Coles &c &c."[16]

James and Dolley needed a strong partnership in order to deal with several serious issues that faced the country and the government and that directly challenged James's presidential power and legitimacy. He had inherited the most fractious Congress a president had yet been cursed with. Congress was riddled with "hostile" factions—mainly Federalists and renegade Republicans—who detested James and meant to destroy him. According to James's long-time political collaborator Albert Gallatin, the day-to-day business of governing fell by the wayside, and the members' openly quarrelsome behavior "embarrassed" the government in the eyes of the world and its own citizenry. The result was an erosion in the people's confidence in their government, as well as their president, since he seemed powerless to rein in his Congress. As Albert gloomily concluded, it was impossible "to produce the requisite union of views and action between the several branches of government."[17]

Albert's assessment came from bitter personal experience. Not only were there no "requisite union of views" between the executive and legislative branches, some members of Congress would not even let James choose his own cabinet. Though nominally of the Republican Party, the "Invisibles," a Senate clique led by Maryland's Samuel Smith, and including Republican representatives William B. Giles, of Virginia, and Michael Lieb, of Pennsylvania, tried at many points to bring down James's presidency. This group of malcontents had bonded over a variety of grievances, most notably those that affected the shipping interests of the middle states—the embargo and spending cutbacks for the navy. They focused on Albert, whom they resented for his power, his connections to Jefferson (whom they also loathed), even his foreign birth and French accent.

James wanted the clever, multilingual Albert as his secretary of state, but he knew that the nomination would never pass the Senate thanks to the Invisibles. The only capacity in which Albert could serve was in the office he already occupied: having become secretary of the treasury under Jefferson, he did not need to be re-confirmed. As an olive branch to the disgruntled Invisibles, James offered the State Department to Samuel Smith's brother, Robert, a charming, lazy man whose ambition far outstripped his intelligence.[18]

The United States was approaching an ever more dangerous time in foreign relations. England and France did not hesitate to use the new nation as a weapon or a bargaining chip in their own quarrels, and the situation abroad was rapidly deteriorating. With the Embargo Act of 1807 an obvious failure, Congress had passed the Non-Intercourse Act of 1809 just before James took office; the act reopened the ports, forbidding trade only with Great Britain and France and barring all foreign warships from American waters. France and England were no strangers to the honor culture; were, indeed, the biggest bullies on the block. In an attempt to force neutral America to choose sides and to benefit from American shipping, both France and Great Britain dispatched to Washington various decrees, orders in council, and other threatening or punitive documents. James responded with a series of increasingly mixed messages. The Non-Intercourse Act of 1809 got as little public support as its predecessor and proved as unenforceable; James would experiment all through his first term with complicated proposals aimed at impelling one nation to lift its embargo against American shipping in a way that would force the other's hand. Misinterpreting these efforts as signs of weakness and cowardice, the two superpowers continued to strong-arm the United States, convinced that its president would not go to war.[19]

As befitted a triangulated conflict, the state of affairs in Europe did not merely divide Congress, it splintered it. Though France, ruled by the capricious Napoleon, remained a power to be reckoned with, Great Britain commanded the focus of the young country's loyalties and anxieties. More than once, James considered whether the United States could wage war against both it and England simultaneously. Of course, the Federalists did not want war with the erstwhile mother country. For the same reason, they also zealously monitored the administration's actions for any sign of favoritism toward France. Their opposition was not purely ideological or perverse: it was New England that suffered the most from the interruption of trade with England.

Cultural and class allegiance to Great Britain, as well as delusions of aristocracy, ensured that the "old Republicans," also known as the "peace Republicans," led by John Randolph, rejected war. Randolph considered himself the last of the pure republicans; on occasion, his "purity" even led him to vote with the Federalists. Of course, the Invisibles took any chance they could get to bedevil the president, and the ever shifting international situation gave them plenty of opportunities. The rest of the Republican Party aligned themselves all along the war spectrum, often changing positions in response to circumstances or interpretations of presidential intent. The work of Congress often reflected this restless multiplicity: in December 1809, that body rhetorically prepared for war while cutting the military budget and reducing the size of the army and navy.

❧

The office of president did not offer many ways to resolve these conflicts. The Constitution did not allow the president to lead Congress or even to take part in its day-to-day affairs. Colleagues and constituents commanded more influence over the average congressman than the president did; voters, not the president, controlled the selection and the advancement of legislators. Ordinary citizens could petition Congress and organize support for legislation; a president could not. The capital city's architecture of isolation, and the customs that grew with it, only enforced the separation of the executive and legislative branches. The president was expected to stay within the White House grounds; government etiquette forbade him making appearances at the Capitol, except for ceremonial functions, such as the inauguration, and to sign bills. Again, Americans of both sexes were free to enter the building at any time to persuade, threaten, or negotiate, but the president was barred. With no constitutionally mandated sticks, James could not dangle any presidential carrots either. Since no one overtly campaigned for office, an early republican president could not offer his coattails or the resources of a national party. Though occupying the highest office in the land, James had no funds, few offices to distribute, and little support for his "friends."[20]

The problem of James's leadership lay deeper still, a question of political style inextricably linked to political substance. The style of a political culture reflects its deepest substance, dictating what issues are important as well as how they are presented. The political culture of the time, as defined by the official men in power, was an undeniably masculine one, not just because only men participated. Contemporaries described James's mentor, Thomas Jefferson, as someone who spoke his thoughts and acted on his feelings, who "fearlessly censured those he blamed as he openly praised those whom he approved." In contrast, James neither "praised [n]or censured"; if he did not feed his colleagues' egotism, he did not challenge it. People loved or hated Jefferson, while James deliberately avoided fostering extreme feelings.

For all James's unquestionable brilliance in the theories of governing, in some ways his political style was more suited to the feminine subtleties of the unofficial sphere: he had always exhibited discretion in print, avoidance of direct conflict, and an unaggressive approach to people. And for all Jefferson's willingness to offend, he had still been considered insufficiently manly by some. Jefferson's more aggressively masculine contemporaries, such as Alexander Hamilton, thought him "weak" and his politics "feminine." How much more feminine, then, did James appear in a time of crisis? Even after he had vanquished the "virile" Monroe and his presidential hopes in the election of 1808, newspapers still expressed their worries about Madison through comments about his lack of strength, potency, and physical stature.[21]

Politics was a man's game, with violence and anger as its tools. In contrast, James's quiet political style depended less on overt shows of power and force than on thoughtful consideration. He examined the subtleties of situations and adjusted his ideas accordingly. At the same time, he refused to commit himself to any position before he was absolutely sure. Reserved but stubborn, James, as Josiah Quincy III commented, refused to "be kicked into a fight."[22] In deciding whether or not to embroil the United States in the European wars, James kept his own counsel as he weighed his options, recalculating his position in response to every move made by Great Britain and France.

Even before he took office, James had resolved that he would go to war if necessary, though the United States was hardly prepared for such an eventuality. Having come to that private decision, he then spent the first years of his administration doing whatever he could to avoid it. His nonconfrontational, cautious, analytical style confused both friend and foe at home and abroad; those impatient for war expressed disgust with what they saw as his equivocal weakness. James's prudence accounted for uneasy shifts in the positions of congressmen who tried to stay loyal to the president. What were they to think when, in December 1809, he sent a budget that cut military spending in half, then only a month later requested an increase in the army and navy?

His congressional followers could not know that he had sent the trimmed budget only to appease Albert Gallatin, who wanted military expenditures cut in order to balance the budget, while strengthening the army and navy were part of James's long-term project of readying the country for war. Having sent the amended budget, however, he could only allude to the "solid state of the public credit" as a funding source for defense. No wonder one congressman compared James's request to "a Delphic oracle," not for its prescience, but "[i]n point of obscurity."[23]

During James's first term, the growing public support for war stemmed not from a serious consideration of economic and political problems, but from a question of male pride. Honor culture focused on degrees and hierarchies of "rights," which participants cherished and defended against any encroachments, real or imaginary. The white male electorate, newly endowed with an ever-expanding list of "rights," comprehended the language of "insult" and "British pretensions" all too well. Indeed, the vacillation among the Republican majority in Congress over the declaration of war demonstrated the struggle in each legislator's mind as he charted the line that separated practical considerations from national self-respect.[24]

James's conciliatory style also doomed him in the heart of the government—his own executive branch. Blocked in his choice of Albert as secretary of state, James constructed the rest of the cabinet to foster party unity and congressional support. Robert Smith proved a spectacularly ineffectual, even perfidious, choice for secretary of state. Uncontroversial appointments, such as Dr. William Eustis (secretary of war) and Paul Hamilton (secretary of the navy), turned out worse than useless when war came.

No person better typified the extreme, almost pathological violence that infused the political culture than John Randolph. Even in an age where the ad hominem attack was a standard political technique, all acknowledged Randolph as particularly excoriating and vicious. Self-righteously occupying the post of the last pure republican, as a congressman since 1799, he had challenged and attacked Thomas Jefferson; but Jefferson's minimalist governing style generally kept John Randolph at bay. James Madison, on the other hand, had been fair game from the start, and during the election of 1808, Randolph had spearheaded the slander campaign against Dolley and her sisters in his attempts to derail the succession. Once James became president, Randolph saw it as his duty to undermine him at every turn, and by any means necessary.

Randolph had a reputation both for brilliance and for an ire that caused his colleagues to wonder about his mental state. When he coupled his eloquence with anger, no one could predict the outcome. As one colleague remembered: "His erratic conduct and more erratic discourse was the delight and terror of the Hall." The sight of his "wizened visage and miraculously bright eyes always produced an electric moment in the House." Randolph was not above name-calling—his particular favorites for James were "weak, feeble, and pusillanimous"—and he accused him of every vice known to man, including corruption, bribery, and whoremongering. On one occasion, he spoke in the House for two and half hours against James, in a speech "replete with invective (the most severe the English language can furnish)." Even supporters and colleagues, such as Samuel Smith, admitted that "he has left stings . . . that never can be extracted."

In a vivid illustration of the savagery of his political discourse, John

Randolph regularly insisted on bringing his dogs into the House. These were not domestic pets, but big, aggressive hunting dogs; according to the *Aurora*'s editor, William Duane, "*no one dared to turn* the dogs out." When one of the pointers attacked North Carolina Republican representative Willis Alston and Alston rebuffed the animal, Randolph beat and almost stabbed him on the floor of the House.[25]

Not surprisingly in a world where a man's power was directly correlated with his masculinity, Washington whisperers attributed the instability of Randolph's character to some defect of his genitalia, though the gossipers could not decide whether size or function was the trouble.[26] People interpreted Randolph's particular hostility toward "the ladies" as an effect of this disability. Randolph did seem unhinged when it came to women, as he regularly railed against women in the gallery, trying to have them barred from the proceedings. He went so far as to cast aspersions on the virtue of these eminently respectable wives and daughters of his colleagues by comparing them with "public women"—that is, whores.[27]

Many thought that he had taken politics too far when he slandered Dolley. A gentleman restricted his attacks to men, who could defend themselves and who, by participating in politics, opened themselves to public comment. In John Randolph's mind, however, Dolley put herself in the same position merely by appearing in public. For Randolph, Dolley posed a double threat—a lushly feminine, sexual persona who asserted a definite public presence. But Dolley had her own way of putting Randolph in his place. After one of John Randolph's diatribes against the Madison administration, her response was typically astute yet elliptical: "It was as good as . . . a play," a comment that at once reduced Randolph's attack to the status of frivolous fiction, not only make-believe but also unimportant.[28]

In spite of John Randolph's vitriol, Dolley continued to frequent the sites of public business at the Capitol and the Supreme Court, almost always surrounded by her friends. Unlike her husband, Dolley could attend congressional sessions, Supreme Court hearings, and all official transactions open to the public. She had led parties of ladies to view the public business since her days on F Street. As the president's wife, she would make female participation not merely permissible but de rigueur. And she hosted "dove parties," meetings with cabinet wives, held at the same time that her husband met with his cabinet.[29]

In addition to actual representatives of "the sex," Dolley also brought the feminine values of civility and emotion into government business. The presence of ladies in the audience at governmental proceedings shaped how the ruling men presented their arguments and chose their issues, with the effect of toning down the usual violent rhetoric. During one court session, former diplomat and Attorney General William Pinkney had just finished his argument and was taking his seat when Dolley and "a train of ladies" entered. Mr. Pinkney immediately stood and delivered his speech again, going "over the same ground, using fewer arguments but scattering more flowers" and cutting his case citations short so as not to be "inimical to the laws of good taste."[30] Mr. Pinkney performed one way for a male-only audience, another way when Dolley and her party arrived. He made changes— "more flowers" and an awareness of "good taste"—designed to please the gentler, more gracious sensibilities of his female listeners. Legislators responded by invoking "higher" morality and love in their arguments and appealing to the "tender breasts of ladies" in their speeches and debates. And, on more than one occasion, they wept.[31]

Not surprisingly, people marveled that "the women here are taking a station in society which is not known elsewhere." What was peculiar about Washington City was that "society" included anywhere that politics took place. "On every public occasion, a launch, an oration, an inauguration, in the [Supreme] court, in the representative hall, as well as the drawing room they are treated with mark'd distinction."[32]

As James embarked on his first term, he had to do something with his rebellious Congress, especially as all indications were that they would have to decide matters of war in the near future. From a management point of view, the president had two choices: to lead them, or to provide a unifying force. Given the limitations of the presidency he could not do the former; given his own personal limitations, neither could he effectively perform the latter. Fortunately, Dolley was more than well equipped to handle the job of unification, though given the level of discord, it was a daunting task indeed. Like every good general, she had a plan for her campaign, and she had begun the first phase even before James officially took office. In her war for hearts and minds, she needed a theater of operations, and for this she turned to the house on the hill.

NINE

Presiding Genius

When Thomas Jefferson first came to Washington in 1801, he approached the task of constructing the president's house with the same creative energy he expended on his beloved Monticello. But the work done by him and his architect, Henry Latrobe, went not much further than ensuring the basic structural soundness of the building. Under Latrobe's supervision, a mostly African-American labor force—both slave and free—shored up the roof, did necessary plastering, and dug a well. Under Jefferson's supervision, Latrobe had finished the classical pavilions on the east and west sides of the president's house and had begun the addition of the impressive north and south porticoes. As the years passed, work on the executive mansion slowed down, partly because of the press of presidential business, but Jefferson's malaise during the second term was also a contributing factor. Consequently, he expended little on the inside of the house, leaving it in "a state of uncleanly desolation" for the Madisons.[1]

Though Jefferson's neglect of the interior could be justified on practical grounds, it also reflected his feeling about the role of the executive mansion in national life. The exterior was more important, for the house was a noble symbol to be viewed from a lofty distance. He did not want it to become a social and political space, to constitute, literally, "corridors of power." So he was content to fill the public rooms with extra furnishings from Monticello and to entertain in a dining room so cold and inhospitable that, according to Louisa Catherine Johnson Adams, in winter dinner guests saw their breath.[2]

The first task that lay before Dolley and James demonstrates perfectly the combination of practical and symbolic politics: the reconstruction of the President's Palace, as it was known in Jefferson's time. As Virginia gentry, presiding over their estate at Montpelier, James and Dolley had experience with houses that transcended the need for shelter. Increasingly through the eighteenth century in America, and even earlier in Europe, leading families in towns and villages built houses that were sites for business and politics as well as being private residences. Any stranger passing through an area—a foreign observer, a traveling cleric, a writer, or an inventor with something to sell—could find the center of local power merely by looking for the house on the hill. There being few or no economic and cultural centers in small towns (in southern rural areas, there were often no religious centers, either), work of all kinds was conducted in the great houses. By design, the material magnificence of such houses impressed visitors and supplicants with the importance of their owners.

Even homes far out in the country were not refuges from the world. The everyday traffic of folks from all walks and classes of life trooping through great houses "on business" would startle modern homeowners. Privacy was an almost nonexistent concept and certainly not highly valued by the upper class. The homes of the powerful doubled as centers of social and cultural life, especially in the South, where the line between business and leisure was often blurred beyond recognition. Friendships forged over food and drink laid the foundation for commercial and political relationships, and men and women transacted business over dinners and barbecues or while sitting and chatting during lazy summer afternoons.

The gentry house, like its ancestor the castle, had long been a seat of power in colonial America. In the eighteenth century, technological innovations that produced a wider variety and number of consumer goods at low prices set off a wave of consumption; the wealthy had increasingly luxurious and elaborate ways to show off. Along with their gardens and attendant buildings, the great houses became stage settings on which the elite could perform before the world, asserting their right to rule by virtue of their aesthetic—indeed overall—superiority. The growing ruling classes of the colonial world had long been using such performances and rituals to confirm their place at the top. By the time the first shots were heard around the world, the message was clear: anyone with a claim to power had to have taste and refinement.

Not surprisingly, men with political ambitions, such as Thomas Jefferson and George Washington, regarded their houses as extensions of themselves and visible measures of their power. Members (and would-be members) of the ruling classes had long had their portraits painted to demonstrate their social and political superiority; in this era, people had portraits of their houses and grounds painted for the same reason.[3] Certainly upper-class women participated, sometimes eagerly, in the process of house building and décor. But for the most part the men took charge, from the initial plans (some gentry men designed their houses themselves) and the landscaping down to the selection of paint colors and china patterns.

Even before James Madison was officially inaugurated, he engaged Henry Latrobe to restructure the Presidential Palace. After all, this was no ordinary mansion, and he had worked on it from the start. As always, personal considerations were as important as professional qualifications: James knew Henry through Jefferson; as the husband of Mary Hazelhurst, one of Dolley's Philadelphia friends, the architect was part of Dolley's personal network as well. As Henry wrote to his brother: "Mary has known his very excellent and amiable wife from a child."[4]

From the start, James "referred" Henry to work with Dolley, turning

over all his accounts to her. In so doing, he entrusted her with his political image and with a task of considerable public power.[5] The need for
extensive interior renovation of the executive mansion was so great that
even Congress could unite around the issue, beginning in 1809 with an
appropriation of $20,000 for the project. That was to cover repairs and
improvements to the house itself, as well as furniture and other household movables.[6]

Dolley Madison and Henry Latrobe did not engage in long theoretical discussions of the project, but their actions—what they bought,
and why—make it clear that they understood they were creating something more than the ultimate gentry house. Dolley wanted socializing
in the new administration to begin as soon as possible, and so they
turned first to constructing public rooms for social and political functions, with three projects taking priority. A large drawing room (also
known as the Oval Room) and a smaller, more intimate parlor occupied
much of their attention; the dining room was slightly further down the
list. In February 1809, Henry began buying and designing for the drawing room and the parlor, with an eye to finishing the parlor first.

Through the winter and early spring of 1809, he and Dolley corresponded, sending suggestions and requests back and forth. Henry, who
lived in Philadelphia, came to Washington City only for short visits.
Though the house lacked many basic furnishings, his mandate was
clear: he was to procure items of luxury and display—rich fabrics,
dramatic-looking glass, silver, and crystal. Cosmopolitan Philadelphia
was just the place to obtain the items on Dolley's shopping list; Henry
also extended his search to New York and Baltimore, famous for its
beautiful painted furniture. In their bid to become the chief supplier of
presidential furniture, the Finlays of Baltimore arranged for a personal
introduction to Dolley.

In early-nineteenth-century America, ordinary houses were crude
affairs, poorly heated, ill lit, with a general roughness that extended
from the uncovered wood floors and tables to the unbolted flour with
which the inhabitants made their bread. The houses of the rich and
powerful, by contrast, strove for the effects of smoothness, illumination, and shine that most ordinary people simply could not achieve.

When Henry Latrobe described one of his first purchases—huge mirrors whose smooth surfaces would reflect both light and the room's occupants—as "the most necessary articles of furniture"—he was making a statement.[7]

By European standards, the Madisons should have built the most luxurious house they could, letting it stand as an uncontested symbol of superiority. But the president's house would be no mere American imitation of an English mansion or a French château. Dolley and Henry worked within the budget set by congressional appropriation, but there were other limits as well: the Madisons had to negotiate the complicated place that aristocracy, represented by material luxury, held in American culture.

On the face of it, there was no room at all for aristocratic trappings in the new republic. True, right up until the Revolution, the colonists had been striving to raise their colonial culture to the level of the mother country's, and everything English set the standard. But then the Americans had fought a war against an absolute monarch, a corrupt Parliament, and everything royalty stood for. As part of their resistance, they eschewed foreign imports and luxury, embracing homespun cloth, herbal "tea," and other material simplicity as manifestations of "republican virtue." American antimonarchism continued after the war. Likewise, Dolley and Henry were committed to creating an *American* house. The Madisons' personal taste ran to French designs; they had filled Montpelier with French furniture and objects. In contrast, all the furniture that Dolley chose for the president's house came from American craftsmen. While the art on Montpelier's walls embraced a variety of subjects, including classical, natural, and religious scenes, the paintings and statuary in the presidential house addressed distinctly American themes, celebrating American heroes and statesmen. Though Henry had to rely on imports for items of both luxury and utility—English Staffordshire china, for example—whenever possible they bought American, a fact not lost on U.S. manufacturers, who soon began sending their wares in hopes that Dolley would display them.[8]

Even if money and ideology had been no object, there were logistical limitations. The items on Dolley's list had to be available, and here politics affected the process. The Embargo Act and the subsequent Non-Intercourse Act of 1809 ensured that many articles were "not to be had for Love or Money," in the words of Mary Hazelhurst Latrobe. (Like most political projects, the renovation had become something of a family affair, with Mary Latrobe and even the Latrobes' young son, Henry, conveying messages, information, and merchandise.) Present circumstances made it difficult to find any "real gold Perl" or "gold thread of any kind," even in Philadelphia, so the team had to make compromises.[9]

Dolley had her heart set on red silk damask for her drawing room curtains, but there was none available in New York or Philadelphia: "I am therefore forced to give you crimson Velvet curtains," Henry informed her in March. Fabric was not the only item in short supply. The Latrobes almost stripped the Philadelphia shops of the countless eating and serving utensils needed for dinners, teas, receptions, and other social events. Henry deferred to the "taste & judgment" of Mary when it came to the small articles, acknowledging that he was lucky to have someone so willing to go from shop to shop, hunting them down. Investigating the matter of china, Mary despaired of the "Miserable choice" available, settling on blue and white "India Stone china" for the dinnerware with the conclusion: "We must have taken this, or none." Writing late at night, after a long day of exhausting shopping, she sent along detailed descriptions of other china items, along with prices. Coffee cups and saucers were $15.00 a dozen, teacups only $10.00 for twelve. "The only thing worth looking at in the way of a tea sett," according to Mary, was one of "beautiful french china," with both coffee and tea cups, pea green in color and gilt-edged, at a pricey $70.00.[10]

For his part, Henry Latrobe found red lacquered serving trays, "the largest I have ever seen," and he bought three. Most Americans had never seen a fork, and indeed, some regarded them with suspicion as an Old World corruption, but Henry and Mary purchased "very elegant white ivory handled knives & forks," as well as knives and forks for dessert, for carving, and for cheese. One of the hallmarks of refined dining was a "buffer" between food and drink containers and the table;

the Latrobes' purchase of wine coasters ensured that no bottle would be set down bare on a presidential table.[11]

Lighting was important as well in a great house; Dolley invested in candlesticks, candelabras, and lamps of the latest technology, along with their attendant accessories. By directing air along the wick, the patented Argand lamps, with their spiral burners and double lights, could give off seven times the amount of light cast by candles. But Henry bought candles as well, for atmosphere as well as illumination. Most Americans burned tallow candles that sputtered and smelled, but the public rooms of the presidential mansion would always be lit by costly spermaceti wax candles, which gave off a soft, even glow.[12]

Henry Latrobe did not lose sight of practical considerations. Even as he worked to create refined and elegant rooms, he also knew that these spaces had to be somewhat flexible, able to accommodate the re-arrangement of furniture and large, diverse crowds. When he ordered the twelve patent lamps from Bradford and Inskeep of Philadelphia, he indicated that he preferred "bronze to brass" and either metal to cut glass. "Lamps ornamented with drops and festoons of cut glass would soon be demolished by clumsy and careless servants of this part of the world and therefore I should wish that whatever is sent should be of a kind to bear handling," he explained to his purveyor.[13]

Every good stage setting needs props, and Dolley chose her objects to signal education, aesthetic judgment, an artistic sensibility, and, thus, a refined character. Henry arranged for a pianoforte and, after a few false leads, Mary tracked down a guitar. They also sent along "1 Sett of Chessmen & board." Mary Latrobe did some personal shopping for Dolley as well, sending along wigs, hats, and turbans, the headwear that soon became Dolley's trademark.

❦

Dolley held the first of her famous drawing rooms on May 31, 1809, only two months after the inauguration. With the large, elaborate Oval Room months from completion, Dolley ensured that the smaller parlor was finished in record time to accommodate guests. The first visitors to "Mrs. Madison's parlor" were dazzled. It was done in the "very latest

Sheraton style" and in "sunflower yellow." Though foiled in their attempts to obtain crimson damask for the Oval Room, the Latrobes apparently had found enough yellow silk damask not only to adorn each window with swags and draperies but also to continue the valance all across the top of the room. Visitors were especially impressed with the silk fringe that trimmed all the draperies and valances. In perhaps a sly political statement, the fireboard in the fireplace boasted the same yellow damask, fluted in a "rising sun pattern." The high-backed sofa and chairs were upholstered in the same bright yellow. Pier tables and card tables allowed the guests to game, as well as to sit tête-à-tête. The parlor also displayed the cherished guitar and pianoforte.[14]

This was a dramatic room, calculated to impress and excite. It contained all the elements of the accepted standards of refinement—its bright color and mirrors reflecting and multiplying light, the shiny satin furniture supplying smoothness. Dolley would play to the room as well, often dressing in buff or yellow when she hosted occasions there.[15] Though it substituted for the Oval Room early on, the parlor was intended for more intimate gatherings. There Dolley received callers and visitors of both sexes, and everyone, from locals to legislators, conducted politics face to face.

Dolley had put the parlor at the top of her list of renovations for obvious reasons. But her eight years in Washington City had underscored the importance of being the caller as well as the called upon, and in a town still famous for its bad roads, she also knew the advantage of being able to offer a stranded congressman a ride: a carriage could serve as a mobile version of the parlor. While Henry was shopping for Dolley's rooms in Philadelphia, he also oversaw the design and building of a chariot or phaeton, as well as a more informal vehicle. The formal carriage in particular was a very expensive item, but the design of both vehicles was crucial, as it would affect function as well as form. Henry delicately offered Dolley options, while expressing his own preference. Did she want her coachie to be open, allowing for more air, or closed, offering more room for decoration? Henry even invented a "*close moveable* front," set with glass, for the chariot. The interior was as important as the outside, so he presented Dolley with the choice of cloth or cotton velvet, and sent samples of English lace for her approval. They pored over drawings of "arms" or a "cypher" to be painted on the chariot as well as the coachie, ensuring that all the Madison vehicles would carry unabashedly aristocratic messages.[16]

Henry Latrobe's suggestions were not only practical; he tactfully intervened with the latest fashion trends when he felt that Dolley's taste was not au courant. (Even as he gave Dolley her choice of lace, he noted his own preference for the "narrowest.") Having pointed out that the current desired shape in a carriage was less rounded, he gently insisted when Dolley demurred: "But the *extreme* Bulges, top, bottom, & sides, are entirely out of fashion I assure you." He hastily added, however: "Your carriage will have a little smattering of the bulging taste about it: just enough to give it an air not entirely different from other carriages, *fashionable here.*" That emphatic underscore reminded Dolley that Henry was on the scene in fashion-mad Philadelphia and so should be the final authority. Dolley's choice of a reddish-brown for the outside of her carriage pleased him, as her "taste in this respect agrees with the fashion."[17]

No story of renovation is complete without a disaster. For Henry, pride went before a fall. The carriage was his pet project; he was full of suggestions and innovations, asking for Dolley's trust: "Will you leave this to me?" He boasted: "I have attended closely to this business & think you will not be disappointed." In his estimation, the vehicle would emerge as "one of the handsomest things Philadelphia has produced." But near completion, it became clear that the "phaeton" was a disaster or at least fatally flawed. Henry expressed himself "mortified" at the result. He laid the blame "at the conduct of the Coachmaker . . . in furnishing to you a Carriage, which even before it has been used is discovered to be so extremely faulty."[18]

But of course, he had chosen the man, so he expended a great deal of ink explaining that he "had employed or recommended him . . . one of the most honest & faithful workmen in Philadelphia." Indeed, Henry assured his patroness, "Mr. Harvie" had built five carriages for him that bore the Philadelphia roads and were the objects of universal admiration. To make matters worse, Dolley's brother-in-law, Richard

Cutts, chose this moment to offer the opinion that she was paying too much for the chariot; Henry had to defend himself on that score as well, assuring her "that [the cost] is below that; which has been given for inferior carriages."[19] Coachmaker Peter Harvie apparently fixed the coach to everyone's satisfaction, though after discomfiture on all sides.

There was another sensitive subject. Henry worried that Dolley misinterpreted his long delay in getting to Washington City to oversee the work himself. In July, he assured her that it was all "business relative to Washington" that kept him in Philadelphia. From there, he sent along not only movable goods, but also structural items, such as chimneypieces, along with instructions on the placement of mirrors and ornaments. He traveled to Baltimore, as well, to check on the progress of his furniture. And throughout his travels, he stayed in touch with the Madisons, even arbitrating between the couple on the use of the portrait of George Washington. Dolley wanted it for her parlor; James determined to make the dining room a gallery of the presidents. Henry sided with James. After apologizing for "counteract[ing] . . . [her] wish," he explained that "the dining room is properly the picture room." "[I]n speaking to the president as to the furniture of the room, I understood it to be arranged that not only the Genl.—but the succeeding Presidents should have a place there."[20]

At other times, Henry deferred to Dolley's taste, even if he harbored doubts. He went along with her initial choice for the Oval Room curtains, perhaps hoping that the light texture of the silk would moderate the intense crimson color. When Henry had to substitute velvet, the heaviness of the fabric combined with the vivid hue undid him. "The curtains! Oh the terrible velvet curtains! Their effect will ruin me entirely, so brilliant will they be." Not only would the color challenge the subtle scheme Henry planned for the Oval Room—cream wallpaper, woodwork shadowed in blue and gray to suggest marble or stone— but the sheer quantity of material would be overpowering. Henry had to buy enough red velvet for five windows and assorted adornments: 150 yards, "exclusive of draperies, chairs and sofas."[21]

No aspect of the décor of the Oval Room, from walls to floor, from chimneypieces to punch cups, escaped Henry's attention. He ensured that the room was "finished" according to the highest standards. Many Americans had paint on the walls; Henry had even the ceiling of the Oval Room painted. Most Americans did not luxuriate in carpet under their feet; Henry installed a Brussels carpet, with a separate border, and a hearthrug. While he followed the latest European trends, he also deliberately presented a political message by utilizing themes of ancient Greece and Rome, most obviously in the design of the furniture. The ancients had been a reference point for revolutionary Americans in understanding their political heritage and goals; modern Greece was at that moment engaged in a struggle to free itself from an imperial Ottoman oppressor, a struggle that would culminate in a revolution. Americans were quite taken with the thought that the descendants of democracy's creators were now claiming democracy for themselves, perhaps in emulation of the American example.

Following the ideal of a Greek sofa expressed by the English designer Thomas Hope, Henry incorporated the ancient device of the anthemion and husks on chairs and sofas, a motif he echoed in the frame for a mirror, which unfortunately broke in transit from New York. Another evocative emblem, the shield and laurel wreath, graced a sofa's back. Nor was he above tracing a more overt connection, explicitly tying together themes of the ancient world with the new. The thirty-six gilded cane-seat chairs supplied by the Finlays of Baltimore were not only made in "a Grecian Mode," but each one bore the arms of the United States.[22]

By September 1809, the Latrobes had arrived in Washington City to oversee the final stages of the project. Like a theater company readying a major production, the Latrobes and their workers felt the pressure, and jealousy and gossip ran wild. At one point, a Mrs. Sweeney, whom Henry Latrobe had hired to take down such curtains that "required Washing" or "would harbor bugs," refused to obey him. As Henry reported to Dolley in Virginia, she said he had no authority because Dolley had told her that she was "so displeased with my conduct especially with my long absence in February and April that you intended I should do nothing more for you."

Still smarting over the carriage debacle, and perhaps recalling

Jefferson's reservations about his abilities, Henry struggled with his outrage. He took the stance of assuming the falsity of Mrs. Sweeney's
accusations—"completely contradicted by yourself in the whole of your
conduct towards me"—while simultaneously seeking Dolley's reassurance. Surely, Dolley would not have added insult to injury by having a
dismissal "conveyed to a man of character and a public officer, at second
hand, by a servant." But the incident shook his confidence, especially as
he received two anonymous letters with the same accusations. He took
them seriously enough that, as he told Dolley, "I have not presumed to
interfere beyond my duties as surveyor of the public buildings, and have
refrained from going into the house more than that duty required."
Henry further betrayed his insecurity by answering the charges at great
length, justifying his absence from Washington City by detailing his
efforts even as he admitted: "You *have reason* to be dissatisfied with your
carriage."[23]

Dolley answered promptly and soothingly: "Incredulous, indeed
must be the ear that receives, without belief the 'Varnished tale.'" She
gently reproved the architect for his lack of faith in her regard, as indicated by her own conduct toward him, as well as on other grounds. "In
the first place my affection for Mrs. Latrobe would in itself prevent my
doing injustice to her husband." Nor would she ever question how he
conducted the "*public business*," wryly adding "(& as it is one of my
sources of happiness, never to desire a knowledge of other peoples
business)." Moreover, "I never for a moment doubted your taste or
honour . . . even in the building of our *Little* Carriage." To the contrary,
she had absolved him on the instant: "The moment we examined the
latter, we declared *you* had been deceived by the maker."

Dolley assured Henry that she would get to the root of all the fuss,
with a strict "examination of the servants." As for Mrs. Sweeney, Dolley dismissed her as "a woman of many words," and so Dolley would
not dream of talking "to her, or before her," on any topic other than
work. She suggested that Mrs. Sweeney might have felt slighted, since
Dolley did not give her as much responsibility as she felt was her due.
Mrs. Sweeney may indeed have had an ax to grind. Though Henry had
assigned her the most menial of jobs, she was a fashionable Georgetown

upholsterer; she had probably confected the elaborate swags and drapes in the yellow room. Reduced to the status of washerwoman—a mere "servant," to Henry—Mrs. Sweeney may have exacted a little revenge. In the meantime, Dolley advised him to ignore the anonymous letters. Always a canny politician, she reassured him: "tho' our enemies may strive to throw around me ungrateful appearances I shall take a pleasure in counteracting their designs." In her public persona, Dolley exhibited only positive emotions; accordingly, as a political advisor she recommended to Henry that in political affairs "most happy would it be, for you, could you listen *without* emotion" to lies that were "framed but to play on your sensibility."[24]

All this drama stemmed from the efforts to ready the centerpiece of the renovation project. When the Oval Room debuted at the 1810 New Year's Day reception, it was one of the most lavish public rooms ever seen in the United States. Designed in 1792 by the architect James Hoban as the chief receiving room of the executive residence, the Oval Room had scarcely been used during the Adams and Jefferson administrations. In fact, it was where Abigail Adams famously hung her laundry. Now, nine years later, it was the centerpiece of the renovation project, the site where the "necessary" mirrors sparkled, where the "brilliant" curtains, as one guest put it, "blaze[d]."[25]

"The President's house is a perfect palace," enthused young Elbridge Gerry, Jr., on a visit to his father, the vice president. A spacious entryway, lined with large lamps, opened onto the dining room, which boasted ceilings "twice the height of modern parlors and 3 times as large." Its elegant furnishings were correspondingly large, featuring a sideboard so huge that it would have taken up a whole wall in an ordinary room. At the head of the room hung the portrait of George Washington, "as large as life."

The dining room led into the parlor, half as large as the dining room. This room was more feminine than the dining room, with "elegant and delicate furniture," and in lieu of the contested Stuart copy of Washington, his rendering of Dolley herself. The yellow room connected to a large oval drawing room. The effect of what would later be known as the Blue Room was light and airy, with a door that opened onto a terrace and with floor-to-ceiling windows, offering a grand view of the surrounding countryside and the river. The curtains that had so worried Henry garnered much approving comment; guests were impressed on economic as well as aesthetic grounds, gossiping about "superb silk velvet curtains which cost $4.00 a yard."[26]

In spite of such costs, Dolley and Henry Latrobe had stayed well within the budget set by the congressional appropriation. From April 1809 to January 1811, they spent $12,669.31, including all construction, wallpapering, and painting as well as all the furniture, ornaments, linens, and china. The sum even covered additions to the presidential library, kitchen furniture, and Henry's 2 percent commission.[27]

❧❧❧

In 1809, as the Madisons engaged in turning the president's house into "a perfect palace," enemies from without and within seemed to threaten the republican dream. European countries, especially England and France, continued to exhibit interest in the former colonies; some Americans even suspected that they exported luxury items to the United States in order to encourage dependence and eventual decay.

Following this logic, then, when the Republican captains, Jefferson and James Madison, took over the helm they should have designed an official residence as simple as a Quaker meetinghouse. But that would not do, nor did either man consider it. Colonial America, and then the new nation, like all of western Europe, believed in rank, believed that some people were born better than others and thus were ordained by birth to rule over their inferiors. Luxurious possessions and the knowledge of how to use them pointed out who these "betters" were. The Revolution challenged these ideas to their very core, but did not eliminate them.

Dolley's presidential mansion had to accomplish two seemingly contradictory symbolic goals. It had to satisfy the still-prominent Federalists and European observers, who interpreted "taste" and the lavish display and use of objects as a sign that the Madisons were leaders ordained by God, and that the republican experiment was blessed too. (Rosalie Stier Calvert spoke for many when she opined, "Just between ourselves, it's time we had a king.")[28] The red velvet curtains, the display of portraits in the dining room, the mirrors, and the silver accomplished that task.[29]

At the same time, the executive mansion had to soothe republican fears that the fragile republic was one palace away from despotism. The purest of republicans had worried about having a capital city at all, and now a castle crowned it. Upper-class Republicans who knew something of European interiors, however, could see that Dolley's choices in objects and décor were not royal but fine—not so different from what they themselves would buy. For those not as familiar with fashion and consumption, the Grecian-themed furniture, the displays of American manufacture that dotted the rooms, and the patriotic art on the walls reassured them.[30]

Some more sophisticated observers, both European and American, recognized the tension between the aristocratic longings of more traditionally minded Americans and the republican rigor of others. But there was a twist. It turned out that on some level, *everyone* wanted the U.S. government's legitimacy deepened and affirmed by aristocratic possessions. Marks of royalty provided the only visual signs of political power and stability. The Revolution had not destroyed the American commitment to aristocratic forms, it seemed, but rather had appropriated and adapted those forms, while inspiring vigorous debate as to what place they should have.[31] Even that foremost guardian of the republic, George Washington, found himself wondering exactly how many matching horses sufficed to convey authority and power without crossing the proper republican line. (The answer was six.) The advice offered Washington by his fellow revolutionary Gouverneur Morris only affirmed what he and other members of the ruling class assumed: "I think it of very great Importance to fix the Taste of our Country people and I think your Example will go very far in that Respect . . . everything about you should be substantially good and majestically plain."[32] Things had changed since the Spartan days of the revolutionary boycotts. Americans were not cooperating with the Embargo Act, because they were reluctant to deny themselves the new luxury items that came over on British ships. Individual Americans had begun to use material possessions to define themselves. Dolley had not only to reconcile two conflicting political styles in the new United States, but also to answer the unspoken desires of all Americans for the good life.

Not surprisingly, while Dolley's renovations leaned toward the aristocratic side, they passed with largely positive comment. Most Americans would never visit the president's house, but they thought he (and, by extension, they) deserved the best, including an executive mansion that was, for all they knew, fine enough for royalty. As a woman, Dolley occupied the perfect position to take on this task of discreetly satisfying aristocratic desires while retaining an overt commitment to republican simplicity. Women of American political families had already assumed that burden; George Washington might be "Mr. President," but Americans crowned Martha "Lady Washington." Since women were unsuited by nature for politics, so the theory went, their presence in a political setting signaled virtues higher than the petty business of increasingly partisan politics. And here was another twist. Much as the nation feared a "party system," it was in the process of constructing one. Each side of the political divide wanted the support of "the ladies," or, in the case of Dolley, a "Lady," whose disinterested patriotism would then seem to ratify their position.

Yet she assumed any trappings of an aristocratic role at great peril. Subtlety was paramount. To ensure the death of monarchy, republican purists feared it was not enough simply to eliminate the king. The influence of "woman" was as strong as nature, as insidious and devastating as a plague. Woman's presence in a political system presaged only destruction; one anti-capital political cartoon depicted the earlier Philadelphia capital as both a prostitute and a transvestite. In America, the fear of the female encompassed more than court women, who reputedly bankrupted a kingdom materially and politically: since women by nature loved pretty things, and since material luxuries both caused and signaled the corruption of inner virtue, *all* women had the potential to foil the republic. Political commentators feared that, tempted by all the imports flooding in from Europe, farm women craving teaspoons and bonnets would drive their husbands into first bankruptcy and then feudalism. More ominously, men might "catch" the female love of luxury, and, like fops at court, would become effeminate in a world that required manly, robust virtues.[33]

In the early days of the Madison administration, Dolley negotiated a balance between this dark judgment of women's potentially disastrous love of luxury and Americans' covert desire for aristocratic display. Later, she would be subject to severe criticism, judged to be "too aristocratic" by some, too "democratic" by others, but her transformation of the president's house was a success. The new Americans showed remarkably little conflict in embracing this particular aristocratic expression. They loved the new house, felt pride in themselves, marking the metamorphosis of the "President's Palace" not only as fitting but also as an important step in establishing the nation. James Madison's presidency ushered in the era when Americans identified themselves with the president's house. As a sign of their affection and familiarity, they even granted the executive mansion a nickname: the White House. Though the structure had always been pale sandstone, people did not focus on the color as a characteristic until they felt connected in some way to it. Before Dolley, the executive mansion had more formal "titles," such as "palace," but, as the Baltimore *Whig* declared in 1810: " 'White house' may be considered the 'people's name.' "[34]

The capital city's planners had sited the house on a rise, intending a kind of loftiness. Because Jefferson kept most of the city and government at arm's length, the location instead had come to symbolize isolation and distance. Under Dolley's care, the White House would become a protective, watchful presence, and, like a gentry house on a hill, it was the place that everyone looked up to when they thought of power.

As befitted the theme of Dolley's political work, her restructuring of the White House had both practical and symbolic uses. On the most basic level, the renovated White House, and the events held there, offered structure to a government that had but little.[35] But the significance of the house on the hill transcended practical needs, affirming both the Madisons' status and the United States' place in the world.

Ritual—defined as "a public ceremonial affirmation of community"—satisfies a deep collective human need. Unfortunately, by definition, democracies lack the impressive shows of power used by absolute governments. Indeed, the only ritual built into the American system is the presidential inauguration, as decreed by the Constitution. When the central character proves less than charismatic, as James did in 1809, the spare inaugural ceremony offered very little to compensate—no trumpets, no ermine robes, no gold crowns. Fortunately, as soon as the official ceremonies were over, "the people" went to the house on F Street (and later, to the inaugural ball), where Dolley created a sense of ceremony around her very person. Through its First Lady, the United States took its first tentative steps toward constructing national rituals, and embraced a national identity.

But though the Constitution did not provide ritual enough for the young republic, the people who built on Washington City's rural landscape also filled the gap. Architecture can supply the same sense of communality, the connectedness to the past, the stability, structure, and breathtaking drama that the best ritual imparts. Like good ritual, a place such as the White House can be embellished, renewed, and changed. If the idea evoked by the building is strong enough, it can outlast the physical structure. The work that Dolley and James, Henry and Mary did ensured that the White House would be that kind of structure, a national home.[36]

"The Great Centre of Attraction"

*I*n January 1811, Samuel and Catharine Akerly Mitchill were hosting a constituent, Mr. John Stevens, and his son, Robert. The high point of the New Yorkers' stay was undoubtedly their visit to the New Year's version of what was known as "Mrs. Madison's drawing room." The excitement began before they even arrived at the White House. "It was really amusing to observe as we rode along, the great number of Carriages, all drawn as it were, by an irresistible impulse towards the great centre of attraction." The Mitchills' driver pulled up to the front door, "the sound of sweet music struck our ears, and young Stevens eyes sparkled."

Ushered into the grand hall by the "enlivening airs" of the musicians, Catharine and her party pushed their way through a large crowd to greet their host and hostess, James and Dolley. "The two great personages" stood in the middle of the room, bowing and "courtesying," as they received their visitors' good wishes for a happy New Year. Catharine spoke a few minutes with Dolley, and then moved on "to take a peep at the company, and spy out my acquaintance."

Since everyone came to the drawing room, no doubt Catharine could spy out all of her acquaintances, as well as plenty of strangers. Indeed, she soon found herself rubbing elbows with "a number of dignified characters, both civil and military . . . in short almost every important person in Washington and Georgetown, both male and female." She also met more constituents, on "visits of business or pleasure," as well as Washington Irving, another fellow New Yorker. With the band playing, she and Irving promenaded up and down the Oval Room, enjoying "considerable conversation." Irving, who had just arrived in town, marveled to Catharine at the sudden transformation from "a dirty stage coach and muddy roads to the splendor of Mrs. Madison's drawing room, where he beheld on every side so many elegant forms," that the writer confessed he almost believed he was in "fairy land." He was not just being polite. By his own account, he enjoyed the "blazing splendor" of the room. "Here I was most graciously received; found a crowded collection of great and little men, of ugly old women and beautiful young ones, and in ten minutes was hand in glove with half the people in the assemblage."[1]

As the festivities came to an end, the Mitchill party took their leave. Catharine had "a few parting words" with Dolley, during which "I observed to her that she ought to rejoice when we were all gone, for then she must be fatigued standing so long." Surprisingly, "she declared she was not in the least fatigued, and that she regretted us going away so early." Catharine mused: "I believed she spoke the real sentiments of her heart, for I never saw a Lady who enjoyed society more than she does. The more she has round her the happier she appears to be."[2]

Dolley brought the drawing room to the city and the government at a crucial stage of their development, and, with a nod to Irving's turn of phrase, it fit like a glove.

Though still a backwater by any other city's standards, in the eight years since Thomas Jefferson and the Madisons came to town, Washington City had made considerable progress. A turnpike now connected the city with Alexandria, Virginia, a major city center. Other bridges and newly created roads linked the capital to nearby towns. New shops had sprouted up, both in the city and in Georgetown, some suited for a capital's peculiar needs, catering to luxury foods, jewelry, and clothes. More hotels and boardinghouses also appeared, offering increasingly varied specialized services, including transportation to the Capitol.[3]

St. Patrick's Roman Catholic Church was consecrated in 1806; Dolley's collaborator, Benjamin Henry Latrobe, had built Christ Church in 1807. A Friends meetinghouse, churches for Baptists, Presbyterians, and Episcopalians, and a Methodist church down by the Navy Yard joined the ecclesiastical landscape. And the advancements were not confined to buildings and shops. With the change of administration and the flourishing urban development, more people flocked to Washington City, including family members of the government officials, visitors, and new residents attracted to the opportunities created by both the city and government.

The workday of a congressman was neither long nor arduous, certainly not in comparison with the lives some of the legislators left at home, whether as farmers, lawyers, or merchants. Legislators did not even breakfast until ten, as they were not expected to be in Congress until eleven. Once there, they did "little or nothing," returning to their respective boardinghouses at three o'clock, dining at four. Unless there was pressing business, in which case Congress might sit far into the night, the workday ended there. At seven or eight in the evening, Washingtonians "took tea," often with one another in local homes, often passing the evening "at cards or in company."[4]

As more senators and representatives brought their wives to stay in the thriving capital with them, the wives and female family members, too, found unaccustomed leisure during a "season" in the capital. Living in a boardinghouse, they were freed from housekeeping duties. Though parents sometimes brought teenaged children to the capital for a little polish, for the most part they left young children at home with relatives.

With so much free time for men and women, socializing became everyone's favorite pastime. Washington City had few public amusements, and with boardinghouse life not conducive to private entertaining, the spectacle of government provided the main attraction. The House of Representatives soon became the "lounging place of both sexes, where acquaintance is as easily made as at a public amusement." Watching the government in action was "as good as going to a play," though, in Washington, all the characters were real and performed their roles ad lib.[5]

Washingtonians, both temporary and permanent, were so busy socializing that they could not even keep their minds on the Divine: "Religion is not much ala mode here." In a metaphor for the centrality of politics to the capital city, many Washingtonians attended "public worship" as they had done since the city's earliest days, in the Capitol building. With no regular clergy, Congress took what it got. Proponents of all denominations of Christianity—from Catholics to Quakers to Unitarians—appeared, and even a woman preacher. In a pinch, members of Congress took to the pulpit. But the variability of the service mattered little. Church had become a place for socializing and display, so well attended that people sat in the Speaker's chair and wedged spare chairs in any available space.[6]

During the service, congregants talked to one another, moving from seat to seat and to the fire, whispering, nodding, "nay sometimes tittering." The most ludicrous moment came at noon, when the postman delivered mail, calling out names over the sermon. Though the marine band looked "dazzling" in the gallery, with their red uniforms and shiny instruments, their attempts at psalm playing proved "*too ridiculous.*"[7]

The Washingtonians' desire for society stemmed from more than the restlessness of leisured travelers or the human desire to have fun. Thoughtful Americans such as Margaret Bayard Smith truly believed that "society" improved people and civilized nations, instilling the ease and polish that made interactions elevating and refining. Moreover, they recognized that getting to know many kinds of people "destroy[ed] the peculiarities & that reserve which are so generally acquired" in solitude.

Socializing with all kinds of people opened the mind, "accustoming us to see those who differ from us" as "equally wise and good."[8]

Washington had not yet developed a set of national manners, and it worried Americans that people who came to the city from across the nation and from Europe brought their own codes of behavior. In their eyes, that variety would prevent the unification of the country. The women of the "Republican Court" of the Washington and Adams administrations had tried to institute a salon culture that would influence public manners. Launching this project in "civilized" cities and towns, such as Philadelphia and Princeton, New Jersey, no doubt helped.[9] From the perspective of Washington politics, it seemed even more imperative that people needed ways to see others as "equally wise and good." The presence of the government, engaged in work on which the life or death of the new nation seemed to depend, and doing this work in an atmosphere of contention, gave the town an urgency and excitement that alternately exhausted and stimulated the members of political families as well as the locals.

The air of change extended into the halls of power. Congress was coming into its own as a political institution. The transition from Jefferson's administration saw enormous congressional growth—from 106 seats in the House of Representatives to 213 seats, and from 32 Senate seats to 48, reflecting the two million Americans added in that time. The United States had gained only one new state, Ohio, during Jefferson's term, but it was one both large and central. More important, the nation had acquired a substantial territory in Louisiana and was expanding westward all the time. As an institution, Congress had existed now for a full generation, almost ten years in Washington City alone, long enough for some members to have made careers in government and for others to consider it a family enterprise. Individual members of Congress also served longer. During the Madison administration, the average congressman served two and half terms, or five years in Washington City. A smaller group of men spent more than one term in public service: three and a half terms, or seven years in the government. Given contemporary life expectancies, seven years constituted a significant percentage of a man's adult life spent in the federal seat.[10]

But, like any other adolescent growth spurt, Congress's did not ensure stability or strength. The increased numbers made it harder to rally a majority; rather, the newcomers splintered the fragile vote blocs formed in boardinghouses.[11] The disruption was more than numerical. The additional representatives and senators came from the new western territories, and the western settlers sent men to Congress who were not members of ruling-class families. Insiders often used humor to express their dismay and disgust with these rough-and-tumble products of democracy. With some amusement Margaret Bayard Smith told of entertaining "two most venerable senators," one a judge, who were amazed at her daughter's piano playing, but only because they had never seen a piano. They touched the strange instrument "over and over," and when Susan Smith opened the lid, they expressed a childlike wonderment. "'Dear me,' said the judge, 'How pretty those white and red things jump up and down, dear me what a parcel of wire.'" Margaret could not get them to understand the concept of reading music, "supposing all Susan's sweet melody was drawn by chance or random from this strange thing."

On another occasion, the same judge approached the French minister, "surveyed him from head to foot, lifted up the flaps of his coat all covered with gold embroidery, asked him the use of the gold tassels on his boots, what was such a thing and such a thing and how much it all might cost." Perhaps mindful of her own call for tolerance, Margaret added: "Do not think now these good men are fools, far from it, they are very sensible men and useful citizens, but they have lived in the back woods, thats all."[12]

More seriously, Federalists used these stories to cast aspersions and doubts on what they saw as a dangerous trend toward democracy. The word "democracy," though its meaning was now undergoing a change toward the positive, still signified "rule by the mob." The British legation's secretary Augustus John Foster had returned to the United States in 1811 as the British minister. When a hapless dinner guest—a local tavern keeper—was caught using Foster's fireplace to answer a call of nature, the Englishman merely laughed. When the Federalists got wind of the incident, however, they played it for all it was worth. Another story had it that a butcher turned legislator took advantage of the free postal franking privilege granted to congressmen to send his laundry home. The Federalist punchline was that it did not cost the government much, since he only changed his shirt once a week.[13]

The humor stung because it had an element of truth. Beginning in the Madison administration, men came to Washington who had never drunk champagne, met a diplomat, or worked with others in a large organization. The presence of such men, and their correspondingly unsophisticated families, exacerbated regional prejudices. Some Americans still referred to the "United States" in the plural and regarded their home state as their "country." People believed that personal characteristics were in the blood and also that environment and climate dictated personality and even morals. Consequently, New Englanders and Southerners, Westerners, and Easterners, viewed one another with suspicion. Indeed, to some eastern members, their western colleagues might as well have come from another country, and they characterized them as "Irish"—ignorant, quarrelsome, and drunk—though only one had been born in Ireland.

Regional loyalty was so strong that it endangered the nation as a whole. Almost from the very moment that the thirteen colonies decided to form a "perfect union," practically every state—individually or as part of a confederation—had attempted to weaken federal power or divide the country. Given the obvious diversity of the states, given that the constant threat of secession was a standard part of political discourse, some despaired that a single government or body of laws would ever prevail. Parochialism worked against the creation of effective parties or coherent coalitions of congressmen. The members of Congress seemed to face insurmountable differences of blood, region, and class, not to mention that they lacked common political ties. The aristocratic plantation mistress Rosalie Stier Calvert had articulated a perfectly tenable position in 1808 when she predicted: "My opinion is that a separate republic of the northern states will be formed, and, after a lot of turmoil, a monarchy in the south."[14]

In spite of the republican commitment to small, weak government, Congress suffered from that malady of adolescence, growing pains.

While the Senate struggled for preeminence over the House, both arms needed stronger internal bureaucratic structure to focus power and to bring legislators together in both small committees and larger bodies—in other words, to become a modern government institution.[15] The obvious lack of structure was evident to even the most casual observer. The day-to-day business of legislation unfolded in an unruly, chaotic atmosphere. Little decorum governed debates. Anyone could bring any topic to the floor, with no time restrictions on orations or debate. The lack of leadership or hierarchy of seniority among the members contributed to the free-for-all atmosphere. The floors of Congress roiled in perpetual confusion, resembling less a parliament than "Hyde Park set down in the lobby of a busy hotel." Members read, caught up with correspondence, talked among themselves or with friends in the gallery and halls, even on the floor itself. Sometimes they even napped, with their feet propped on their desks, but at least the sleepers were quiet. Spectators roamed the main halls and anterooms, while messengers darted back and forth on the congressional floor, delivering food, messages, and mail, calling out members' names even during speeches. Little wonder that a congressman called the ruling body of the new United States "Babeltown" and that the rowdy tone of the congressional milieu spilled over into Sunday services.[16]

❧

Like Congress, the Madisons' presidential household was lively from the start. At any one time, the household included not only James, Dolley, and Payne, but also Anna and Richard Cutts and an increasing number of children, who lived in the executive mansion while Richard served in Congress. Sister Lucy and her boys visited often, and, creating their own excitement and uproar, an assortment of young nieces, nephews, cousins of all degrees, and friends filled out the family circle.

In his capacity as presidential secretary, Dolley's cousin Edward Coles quickly became a constant and welcome presence. He was also following a family tradition; his older brother, Isaac A. Coles, had been Jefferson's secretary. A charming, intelligent, deeply thoughtful man,

Edward Coles also was a bachelor; he devoted himself to the Madisons, and Dolley especially responded in kind. Marrying off cousin Edward remained a playful joke for the Payne women. Dolley characterized him to Anna as "a great fidget & is hard to mary."[17] (He did marry, years later, when he had resolved the dilemma of his life. The immorality of slavery troubled Edward Coles, and he often argued with James about it. Edward would go on to move his slaves to Illinois, free them with land of their own, and settle there himself for a time, his life a reproach to slaveholders and to his Albemarle County neighbor and friend, Thomas Jefferson.)

Dolley's son, Payne Todd, came of age during the Madison administration. Payne finished school, but he was no scholar and could not hope to follow in his stepfather's footsteps to his alma mater, Princeton. With no occupation or interest in anything except pleasure, Payne was developing along worrisome and, considering his uncle, ominously familiar lines. Dolley could not discipline him; something within her collapsed at the prospect of restricting her only child. James could or would not either. He may have felt the delicacy of his position as Payne's step-, rather than "real," father. In this culture of early death, however, many families were blended, and, for all the cultural preoccupation with blood, other men unambiguously ruled over stepchildren. More likely, James wanted to "spare" Dolley, and the two of them began a pattern of bailing Payne out of his various scrapes, each sometimes hiding their efforts from the other. Payne soon figured this out and played on their dynamic.

With barely a brother and a son growing more distant by the day, cousin Edward Coles remained Dolley's closest male kin, and politics deepened the connection. Edward Coles and Payne Todd could not have been more different, the starkest contrast coming from direct comparison. During Edward's long illness in 1813, Payne assumed his duties; even as a temporary replacement, he gave no satisfaction, and Dolley took over.

The Madisons' circles included not only family, of course, but also allies. Dolley was intent on drawing people into the Madisons' circle of supporters. As always, she relied upon calling to open relations between families, and often used the first visit to invite the called-upon to a social event or excursion. Even when occasions were open to the public, such as her drawing rooms or a Supreme Court session, she sometimes delivered a personal invitation. Charmed by the leading lady of the land taking the subordinate role in "waiting" upon *them*, people rarely resisted. Dolley's use of these visits to make contacts was all the more important because James could not call. Indeed, in order to avoid any hint of favoritism, James had decided to refuse all dinner invitations, so Dolley became his sole public representative in the outside world.

If James would not travel out to meet political families, Dolley would bring them to him; over the course of the next eight years, she held more formal dinners than any other president's wife in history. Under Dolley, the official social season in Washington City lengthened from six weeks to ten—spanning the first Wednesday in December until the middle of February. She continued her project of readying the new White House for society, installing bells in every room and more than doubling the size of the staff, using her own slaves and hiring others from nearby plantations and households. Sometimes at dinner parties, the number of people waiting on table equaled the number of guests.[18] Dolley also instituted a new job for the president's house: master of ceremonies. She probably invented this position because she had found the perfect candidate. Jean Pierre Sioussat was a refugee from Napoleon's France, who deserted from the French navy by jumping from his ship while it was anchored in New York harbor, and swimming ashore. He had come to Washington City in the employ of the Merrys; when he left them, Dolley and James hired him on. "French John" (as he was called to differentiate him from the black slaves) proved more than a servant. Dolley described him as "my faithful domestic," a man of "unusual activity and resolution." His official duty was that of doorkeeper, a post that put another layer of formality between the president and his guests. Even more important, his language skills and his experience with French customs and points of procedure aided Dolley as she constructed a workable American form of precedence.[19]

When the Madisons moved from F Street to the White House,

their meals underwent a corresponding rise in lavishness. Guests offered endless praise for Dolley's White House dinners, because they recognized, as one etiquette book put it, that "to perform faultlessly the honours of the table, is one of the most difficult things in society." Louisa Catherine Johnson Adams, a hostess extraordinaire in her own right, concurred: "To entertain well you must forget that you are so engaged and your company will feel perfectly at their ease and forget they are visiting." "This," she wryly concluded, "like most things is easier in theory than in practice."[20] But putting people at their ease was Dolley's forte.

James was a chief beneficiary of her deftness. As Sarah Gales Seaton, whose husband and brother published the *Intelligencer*, observed, Dolley often headed the table and led the conversation, sparing James the responsibility. Freed from having to direct the conversation, a more relaxed James could be convivial and charming. But notwithstanding his seemingly secondary position, James played an active role. He, too, knew the power of dinner party politics, and he planned the format and seating for the dinners as meticulously as he did every political project.[21] He understood that with Dolley at the helm, no one would feel slighted or ignored; typical was this assessment: "I never felt more at home, or spent a more social time."[22]

During one dinner party, making what he thought was a gallant offer, Elbridge Gerry offered "to aide Mrs. Madison in doing the honor of the table; 'O no' says she Mr. G see with how much ease I will do it." Gerry happily "witness[ed] . . . her ease, & glad she officiated herself; for it was impossible for me to have equaled her in this instance." He added to his daughter: "Indeed every thing she does is with such elegant ease as would delight you." Dolley seemed "as easy as if she had been born & educated at Versailles."[23]

It is no accident that Gerry used the word "ease" or "easy" several times in that description. The quality of "ease" was highly prized in aristocratic circles; the perfect hostess, possessed of this gift, polished yet accessible, would soon put her guests at ease. No better judge of "ease" exists than a painter, and while Eastman Johnson, who painted Dolley many years later, remarked approvingly upon her "taste" in dress—for the sittings she wore a "white satin, turban, black velvet dress"—it was her way of being that drew his highest praise. With a "countenance full of benignity and gentleness," along with "polished and elegant manners," Dolley epitomized the ease of the natural aristocrat.

In genteel company, the ultimate test of a truly refined, superior being lay in the art of conversation. Tellingly, participants in the "best" social circles tended not to record the actual content of talk—*what* was said—but instead commented on the general quality of the conversation—*how* things were said. Like the most accomplished salonnières on both sides of the Atlantic, Dolley could converse on any subject likely to come up in genteel company. Eastman Johnson also commented on her ability to acquit herself in this arena: "She talks a great deal and in such quick, beautiful tones."[24]

What was for dinner at the White House had significance as well. Sarah Gales Seaton was surprised to note that "the dinner was certainly very fine; but still I was rather surprised it did not surpass some I have eaten in Carolina." Dolley continued to serve southern foods in the Old English style —plain meat with separate dishes of vegetables—but, like other American hostesses, she had also begun including newer French dishes, with their emphasis on subtle seasonings and sauces.[25] Her table reflected some of the natural abundance of the area, which, declared one gourmand, "furnished better viands than Paris, and only wanted cooks." Wild game such as deer, turkey, canvasback duck, as well as oysters, turtles, fresh- and saltwater fish, and seafood were among the delicacies served. In the early days of the capital, the only luxury was found in the households of the diplomatic corps; among the local and official families "very few . . . aimed at great ostentatious display." Availability had also limited one's aims: in the first years of the Jefferson administration, the city lacked confectioners and pastry chefs, and a table was only as fine as the lady of the house knew how to set (or how to instruct her servants and slaves to set). By Dolley's reign in the president's house, "luxury increase[d] daily" in the capital city.

In addition to luxurious and impressive meals, Dolley also served political messages. According to Washington legend, she actively sought out recipes from the female members of leading families across the country. This, too, was a typical Dolley transaction, one that left everyone feeling satisfied. Women from the hinterlands were honored and delighted to think of their dishes adorning "America's table," and Dolley could then evoke authentic "Americanness" for her guests. Moreover, to cement the connection, Dolley offered her own recipes in return, both equalizing and elevating the exchange. One of the recipes Dolley may have proffered was the prized "receipt" for ice cream, possession of which afforded a hostess the social advantage of being the first in her area to serve the delicacy.[26]

In making her dinner table yet another political space, Dolley built on a long tradition in politics. Sitting down with people to share food constitutes an act of power in all societies, the first step in network building. This had been true in colonial America, even as it prepared for revolution; indeed, one might say that the whole revolutionary enterprise unfolded in a series of conversations, with many of the conversations, such as the political bargain involving the capital city, taking place at dinner tables. Dinner with Dolley represented an initiation rite, a passage into the circles of power. The superior food, the lovely setting, and the refined behavior allowed people to feel open, relaxed, and included. The power of dining, of course, went both ways. Even the most backward rube understood this, as when one southern representative responded to a dinner invitation from James Madison: "I won't dine with you because you won't dine with me."[27]

For diplomats in Washington City, the dinner table was their office, and they spent plenty of money in the primitive city on dinner parties, leaving guest lists and tactical memoranda for their successors. By 1809, other official families had begun to hold dinners and parties. But Dolley had no equal as a hostess, and her events reigned preeminent. On the surface, her social events were all that such occasions should be. In her skillful hands, people could be their best selves, easy, elegant, even a tad aristocratic. But the social atmosphere successfully masked the high political stakes.

If food acts as a system of communication and a medium of exchange, Dolley's table, laden with luxury foods such as duck and ice cream, made her guests feel privileged and honored. Dinner at Dolley's bought nothing so crass as to be measurable in monetary terms, or so crude as a vote in Congress. Rather, it built goodwill and a social allegiance that, in early Washington, easily translated into political alliance. Dining was most often a family experience; by inviting prominent people to dine with her, Dolley made them part of the Madison family.[28]

✻

At the time of James's inauguration, Dolley's Philadelphia friend Eliza Collins Lee had written to convey her love and best wishes: "Allow me then to offer my congratulations at a moment when you are about to fill a character the most dignified and respectable in society." Eliza knew well Dolley's gifts, temperament, and talents, and how her background had prepared her for this task: "And I assure you I feel no small degree of exultation in knowing that the mind, temper, and manners of my Philadelphia Quaker friend, are peculiarly fitted for the station, where hospitality and graciousness of deportment, will appear conspicuously charming & conciliating."[29] Eliza's focus on her friend's "mind, temper, and manners," and the qualities of conciliation and charm, acknowledged not only Dolley's strengths, but also something important about her political context.

The era of the early republic may be characterized as "a nation of men," of individuals and personalities enmeshed within a "resolutely personal" form of politics. The leading men personified political issues and in turn, the issues shaped them. Trust was a crucial component of the system; so, correspondingly, was its flip side, betrayal. Personal, face-to-face politicking had the potential for disaster, as the bad behavior in Congress demonstrated, but it also had the potential for forging bonds and creating avenues for political work—provided, of course, that a strong, charismatic personality could guide it to positive ends.[30]

Thomas Jefferson was just such a personality; James was not. Socially graceful, a master of the dinner table strategy, Jefferson came close to his goal of controlling government. A brilliant politician and charming man, he did not need a wife to do his unofficial networking. Throughout their political partnership, but especially in the 1790s, James Madison had played a subordinate role to the more flamboyant Jefferson. He performed wifely duties, such as passing on information and acting as a messenger, as well as restraining Jefferson when his passions moved in an imprudent direction. Like the perfect spouse, James guided his leader gently, while not challenging his own status as a subordinate, even though his was a more formidable intellect than Jefferson's.[31]

For much of his later political career, James existed in parallel "marriages" with Jefferson and Dolley, though the tasks were divided differently in each partnership. Obviously, James took the leading role with Dolley, but Dolley constituted the Jefferson of their collaboration when it came to charisma and personality. Her style, like Jefferson's, could offset the era's enormous political contentiousness as well as its lack of party structure and bureaucracy. While she had her own political goals, however, Dolley did not strive for the control that Jefferson sought; indeed, as a woman, she could not ever hope to achieve it. Her political style centered on working together, building bridges rather than bunkers.

The face-to-face politics that ruled the day was precisely the politics at which Dolley excelled. Unlike more timorous wives, she did not merely provide a social setting, then retreat from the field, hoping that all would behave well. Rather, she offered the positive side of personal politics, a politics of intimacy. Moreover, she dealt with people and situations one at a time. Not for her airy abstractions and theories about how politics should work in an ideal world. She focused on politics on the ground, providing an arena for power in her home and addressing specific political needs, whether for a job, an introduction, or an intercession.

As it turned out, the politics of a budding democracy relied on face-to-face personal relations more than a royal court did. An absolute monarch need not seek or heed counsel, but a democracy depends on consensus and collaboration, so legislators and bureaucrats must discover where their mutual interests lie. Happily for the future of Washington City and the nation, Dolley Madison constructed an alternative to the fragile governmental structure, one that provided the space for such discoveries.

Members of Congress, along with their families, had to find ways of working with each other and tolerating the conflict that would be an inevitable part of democracy. The first step lay in seeing each other as human beings, rather than as simply political figures or as the inhuman monsters of early American rhetoric.[32] At Dolley's dinner table, male politicians began to see political enemies not as villains to be attacked from the floor of Congress but as people like themselves "wise and good." As this incipient ruling class interacted on a variety of levels—from sharing food to meeting each other's families—they began to develop personal relationships, creating mutual feelings of loyalty and obligation. The presence of women and other family members was instrumental in achieving that goal, not only because they had a "softening" effect but also because they humanized their menfolk in the eyes of others.

Dolley's drawing rooms or, as they soon became known, "Mrs. Madison's Wednesday nights," began only two months after James's inauguration and remained a fixture on the Washington scene for the next eight years. Though Dolley held the first drawing rooms in her sunny yellow parlor, she moved them into their proper space—the Oval Room—as soon as it was ready, on January 1, 1810.

In creating her Wednesday nights, Dolley adapted a form of the European royal levée. By calling them drawing rooms, Dolley made them seem less continental, while still evoking a touch of the British gentry. Indeed, her drawing room echoed the old British tradition of "public days," when the great houses of the gentry were opened to all, awing the lower orders and commanding the respect of other denizens of the ruling class. Initially, Dolley put a general note of invitation in the newspapers. The only qualification for attendance was the usual: that one have been "introduced" to the Madisons, either personally or through letters of introduction. Soon both the introduction requirement and the general invitation faded away. Everyone knew where to be on Wednesday nights, and everyone went.[33]

Obviously, official families regularly attended, as did the local gentry and members of the diplomatic corps. But visitors to town and other classes of people also made their way to Mrs. Madison's Wednesday nights. A congressman might encounter his boardinghouse landlady and her daughters in the Oval Room. Ladies and gentlemen who came by hired carriage would be joined in the "spacious hall" by the drivers who had transported them.

Dolley's drawing room swirled with excitement, crowds, color, and movement. Before long, these events became known as "squeezes"—some called them "a genteel squeeze"—for two or three hundred people crammed into the White House rooms. To accommodate these crowds, Dolley opened the three front rooms; the guests moved back and forth through the dining room and the parlor, spilling into the grand Oval Room, "where the company were at liberty to walk about, make new acquaintance, or chat with the old ones."[34]

Unlike the staid gatherings held by Martha Washington and Abigail Adams, where all guests stood or sat in ceremonious fashion, waiting to be greeted, Dolley's guests had the freedom to meet, greet, and move among groups of people as they wished. Side tables held punch, wine, coffee, tea, nuts, cake, fruit, ice cream, and other light comestibles. Food also came to the guests, on those scarlet "japanned" trays that Henry Latrobe had bought, carried by slaves and hired servants. But one had to be quick. As the ice cream and other dainty fare passed through the crowd, people were not shy about helping themselves.[35]

Anything could happen at a drawing room. One evening, guests were treated to the sight, from a White House window, of what they thought was "a rolling ball of burnished gold, carried with swiftness through the air by two gilt wings." It was the carriage of the French minister, who "alighted, weighted with gold lace." What the astonished guests thought were wings "were nothing more than gorgeous footmen with chapeaux bras [brass helmets], gilt braided skirts and splendid swords." No one had ever seen anything "so brilliant and dazzling—a meridian sun blazing full on this carriage filled with diamonds and glittering orders and gilt to the edge of the wheels—you may well imagine," rhapsodized Sarah Gales Seaton, "how the natives stared and rubbed their eyes to be convinced 'twas not a fairy dream."[36]

At the center of it all was Dolley. Like a European woman to the manner born, she knew how to manage a room full of people, when to distinguish and when to detach. Wherever she went, the crowd followed, "the towering feathers and excessive throng distinctly point[ing] her station wherever she moved," as one guest noted. The garments Dolley chose were of fabrics and colors not usually seen even among the wealthiest men and women. At the 1811 New Year's Day drawing room, Dolley dazzled in a loose-fitting silk robe that formed a cape at her neck. Trimmed with white satin ribbon, the material was woven in such a way that it changed color in the light. Dolley's white satin head-dress matched the trimming, sporting a flower in the front.[37]

Dolley's effect proved more than sartorial; as Sarah Gales Seaton noted, " 'Tis here the woman who adorns the dress, and not the dress that beautifies the woman." She spoke for many when she declared: "I cannot conceive a female better calculated to dignify the station which she occupies in society than Mrs. Madison—amiable in private life and affable in public, she is admired and esteemed by the rich and beloved by the poor."[38]

The secret of Dolley's charm, as countless friends and admirers noted, lay in her generosity and tolerance. As Catharine Akerly Mitchill marveled: "Really, she makes herself so agreeable and by her civil & polite expressions, puts every one in such a good humour with them-selves, that no one who has once seen her, can help being pleased with her, or quit her house without feeling a desire to renew their visit." Dol-ley's "affability" had political implications, and her evaluators could not resist comparisons to her husband. While Dolley struck people as "a very suitable person for the station she fills," James, by contrast, did "not appear to have so high a relish for these exhibitions. The little Man looks sometimes, as if the cares of the nation and the toll of seeing so much company had almost exhausted him."[39]

❧

"Mrs. Madison's Wednesday nights" offered an event Washington soci-ety could count on. Especially near the end of congressional sessions, a week or more might go by with no party, "except the drawing room, which was most magnificently attended." It was the one occasion where you could find anyone, from a Senate colleague to a visiting constituent. People understood the inherent political opportunities, and no one could keep away. Right from the start, even "Federalists generally were present," according to Timothy Pickering, a rabid member of the opposition party. When he himself needed "to introduce a friend into society" (bearing in mind that "friend" stood as a euphemism for a political supporter), he set his sights on the "splendor of the drawing room." When wind and fog "disappointed us" in the task, Pickering took comfort in the fact that he and his "friend" could go the following week.[40]

The weekly event afforded everyone in Washington City access to the president unparalleled before or since.[41] George Washington and John Adams had held weekly functions for a small numbers of select men, and they might also speak to ladies at their wives' levées. In contrast, at Dolley's Wednesday nights, all kinds of Americans, male and female, as well as European visitors, had a chance to talk with James.

Just as generosity and openness were the key to Dolley's charm, a large measure of her social success lay in her willingness to supply members of the federal government with access not only to herself and her husband, but also to one another. Then, as now, "access" to key personnel and points of decision was a crucial factor in the political process, and one most available in an informal situation rather than in a formal structure. (Hence the success of the lobbyist profession.) Access proves particularly important in a government like that of the United States, where the branches are separate and where membership in one branch does not automatically convey affiliation with the others.[42] While contact with the Madisons was obviously an advantage, the more numerous and less dramatic connections that members of political families made with each other formed the core relationships of the federal government.

Interacting at social events, people appeared at their most fully human, allowing others to approach them in all capacities—not just as an official or the wife of an official, but also as a mother, a cousin, or a fellow spirit. Washingtonians deliberately conflated society with politics, partly from political expediency, partly to mitigate the ruthless nature of power. The language and conventions of personal relationships both veiled and signaled political purposes.

At a Madison drawing room, presided over by a charismatic lady, people could move beyond partisan politics if they chose. Official men and "unofficial characters" of all kinds made rapprochements, proffered suggestions, and brokered deals outside the glare of the official spotlight. While the music, dancing, wine, and "social" conversation permitted Washington's political players to entertain possibilities too risky for the floor of Congress, these same elements allowed them to deflect or refuse without offense. The large crowds and noise, ironically, permitted more private conversation than, say, a seat at Jefferson's tightly controlled dinner table.

The style of Dolley's socializing, like political style generally in the first years of the republic, was southern, specifically Virginian. Europeans regarded the "southrons" as the most sociable and urbane group in America, an understandable view considering the alternatives.[43] New England socializing concentrated more on adherence to stiff-necked notions of propriety than on enjoyable human contact. Dolley's extension of the Virginia dynasty's ruling style encouraged people to be at their most available and open, rather than at their most proper. A willingness to reach out, to take modest social risks, was precisely what the Washington political community needed.

The regularity of Dolley's drawing rooms had uses beyond immediate practicality. The events answered Washingtonians' need for ceremony and ritual. Whereas, in a pinch, architecture such as the White House's substituted for ritual in an austere republic, the drawing rooms were the real thing. They were regular and episodic, each evening having a rhythm and a feel different from ordinary life. Partygoers responded to the heightened emotions, sensuousness, and atmosphere of ceremony at these events. For the group, these rituals strengthened bonds and boundaries, confirmed identities, and provided structures to the society. Just as families enact ritual in order to bring members together or to incorporate new members, Dolley's drawing rooms brought disparate parts of the capital together, like one large, diverse family. And though she could not have foreseen this, Washington City and the nation would need the stability of rituals to ease transitions and foster change.[44]

Not everyone admired Dolley or enjoyed the drawing rooms. But they *went,* and their detractions only attested to the events' power.

Alexander Dick, a member of the British legation, remembered a time in Washington when the president's house had "no ladies parties, nor indeed Public levees . . . dancing and cards." Truth be told, he was not all that impressed with the change the Madisons brought. For him, the drawing room seemed merely a large gathering of people with only "tea Coffee, Ice Creams Cakes & refreshments" being "all the entertainment." However, he admitted, "in a place like Washington where there are Scarcely any public places at all, Such a Meeting Seems to be much relished, & then there is the honor of Seeing the President & his Lady & other Public characters."[45]

In 1812, the *Alexandria Gazette* would accuse James Madison of seducing Congress into declaring war by means of the "extravagant imitations of a royal court" that were his "levées." At the drawing rooms, asserted the *Gazette,* good republicans became courtiers—"congressional attendants"—and they would "bow and cringe, and dangle and play the parasite."[46] If the drawing rooms seemed a dangerously aristocratic holdover to some, they presaged another, more modern fear for others. By literally inviting everyone to the party, Dolley made her drawing rooms an experiment in democracy. This genre of criticism reflected a shift from old fears to new. Now elite families worried less about royalist plotters taking over and more about a coup by the unwashed hordes.

Upper-class Americans and Europeans appreciated the properly sumptuous setting of the drawing rooms, but the freedom of access and movement troubled them. Augustus John Foster, who generally admired Dolley's skills, characterized the drawing room as an event where "anybody might introduce at the President's, where every blackguard might go . . . the dirtier the better." As a symbol of their distaste, critics focused on the fact that some men came to the event in rough workaday boots, rather than more refined and formal shoes. In conservative minds, the consequences of such tolerance could be dire. The Cassandra of the Federalist Party, Rosalie Stier Calvert, who scorned Dolley, thought that under the Madisons the Republicans had already devolved, and she predicted: "If the Democratic party continues to rule, a dissolution of the Union will be the result sooner or later." In their critique of Dolley and her ways, Rosalie and like-minded Americans were partly right. Though Dolley came from the traditional ruling classes, by letting the dirty boots into her parlor she did foreshadow the dreaded democracy.[47]

Even as some criticized Dolley for allowing the footwear of the lower orders to tread the White House floors, the *Baltimore Whig* tried to prove that Dolley was a secret Federalist, claiming that she barred a boot-wearing guest from her drawing room. But that was not true. Though most male guests adhered to standards of gentility by wearing shoes, even a rigorous Republican, Pennsylvania representative Jonathan Roberts, had to admit that one could indeed attend the drawing room in boots. From that he concluded, "Mrs. Madison I understand has unequivocally declar'd she is a democrat tho the world have strong doubts about it." Dolley used her drawing rooms as a public stage, on which she performed "Americanness."[48]

Like it or not, the drawing room had become the indisputable power center of the capital city. No one could afford not to go, and few circumstances prevented attendance. When Vice President George Clinton died in 1812, a young visitor, Sophia May, reported: "It was generally thought upon the Hill that there would not be any Levees altogether but they would not pay even that poor compliment to his memory." How could they, when, according to Dolley, "Eletioneering for his office goes on beyond description"?[49]

⚜

The very openness of the drawing room operated subtly in a culture where attendance implied a political loyalty to the host. In contrast to an intimate dinner or an invitation-only occasion, the drawing rooms— so open, so public—implied that no such commitment was expected. At the same time, of course, as people of all political stripes flocked to the White House, they opened themselves up to the many implicit and explicit messages that Dolley sent. At Dolley's social events, Washingtonians began to cohere into the two collectivities that would make up institutionalized political parties. Together they formed a ruling class with whom they could share values, manners, assumptions, and a vision of nationhood.

Dolley worked to make the drawing room as politically neutral as possible. People marveled at her ability to entertain everyone; as Congressman Jonathan Roberts noted: "By her deportment in her own house you cannot discover who is her husband's friends or foes. Her guests have no right to complain of her partiality."[50] Even John Randolph was welcome. And by all accounts, he behaved himself: in accepting the hospitality of a lady, everyone understood, one also accepted that this was a social event set apart from the culture of violence, and so put on one's best behavior.

Dolley also worked hard to appear to be above politics, moved simply by love of humanity and social life. Under the cover of "entertainment," however, lay the calculated purposefulness of her efforts. The most obvious clue was the regularity of those entertainments, the work and energy it took to make Dolley's drawing room the place "to see and be seen," as Catharine Akerly Mitchill put it. No one just happened to host a party on the same day every week. Neither preference, weather, nor death halted the drawing rooms, so they must have stemmed from more than a fun-loving spirit or a good heart.

In some ways, Dolley *did* enjoy society as much as Catharine Akerly Mitchill suspected; she thrived on human interaction. One evening, even though she was ill, upon finding friends (and "strangers") "impatient for an open room," Dolley "ventured down to pass the ev[enin]g." She found herself "re-novated by the kindness & sympathy expressed by a numerious circle." She once philosophized to her protégée, Phoebe Morris, that "to have conciliated the regard of those, by whom we are surrounded—it is a sensation, my dear girl, *worth all the pains you can take.*"

But as the political stakes rose, so did the need for the social sphere, taxing even the indefatigable Dolley: "We have new Members in abundance—their wives daughters &.&. and I, never felt the entertainment of company, oppressive until now." No one outside her intimate circle saw it, but to friends and family, Dolley complained: "I have been engaged all the session, without an hour's leasure, & have still, a weight of cares." It took a lot to oppress Dolley; in any case, the work had to go on.[51]

Dolley was a woman of strong emotions, who knew how to control them, however. She eschewed open shows of anger and, when she did not trust her capacity to behave calmly, she hid herself, as when the "violence of evil sprits" denouncing James from the floor became too much for her and she stayed "quietly at home—as quietly as one can be, who has so much to feel at the *expression, for & against their [Congress's] conduct.*"[52]

The presence of Federalists at a Republican president's drawing room reaches the heart of the drawing room's significance. In or out of the government, only at Dolley's events could political enemies get to know one another in circumstances that demanded the best of them. Government officials fought physically on the floor of Congress, in their boardinghouses, and on the street; but they dared not strike one another with ladies present. Social events required manners, which aimed at controlling emotion and adhering to rules of civility.

If for no other reason than this, the drawing room contributed to the construction of a workable government in Washington City. To be sure, more concrete and specific political activities transpired, but one of the difficulties in documenting the workings of the unofficial sphere lies in the very dynamic that makes it successful: it hides relations of power. Because the strength of the unofficial sphere lies in its unconsidered nature, which draws a veil over political process, it is hard to reconstruct its precise effect on official happenings. Direct documentation, such as Jefferson's "Anas," is rare.[53] Mostly, the significance of the unofficial sphere in Washington City comes from evidence glimpsed at the edges.

The drawing room offered many political opportunities that people readily embraced—they made connections, sought or dispensed jobs, proposed and marshaled support for legislation, and conducted other such meat-and-potatoes politicking. Dolley used personal invitations as diplomatic statements, as when she informally "recognized" the Chevalier de Onís from Spain when James could not.[54] As with all social events, however, the primary political activity was the collection and dissemination of information, a desirable commodity to anyone in government. Through gossip—the language of the unofficial sphere—people imparted and obtained information in a variety of ways, overtly and covertly, consciously and inadvertently.

Gossiping allowed an exchange of information different from the data in a memo or any official document. How gossip traveled varied. At Dolley's drawing room, information was both overheard and broadcast. On the eve of his departure in 1806, when Anthony Merry informed James Madison that "before we went to war, we ought to be very sure that no other measure of a conciliatory nature remained," the remark was clearly meant to "go public," and indeed, it sparked much talk and political maneuvering.[55]

Information was in short supply, whether about the opposing party or the increasingly tense foreign situation. Since only Congress could declare war, legislators from both sides eagerly tried to discover where their colleagues stood. Of course, as the person who would request a declaration of war, the president was the best source of information. Consequently, at the drawing room, the only public place in which James appeared, everyone was on the lookout for signs, trying to interpret his slightest gesture in order to discern his mind. One Washington newspaper correspondent would use the ominous sight of James and the new British minister, Augustus John Foster, in 1812 "in very familiar chit-chat at the levee tonight" to hypothesize that James would use French outrages on American shipping as an excuse to go to war with France. (Foster wished it were that simple. During the year leading up to the declaration of war between the United States and England, Foster frantically relied on the social sphere both to forestall hostilities and to read the political winds. He talked issues and policy with James at the drawing rooms and during innumerable "social" calls. In spite of presidential "asperity," cabinet civilities shown Foster at Dolley's Wednesday nights would encourage him to ask James for a suspension of the current nonimportation policy. Gloomily, he concluded from the way James behaved at a drawing room in April 1812 that the president "really wishes for war now—become desperate.")[56]

In 1811, it was at the drawing room, where he was "received as the envoy of the emperor ought to be," that Louis Sérurier first learned that the United States might be on the brink of declaring war on Great

Britain. With deportment and language now standard at the drawing room, the company paid him suitable honor; afterward, Secretary of State Robert Smith took the French envoy aside and informed him that "he was authorized to give assurance that, in case England once more showed resistance to recalling her orders, the government had decided to re-enforce the non-intercourse, and to give to this measure all the consequences." In other words, if England would not repeal their sanctions against the United States, the Americans would retaliate with their own sanctions, which would have the effect of favoring France (Smith's revelation to Sérurier was correct though premature).[57]

As important as information networks were to politics, the gossip at Dolley's drawing room or parlor served long-term purposes as well. The "world's talk" allowed the gossipers to form human connections and to carve out a sphere of intimacy. Gossip is, after all, a profoundly human activity, here put to political purpose. Gossiping can have nasty, exclusive results, but, like any ritual, it can also help form a community and multiply connections.[58]

Washingtonians, like many other Americans, saw their capital and, indeed, their nation as fragile. They needed any activity that could provide reassurance in an insecure world. In Washington City and all across the country, America was deciding what constituted its ruling class. By sharing views, opinions, and judgments in the hidden world of gossip, the new ruling class determined proper standards of behavior. They exchanged not only information but also points of view.

At Dolley's drawing room, politicians and members of political families gossiped to form alliances, develop strategies, and agree on common goals. Again, like other elements of the unofficial sphere, gossip accomplished some of the structure building that the government sorely needed and that the Constitution did not provide.

❧

With her weekly drawing rooms, Dolley had created an institution. Unlike French salons, which aimed at creating an uplifting, artistic milieu, these American versions concerned themselves almost solely with politics and government. Never again would a president operate without a "social lobby" located within the White House walls.[59] In the first years of the nineteenth century, as politicians struggled to make republicanism work, Dolley and others translated political theory into a living, breathing reality. Her husband and the other founders may have dreamed of and drafted the plan for the "Grand Federal Edifice," but Dolley built it brick by brick, one cup of tea, one favor, one connection at a time.

In doing so, she changed the course of the republican experiment. Republicanism stressed depersonalized authority; Dolley's personalization of authority for her husband's politics demonstrated that republicanism would not suffice to meet the nation's needs.[60] In the absence of other models, Dolley fell back on older forms, and, however unwittingly, laid the groundwork of a new and democratic political style. Paradoxically, she used old-fashioned court ways to create a "new-fashioned" democracy, making bold choices all along the spectrum of aristocracy and democracy: on one hand, insisting that ladies curtsey to the president, on the other, mingling "the Minister from Russia and underclerks of the post office." By transmuting republicanism through selective borrowing from court culture, she adapted it to the nation's peculiar needs. Indeed, Dolley provided a social solution to the central problem of republican politics, namely, how to make the federal government cohere without threatening the underlying values of republicanism as James Madison and Thomas Jefferson had defined them.[61]

Dolley's major accomplishments as the president's wife always had two dimensions, encompassing both immediate political results and lasting benefits for the federal government and the country. In her public persona, and especially at her drawing rooms, Dolley created an American ruling style, one that served political Washington well and would evolve over the centuries.

She favored extremes. In the White House, she created a lavish and sumptuous stage setting, in which she dressed like an American queen. But she also invented presidential ceremonies to which she invited everyone to politick as they liked. Though her style had little in common with the movement toward a middle-class vernacular gentility of quiet taste, Dolley did concur with emerging opinions on one crucial point. She was always careful to differentiate "etiquette," which was associated with the empty show of courts, from "manners," which, in the Scottish Enlightenment formulation, reflected inner virtue. Her niece, Mary Cutts, insisted that "etiquette she delighted to throw aside at all times, she liked no form which separated her from her friends."[62] Dolley recognized the need for civility in a democratic society, but borrowed little from older caste systems and institutions of privilege.

Style—especially in politics—proves inseparable from substance. The "style" of governing, the way that power is implemented and circulated, has everything to do with how the governed experience being ruled. Style also encompasses the symbols and institutions that bind the people to their government.[63] The American style that Dolley created combined modern, urban standards and older, courtly forms from the South, blending the manners of the European gentry with the refined republican morals of the new United States. That everyone could go to the "Palace," even in boots, speak to their president, and be spoken to by a "Lady," made a difference in how Americans felt about themselves and their government. One need only imagine how badly the opposite situation would have been received, with an executive mansion occupied by distant leaders and forbidden to the public. That scenario had almost occurred under Thomas Jefferson.

All those who feared that the capital would become a magnet for hordes of power seekers need not have worried. The roads that stopped at the city limits symbolized the lack of connection between the capital and the rest of the country, as well as the relationship most Americans had with their federal government. A very slow mail service and the occasional request for troops provided the sole everyday contact Americans experienced with their government. No citizen delegations or lobbyists acted as a bridge between the citizenry and it. This lack of connectedness could prove a liability, for public apathy in a representative republic was more than ironic; it was dangerous.[64]

Dolley changed that. Her creation of a vibrant social life directly connected with politics attracted people looking for excitement, pleasure, and political involvement. Her personal style of openness and accessibility encouraged interaction. Travelers from the United States and Europe might venture to the capital to observe the federal government in any case, but the world that Dolley created encouraged them to stay and partake. With no party machines in place, the only links in the system existed among leading families of various regions. As the capital city became a "resort" of fashion and power, these families came to visit. Dolley brought them into the executive mansion, putting them in contact with her husband and with one another. But no matter the event, the guest list, or the political issues at stake, Dolley was always the center of attraction.

ELEVEN

Family Matters

*I*n June 1810, as the government was deciding whether to go to war with Great Britain, France, or both, Dolley sat at her desk in the White House to write a short but urgent note. A mix of discretion and expediency, the letter was vague—she did not name the recipient nor specify the situation—but its tone was insistent and determined.

Dolley began with a disclaimer—typical of political women: "I am about to take a liberty my good friend, which *must remain a secret*"—then invited this person to come to Washington "*immediately.*" After deliberating for two weeks "on the propriety of my doing this," Dolley had finally decided to summon him or her, especially upon "finding that you are not likely to be made acquainted with the *necessity* for *your aid.*" She closed: "[C]ome then, as soon as possible to my Husband who will not call, though he wishes for you every day."[1] It was unclear whether

James knew that Dolley was taking the step of calling for this person; he may even have used her letter as a cover for his own request. What were the other systems, that in this case failed, which would "acquaint" someone with James's political need? The letter remains unquestionably important, forever obscure.

During the Madisons' first term, Dolley used her correspondence as she used her social events, to aid her husband politically. She wrote to family and friends, seeking and giving information, shoring up support, granting political favors, all to help James in two important arenas: his relations with his cabinet and Congress, and the decision to go to war with the European powers. As at a White House drawing room, the "space" offered by Dolley's letters granted participants a freedom unavailable in more official settings, while allowing Dolley and James to perform more emotional and psychological political tasks than the official sphere of government business would permit.

Unfortunately for the Madisons, 1810 had seen numerous catastrophes that could qualify for "the necessity for [your] aid." The year had not started off well. At the New Year's Day levée, a merchant from nearby Alexandria remarked that the president "appears to be bending under the weight of cares in office," and a Federalist representative from Massachusetts, Ezekiel Whitman, amused himself by counting the number of "wrinkles in little Jemmy's face," deciding that he sported far more that winter than the previous summer.

Whitman also unearthed a luscious piece of gossip that offered a glimpse of James's contentious cabinet. "It is said," the congressman related with some glee, "that Secretary [of State Robert] Smith's wife declares that it is infamous that we should have a French schoolmaster for our Secretary of the Treasury [Albert Gallatin]." No doubt stung, since Albert had been James's first choice for secretary of state, "Mrs. Secretary of the Treasury in her turn says that it is a vile shame that we should have a pettifogging lawyer for Secretary of State." Using wives as stand-ins for their husbands, Whitman concluded from such a public display by ladies that James's Republican enemies "control[led] the nation."

James and his Congress began the new year as they had left the old, wrestling over various alternatives to total embargo and all the concomitant foreign policy issues. But he had enough to do trying to control his own government. In February, the administration was embarrassed before the nation when a scathing newspaper attack on Secretary of Treasury Gallatin was discovered to have been ghostwritten by an operative of Secretary of State Smith.[2]

As always, Dolley remained her husband's unwavering supporter while the first term seemed to spiral downhill toward a declaration of war. "Knowing the turbulence & miseries of a publick life" in those years before the war "convinced" Dolley of the value of "independence & peace." Even as she bravely carried on in the face of that public "turbulence," Dolley was also enmeshed with various issues involving her family, the source of her greatest joy as well as her deepest despair.[3]

Next to James, Dolley's sisters remained her closest emotional connections. Relationships with her female relatives and with women friends had always been paramount. Her tendency to bond with women may be traced to her relationship with her mother, as well as to the fact that in the world of the nineteenth century, relations between men and women were so unequally structured that a woman's greatest chance for a peer relationship, or one that would allow her to dominate, was with another woman.

Little sister Anna still reigned supreme in Dolley's heart. Happily for Dolley, Anna Payne Cutts and her growing brood joined her in the White House for most winters. Anna was proving a prodigious mother, who would give birth to and raise five sons and two daughters during the Madisons' time in Washington City. Not surprisingly, Dolley was a loving aunt, but though she waxed enthusiastic over each new addition, she seemed to take particular delight in the girls. In July 1811, she wrote to the new mother: "Joy Joy! to you my beloved brother & to you Oh my dearest Anna—but are you sure it is a girl? Now do not hum [tease] me, because you know I have set my heart on haveing a girl, & I tell you plump, that I shall be sick if, in your haste to write, you have mistaken."

Playfully, Dolley warned the new arrival's big brothers, James Madison, Thomas, Richard, and Walter Coles: "Yes Mad Tom Dick & Wat—sweet as you are, stand aside, that I may kiss & squeeze the cherub—Dolley—Lucy—Ann—Mary—Julia, or what ever else she may be named, I claim her as my pet." And not only as "my pet." Indeed, Dolley claimed the little girl (who turned out to be Dolley Payne Madison Cutts) as "my darling daughter." She even made a suggestion that seems a little extreme, even in a culture of marrying cousins: "I wish Payne could marry her at once to put it out of doubt, her being my own."[4]

With nieces and nephews alike, Dolley happily and easily entered into the world of child's fancy. She teased her little nephew, bidding Anna to "tell my sweet boy that I don't like the story he tells on me & that I'l give him another to lern—Aunt D. will come & take me to see the Seals dance on the rocks & then cary me, her little son, to her home to go a-guning with cousin Payne."[5]

As always, to the world, Dolley presented a picture of health and vitality; following the pattern in Philadelphia, to Anna she fretted freely about "a pain in my face for several days," and on other occasions, "sore ears & deafness—the deafness continues, & distresses me beyond any thing that ever ail'd me." Dolley hoped the loss of hearing was a temporary condition, brought on by cold, and that "I may throw it of[f]."[6]

Dolley also confessed to "low spirits" and to her worries, Anna's own health chief among them. Anna's steady childbearing took its toll. She suffered a variety of ailments related to childbirth and recovery from it, including, probably, what would today be termed postpartum depression. Dolley worried about her baby sister's "poor breast," which had developed an abscess. She reassured Anna that "the Milk & bread [applied as a poultice] I am told, will cure, of itself—especially after lanceing." A report from Anna about her health "cause's me more greaf than I can speak—your constant indisposition your low spirits—every thing that disturbs you never fails to vibrate thro all my heart." Always ready to mother Anna, Dolley had lots of good advice: "I wish & seriously advise the simple weak french brandy & Water for your Eyes and ears—don't take phisick, unless but a little cream of tarter, as a drink, & Magnesia now & then."[7]

Dolley put a good deal of faith in the power of her love, feeling sure that she could heal her darling with her own brand of physic. "Try to get ready & come to me—I think you would soon be well if you once set of[f] on your journey to your sister who longs to fold you to her heart & to restore your system to its naturel strength by her cares." Writing to Anna brought out the Quaker locutions of their shared childhood: "[T]is weakness that continues thy sad complaint so long."[8]

The only thing that made Dolley happier than the winters that Anna and her family spent at the White House was the period when middle sister Lucy lived there as well. When George Steptoe Washington died in 1808, and Lucy found herself a young widow, she and her three young sons joined the Madison clan in Washington. Like many a middle sister, Lucy used her personality to forge her own place in the family, distinguishing herself from older, responsible Dolley and from Anna, now the baby of the three girls. In 1809, Lucy was "still young, very pretty, animated, full of repartee and impulse forming a contrast in figure as well as dignity" to Dolley. When James came trudging from his office into midday dinner "greatly fatigued and exhausted with the grave affairs of state at that harassing period," Lucy amused him; he declared the laughter she elicited "as refreshing as a long walk."[9]

A rich and pretty widow with impeccable political connections, Lucy found herself besieged with beaux, and she joked about her suitors with her sisters. When stranded in Virginia, declaring that "I am almost kill'd here with *ennui*," Lucy could still try to make Dolley laugh with her pert observations: "Edward Coles promised to write and tell me all the news of Philada, but I expect he is like a goslin let loose out of a pen, and so wonder struck at all he see's that he thinks of nothing."

If Dolley always had to exercise tact and forbearance, Lucy could act the enfant terrible. She sympathized with her sister about an old friend, Anthony Morris, and his daughter, Phoebe, who were outstaying their welcome: "I wish indeed you cou'd be reliev'd of their *agreeable* company—for it must have arriv'd to a trying point." She also relished a "scene" between Edward and young Phoebe Morris: "I expected cousin Edward & herself wou'd scarcely part without blows—they were very near it when I left them." While her sister had to be discreet about an eccentric neighbor, Lucy could give full vent to the extent of her sisterly loyalty: "I feel very much provoked at that old hag Mrs. Duval—yet I scarcely think her worth your notice every body knows her disposition to venom and no body loves or respects her—tho if I had her head here I'd box her ears."[10]

Lucy cultivated the image of flibbertigibbet: "I am a bit of a fool, always was, and I fear always will be—or rather shall be." She also played the clown, indulging in breezy, slightly racy, even slangy language—she shopped for "tasty" glass and "a little snuff to comfort us"—perhaps as a way to compete with young Anna. After joking that Anna could only try to fill the void for Dolley after her own departure, Lucy commented wistfully: "Dont think me selfish dear sister—you know I always was jealous of you because I wish to be first in your affections."[11]

Much as she might affect a certain flightiness, when it came to the serious business of marriage, Lucy shared her sister's considered judgment. Her youthful elopement had allied her with the preeminent American family. In 1812, she married again, and again well, to Judge Thomas Todd of Kentucky. Contemporaries described him as a dark, good-looking man with a "kind heart and popular manners." Dolley regarded him as "a Man of the most estimable character, best principles, & high talents," and commented approvingly to Anna, "I told you how amiable & respectable Judge Todd is—how wise Lucy was to chuse him in preferance to the gay flirts who coarted her."[12]

Lucy's three sons now had a father; Lucy gained five older children and a beautiful Frankfort home in "fine society." The best part of the marriage, from Dolley's point of view, was that, as a Supreme Court justice, Todd had to come to Washington for at least two months a year, and he promised to bring Lucy. This almost made up for having a sister living so far away, a prospect that Lucy dreaded as much as Dolley. Her big sister reported: "Lucy is in deep distress & you may suppose that my greaf is not slight."[13] Lucy's wedding was the first in the White House. It was a modest affair; still, belying her reputation as the most feminine of women, Dolley did not indulge in discussions of the details.

Marriage did not change the impetuous Lucy. When they lived all together in the White House, James often teased his sister-in-law by kissing Dolley in front of her. Cheeky as ever, newlywed Lucy got her revenge with a message sent through Dolley: "Tell him I hope he

Misses me at Meals . . . and when he Kisses you—he was always so fearful of making my *mouth water—tell him I get kisses now that wou'd make his mouth run over.*"[14]

⁂

A good deal of the sisters' concern centered on their brother, John, who was precious to them—doubly so, because he was truly the baby of the family and also the last of their brothers. The fates of the men in his family did not bode well for the sole surviving male Payne. His father had died bankrupt and emotionally unstable, and his older brothers died untimely deaths after dissolute youths.[15]

John had been in North Africa since 1806, serving as a secretary to the American representative in Tripoli, George Davis. He wrote only sporadically; by 1809, it had been at least two years since Dolley had heard from him. When he finally made contact, Dolley wrote back that she "griev[ed] more than I can express," having "written you vols.," apparently to no avail. (Dolley chose to believe that John never got her many letters.) She now had bad news, of "the many & sad changes in your family. you are yet to weep over." Dolley wrote of the death of their mother, of his closest sibling, Mary, and of Lucy's husband. But, she assured him, the remainder of their family were together, along with Anna's "three fine boys" at the president's house, "where you know we now reside, . . . & where I wish you my Dear Brother was also a resident." Then, with the awkward pause almost palpable, Dolley reconsidered his situation, adding, "Mr M. who you *must know,* is President of the U.S."

Dolley could not assume that John knew that James was president, no matter that he was nominally a government official. For all her present and future optimism that John would reform, on some level she understood how dissipated her brother had become. She begged him to come home, and, no matter what he had done, not to let shame "stay you one moment from my arms & heart, that are open to receive you." In addition to the assurances of her love, Dolley added that their mother had left everything to him, "a respectable independence if properly managed," which Dolley offered to arrange in his absence.[16]

Astonishingly, Dolley decided that more responsibility would bring

John back into line. She assured him that if George Davis decided to leave Tripoli, he had a good chance to be promoted to consul. If it turned out that another candidate got the job, John would have "the choice of remaining or not" in his present post. In February 1811, when James appointed her friends Joel and Ruth Barlow to the ministry to France, Dolley obtained the much coveted post as Barlow's secretary for John, though author, translator, and diplomat David Bailie Warden wanted it, as did Washington Irving, among others. Since John was already abroad, it made sense for him to meet the Barlows in Paris, but it transpired that, because of his debts, John risked arrest if he showed his face in that city. The new plan was that John would come home first, and the whole party would leave together as soon as possible for France, presumably with John's debts settled. But John did not come home. Partly on his account, partly because of political concerns, the Barlows waited, although the international situation demanded an American presence in Paris as soon as possible. Finally, almost four months after John had been informed of the position, the Barlows sailed for Paris. When John finally arrived in America, in what became a familiar pattern, he took a detour on his way home, and once again dropped out of contact with his family.[17]

When John eventually surfaced in New York in June 1811, no one could have noted it as charmingly as cousin Edward, who acknowledged his arrival without acknowledging the difficulty. "I congratulate you on the safe arrival of your Brother John. The pleasure of seeing him must have been much enhanced from its having been unexpected." Sadly, John was forced to sell everything he owned to pay his debts. With an unemployed and insolvent brother on her hands, Dolley informed Anna with dismay that "he has returnd in greater difficulties than he went, being oblidged as he thought to borrow mony." Dolley even had to give him an extra $150. "[A]lass!" she confided to Anna, "I wish often that he had been never in Tripola with Davis." Dolley wondered what had gone wrong with John. In looking over the past, "I know not what to wish . . . more than that he had allways been prudent & wise. he is now entirely dependent even if he sells his lands to advantage." Dolley abruptly pulled back: "But let me stop—you are at a distance & so is Lucy." If they had been together, the sisters would have understood her outburst and comforted her. Her feelings seemed too dangerous to put on paper.[18]

Lucy mourned as well, casting John's situation as an unlucky family circumstance, rather than the result of an individual's bad choices: "How peculiarly unfortunate we have been." She could not see how any of the sisters could help him without ruining herself financially.[19] Still, the three sisters hoped that "by kindness and attention he may be brought to reason yet," and committed themselves to reforming their little brother. Dolley, in particular, never gave up hope. At least initially, the Payne women wisely decided to keep him near his family and far from perfidious influences. However, the logistics were complicated: John was shuttling back and forth among Dolley at Washington City and Montpelier, Anna in Maine, Boston, and Washington City, and Lucy, who still kept a residence, Harewood, in Virginia, but after her marriage lived mostly in Kentucky. To everyone's dismay, John made a habit of disappearing while en route from sister to sister, just as he had done on his return voyage from Tripoli. Days and weeks went by when no one knew where he was.[20]

In one letter to Anna from Montpelier, Dolley admitted that as John had not appeared, "you may guess at my anxiety." She returned to the usual topics, listing visitors and describing all the bustle attendant on returning home, but could not let go of her family worries: "I am miserable for John, & anxious for you." Though she had just arrived in Virginia, all Dolley could think of was that "we shall be in W[ashington] early in Octor. Pray get well & come to me."[21]

As part of the rehabilitation process, Lucy took John with her when she and her new husband went home to Kentucky. On the road, Lucy saw aspects of the charming, good-hearted boy they had once known. She pledged to her sisters: "I will do all in my power towards our poor dear brothers reformation and am not without hope that he may return to you an alter'd Man—I cannot believe that with his heart and understanding he will prove incorrigible."[22]

While John was in Washington, Dolley continued the effort. She tried to get him a military commission and to talk some sense into him—"he has *taken up* a good deal by my persuasion. I have dressed him & forced him to change bad for good society." But to no avail. At times, Dolley exhibited a breathtaking naïveté. During one of his "disappearing" acts, she asserted to Anna: "I have not heared from Jno, but have no doubt of his being at Hairwood & doing well with *them*." Yet she was also grimly aware of the realities of the situation. After bailing out her brother yet again, she dryly remarked: "It is not worth while to tell you the particulars of his *last* frolick, or the sum he spent on it. I *re-fixed* him, *with my all even* my *credit*." Dolley blamed other people for John's failings, and after this particular "frolick," she sent him away "*from this den of Theaves*."[23] However, Dolley had learned her lesson: she sent an escort to assure a safe and timely arrival.

❧

Like links in a chain, Dolley's family circle overlapped and connected with the family circles of slave families in Washington and at Montpelier. With respect to the issue of slavery, Dolley was probably one with James, as she was in most things. Like other planters with a conscience, James abhorred the institution, and, like Thomas Jefferson and others, he regretted that it had ever come to the colonies; but, given that enforced, lifelong, hereditary servitude lay at the base of the regional economy, he could not see how he or the South could survive without it. Even if the South could do without slaves, James could not conceive of a society with blacks on the same level as white Americans. In a characteristic move, he soothed his misgivings with an abstract formulation. He convinced himself that the experience of slavery had improved since the Revolution. He imagined that the "sensibilities" to natural human rights aroused by revolutionary rhetoric had mitigated masters' treatment of slaves. In addition, he figured, subsequent economic events, such as the 1808 abolition of the overseas slave trade, must have made masters value slaves more highly, treating them better if only out of their own self-interest.[24] This formulation was pure James: a logical theory that did not take into account actual human motivation and behavior. His guilt and sense of helplessness increasingly led him to grasp at unlikely straws in order to resolve the dilemma.

From the evidence of later years, James apparently treated slaves comparatively well at Montpelier and their day-to-day life was not as violent or harsh as it was in many other settings. Enslaved workers had Sundays off, a customary, though by no means universal, concession. One visitor found that Montpelier slaves possessed "more independence of manner . . . when conversing with their master" than he had expected. When one slave complained to James of illness, he did so with "great confidence of having a favorable hearing," and indeed, James sent him to the house for medicine.[25]

James's long-time valet, Paul Jennings, famous for writing his *Reminiscences* and for proclaiming James "one of the best men that ever lived," testified that the lack of "passion" that characterized James's political life translated favorably into his role as a master. In some ways, Jennings's assessment of James's character carries even more weight than similar evaluations by white colleagues and contemporaries. It is one thing to control one's temper in front of peers, but for many years, Paul had been a subordinate, and, as a valet, an intimate one. But he had never seen James strike a slave or allow an overseer to physically punish one. When an enslaved worker needed "correction," according to Paul, James would "admonish them privately, and never mortify them by doing it before others."[26] Nor is his testimony tainted by his enslaved status, because it was written long after he had gained his freedom and became a friend to the Madison family.

To bear to live under such a system while reaping its benefits, white masters and mistresses adopted all kinds of defense mechanisms. Thomas Jefferson, for instance, solved the problem in his own compartmentalizing way, by putting the working slaves literally out of sight.[27] One conceit adopted by the planter class was to consider all the plantation inhabitants as "my family white and black," thus transforming slavery into a domestic institution rather than the legally sanctioned system of enforced labor that it was. Like all proper families, these household amalgamations were to be ruled over by a benevolent patriarch. James no doubt strove to fulfill that role; his concern for the health of his slaves and even his approach to "correction" suggest a model of paternal care. He made his best deal with the devil and tried to put his abstract despair about slavery to some practical use, easing the conditions of the slaves' lives without fundamentally challenging or changing them.

Dolley was not unaware of James's discomfort, or of the growing abolition movement among a newer generation of Americans who had come of age with the ideals of the Revolution. She certainly could not ignore the issue, not with her cousin Edward Coles in the household. Edward did not keep his abhorrence of the institution to himself but challenged Virginia slaveholders, including Thomas Jefferson, on the issue. She may have even overheard him sarcastically "congratulating" James on being "the Chief of our great Republic," a nation "boastful" of the rights of men but marred by the "revolting sight" of enslaved people in the streets.[28]

Without minimizing the legal and economic realities, slavery *was* a domestic institution, though not in the way that its apologists meant. At Montpelier, as everywhere in the South, slavery as a system and the enslaved workers as individuals made up not merely an important part of the plantation's everyday existence but its lifeblood.

From Montpelier and Washington City, Dolley's letters passed on and received news of family members separated by slavery, reflecting the interweaving of "families, black and white." In 1814, her ne'er-do-well brother married Clary Wilcox and settled in Louisa County, Virginia. Before launching into the news of "ourselves," the white Madison family, she acknowledged that "Paul is much oblig[ed] . . . by news from his wife & children." She also asked John to relay the information to Sarah's husband that Sarah's health was better, adding "*tell him* & [she] waits to hear from him." Sometimes the messages Dolley passed between her enslaved people sound uncannily like her letters to her own family, which mixed professions of devotion with practical care. "Tell Ralph his mother sends her love to him & says shel bring him something." Dolley's "black family" echoed her white one in less attractive ways as well. She probably did not appreciate the irony of adding in her letter to her own troublesome brother that "Sam is well & sober so his wife may also be regaled by the *news*."[29]

Not that Dolley regarded the people enslaved to her husband as truly members of her family; rather, she exhibited that curious mixture of familiarity and distance common to people of her culture. Madison slaves bore Madison family names—for instance, "Jamey," "Jem," and "Dolley" (indeed, Jem and Dolley had a child together). The names of Sukey, Susan Ellen, and many other men and women cropped up casually in Dolley's letters, interspersed with news of friends and family, sometimes with concern—"my most efficient House servant Sucky lies very ill with bilious fever." At other times, Dolley expressed exasperation with "her people," and like others of the slaveholding class, exhibited a willful blindness to the logical outcomes of enforced servitude. She complained: "Sucky has made so many depridations on every thing, in every part of the house that, I sent her to black Meadow last week but find it terribly inconvenient to do without her . . . so I must let her steal from me, to keep from labour myself."[30]

Like other men and women of her class, Dolley seemed unable to attribute understandable human motivations or drives to people of color. This lack is all the more remarkable given her usual capacity for empathy. Discerning what others wanted and expected was a skill inculcated in females of the time, and in her political dealings with white people, Dolley had parlayed that skill into an art form. To serve the family's political goals, she had put her understanding of human motivation to good use. But Dolley could not comprehend why Sukey would steal, seeing the situation only in terms of the hardship it visited upon her. On occasion, Dolley acknowledged emotions in enslaved people but only for the purpose of manipulation, to ensure good and dependable service. She advised Anna to "attach" her "Woman" to herself and her children "now that she is your own."[31]

The Madisons sold slaves, though generally they did so only in extremity. When it came to buying and selling human beings, Dolley could talk in the cold language of commerce—"Mr. Madison is willing to take David for 400 dolrs. to be paid at the end of one year from the time of his comeing into service with lawful interest." True, Dolley did not know David, but it is unlikely that the mercantile language would differ even if she were selling an old friend rather than buying someone unknown to her. The Madisons, in direct contrast to some of their neighbors, also freed slaves on occasion. In addition to prices and terms, this transaction also specified that David would receive his freedom after five years.[32]

Celebrated as she was for her good heart and her warm personality, Dolley seems to have been quite cold on this particular subject. This affect, along with Dolley's refusal or inability to understand why her slaves might steal or otherwise resist, might well have stemmed from the need to distance herself from the reality of the situation and to deny her participation in it.

⁂

For many of her relatives, Dolley was the heart of their circle of kin, but in a family for which politics was the family business, Dolley and James together formed an important nucleus. For the Madisons—along with the Paynes, Coleses, Todds, Symeses, Allens, Jacksons, Skipwiths, and Winstons on Dolley's side and the Taylors, Willises, Conways, and Throckmortons on James's side—the Madison presidency was the focal point around which their lives revolved.

Writing to her relations was the way that Dolley could keep close. In her family letters, politics wove through all of everyday life, the trials and tribulations as well as the trivia. Dolley's letters did not contain long political discussions of the kind indulged in by John Adams and Thomas Jefferson. In their late-in-life correspondence, they expounded on political "topics," well aware that they were positioning themselves in the historical pantheon. In contrast, with bits of politics and pertinent information larded among family news, gossip about love affairs, travel schedules, and shopping lists, Dolley's letters also used a language of emotion and family to make political requests or express opinions.[33]

Dolley struggled with discretion in her correspondence, especially with Anna and her closest relatives. Generally, in his private writings, James avoided long political discussions and self-classifications as well. In this, as in other arenas, Dolley was his pupil, and for the most part she succeeded. Interestingly, she found it easier to exhibit discretion when she appeared as the public Dolley. She wanted to be more authentic and free with her familial correspondents, so it was an effort to juggle the need for obliqueness with her more open, free-and-easy style.

She knew all too well how even personal letters could become public property. As her political career progressed, Dolley added reassurances: "No eye but your sisters shall go over our family letters," and "No one shall lay Eyes on your letters."[34] She expected reciprocity; given the climate, it was reasonable caution, not political paranoia, that led Dolley to end letters filled with family news and political information with instructions such as "I enclose Lucy's last and Mrs. Bomford's you may burn L-s and return the latter."[35]

And Dolley had reason to be worried. In 1812, Joshua Gilpin, a Philadelphia merchant who had known Dolley since their Philadelphia days, was now living in England. He wrote to Dolley that, in the course of an arrest, several of her letters had been seized by the mayor of Liverpool. The mayor offered to release them upon Gilpin's identification. Anthony Morris, providentially on the scene, took charge of his old friend's correspondence.

Dolley wrote like a busy person. At times, her elegant Italianate hand broke into a scrawl, especially when she wrote quickly to someone close to her. She deprecated her abilities, aware that when it came to "all that is good & smart in letterwriting," she "fe[lt] a deficiency when I attempt the flourishing stile." The queen of style in her public life, Dolley eschewed that effort when it came to finishing a letter in order to catch the post. She skipped from topic to topic, often closing with crammed lists of news and good wishes, as though she worried that she might forget something. Her tendency to revert to subjects that preoccupied her intensified during the White House years, so that in between news and practicalities, she returned twice or even three times in a single letter to an issue that worried her—the bad behavior of her husband's enemies, or the misfortunes of her brother John.[36] At times, her letters overflowed with emotions, revealing love, worry, joy, anger, and grief. And woven subtly through them all was politics.

As with emotional issues, Dolley expressed her political opinions most freely to Anna, revealing a Dolley quite at odds with the public persona. To the world, Dolley displayed a placid serenity, far above politics; with Anna, she expressed anger and contempt. But Anna and Lucy were not the only family members with whom Dolley shared political news. She swapped information and intelligence with her brothers-in-law, both congressmen. Death did not sever family bonds; indeed, shared grief cemented them. Even after his wife's death, John G. Jackson still called Dolley, Mary's sister, his closest confidante "in all things."[37] Imitating the heroes of epistolary novels, he even had a nickname for her—"Dorah."[38]

To his sister-in-law, John G. Jackson poured out his heart. He had never fully recovered from the death of his wife and daughters, and continued to write in what Dolley called "his old stile of melancholy." When his remaining daughter had any episode of illness, it drove him to distraction. "Great God!" he wailed to Dolley in one letter before James's election in 1808. "When shall sickness & death cease to terrify & distract me?" But in this same letter, he also reported on the "political warmth" in his Virginia district, as well as quarrels over the embargo. He even had enough emotional reserve to wax vehement on James's behalf, "depend on it those little great men are filled with venom & Gall."[39]

Their close relationship continued after Jackson remarried, to Mary Sophia Meigs. Not only did Mary Meigs share the same first name as Dolley's sister, she was, as John reported to his "Dorah," "about the size of our dear Mary, [and] much such a person." Dolley welcomed her as the "sister of my adoption" and continued to confide in her brother-in-law, feeling close enough to him to give full vent to political feelings unfit for public observation. She commented with bitter sarcasm on the attempts of Federalist newspapers to cause trouble in the Madison cabinet and with Congress: "Duane & & [newspaper editors] take a *few liberties* with M on the subject tho they do not deny *his right* to make a Secry to *suit him* & the Office." Again, Dolley curbed herself, hinting darkly: "I could tell you many curious things my brother, but as *people say I have my oppinions && I must not trust my pen*."[40]

In October 1809, Jackson had laughed off rumors that had reached Dolley's ears: "Why, my dear Sister, do you distress yourself on my account & allow alarms of danger & of Duels to reach you." Dolley had reason to pay attention to rumors, however. The previous June, the North Carolina Federalist Joseph Pearson had fiercely assailed James and Thomas Jefferson in House debate. Jackson had risen in Congress to defend them as vociferously. All through the summer, the men had been sniping at each other. On December 4, a few months after her brother-in-law teased Dolley for believing "talk," the loyal and volatile Jackson dueled with Pearson. Neither died, but John suffered a gunshot injury serious enough to cause him to take a leave of absence from the House.

Anna's husband, the Maine congressman Richard Cutts, provided a more stable source of support. Dolley called on him for political favors and reciprocated with political information. Even as he and Anna honeymooned, Dolley urged them to find out what the Philadelphia gentry thought about the issues of the day, namely the French, "Bonopartee & so forth."[41] Twice, in 1811 and 1812, when James thought that he might need a vote for war, Dolley summoned Cutts to Washington. Safely ensconced in Federalist New England (he was conveniently nursing a shoulder hurt in a carriage accident), Richard may not have wanted a vote for war on his record. His own shipping interests added to his reluctance. Dolley insisted, not hesitating to employ a veiled threat: "You may rely upon it, if Mr. Cutts does not come it will be a disadvantage to him as well as to his party—some of them have reproached him already, but he will be here, we hope, just in time—not a moment too soon, it is supposed, to give his vote for War."[42] Like a dutiful brother, he did—in a way. Though Cutts arrived too late for the first round of voting in 1812, he arrived in time to vote for a postponed war.

James Taylor, a distant cousin of James Madison and a minor government official in Kentucky, became one of Dolley's closest correspondents, with whom she shared information about "the state of our Relations in Europe . . . [and] *some very wicked, & silly doings at home.*" To cousin James, Dolley reported on the return of the *Hornet*, a brig that carried information back and forth across the Atlantic. In 1810, it brought "us nothing contradictory of the *affectinate* intentions of Napolian."[43]

Dolley continued: "I know, however, by the intense study, of Mr M & his constant devotion to the Cabinet, that affairs, are troublesome & difficult." She explained: "You see the English are stuborn yet, but we anticipate their yealding before long—in short, the Proclamation [of non-intercourse with Great Britain] gives you the state of things *now*." Again, Dolley buried her hints, in this case a request for information, in a postscript. "When any thing interesting occurs I will write you again in the mean time, let us hear from you."[44]

Much of the discussion in Dolley's correspondence concerned foreign affairs: the declaration (or not) of war, and the comings and goings of various ships, important because they carried information. The preoccupation with shipping reflected the many prewar experiments James made, as secretary of state and then as president, with all combinations of embargo and boycott.

Of course, the various nations responded in kind. Degrees of loss existed as well. As unprofitable as it was to have a ship sitting idle in a home harbor, worse still was to have one unable to come in, forced to sit outside the harbor or return home with a spoiled cargo. Fortunes rose and fell with each new development in the various embargos, nonintercourse acts, and European decrees in the schoolyard bullying that characterized U.S. foreign relations.

The knowledge of when a new policy could result in any of the above remained a most valuable commodity. No laws prohibited passing on such intelligence; when it passed between women, especially within families, the transmission of information was just another way to demonstrate care. Dolley's nudges in a letter she would send to Anna in 1812—"Where is Mr Cs vessells? Why dont he get them in? What can be done for him?"—reflected more than simple older-sister bossiness, even as they appeared seemingly at random in a letter with news about misbehaving Federalists and "the War business." What Dolley meant became clear in her next letter, though typically, she buried these tidbits among the other family matters: "I wrote you that the Embargo was to take place, but I fear they intercept my letters." In the next sentence: "did you get my Childs Necklace and earings?"[45] For all of its "aside" quality, information about the embargo was important to Anna, as Richard Cutts had a great deal of money invested in shipping. In the letter that followed, Dolley seemed aware that she might be crossing some kind of line: "[I wrote you] that the Embargo would ta[ke place]

3 or 4 days before it did, & I had a bet[ter right] to do so than the Fedl. Member."[46]

Probably because of the urgency of the matter, on this occasion Dolley was fairly direct with her sister. Most of the time, she imparted such inside information within other contexts, as when discussing the logistics of shopping. Cousin James Taylor, for instance, learned that "the Non-intercourse law will prevent" his shipment of china from coming in, "unless it was shipped before the 2nd of Feby."[47]

Surely Dolley would not have passed on certain information without James's sanction. And clearly, he sometimes used the cover of her correspondence to convey his own wishes. At some points, the president even sent along "some papers" with his wife's letters.[48] In this era, the presence of women in political transactions always signaled something hidden, and, by using Dolley's "personal letters" to sidestep official channels or to reward a political supporter, James acted within a well-established tradition.

Like social events, letters formed part of the unofficial sphere. Much like the socializing at a drawing room party, the conventions of letter writing allowed a more flexible, more freewheeling, and yet more hidden place to politick. The Madisons and their circle sufficiently disguised their aims under the womanly veil of feminine activities and topics. Only rarely did that veil slip.

❧

In 1809, Dolley's nephew from her first marriage, Samuel Todd, asked her for help in obtaining a post. Samuel was the son of James Todd, who had played fast and loose with Dolley's inheritance from John Todd. Perhaps that was an intimation of things to come. In 1805, James Todd, who was a banker, fled Philadelphia after embezzling $3,000 in cash and $1,500 in credit, leaving his family ostracized and in dire financial straits. Young Samuel Todd, then, needed a job to rescue his family both financially and socially.

Dolley's quarrel was with James Todd only; in a typical show of family loyalty, she maintained a close relationship with his wife, Alice Poultney Todd. Dolley responded to Samuel Todd's request within days, reassuring him "that nothing would gratify me more than to be of use in promoteing your wishes & your good." But of course Samuel's individual good played only one part in Dolley's motivation; she also cited her love for his mother and family. Whatever his professional qualifications for a post, Samuel possessed the chief one for Dolley: "As I understand you have been an excellent son I hope it will still be your good fortune to smooth the way of your Parent & dear sister's." She happily informed him that James was "fully disposed to be your friend."

Sentimental disclaimers out of the way, Dolley discussed details. Samuel wanted to go to sea, but Dolley cautioned that few positions were available. Instead, she suggested a clerkship in one of the departments. "Write me accordingly," she instructed, "& I will apply to the Heads of the Depts. to obtain one for you."[49]

Samuel agreed to this plan, but heard nothing from his aunt for weeks. Dolley anxiously wrote to Samuel to allay his fears. None of the secretaries whom she planned to approach had arrived in town. "I trust you will be patient, under this delay & rely on my assurance of a sincear & affectinate interest, which, shall not be inactive." Again, Dolley concerned herself with professional practicalities: she wanted a clerkship with a salary of seven or eight hundred dollars a year for Samuel. Even if this did not suit him, he should take it, Dolley advised, since being in Washington would increase his chances for obtaining a better job. Perhaps used to the disastrous decisions made by her other male kin, Dolley also felt it necessary to add: "You will not resign your situation in the Bank until the other is secure." In the next breath, Dolley dropped the imperative tone, ending, "With best love to your Mother & sisters."[50]

By May, additional possibilities had emerged, but still nothing definite. Dolley had obtained "positive promises" from the secretary of state and, though nothing had happened yet, she remained optimistic, although "I believe you cannot have felt more anxiety than I have on this subject." Finally, in November 1809, Paul Hamilton, the secretary of the navy, wrote to Samuel Todd that the job of accountant in the Navy Department was his. This was good news, indeed, better than even Dolley anticipated. The salary, according to Paul Hamilton, was $1,300. And, Hamilton assured young Samuel, he had obtained the office at the behest "of your friends Mrs. Madison and Mr. Cutts."[51]

Over the course of her Washington career, Dolley had assembled a network of influence. Even as the wife of the secretary of state, she had received requests for jobs. As part of a network of local and official women that included all of her friends—Margaret Bayard Smith, Marcia Burnes Van Ness, Catharine Akerly Mitchill, Hannah Nicholson Gallatin, and Anna Maria Brodeau Thornton, among others—she helped sponsor good works, dispense charity, open schools, and engage in what can only be called influence peddling.

Petticoat politicking and patronage may have been anathema to pure republicans, but Dolley operated freely in her quest for a job for her relative, contacting all the heads of the department and even Secretary of State Robert Smith. No one reacted with horror or accusation; Paul Hamilton's tone seems remarkably matter-of-fact. For all her language of love, too, Dolley played more than a passive role. While engaging others on her behalf, she did the actual soliciting herself. Not only did she know the details of salary and personnel in the secretary of state's office, she was obviously in the loop in an immediate way. When Samuel Todd did not answer Paul Hamilton's letter quickly enough, Dolley pressed: "I hope you will attend to [Hamilton's letter], as I am truly anxious that you should fulfill my promises."[52]

Everyone acknowledged Dolley's power of appointment. Washington Irving made his way to Dolley's drawing room, as he told Catharine Mitchill, almost immediately upon his arrival in the city in January 1811. Irving's eagerness had nothing to do with sociability. He had an object—he had come to the capital in order to obtain the job of secretary to the American minister to France. As he fancifully depicted the situation, he was "a vagabond knight-errant trust[ing] to Providence for success." But Irving did not put his trust entirely in Providence; instead, he immediately began working for the appointment. After making his debut at Dolley's drawing room, he embarked on an extensive round of socializing, reporting with confident glee that he had every hope of success, "especially as Mrs. Madison is a sworn friend of mine, and indeed all the ladies of the household and myself are great cronies."[53]

Irving did not succeed in his quest—this was the job Dolley intended for her brother John—but he had gone to the right address. In a political culture that eschewed court practices, patronage—the practice of awarding jobs, money, land, titles, or other goods and honors to political supporters and friends—stood as a hallmark of courts. It also stood, of course, contrary to republican theory, which rejected personal, preferential treatment in favor of a depersonalized approach.[54]

In the years before the "Revolution of 1800," Thomas Jefferson, James Madison, and other "pure republicans" attacked the incumbent Federalist Party for any sign of this sinister, loathsome Old World practice. When Jefferson and his followers came to power, however, they realized, with some dismay, that rulers need patronage. Friends and supporters who worked for them, expending their personal political capital, expected some recompense. That seemed only fair. It also made sense for a leader to surround himself with people who supported him, with friends rather than enemies.

Presidents were not the only officials who wanted and needed the power to convey favor. The humblest backwoodsman sent to Congress by his hardscrabble constituents faced the same dilemma as his English counterpart dispatched to Parliament by gentry voters. Sent to the capital by his local connections, a man had two jobs—to maintain ties to his home region in order to ensure his return to high office, and to make his presence felt in the capital as a man of importance.[55]

Fortunately, a congressman could do well for his supporters and add to his own power base at the same time in several ways: by sponsoring legislation for a constituent, for instance, or working with a congressional committee around an issue of local interest. Patronage served this dual purpose as well. If one obtained a job for a constituent, one had done a favor to a whole family. In the process of lobbying his fellows and their families, a man could build his own set of contacts, creating networks of obligation with powerful people. Putting a supporter in place also had more long-term advantages, as one's protégé could easily become one's patron.

Patronage linked citizens and political families in other regions with the government in Washington. Apathy had emerged as one of the biggest challenges facing the administration and the capital; the people of the United States did not feel a strong connection to either.[56] Rewarding loyal followers from around the country could help secure the regime, building ties between federal and state powers, nurturing national loyalty in far-flung regions. More parochially, involving local gentry in the federal government fixed the capital's presence on the landscape. Patronage nurtured connection even between branches of government. The federal government needed to accommodate power and build a bureaucracy in order to become a democracy and a nation-state.

In spite of patronage's "dirty" connotations, no nation needed patronage's power to order and connect more than the young United States. In reality, few government jobs available for patronage existed. There were a handful of posts around the country—for customs officers, postmasters, judges, and all the personnel required to expand and rule new territories—as well as naval and military officerships. Jobs based in the capital, especially for the clerks and bureaucrats who ran the various departments, were the most desirable situations. Competition for such posts was fierce, with hundreds of official applications "overlooked and thrown aside" on the desks of the departments.[57]

Everyone knew that the greatest chance for a candidate lay in informal channels, in having "a friend at court," as they would say. As Jefferson had noted earlier, women had always been associated with patronage. This became even more true in early republican Washington City. In colonial America, men and women alike had dispensed patronage as part of their political work. But in the official sphere of the capital, men had to exercise more discretion. As with other issues where power needed covering, women stepped into the breach. Women as the purveyors of patronage became part of business as usual in Washington City. By constructing a patronage machine, these women acted much as modern interest groups do. Instead of applying an outside "group pressure," however, they worked from within the political culture. They approached government officials to fill their requests, and their successes and failures became part of the public conversation.

For ideological reasons, patronage remained a very touchy subject;

female involvement made it doubly dangerous to discuss. It proved quite in the interest of these early players to leave a trail that one historian calls "epistolary, anecdotal, unquantifiable."[58] Patronage activities moved through the politics of the early republic like a powerful underground river, visible on the political landscape only when it intermittently came above ground. Otherwise the currents, the meanderings, and the eddies of power remained hidden. Like other activities in the unofficial sphere, patronage happened in the spaces in the formal framework of government.

Gossips might openly discuss patronage, but participants typically disguised the actual transaction, using a special code that allowed them to trespass on dangerous political ground. This language came straight from petitioning, another political activity associated with women since Queen Esther. The language of patronage stressed feminine attributes and activities, most notably passivity, piety, emotion, and, above all, family. It dissembled and obscured, disguising politics with concerns for hearth and home, family and love, health and personal happiness. Women did not employ such language cynically. If they were hiding from the official spotlight and cultural censure, they were also hiding from themselves. In justifying influence peddling on the grounds of family, or justice, they enabled themselves to understand their actions as properly womanly, and as being not only above politics but also within the realm of morality.

Dolley came to the White House with a record of patronage, and with a network of female colleagues already in place. Her position as the first among ladies only increased her visibility and, at least from others' perspective, her power. The drawing room, with its almost unlimited access, its exponential networking possibilities, and its cover of sociability, was the perfect place to find and dispense jobs. The terms "patronage" and "influence-peddling" evoke images of men wangling deals in smoke-filled back rooms. In early Washington City, the scene was more likely Dolley's crowded and colorful drawing room. Though a stranger to Dolley and to national politics, Washington Irving had come to the capital with certain assumptions about her power, and he restricted himself to the unofficial sphere in his pursuit of a position.

His behavior demonstrated his presumption that women were the way in and that cultivating Dolley as the most highly placed lady constituted his best strategy.

Critics also recognized the drawing rooms as an important employment agency. The Federalist congressman Josiah Quincy III spoke against a bill to increase the size of the army and navy, by lashing out at the extensive patronage this would engender. And where would these "little men who sigh after great offices," these "toads that live upon the vapor of the palace," "whose full-grown children are at suck at the money-distilling breasts of the Treasury," congregate? At Dolley's White House, of course, where they would "swallow great men's spittle at the levees."[59]

Officials groused about Dolley's patronage activities. In a letter home, Representative Abijah Bigelow, of Massachusetts, reported that some attributed the (failed) nomination of Alexander Wolcott for a Supreme Court justiceship "to Joel Barlow, others to the influence of Mrs. Madison, observing that Wolcott being a handsome & gallant man, she is pleased with him." Bigelow could not resist that dig, but the words of enemies often provide the best proof, as revealed by one newspaper's evaluation of James's military appointments: "There seems also, to be a little *family influence* creeping into the business of appointments. Mr. Cutts, who married one of Mrs. Madison's sisters, holds the lucrative office of Supt. Gen. Of Military Supplies."[60]

Like modern lobbyists, the ladies of Washington worked on developing and improving their access, taking control by instigating social events. Expediency ruled the day, however. When it came to patronage, people did whatever worked, and though men and women played different parts, patronage allowed a certain amount of fluidity. Both women and men visited official men in offices, and everyone made patronage connections at social events. Men, as well as women, used "family," meaning both that they operated within families, and that they applied the idea of family as a way of understanding their work. Men even employed the same sentimental language of the heart in making their pitches. Patronage, at least in early Washington, was women's work, and successful men played by their rules.

Dolley had long adapted the southern obsession with tracing family connections to her own political purposes. She exploited and even manufactured kin connections with powerful individuals, promising protégés, and prominent families, in order to draw people into the Madison political network. She formed one such fictive family connection with the Morrises of Philadelphia. Dolley Madison and Anthony Morris had known each other as young people, and they stayed connected even as Dolley moved with James through his career. Dolley declared Morris's eldest daughter, Phoebe, *her* daughter, a decision she reinforced with the language she used in writing to and of Phoebe, and which both Phoebe and her father regularly affirmed.[61]

Through the years, Anthony Morris and Dolley had worked together on several patronage projects, mostly getting jobs for his law clerks. But in 1811, Anthony Morris himself needed a job. A savvy political player, he began lobbying for a diplomatic posting abroad first through official channels: that is, he applied to James Madison. But at the same time, he wrote to Dolley apologizing for not going directly to her, and imparting confidential information about other candidates for the post, information that would have been inappropriate in an official application.[62]

No matter that he was one of Dolley's oldest friends, in this letter Anthony Morris followed certain conventions. His penmanship was more formal than his usual hand. With James, Morris discussed his qualifications; with Dolley, he talked family, couching his desire for a job as a way of securing his children's future. A more cosmopolitan venue than rural Pennsylvania would give his daughters a chance at good matches and his son a fine education. He even played the "daughter" card, mentioning "*our* darling Phoebe's" health, which he thought necessitated a change of scene. When Phoebe joined the letter campaign to Dolley, she concentrated on concerns about her *father's* health. Phoebe felt quite justified in treasuring hopes about an appointment for her father through her correspondence with her "Mother"—as a houseguest in 1812, she had observed Dolley being petitioned by "Ladies for their Husbands, or Brother, or Cousins."[63]

Dolley responded to Anthony Morris in the feminine and obscure language of patronage—"I pray that you may be gratified." In contrast, to Phoebe Dolley passed on "interesting communications," including "political hints" for Anthony. To Phoebe, Dolley related the disappointing news about Anthony Morris's official petition: a recalcitrant Senate, which had to approve diplomatic posts, had denied him an ambassadorship. Dolley exclaimed: "There is *nothing* to be *done*—in such times as these! Mr. M.[adison] is anxious to employ your Papa in some good place, entirely within his own gift, when *we* should not be subject to the political or personal objections of a capricious Senate (allmost treason my dear) but it is really true that M[adison] has but a small voice, at present, in appointments that go into the House."[64]

This was no doubt true. Always uneasy about patronage to begin with, James had his hands well and truly tied by Congress in the months before the declaration of war. At this point in the story of Anthony Morris, the official record falls suggestively silent, because the end of the transaction took place in the unofficial sphere, the world of women. Shortly after Dolley's discouraging report, James appointed Anthony Morris as a secret envoy to Spain, to help negotiate the purchase of Florida.[65]

From the ship to Spain, Anthony Morris wrote his thanks to his dear friend Dolley for securing this opportunity, invoking images of piety and religion, calling her "our ministering Angel." (He had earlier deemed her influence peddling "Acts of grace.") He ended his letter by reaffirming his debt for his good fortune "to Heaven, & you."[66]

Presidents, of course, had to distance themselves from patronage, as James once nervously admitted to Richard Cutts: "This is a subject on which as you may suppose it is the inclination & practice of the Ex[ecutive] to enter as little as possible." Discretion drove James into circumlocution, his prose becoming more tortured as he endeavored to explain how an "expression of sentiments" (a patronage promise) might be "disagreeable to others" or would "embarrass future arrangements." That is, James did not want to be caught practicing patronage, as it would give his enemies ammunition and might defeat his objectives.

But James depended on Dolley. In this same message to Richard, he alluded to the larger package that the letter accompanied. Intimating that he knew nothing of its contents, he declared, "From the size of the enclosed I perceive Mrs. Cutts is supplied by her sister [Dolley] with whatever in our present situation may be interesting to our particular friends." In political code, "interesting" meant of professional self-interest, "particular friends" were those who would be politically rewarded.[67]

When men and women wrote to Dolley, seeking an official position for themselves or a relative, they understood that they were in effect petitioning James. After all, Dolley did not have the power to nominate or put someone on the payroll; her role was significant but subtle. Immediately after James's first inauguration, because Dolley "expressed a wish to promote my wishes," the former diplomat Stephen Sayre asked her to "prevail on the president." In 1811, when David Bailie Warden wrote to Dolley about an appointment as American consul at Paris, he understood that "the President will nominate me." But he assumed a personal appeal would have an effect, and indeed, two months later, he wrote to Dolley to thank her for "communicating certain information which so deeply interests me."

One of the Madisons' "particular friends" was John Jacob Astor. A German immigrant, Astor made his fortune in the fur trade, becoming one of America's early multimillionaires. By 1800, he was looking for expansion opportunities, which he found abroad, especially in China and Russia, and at home, with the acquisition of the Pacific Northwest. A man with plenty of money and power in his own right, he realized the way to even greater power lay in alliance with the federal government. Knowing that a direct approach to men in office might attract the wrong kind of attention, he began by assiduously courting political women. He well understood the power of such women, having married a well-connected New Yorker, Sarah Todd, who knew both the fur business and the right people.

Astor had become one of Dolley's circle during the White House years. Dolley and he performed patronage favors for each other, and he would provide services for the government, for instance allowing official personnel to travel on his ships during wartime.[68] Astor was famously generous. He bought the Madisons a set of china on commission, but never sent a bill. When a White House guest exclaimed at its beauty, Astor sent *his* family a set as well. An importer of goods from all over the world, he could offer the choicest items of exchange, as he did in an 1812 letter to Dolley, presenting her with "the very best" tea from Canton, China, "two boxes of Superior Sweet oile & two Small Boxes containing Madeira wine," that no doubt James would appreciate. After listing all these delights, Astor made the situation clear in the heavy-footed way of a businessman.

Others suffered shipping losses, but "Mr. Astor recollects with Greate pleasure all the good wishes which Mrs. Madison expressd for him when he was Last at Washington—and he has not forgotten The bargain made at that time—he well remembers Mrs. Madisons Assurances that all Mr. Astors Ships should arrive and he is happy to say that two have arrived from Canton with valuable Cargoes two are yet out both to China should they arrive agreeable to Mrs. Madisons good wishes one of them shall be transferred to Mrs. Madison and it shall *be the best* of them."[69]

Clearly, regardless of official policy, Dolley and James could somehow arrange that Astor's ships would dock in a U.S. port. The China trade was lucrative at any time; during this era of embargo and restrictions, prices for imports skyrocketed, all pure profit for Astor. No wonder Astor called James "the founder of his fortune." Politicians from the founding onward had tried to avoid any intimation of quid pro quo in political transactions, but Astor was a businessman, used to the clarity of contracts and terms. He had not quite developed an ear for political language: the term "bargain," which to him simply meant an agreement, stood as a codeword for corruption in early republican politics.

Though it included a request that Dolley present the wine to James (Madeira was his favorite), the letter was addressed to her. Still, this transaction must have involved James, if for no other reason than that as a married woman, Dolley had no easy legal way to "own" a ship or its contents. Why might James risk the censure that would surely follow if a transaction of this magnitude came to light? The answer was as clear as the balance on a ledger sheet. Astor stood ready to help the Madisons in a way few others could. In 1813, after James had finally declared war and the Treasury was nearly bankrupt, Astor would help to raise $12 million in government bonds.[70]

When Dolley wrote in 1810, "[C]ome then, as soon as possible, to my Husband who will not call, though he wishes for you, every day," she was operating within a well-established system that mixed political and family concerns. Since she often wrote as a surrogate for James, the recipient might reasonably assume that James, though he could not openly request a favor, was indeed calling upon a friend. On the other hand, Dolley had a long record of independent political action, so the plea may have come directly from her. In either case, the recipient had to take the request seriously. Reflecting the political climate, the letter's vagueness was deliberate; Dolley did not outline specifics, not because she did not know them but because the political use of personal letters required prudence. Perhaps the most striking aspect of the letter—and the one that would make the request hard to refuse—lies precisely in the fact that it came not from James, but from Dolley. An appeal from a woman famed for her good heart, using the language of friendship, made this request, like so many that came from her pen, emotional, personal, and ultimately irresistible.

TWELVE

The Republican Queen

*S*enator Henry Clay once gallantly remarked to Dolley, "Everybody loves Mrs. Madison." Without hesitation, she replied, "That's because Mrs. Madison loves everybody." That simple exchange captured the essence of Dolley's public image. She operated in the guise of disinterested "pure" emotion, which seemingly included everyone. Unwittingly, through her playful echo of the third person, she also revealed the constructed nature of this persona. There was Dolley herself, and then there was "Mrs. Madison." Her presentation of lovable "Mrs. Madison" became so successful that, notably in this formal era, many people even called her "Dolley," as though her very publicness and inclusiveness gave them permission.

Another Dolley admirer hazarded that she exemplified the motto of her birth state, North Carolina—"Esse quam videre," "To be rather than to seem." Her charm appeared genuine, and in truth, she did draw upon ample reserves of goodwill in creating her persona. At the same time, she also had wells of anger, depression, and a sharp, arguably cynical, view of the political world, all of which she quite consciously chose to conceal. Dolley knew from past experience that visibility brought censure as well as admiration. At the beginning of the first Madison term, a foreign observer had noted the double-edged sword of presidential success: "If her ambition has been pleased [by the election] her tranquillity has also been invaded." On one hand, "clumsy courtiers whispered flattery," while on the other, "illiberal libellers loudly published accusations and disseminated slanders."[1] To Henry Clay she professed her "love" of "everybody" but to herself, she wrote a reminder: "Warning words of my husband: 'Be always on your guard that you become not the slave of the public nor the martyr to your friends.'" The warm and generous Dolley was real; so was the cautious, prudent, privately doubtful, and politically savvy Dolley. Together, they became "Queen Dolley."[2]

Decades of tutelage under James Madison also enhanced Dolley's natural gifts. Her elliptical, discreet style of politicking, so appropriate for the unofficial sphere, characterized both husband and wife. Charles J. Ingersoll, a converted Madison supporter, noted with awe that as a candidate, not only did James have the self-control never to discuss the campaign, he suffered "threats of calumny without the slightest complaint."[3] Dolley took this stance even further, becoming famous for entertaining everyone, seemingly oblivious to political divisions. One of her more famous proclamations, passed on late in life to her nieces, was "I confess I do not admire contention in any form, either political or civil."[4] Few ever heard a bitter or negative remark pass her lips, in public at least.

A certain amount of effort, even posing, underlay this conciliatory approach, of course. Dolley's declaration to Henry Latrobe—"it is one of my sources of happiness, never to desire a knowledge of other peoples' business"—was disingenuous at best. Evidence abounds that Dolley took a great deal of interest in "other people's business," as well she should have, since that knowledge was crucial to James's political career, as well as to hers. So was political talk, and Dolley's well-documented willingness to entertain it and pass it on belies the second half of her famous disavowal of contentiousness. If she did *"not admire contention in any form, either political or civil,"* she went on to declare, "I would rather fight with my hands than my tongue." Though Dolley presented herself as a proper lady, when there was fighting to be done, as there always was in early Washington City, she was willing to do it. Passion and power lay beneath Dolley's public charm.

The construction of Dolley's persona began with the exterior. She loved pretty clothes, and if she had remained a Virginia gentry woman, she would have been one of the best dressed. What she set out to do in Washington, however, went beyond merely looking her best or keeping up with the latest style. To legitimize her husband's administration, she drew on the age-old ruling-class techniques of using material display, especially clothing, to assert power. Like her White House, her impressive garments and jewelry reassured everyone, from ordinary American visitors to skeptical and scornful European observers, that the very best people ruled America.

Rulers have used clothing as a vocabulary of power throughout human history. The great number and variety of consumer items available in modern times have only enlarged that vocabulary. Though both male and female royalty used clothing for effect, women's bodies, clothed and unclothed, possessed a special significance and power. Dolley, along with other Americans, had watched in horror during the French Revolution as Marie Antoinette's image inflamed the radicals, and as, in an extreme enactment of politics on a woman's body, in 1793, she paid the ultimate political price.[5]

Like a military uniform, elite women's dress signaled power and status. Unlike modern styles of female "power dressing," which borrow elements of male clothing, the fashions that Dolley and her class embraced were completely feminine and as different from their male counterparts' as possible. In the eighteenth century, women literally took up space, horizontally with wide skirts and trains and vertically with hats and other headgear. Upper-class women's dress combined heavily draped, luxurious materials that, gathered strategically, provided sharp contrast to breathtaking displays of bare skin on the arms, neck, and bosom.[6]

The Madisons expended a great deal of money on Dolley's wardrobe. No one in her circle who traveled to a major urban area escaped the obligation to shop for their friend. American diplomats in Paris, Ruth and Joel Barlow, Ruth's sister, Clara Baldwin, and the U.S. commercial agent, William Lee, spent a good deal of time and effort on this project. Lee in particular took his mission seriously; for two months in 1811, he did nothing but make the rounds of Paris shops and pore over fashion magazines, choosing items with "taste & judgment."

When the substantial shipment of clothes and accessories arrived from Paris, Dolley appreciated Lee's selections, especially the beautiful dresses. Unfortunately, the wigs were too tight and so expensive that none her friends would buy them or swap for them. She was also horrified to discover that the shipment, including purchase price and customs duties, cost $2,000. She confessed to Ruth: "I'm affraid that I never shall send for any thing more."[7]

Such purchases, though, ensured that Dolley dazzled most Americans who attended her drawing rooms. The colors of ordinary American clothes were limited to dull browns and greens that came from simple vegetable dyes. Standard dyeing practices could not produce "pure" hues very easily; white, in particular, was difficult to achieve. And everyday fabrics, with their homespun weaves, were rough in texture. Even the layers worn next to the skin, such as stockings and the all-purpose shift worn by both sexes under their outer garments, were made of coarse wool or cotton.[8]

The same qualities that differentiated gentry décor from ordinary settings—smoothness, shininess, and the reflection of light—marked upper-class clothing. Dolley set herself apart from the crowd when, at one of her drawing rooms, she wore a satin dress with a train several yards long. The gown was rose-colored, and the train was white velvet, lined with lavender satin, edged with lace. Her accessories included a gold girdle, necklace, and bracelet, along with a white velvet turban, festooned with white ostrich-feather tips and a crown embroidered with gold thread. Dolley used not just fabrics, but solid, precious metals and luxury items, such as ostrich feathers and, on one occasion, swans-down, to create an image of material (and thus political and moral) superiority.[9]

She began her day in plain dress, often Quaker in style, changing into simple but fine fabrics, such as cambric, for daytime visits and calls. Details such as a ruffle around the hem and tiny buttons with elaborately worked buttonholes running the length of a dress, however, rendered these garments far from ordinary; she also harmonized her accessories with an eye to texture and color. With one white cambric gown, she chose a short, close-fitting jacket and a silk scarf, as well as a gauzy turban, all in peach.[10]

Women with heavy social schedules often "made do" with their best dresses, changing trimmings and other design elements to freshen them up. At almost every drawing room during the congressional season, Dolley wore a different ensemble. Her dresses were so unusual that they could not be easily adapted for second or third wearings. The vivid colors and patterns and the fine trimmings made them memorable, whether she wore a gown of "sky-blue striped velvet" or used lace as a handkerchief, a turban, or a ruff. Coming to Washington from Salem, Massachusetts, a prosperous American port, the elite Mary Boardman Crowninshield was no stranger to luxurious and exotic items. Yet even she was amazed by Dolley's yellow satin gown, "embroidered all over with sprigs of butterflies, not two alike."[11]

Clearly, Dolley's dress exceeded the standards of her best-dressed contemporaries. Principles of republican simplicity, as well as the developing notion of genteel "taste," dictated that even the richest Americans should avoid excess. Unlike upper-crust Europeans, Americans of this period aspiring to gentility did not tend to ornament themselves with gold and silver buttons and buckles or flows of lace; they eschewed bright colors that seemed flashy or pretentious. Muted colors, especially black, prevailed. In fact, the deeper the hue of black, the more expensive the garment and the greater status conveyed, since a true black could be achieved only through an expensive dyeing process.[12]

But these newly emerging styles of middle-class gentility would not do for Dolley's mission. The only black that Dolley is recorded as wearing at this time was a regal velvet gown that was anything but discreet. She drew on royal themes and older models of lavish display when she wore, as the Gallatins' niece, Frances Few, described, a "gown of brick coloured silk with a train two yards long trimmed with white—on her head a small cap with a large bunch of [calico] flowers." Frances responded with disapproval: "Most preposterous."[13]

That Dolley deliberately invoked royal themes in her choice of ensembles did not escape notice. For the most part, people approved. Sarah Gales Seaton used appropriately royal vocabulary to praise one particular outfit: "Her majesty's appearance was truly regal—dressed in a robe of pink satin, trimmed elaborately with ermine, a white velvet and satin turban, with nodding ostrich plumes and a crescent in front, gold chain and clasps around the waist and wrists."[14]

But employing lavish clothes to command the spotlight carried some risk. Not so long ago a profusion of gold lace on the French minister's coat had so displeased Jefferson that he jokingly predicted that "the boys on the streets will run after him as a sight." Dolley's aristocratic imagery shocked some observers, who often focused on her headdresses, especially when her trademark turbans sported embroidered crowns or other monarchical insignia. On occasion, Dolley skated dangerously close to crowning herself queen, sporting accessories such as a "silver headdress . . . in the form of a crown." On this score, her harshest critics were not dyed-in-the-wool "democrats," as the Republicans were beginning to be called, but rather "aristocratical" New England Federalists.[15] Appalled by Dolley's "pretensions," Harriet Otis, a young lady from a prominent Boston Federalist family, used the language of royalty not to praise, but to bury. She related that on a visit to "the palace," she approached "the royal circle" to greet "the Queen" ("of January [not May]," added Harriet, a slap at Dolley's middle age). On that day, Dolley was adorned in white satin, invoking the royal custom of wearing white on state occasions, and boasted a *"sparkling diadem on her head."* In an antimonarchical jeremiad worthy of John Adams, Harriet shook her head at the laxity of her fellow and sister Americans: "If this people were as jealous of all approaches to royalty as the ancient Romans, what would they say[?]"[16]

Harriet was right about what good republicans *should* say. After all, even after the Revolution, some states tried to reinstate sumptuary laws, and clothing remained a way to demonstrate and measure patriotism all through the era. Most people raved about Dolley and her dresses, however, and "this people" accepted her royal messages with few objections. As with her White House project, Dolley walked a fine line, playing on older cultural and political commitments to rank in order to reassure everyone of the Madisons' fitness to rule.[17]

Yet, Dolley's clothes, while gorgeous and unprecedented, were not up to the standards of European courts. Though she wore velvet, satin, and silk, Dolley also dressed in muslin and fine linen, in proportions and styles that allowed her the freedom of movement to welcome all her company at the drawing rooms. Echoing the décor of her White House, her wardrobe invoked royalty, but it remained firmly in an American mode.[18]

And just as Henry Latrobe used symbols of the ancient world to make political analogies, so did Dolley. In this, she was aided by fashion. By 1800, women's dresses were being modeled on ancient Greek styles. The silhouette was slim, with an Empire waist and low neckline, the fabrics gauzy and clinging. In its "highest" form, the fashion could be quite shocking. When Elizabeth Patterson Bonaparte debuted the French couture in Washington City, people considered her "nude," and boys lined up to see her. During the Madison administrations, Dolley adapted, rather than adopted, the new, more revealing styles. With her impressive stature and her dark curls in a neo-classical chignon, Dolley must have seemed like a Greek goddess to the new Americans, for whom the ancient world remained a national touchstone.

Similarly, Dolley did not invent the turban style of headdress, but it became her trademark, and women imitated it on her account. The turban was an evocative choice; drawing attention to Dolley's head and face, it carried a sense of the exotic as well as the regal. It also offered additional space for fashion statements: she could highlight jewels by pinning them to the headdress, or even "crown" herself. Dolley often fastened feathers and plumes to the turbans, as she famously did for the first inaugural ball. As many guests noted, they had the effect of adding to her height and marking her in a crowd. Plumes attached to a glamorous headdress served a symbolic purpose as well. Visual culture played a large part in anchoring the nation, and images of America, especially allegorical images, abounded. Not surprisingly, artists looked to the ancient world for models of the new nation. The most famous of these was, of course, Columbia, the symbol of America, a beautiful woman in ringlets and a dress like Dolley's. Other representations of America featured a female figure in a helmet or a hat adorned with ostrich plumes. With her plumes and her Grecian-style dress, Dolley personified the new republic. These signifiers, with their political implications, were not lost on her audience; portraitists and engravers highlighted classical elements in their depictions of Dolley. One observer referenced King Henry IV of France, describing Dolley's headdress as the "plumes of Navarre."[19]

Physical descriptions were so tied to political assessments that another European admirer compared her black hair and blue eyes to those of the powerful, though despotic, Napoleon. This observer thought that the eyes of the two leaders differed in one significant way: those of "the Corsican bespeak the ferocity of his heart; the look of the fair American indicates the tenderness, generosity, and sensibility of her noble mind." According to the visitor, this should satisfy the most punctilious republican American, for whom it was not enough to "elect a Brutus for their chief, they must also be convinced that his partner possesses the soul of a sister of Cato—the sentiments of the wife of a Brutus."[20] For him, classically-clad Dolley met that standard.

Jewelry, yet another important element of formal dress, formed a crucial part of the vocabulary of power. Emeralds, rubies, and sapphires carried the mystique of legend and had always been prized for their rarity. Not only did these glittering objects mark status, but individual pieces often carried family and historical pedigrees, recognizable to all. Like the medals on an officer's chest, a woman's jewelry commanded respect and attention.[21] De rigueur for any court lady, diamonds stood above the rest as the ultimate jewels, yet while Dolley did not hesitate to wear large, warm, glowing stones (a pair of emerald earrings in the shape of "M"s, for instance), she avoided diamonds. She knew her

Washington crowd and was well aware that Elizabeth Leathes Merry had been refused admittance to a party to celebrate the acquisition of Louisiana on account of her "undemocratic" diamonds. Dolley instead favored pearls, which, with their more modest message of purity and quiet elegance, could be seen as the official jewel of the early republic.[22] By dressing like a queen, Dolley asserted herself as part of a new ruling class. By making herself a charismatic figure, she assured that all eyes would be on her. Of course, supporters and foes alike perceived her public image for what it was—a political statement, rather than personal paradings.

❧

William Campbell Preston, the young scion of a South Carolina family, came to a Wednesday night, shy and disconcerted by the elegant scene and the crowd of fashionables. Though William had been introduced to President Madison as "a kinsman," James exhibited "an abstracted air and a pale countenance, but little flow of courtesy." Awkwardly, the young man stood by the silent president until Dolley entered the room. As every eye turned upon her, she walked directly up to William, asking, "Are you William Campbell Preston, son of my old friend and most beloved kinswoman, Sally Campbell?" Upon his assent, Dolley bade him, "Sit down my son, for you are my son, and I am the first person who ever saw you in this world." Dolley then reintroduced the dazzled young man to the president as *her* relative, and President Madison shook hands cordially. With an "easy grace and benignity which no woman in the world could have exceeded," Dolley proceeded to introduce Preston to the important men and the reigning belles at the party, admonishing all to consider him her "protégé," and insisting that he stay in the White House as "I stand towards [you] in the relation of a parent." By singling out this young man and underscoring his relation to her so publicly, Dolley made a friend and potential ally for life: "My awkwardness and terror suddenly subsided into a romantic admiration for the magnificent woman before me." Dolley proved as good as her word, and William Preston soon became a White

House favorite. As regards the young man's future, Dolley's instincts proved correct. Preston was elected to the Senate, and he later became the president of the University of South Carolina.[23]

More than one observer qualified a description of clothing by mentioning that Dolley wore the clothes, not the other way around: it was "the woman who adorns the dress and not the dress that beautifies the woman." What she wore played only a part in the powerful and reassuring message that Dolley sent; how she wore her outfits mattered, too. People regarded the way one held oneself as even more significant than the possession and use of material culture. Gowns and jewelry could be acquired, after all, but bearing revealed the real person, and superior posture and carriage signaled true breeding and inner nobility. Her admirers insisted that Dolley was more than the sum of her sartorial parts: "'Tis not her form, 'tis not her face, it is the woman altogether, whom I should wish you to see."[24]

Without question, Dolley possessed that ineffable but instantly recognizable quality of charisma, the "gift of the gods," outward sign of an inward grace. She not only passed cursory inspection, but the closer the view, the more to advantage she appeared. Even those who did not fall under her spell grudgingly acknowledged that she had magnetism. Dolley had never been a classic beauty, and that, in its own way, made her power as a public figure even more impressive. When the British minister Francis James Jackson and his haughty Prussian-baroness wife came to America in 1809, they were determined to be displeased, and so they were. Francis described Dolley as "fat, forty, and not fair," and Mrs. Jackson dismissed her as a plump bourgeoise. Cruel but correct assessments; during her White House years, Dolley *was* middle-aged and plump. But even the Jacksons conceded her refreshing lack of pretension and, at dinner with Dolley, a surprised Francis admitted: "I do not know that I had ever had more civility and attention shown me."[25]

The standards for mien came directly from European courts, where speech and action took on meanings beyond the aesthetic. The way court personages stood and moved, how they held their faces and hands, all conveyed policy as well as personality. Royal observers and participants read the gestures and movements accordingly. Even as they applauded the "art" of conduct, they understood that this was not for art's sake but for the sake of state power.[26]

This meaning-making function of posture and movement explains the many and minute descriptions of men from the founding period. Americans remained nervous about the republican experiment, especially as it seemed to rest on the shoulders of certain specific individuals. George Washington in particular had become the focus of almost obsessive attention. Whether getting out of a carriage or reading an address, high and low alike evaluated him for "inner majesty and grace." Simply standing on the steps of a public building, as he did at a 1790s opening of Congress, Washington could still convey "civic duty and moral grandeur," as he stood "erect, serene, majestic."

As a matter of fact, on that occasion Washington had merely paused to allow his secretary to catch up with him. The crowd that gathered at the bottom of the steps, gazing "in mute unutterable admiration," was simply projecting onto their leader the qualities they admired. As Richard Rush, the son of Dr. Benjamin Rush and himself a future politician, described it, "Every eye was riveted on that form—the greatest, purest, most exalted of mortals." As the two men went into the building, "the crowd sent up huzzas, loud, long, earnest, enthusiastic."[27]

When Washington exhibited public clumsiness, people worried, as did Senator William Maclay upon observing him delivering a speech at the opening of Congress. The president "had too many objects for his hands," as he attempted to juggle his speech, his spectacles, and a hat. According to Maclay's critique, "he did as well as anybody could have done the same motions," though receiving the company with his spectacles already on "would have saved the making of some uncouth motions." If only, William Maclay sighed, "the laws of etiquette" had permitted him "to have been disencumbered of his hat."[28]

Dolley, by contrast, almost never took a false step. It is not a quirk of history that so many descriptions and evaluations of Mrs. Madison were recorded. Evaluating the performance of one's betters had long been a part of elite life, with observers analyzing bodies and behaviors for signs of superiority; hence the in-depth dissections of Dolley's

ensembles and of her effects on others.[29] Not coincidentally, people re-
sorted to royal or even divine imagery when describing her bearing. Almost every commentator, male or female, described her moving "with
the grace and dignity of a Queen." And she moved freely and often at
her drawing rooms, with a "stately and Minerva-like motion."[30] Little
wonder that she, like George Washington, captured the crowd's gaze,
and that they looked at her, as they did at Washington, to find confirmation of the inner qualities on which to build a nation.

The secret of Dolley's successful political persona, however, lay not
in her appearance but in her character, as discerned through her behavior and her treatment of other people. The whole point of her creation
was to use her inner gifts in order to attach people to her and, by extension, to her husband and his politics. Dolley's interest in and enjoyment
of people was genuine, and they felt it, responding almost uniformly
with positive assessments of her presence and her character. Like her
clothes, her gracious goodness also answered fears about both democracy and demagoguery. Part of her appeal was simple: Dolley was viva-
cious, quick, and lively. Members of the upper class cultivated these
qualities, because "better" persons exhibited vitality and vivacity, in contrast to the torpid peasants. They took the term "high spirits" seriously,
considering an animated affect "elevated," an almost divine gift.
Though Dolley possessed a genuinely vibrant, energetic personality, no
doubt she also cultivated the appearance of vivacity, and some detractors accused her of being affected.[31]

Dolley's extroverted approach spoke to an aristocratic standard of
ease; by extending it to everyone, she also embodied an ideal of democracy. No matter "how great a person greeted her or how comparatively
unimportant a guest, her perfect dignity and her gently gracious interest
were the same to all." If she showed any preference, "it was to the modest and diffident." Her cousin, Sarah Coles, observed that Dolley "certainly ha[d] the most agreeable way, of saying the most agreeable
things." Dolley's niece put very simply the secret behind her aunt's success: "You like yourself more when you are with her."[32] Under the spell
of her "free and friendly manner," absent any snobbish airs, even shy
guests would soon be "put at ease by her affability." This "free and

friendly" manner struck some as a little too down-home. Proper Sophia May, a visitor to the city, was one of those taken aback when Dolley called her "honey"—which "sound[ed] queer to a Yankee"—but even Miss Sophia found herself won over by Dolley's "sweetness." Dolley was not only "humble-minded, tolerant, and sincere," but the source of her popularity lay in her "desire to please, and a willingness to be pleased." Contemporaries understood her seeming meekness in the face of partisan conflict as a manifestation of her "power of adaptation" to circumstances, the pre-eminent and praiseworthy feminine quality.[33]

Dolley's generosity of spirit and lack of censoriousness (at least in public) made her seem as if, according to one admirer, "she could disarm envy itself." By the time she got to the White House, Dolley had endured decades of political strife. She still had plenty of spirit left for a fight when the occasion called for it, but she also acquired a disregard for personal pettiness. Possessing "colloquial powers of a most rare and extraordinary character," she appreciated the seemingly quotidian and the cumulative effect of small moments of goodness. These powers manifested themselves in "a fascinating manner in bestowing those trifling but delicate attentions in a large company, which are so acceptable to strangers."[34]

And she knew the obverse was true, remarking to sister Anna "that the inconveniences which may be borne for a time become intolerable by their continuance"; that "'from small vexations continually repeated flows the misery of man, not from any heavy crush of overwhelming evil!'"[35] Exquisitely tuned to nuance in human behavior, Dolley paid a great deal of attention to detail, both internal and external.

She understood that guests' comfort trumped the rules of etiquette. At a drawing room, one of those "backwoods men" at whom Easterners laughed had been standing uneasily against a wall for half an hour, intimidated by the grand setting and company. He suddenly moved to take a cup of coffee, just as Dolley walked over to him. She greeted him by name, flabbergasting the young man so that he spilled the coffee, dropped the saucer on the floor, and, completely at a loss, stuffed the cup into his pocket. Dolley waved aside the broken saucer as a consequence of the crowds, and appeared to notice neither the gentleman's embarrassment nor the inadvertently pilfered china. Instead she spoke of his "excellent mother," whom she "once had the honor of knowing." The topic of his mother broke the ice, they chatted for a time, and when the young man felt quite at ease, Dolley asked a passing slave to bring him more coffee.[36]

Dolley's charm was not a passive ornament; she actively drew people to her. With women, she used physical familiarity and customs of intimacy; she charmed the wife of the secretary of the navy, Mary Boardman Crowninshield, by remarking on "how much we think alike" when they both came dressed in blue velvet with flowers in the hair. On another occasion, Dolley remarked, "Oh Mrs. C., your butterfly is too much hidden," meaning "that elegant ornament in your hair—it is superb indeed."[37] Mary did not say, but it is easy to imagine Dolley reaching over and adjusting the ornament in Mary's hair.

She did not always enjoy company, and she worked at making conversations flow. To young William Preston, Dolley confessed that sometimes "the necessaries of society . . . wearied [her] to exhaustion." When William saw her with a book in her hand, he said: "Still you have time to read. 'Oh, no;' said she, 'not a word; I have this book in my hand—a very fine copy of Don Quixote—to have something not ungraceful to say, if need be, to supply a word of talk.'"[38] Cervantes's novel was a good choice as a conversational prop, because it offered several levels of discussion. Guests could simply admire her copy as a "very fine" volume, chat about the content on the simplest story level, or, if they were shrewd, discuss the deeper meanings of the satirical story of a man who tilted at windmills.

William also noted that when not in company, James called his wife Dolly. His description of the "influence" this had on her poignantly illustrates both the couple's tenderness toward each other and the extent to which Dolley lived onstage. At the sound of her name, "the lady, and on no other occasion, relaxed the deliberate and somewhat steely demeanor which always characterized her." Effort lay behind Dolley's seemingly casual, yet elegant ease. William knew that some artifice formed part of Dolley's public face, that it was a kind of "steely" armor, but he did not think any less of her.[39]

She was famous for her ability never to forget a name, a face, or a pedigree. On one hand, this skill was indubitably hers, the gift of a superior intellect and a capacious memory. On the other hand, she was famous for it, because she employed it often and publicly. Perhaps it overstates the case to claim, as did a nineteenth-century historian, that "it was this intellectual power, combined with all the graces and elegances of her sex, that made her once almost the center and source of power in the government." Certainly, though, it was the skill of a professional politician.[40]

Even in a world that frowned upon "petticoat politicking," analysts of Dolley's persona acknowledged the political uses of her personality. They took pains to establish the genuineness of her qualities, while obliquely acknowledging that she used her inherent goodness to good effect. They depicted her drawing rooms as places "where all parties appeared, knowing that they should all share her kind welcome and benignant smile." But Dolley was more than a gentle, passive presence. When an argument between James and the British minister Francis Jackson became too heated, Dolley sent in punch and cake. The imperious Jackson found both offerings "distinctly inferior," but the gesture calmed the situation. She also used a dinner invitation to derail Congressman Samuel Dexter's anger as he argued the Federalist position with James.[41] "She felt that it was her duty to pour oil on the waters of discord and draw malcontents into the fold of her husband, and successful she was for few would oppose the partner of such a wife!"[42]

Her persona affected people on several levels, as they perceived her efforts as both personal and political. Some, of course, distrusted "those smiles which no doubt helped to make the dominant party adhesive in . . . her presidency." "I do not think it possible to know what her real opinions are as she is all things to all men," sniffed Frances Few, inadvertently offering a perfect, albeit cynical, description of a politician. That some people criticized Dolley for her politesse merely affirmed the extent of her power, if in a backhanded way. Dolley's "inordinate love of pleasing" was seen by some as a sign of "insincerity, and even 'toadyism.'" But even for the mistrustful Frances, "[Dolley's] face expresses nothing but good nature—it is impossible however to be with her & not be pleased." She had to conclude with a sigh, "There is something very fascinating about her."[43]

Dolley succeeded so well in establishing her image that early into the Madison administration, she acquired the semi-official title "Queen Dolley." Though a lofty appellation—the revered Martha had been only "Lady Washington," after all—the nickname expressed as much affection as awe. Americans had a remarkable appetite for titles. People needed Dolley to function as a queen, and she happily obliged.[44]

She could be a Republican Queen because she worked in harmony with James, and her genuine kindness and regard for others mitigated any charges of "swanning." One perceptive guest, after detailing her majestic outfit, added: "Her demeanor is so far removed from the hauteur generally attendant on royalty, that your fancy can carry the resemblance no further than the headdress." And even for people who thought her manners a bit over the top and her dress too gaudy, her sincerity saved her. She may have been a queen, but she was, as one famous nickname characterized her, "a *queen of hearts.*"[45]

The Danish minister, Peder Pedersen, appreciated the aristocratic image coupled with down-to-earth kindness and consideration for others: "I have, by turns, resided in all the courts of Europe, and most positively assure you, I never have seen any Duchess, Princess, or Queen, whose manners, with equal dignity, blended equal sweetness." He saw "dignity" in the form of a "stately person," with a "lofty carriage," but also noted a "sweetness" in an "affable and gracious manner" that would bring her distinction "at any court in the world." Pederson recognized this new hybrid, the Republican Queen, pinpointing the source of Dolley's charm: "I have seen her moving through admiring crowds, pleasing all, by making all pleased with themselves, yet looking superior to all, I often have exclaimed—'She moves a goddess, and she looks a queen.'" Moreover, he understood Dolley's political function, rhetorically asking the American people: "What need you manners more captivating, more winning, more polished, than those of that amiable woman?"[46] To European men and women, if James resembled "a schoolmaster dressed for a funeral," "Mrs. Madison has become one of America's most valuable assets. She would be equally at ease in any of the world's capitals."[47]

Dolley's old friend Anthony Morris saw both the genuineness of Dolley's personality and its politic effects on others. He lauded "her courtesy of character, all her kindness, her mildness and her engaging manners," but these rather formulaic encomiums did not cover the full extent of her "virtues and attainments." According to Anthony, Dolley had the "peculiar power . . . of making and preserving friends and of disarming enemies, for even ladies . . . will have enemies when they come into conspicuous stations in Society." He marveled at her "magic power" over her enemies, that she "convert[ed] them into friends." Morris no doubt played on the double meaning of "friends," a euphemism for political supporters.[48]

Many descriptions evaluate Dolley in the context of the mission to create national manners. In this regard, she succeeded as well, since her "manners" seemed to spring directly from her good heart, rather than out of empty etiquette, and could not "be imitated by those who have not the love and sympathy ready to be called forth at all times." The mandate to create manners was not meant to be directly applied to politics, but, as the president's wife, Dolley actively championed a policy of noncontention, promoting her own values of harmony and civility in the political arena. This strategy required manners, understood as ways of behaving, talking, and interacting that reflected these ideas. For her model, she drew on the deepest part of her personality as well as on cultural ideals of ladyhood, according to which women embodied the delicate sensibilities of sentiment.

Dolley transformed personality into a self-conscious tool of policy. Success in the unofficial sphere required a subtle, circuitous political style, one that called on emotions and the softer side of personality: a "feminine" style of politics. The unofficial sphere was not the place for direct confrontation or coercion. Rather, it utilized emotional control, the interpretation of nuance, the subtle use of words and actions, and self-consciousness about how one was being perceived. In all these areas, Dolley reigned supreme.

The rebelling colonists had had a vocabulary for revolution, one with a long history, full of well-grounded concepts that all participants more or less understood. Dolley's generation had no such shared language for the practical task of governing the nation and for the political system that they were developing, a democracy with a two-party system. In her words and deeds, Dolley brought a new language to the table of early American politics, a feminine vernacular of sentiment and feeling, with an insistence on civility.[49]

Obviously, not everyone loved Dolley, any more than everyone loved her drawing rooms. Even her best qualities could be twisted by her enemies: "Her frankness . . . her loveliness, and sincerity have long excited the suspicions, alarms and apprehensions" of radicals both democratic and elitist. Dolley's bipartisanship drew suspicion; rumors persisted that she was a closet Federalist who obtained offices for members of the opposing party. Like the reactions to her drawing rooms, these criticisms focused on both an excess of aristocracy, at least from the point of view of snooty New Englanders, and a dangerous tendency to democracy. In spite of the pink satin and ermine, some considered Dolley not aristocratic enough, even common. Rosalie Stier Calvert referred to her as "Queen," but mockingly: "Queen Dolla lolla." (She derisively dubbed the Madison supporters "'the Court.'") Dolley took snuff; the habit, aristocratic in the eighteenth century, increasingly was regarded as crude, old-fashioned, and vulgar. Mary Boardman Crowninshield still kept a snuffbox at her house for the ladies, though she regarded it as a "bad habit."[50]

Racy stories about Dolley's behavior made the rounds. Unlike the obviously manufactured slanders of zealous partisans, these tales were more likely to be misreadings of actual events, in some cases stemming from regional prejudices. Like many southern women, she hugged people, and, when asked for a kiss, presented her lips. Dolley famously wore low-cut gowns that made the best of what Frances Few reluctantly conceded was "the most beautiful . . . neck and bosom . . . I ever saw." Women used kerchiefs tucked around the necklines of their fashionable gowns to shield their cleavage, as Dolley had herself when she first came to Washington. As the administration's leading lady, Dolley eschewed that modesty. On one occasion, Dolley met a Quaker gentleman who had not covered his head in the traditional manner. In a salute to a fellow apostate, Dolley raised a glass and toasted: "Here's to thy absent broadbrim, Friend Hallowell." To which Hallowell replied, "Here's to thy absent kerchief, Friend Dolley."[51]

⚜

As in real life, the image of Dolley did not stand alone, but worked in the public mind in concert with her husband's persona. James Madison's talents lay not on the surface but in his capacious intellect, his subtle and perceptive ability to understand and synthesize sound, intellectually exciting ideas, as he did for the Constitution and Bill of Rights. But even in the world of his ideas, his words do not sparkle or shine; his writings contain few immortal phrases or quotable quotes. His intellectual soundness, coupled with the self-effacing messages he sent through his person, might have reassured or impressed his public but could not captivate or comfort them.[52]

It was hard not to compare him with his charismatic wife. The hostess with the warm smile, flowing garments, and waving ostrich plumes stood vividly in contrast with the "very Small thin Pale visag'd man of rather a sour reserved & forbidding Countenance." Though James was hailed by all as "a Man of talents," most people agreed that "he seems to be incapable of smiling." At social events in the White House, "being so low in stature, he was in danger of being confounded with the plebian crowds and was pushed and jostled about like a common citizen—but not her ladyship."[53] As opposed to his wife's modern glamour, James consistently dressed in the "old style," wearing the traditional breeches, stockings, and buckled shoes of the revolutionary generation. He even wore his hair gathered in the back and powdered.

Some admired Dolley, some did not—all acknowledged James's lack of charisma. To Washington Irving, Dolley seemed simply "a fine, portly, buxom dame, who has a smile and a pleasant word for everybody. . . . [B]ut as to Jemmy Madison—Ah! Poor Jemmy!—he is but a withered little apple-John."[54] Irving's New York Federalist politics may have influenced his assessment, but even James's strongest supporters could claim for him only modest sociability in large companies.

In contrast to James's rather sickly looks, the appearance of blooming good health and vigor formed part of Dolley's carefully constructed persona. In reality, during her White House years, she suffered from an eye ailment and from rheumatism. She also had trouble with her ears, at one point going temporarily deaf. The stress of public life, and her personal griefs, may have caused or exacerbated these conditions; Dolley also vaguely alluded to several bouts of ill health that were "dangerious & severe," making her "very sick" and "extreamly ill." These may have been miscarriages. But whatever the actual state of her health, she saw to it that others had before them only a robust and energetic figure.

Times of actual illness aside, Dolley's seemingly unflagging reserves of energy and good health allowed James to sidestep that issue when it came to his public image. A confident, easy Dolley, cheeks ablaze, dominating the room, not only balanced James's lack of vigor, it also allowed him to be himself. He did not need to compensate, to try to be both the strong, masculine leader and the embodiment of a republican, and therefore weak, central power. Of course, this disparity could be used against the couple, as whisperers surmised that Dolley's excessive "heat," in the form of sexual appetite, made her husband sterile.

In her ability consciously to create and implement a persona deeply rooted in her authentic self, Dolley was a genius, an artist. Had she been born in a later era, she might have found greater scope for her powers, but she took the opportunities her culture offered and made the most of them. In a world where women were above all wives, Dolley became the wife of the most powerful man in the nation. As is true of other geniuses, nothing in her background can account for her accomplishment. Indeed, her upbringing provides an interesting counterpoint, for her parents raised her as a modest Quaker woman—in the world but not of it—yet she lived her adult life not only in the center of fashionable society, but at the apex of the very kind of coercive political power that Quakers abhorred.[55]

Geniuses make art by transforming individual essences into something larger than personal traits. In creating her political persona, Dolley drew on her deep need to please and on her personal insecurity. From girlhood on, she had suffered loss, and she felt and feared it keenly. In its positive form, her need for connection made her a wonderful kinswoman. She proved consistently caring, nurturing, and deeply loving, especially with her female relatives and friends. To be Dolley's sister or niece was to be blessed with a constant and steady source of love. The negative side of Dolley's need for approval emerged in her relationship with her male relatives. Raised to defer and submit to men, fearful of criticism from the men in her life, Dolley was often too uncritical and protective. Her son, Payne, was growing up to be a reckless, spoiled young man, far too indulged and petted for anyone's good. Dolley did not have the inner strength to discipline him, for she could not have tolerated even a child's displeasure.

Dolley's need to please took another form, too: an almost pathological avoidance of conflict and an overriding impulse to defuse tension and contention. In an era that equated complete self-effacement with ladylike behavior, her contemporaries recognized these tendencies and mostly registered approval. Still, even by her culture's standards, she could be excessively appeasing, even prompting some to suspect hypocrisy. This eagerness to please might be traced to her unsettled childhood, a mixture of the Virginia hospitality of her early life with the deference of the commercial class, befitting the daughter of a tradesman and a boardinghouse keeper. But her need to avoid conflict and confrontation was so deep-seated, so urgent, that its roots must have been even closer to home. Temperamentally, John Payne was clearly a difficult man; life with him may have been stormy enough to teach a daughter the value of smoothing things over. What is unique to Dolley is that, rather than become simply an appeaser, she actively exercised a strong sense of self and of will. She did not merely sidestep conflict, but actively reached out to charm and disarm. Dolley was always willing to beard the lion in his den.

As a person who pleased, Dolley was highly attuned to people and their needs and desires. She put this knowledge and her own passions to the service of something larger than herself: James's political goals for the country. And, for all her inner sweetness and goodness, Dolley's will asserted itself in another way that served her well. Plenty of quiet, meek, and culturally sanctioned ways existed for a woman who strove to be kind and loving as well as politically effective. Dolley wanted to be the ultimate pleasing woman, but she wanted everyone to see her do it. She liked being the center of attention, and even sought out the spotlight. Dolley used her own self writ large to create a Republican Queen, a charismatic figure around whom people could rally, a figure who commanded the focus of any room and who radiated calm goodness.

As in all of Dolley's work, the immediately practical and the long-term symbolic existed simultaneously. As the charismatic figure, she won her husband supporters and affirmed existing loyalties, crossing party lines as he could not. As the leading inventor of Washington City's ruling style, as well as the center of attraction, she functioned as a national figure, one of the first in American history. To put it simply: in an age before celebrities, Dolley became a celebrity.

In a time when it was inappropriate for a woman's name to appear in the public press, Dolley had her picture on the cover of the famous Philadelphia literary magazine *The Port Folio,* and flattering coverage in the Federalist magazine *New England Palladium.* American manufacturers sent gifts and fulsome addresses, hoping to link her endorsements to their wares. John Jacob Astor, in his capacity as the head of the American Fur Company, sent her free clothes "from Motives of Patriotism." Ordinary people, too, sent gifts, some purchased—clothing, books, pictures, porcelain—some household productions—blankets, a counterpane, and handkerchiefs intended to "shad[e] her lovely bosom from the admiration and gaze of the Vulgar." One admirer even sent her some white mice. She became Washington City's chief tourist attraction, and ordinary people showed up at the White House door at all hours of the day to meet her. Ironically, considering the political contention around transatlantic shipping, merchant Jacob Barker named a ship, *Lady Madison,* after her. Her fame was durable; she appeared as a character in novels and stories long after her heyday, most notably, in Margaret Bayard Smith's *A Winter in Washington* (1824) and *What Is Gentility?* (1828).

Several authors asked permission to dedicate their works to her.

The writer and librarian of Congress George Watterston begged her to accept his dedication of a play "in expectation that under your patronage, it will survive the nipping blasts [of] criticism, & out live the noisy storms of malignity." In other cases, authors merely wanted her to promote their work among her public. Joseph Milligan begged Dolley to start the list of subscribers for a new volume, *Tales of Fashionable Life*, by the noted Irish writer Maria Edgeworth. "If Mrs. Madison should think fit to begin the list he has no doubt [but] most of the Ladies would follow [her] example."[56]

Politics requires a "charismatic figure," especially in a new nation. The biggest crisis that faced Americans in the early nineteenth century was one of national legitimacy—in the eyes of the outside world, as well as in their own. The United States had not been in existence long enough to rest its authority on long-standing tradition; the traditions and systems of Great Britain, which had supplied colonial Americans with a sense of self, had become too alien.

In those early days, people relied on public figures to generate unity. George Washington emerged as the first charismatic figure to hold the fragile republic together, symbolizing the values and aspirations of the nation and legitimizing the new government with a "gift of grace." The stakes were slightly different by the time Dolley and James had settled into the White House. Americans had begun the process of transferring their loyalty from one or another individual to a national collective—the United States of America. The republic had survived for a generation, but these were more complicated times. The psychological boost of victory over British oppression that had carried and united the nation for the first years had dissipated. Foreign relations could not be summed up as a simple "David and Goliath" tale. Partisan conflict, symbolized by the obstreperous Congress, now threatened the existence of the Union. Although Americans could celebrate the survival of their experiment thus far, the future of the republic remained uncertain.

During her husband's administration, Dolley emerged as arguably the most famous and loved person in the United States. George Washington was dead, and the rest of the official men identified too closely with one party or the other to inspire universal admiration. In these partisàn times, perhaps only a woman could have emerged as a national symbol, a charismatic figure. The Republican Queen masked more than the aristocratic and democratic tensions in American culture. Because, like other women, she was excluded from holding official power, Dolley occupied a place "above" party politics; the very picture of disinterested-ness, she could unify the country. Increasingly, women were called upon to veil partisan conflict, allowing men the freedom to conflict and contend as they created the political machines of the two-party system.[57]

THIRTEEN

Affairs to Remember

On February 2, 1811, Congress was debating yet another carrot-and-stick variation on embargo. Macon's Bill, while removing trade restrictions with both Great Britain and France, would give the president the power to reimpose the ban on either country if the other ceased to violate U.S. neutral rights. During the interminable wranglings in the House, Congressman John Randolph, of Virginia, rose to speak. Just the sight of him getting to his feet brought a nervous energy to the House. Would the distinguished gentlemen be treated to a show of brilliance and eloquence, or would Randolph go off into one of his "mad fits"?

On that day, it was the latter. In his surprisingly high-pitched, feminine voice, which, as he warmed up, "assume[d] a more manly tone . . . distinctly heard in every part of the House," Randolph attacked the bill and the president. "It is a bargain in which credulity and imbecility enters into with cunning and power." Though, according to a congressional reporter, Randolph declared that "really, nothing was farther from his wish, nothing was farther from his policy, than a desire to create an unpleasant sensation or reflection in the mind of any member of this House," in his usual fashion, he unleashed a volley of "satire and invective" not only against the bill, but against one of its sponsors, his fellow Virginian John Eppes. Enraged, Eppes replied in an equally hostile matter. Sharp words were exchanged, and Eppes challenged Randolph to a duel, right from the floor of the House.[1]

John Randolph's objections to the Macon Bill were both personal and political. He harbored legitimate concerns about giving James the power to reinstate the embargo, suspecting that the president would use his power to favor France. But John Eppes also spurred his wrath: Eppes was Thomas Jefferson's son-in-law, the widower of Maria, and Randolph hated Jefferson. Eppes was not the first Jefferson son-in-law that Randolph tried to take down; in 1806, he almost dueled with his own cousin, Thomas Mann Randolph, Jr., the husband of Martha Jefferson Randolph. Randolph's loathing of Jefferson had both political and personal dimensions. He sincerely distrusted and disagreed with Jefferson's philosophies, but he was also jealous of the meteoric rise of a member of what he considered the second rank of Virginia gentry. Moreover, having risen, Jefferson did not share his political largesse with anyone but his own kin and closest friends. John Randolph especially resented being passed over for the post of minister to Great Britain, a position that went to William Pinkney of Maryland, one of the then-president's supporters.[2]

Though it was Randolph who enjoyed a reputation for excessive violence, in this instance the outraged John Eppes took the initiative. Like boys arranging an after-school fight, the French minister, Louis Sérurier, reported, Randolph had "so violently called the name of Eppes [that] the latter answered with a challenge to a duel at the end of the session next Monday." Most shockingly, Eppes had issued this challenge from the floor of Congress. Sérurier gloomily predicted that, following "what usually happens in these duels in America," one or both would die, an outcome that seemed likely given that the pair settled on pistols as the weapon of choice.[3]

Suddenly James Madison and the entire federal government found themselves in a grave situation, one that would call into question the reputation of the United States. Although some men viewed dueling as a defense of sacred honor, it was illegal in the District, and many objected to it as an immoral and sinful practice; hence the infamy that fell upon Aaron Burr after his duel with Alexander Hamilton in 1804. Correspondingly, men for the most part dueled in secret, with the various negotiations happening between private parties, usually intermediaries. In contrast, as Sérurier's account demonstrates, everyone knew about this duel. To have such a challenge—and indeed, the very event—be part of the congressional business day did not cast the federal government in a good light. With the world watching, Randolph and Eppes stood to shame the people of the United States in both their own and international eyes for this barbaric and un-Christian practice.[4]

James Madison found himself in an awkward position. The year before, he had been embarrassed by the duel between John G. Jackson and the North Carolina congressman; there had also been an uncomfortable incident involving a horsewhipping given to a Maryland congressman, Roger Nelson, by Isaac A. Coles. The House fined Coles $20 and he apologized, admitting that administering the whipping in the Capitol showed a lack of respect. James did not personally favor dueling, but in his view it was akin to suicide: he reckoned that if a man wanted to do it, "no law can hinder." Certainly as president, he could not be seen sanctioning an illegal act. On the other hand, he was a Virginia gentleman, and he understood that a heavy-handed reaction could hurt the participants' pride or even escalate an incident that could be still defused. Moreover, he had to exercise discretion; if he took a very public role in stopping a duel, the information might surface that he had served as an adviser to duels in the past.[5]

Once a challenge was declared, there were very few honorable ways to back away. A woman's entreaty was one such way, and to everyone's relief Dolley stepped in. According to Sérurier, the duel "was converted into an accommodation by Mrs. Madison." She even wangled an apology out of John Randolph. Not surprisingly, "everyone is astonished at an issue so contrary to custom, and all the honor of the affair remains with Mrs. Madison." Dolley may have intervened to save John Eppes, for reasons of family or sentimentality; given John Randolph's attacks against her and her family, she probably did not care much what happened to him. Precisely how she worded her appeal was a mystery: "Nobody knows what she said, but everybody can know what she accomplished."[6]

Undoubtedly, politics played its part in Dolley's calculation. Gentlemen might be willing to spill each other's very blue blood over their principles, but Dolley did not want them to do it as representatives of the government. Division over James's proposed non-intercourse policies was bad enough; she would not have the bill covered in gore.

Bad behavior soon broke out in the executive branch as well. Secretary of State Robert Smith, whose brother Samuel was one of James's enemies in Congress, not only was proving wildly incompetent, but was also taking every opportunity to undermine the president. Indiscreet to the point of treason, deliberately disruptive in his personal interactions with diplomats, Smith turned the centrality of the unofficial sphere on its head. Diplomacy depends on informal social interactions outside of the official spotlight; such interactions enable individuals and families to establish trust. The stakes are so high, of course, since these particular individuals and families represent nations. In an age when slow communications entailed lengthy reaction time, the judgments of national representatives on the spot in Washington City *became* their countries' foreign policy. With a loose cannon like Robert Smith dealing with the diplomatic community, the social arena became unstable and dangerous rather than useful to the Madison administration. In order to keep Smith in line and accountable, James had to restrict the secretary's communication with diplomats to official correspondence. Moreover, Smith was so inept that James had to write the communications himself, over Smith's signature. Not surprisingly, one British minister, the prickly Francis Jackson, expressed dismay at being deprived of the face-to-face relations so necessary to the business of diplomacy. He misinterpreted James's insistence on written communication suspiciously, but not unreasonably, regarding it as a hostile act.[7]

Finally, in the third week of March, James asked for Smith's resignation, softening the blow by simultaneously offering him the ministry to Russia. At first Smith, perhaps taken aback, agreed, setting April 1, 1811, as his resignation date. James wasted no time and offered his old rival and neighbor, and now governor of Virginia, James Monroe, the post of secretary of state.[8]

When Robert Smith's initial acceptance of his new appointment quickly (and predictably) gave way to anger and resentment, he rejected what he regarded as a Siberian exile. He used a social event to express his displeasure, signaling to James and Dolley that hostilities had commenced by failing to show up at a state dinner to honor the Russian diplomatic staff and introduce them to the Smiths. In fact, Robert reported righteously in a letter to his brother Samuel, the Smith family had not crossed the White House threshold since "the day of the insidious offer."[9]

The following day, Dolley, Anna, and Lucy called twice upon the Smith family with great professions of affection. Unfortunately, no rapprochement was possible; when Congress adjourned, the Smiths returned to Baltimore. The Madisons assumed that, safely ensconced on their home turf, they would interact with other ruling-class families along the Eastern Seaboard, using gossip in private letters and at social events to spread their side of the story to the detriment of the president and the administration.

Consequently, in June, the Madisons sent the devoted and astute Edward Coles, with Payne to assist, on a fact-finding mission. They stayed and socialized with the same families within the Smith network, attempting to discern what (if any) retaliation the Smiths planned, and gathering reaction to James Monroe's appointment. Edward even paid a visit to the Smith family on their home ground of Baltimore, hoping to mend fences, forestall future trouble, and get information. As requested by Dolley, he reported back to her on the day of the event, describing his reception by the Smiths in detail, noting that while they treated him "very civilly," "their displeasure with the President and yourself was very apparent."[10]

Edward proved a great correspondent, supplying all the particulars of people and places that Dolley needed to know. Like a seasoned courtier (or a perfect lady), he probed every word and gesture for meaning. With some amusement, and sparing no detail, he related how none of the Smiths "made any enquiries after you, or the President," except Margaret Spear Smith, Samuel's wife, "who ask[ed] after your health." Edward also reported being "quite diverted" at the Smith party line, which answered the dictates of good manners without conveying any regard: "I hope you left our friends well in Washington."

From his canvass of the other families, Edward concluded, as the Madisons suspected, that "the Smiths are said not directly to vent their spleen, but to spur on their relations & friends, many of whom are extremely abusive of the President & Col Monroe." Edward even ferreted out the information that a Smith kinsman was printing "abusive & scurrilous pieces" in the newspaper.[11] Dolley in turn related that they were "precisely in the [same] state of suspence that you left us as it regards European affairs," as well as news of upcoming marriages and the parties of "great belles." By then, Edward was staying with the Cuttses, so Dolley included a political hint, asking her cousin to tell Anna "to hasten her preparations for Washington as *I* have no doubt, but that Congress will be call'd before Novr." This was actually a message to everyone, including Edward. James expected that the Congress might vote for war, in which case, he would need both Richard and Edward on the scene.[12] The underscored "I" may be interpreted in either of two ways: as making clear that this was not an official summons from James, or as obscuring the fact that it was.

❧

Dolley's patience with the sulkiness of the Smith clan wore thin, as reports of their malicious gossip against the Madisons reached her ears through the early summer of 1811. Having someone as talented and experienced as James Monroe in Smith's place more than made up for it, however. Dolley wrote to Edward: "Payne gave me the *little* account you directed & I exult in my heart at the full indemnifications we have for all *their* Malice, in Colo. Monroe's talents & virtue."[13]

But neither the Madisons' initial attempts to soothe nor the passage of time worked any magic. Robert Smith was determined to "humble" the great little Madison, and only a week or so after Edward's visit, Dolley grimly reported to Anna: "We expect too *Mr S——s book opening the eyes of the world on all our sins* &. &." Indeed, the pamphlet, "Robert Smith's Address to the People of the United States," broke upon the political scene, full of outrage and accusations. The classic disgruntled former employee, Robert Smith used his forty-page opus to present himself as a man who resigned out of principle, not an incompetent who was fired. More generally, it also rehashed the foreign situation, presenting James as corrupt, weak, "unmanly," and with a truckling bias toward France. In his zeal to bring down his enemy, Robert Smith overreached himself, inciting charges of disloyalty as he indiscreetly revealed "facts that relate[d] to pending negotiations." To support his position and contrast himself to the pusillanimous James, Smith put his own papers into evidence, even, incredibly, those that James had written for him.[14]

While James arranged that his supporters refute the pamphlet in the press, he attempted to downplay its importance. Dolley was less sanguine; as she wrote to Anna: "[Y]ou ask me if we laughed over the Smith Pamphlet. . . . I did not—It was too impertinent to exite any other feeling in me than anger." In spite of her personal reaction, Dolley knew politics and people and went on to predict: "He will be sick of his attempt when he reads all that will be replyed to it." Later in the letter, she returned to the irksome subject, noting the loyalty of her husband's cabinet: "[Secretary of War William] Eustis declared against Smiths Pamphlet, as soon as he saw the Book. [Secretary of the Navy Paul] Hamilton is enraged, & writes, or intends it on the subject you may guess how the Secys feel & speak." She predicted: "In short, the Smiths are down whatever harm they may have done to M."[15]

Once again, Dolley proved prescient. Even sworn enemies of the Madisons greeted Smith's pamphlet, with its slippery use of evidence and obvious spite, with near universal scorn. No one appreciated a good diatribe (and hated the Madisons) as much as John Randolph, but even he wondered of Smith, "Does not he outcant all his outcantings?" Even as they reprinted the "Address" for all the world to see, newspapers, for example the *National Intelligencer,* pointed out to their readers the "nefarious principle" underlying the text, begging them to "notice its glaring absurdities." Smith's attack on James was such an utter miscalculation that he lost even his family as supporters. Another member of the Randolph clan, John's half brother, Henry St. George Tucker, mused: "It is one of the rare instances of a man's giving the finishing stroke to his own character, in his eagerness to ruin his enemy. I hear but one opinion of Smith: he has signed his death-warrant," politically at least.[16]

By November, even Dolley couldn't help but express some sympathy for Smith. Writing to Ruth Barlow, Dolley passed on the news that an attempt to slander William Lee, the United States' commercial agent in France, had failed. "From all *I lern* good sense & principle will prevail over *Intrigue* & *vanity*—The instance of Mr R S is strikeing. The poor man is down! [E]ven his Brother professes to have borne no part, & comes *here* as usial."[17] Of course, as this letter was part of a semi-public diplomatic correspondence, Dolley may have exhibited more Christian charity than she might actually have felt.

In the course of a presidential administration or political era, some events come to be called "affairs." Even when used in a political sense, the term carries a sense of the clandestine, the slightly scandalous. "Affairs" are usually events that prove too slippery for the official sphere of laws and decrees to handle. Major incidents in "affairs" often take place in social spaces or behind the scenes; often they involve troublemaking women, as did the "Merry Affair." Even if some events, such as the abortive Randolph-Eppes duel, do not carry the label, their nature classifies them as "affairs." During James's first term, he and Dolley, along with others, tried to control such "affairs" using the unofficial sphere of reconciliation and harmony that Dolley had nurtured.

In the Smith Pamphlet Affair, Dolley had rallied her kin, hoping to contain bad feelings and to restore relations between the families by a series of visits. But the damage was too great, from the Smiths' point of view. The greatest miscalculation, however, was not Dolley's. Using gossip (both written and oral), the Smiths tried to harm the Madisons politically. They also attempted to rouse emotion, righteous indignation, in order to soothe their own feelings of betrayal and hurt. But negative emotions can backfire. No one could have said it to their faces, but Robert Smith had had a reputation for incompetence for too long for people to believe his account of events.

Though men and women used the unofficial sphere all the time to spread rancor, it worked best to conciliate, as Dolley tried to do. If the Smiths' gossiping tales carried one-tenth of the obvious venom that Robert's pamphlet did, people would have found themselves confronted and, thus, uncomfortable. Uncomfortable people become censorious. Had the Smiths apprehended the tenor of the face-to-face relations they had experienced, they would not have committed their views to print. In the end, even Samuel Smith had to capitulate, abandoning his brother in order to restore the "usial" social intercourse so necessary to politics.

In the event, though Dolley and James could not prevent Robert Smith from publishing the pamphlet, it improved James's position. In the face of such crass partisanship, his enemies had to stay silent for a while, in print at least. The exposure of Robert Smith's true character also justified his removal from office and increased support for his replacement, James Monroe. The best summation of the situation came from James's attorney general, who paraphrased the book of Job: "O that mine enemy would write a book!"[18]

❧

Less than a year later, James and Dolley dealt with another "affair" that more than deserved its illicit intimation. It included covert operations, national security, international glamour, a slick con man, and a lot of money. In January and February 1812, James Madison and James Monroe engaged in secret negotiations to buy a set of letters from a British spy, John Henry. Partly because of Anthony Merry's earlier reports, Great Britain had sent Henry three years earlier not only to ascertain the degree of disaffection in Federalist New England, but also to encourage it. John Henry found the rocky New England soil fertile ground indeed, as his reports testified. James Monroe eventually paid Henry $50,000 in federal funds in order to prove the treachery of the

Federalist Party and "as a last means of exciting the nation and Congress" to war against Great Britain.[19]

In one way, the strategy worked. When James proclaimed to Congress that "in the midst of amicable professions and negotiations" Great Britain had also been "fomenting disaffection to . . . destroy the Union," he played on an old and deep American fear. The vision of a foreign power conspiring with dissident elements to break up the union, and "making the eastern states part of the British empire," had long been a staple anxiety in the republican lexicon.[20]

In reply, Federalists cried foul. Though it was no secret that a secession movement was afoot in New England—ministers preached disunion from the pulpits every Sunday—Federalists pointed out that the very expensive letters named no American traitors, unless one counted the entire state of Massachusetts. The taint of Francophilia added to their case. They quite rightly suspected Minister Sérurier of having forwarded the business, and one of the agents Henry employed to make the sale was a self-styled French nobleman loyal to Napoleon, Count de Crillon. That Crillon turned out to be an imposter and a swindler only added to the Federalists' outrage and malicious satisfaction; but in any case, he was still French. In addition, the New Englanders lived up to their reputation as a thrifty and parsimonious people, complaining that James had used federal funds to pay so much for so little.

From the start, the very vastness of the sum seemed to indicate something criminal or at least shady. Some hinted at forgery, but, even though Crillon was clearly a crook, the Henry letters were undoubtedly authentic. As for the lack of specifically named traitors, James Madison took the high road, pointing out that he wished to keep the focus on "only the crimes of the foreigner." The letters *had* named Federalist names, but, at the request of the president, John Henry had erased them before he handed the letters over, so that, rather than airing their dirty laundry to the world, the "great American family should see in this fortunate discovery only reasons for coming together and reuniting against the common enemy." But these were all side issues; the letters themselves proved damning. They were, in essence, reports of conversations with New England Federalists. The very anonymity of Henry's sources made it seem that every resident of New England was cheerfully and openly planning sedition, the overthrow of the presidency, and the breakup of the union. Moreover, with no malefactor named, anyone could be suspected of such treasonous talk, and when read aloud in Congress, Federalists paled, paced, squirmed, and sweated profusely.[21]

The Federalists had to respond quickly. In early nineteenth-century Washington City, social events functioned as polls and mass media do today, providing rapid communication and a way to register a reaction or position quickly. It might take weeks to write, publish, and distribute a pamphlet. The flexibility and visibility of a social event, on the other hand, guaranteed a quick response. On the theory that the best defense is a good offense, the Federalists decided to register, actively and publicly, their disapproval of the president's backroom dealings, and they used Dolley's arena as their venue.

Augustus John Foster, who had returned to the United States in 1812 as British minister, kept a strict eye on the social scene. He noted: "Seven Federalists refused to dine at the President's without having concerted it," suggesting that this strategy had occurred to several opposition members simultaneously. When an eighth realized he would be the only Federalist at dinner, he also withdrew his acceptance. Dolley wrote to Anna that the Federalists were "affronted [to a] Man—not one (I mean of the 2 houses of [Cong]ress) will enter M[adison]s door since the communication of (Henry) to Congress." The North Carolina Republican representative Nathaniel Macon agreed that they were "as mad as they could be," and on March 18, 1812, only a single member of the Federalist Party, Robert Le Roy Livingston, went to the White House drawing room. Livingston found himself in a sticky situation. As a Federalist, he should have stood with his brothers. But in the end, loyalties engendered by patronage and self-interest won out. According to Dolley, he "*consider*[ed] him self attached by his appt. of Colo. to the Gov."[22] Lacking solid evidentiary grounds to protest the Henry letters, the opposition party decided to signal a public breach, hoping (like Robert Smith) to cloud the issue with emotions of outrage and betrayal.

But Dolley remained the social leader of the capital, who had many connections of her own. Even as she reported to Anna that "the Feds. as I told you, ware all affronted with M, refused to dine or come," she gleefully added, "but they have changed their *tack*—last *night* & the *night* before our rooms ware crouded with republicans." She reported triumphantly that "such a rallying of our party has alarm'd them into a *return*. They came in a large party last night also & are continually calling." A New Hampshire Republican congressman, John Harper, confirmed the misfire, noting that nothing had mortified the Federalists more than "finding that the Republicans, in consequence of their conduct, paid their respects to Mr. Madison almost to a man."[23] In fact, Dolley had to hold two drawing rooms that week to accommodate the "political statements."

❧

In February 1811, James Madison had appointed the writer, diplomat, and businessman Joel Barlow American minister to France. Rumor had it that Dolley had secured this plum position for him, and indeed Barlow was undoubtedly a favorite with her, but he possessed ample qualifications. An epic poet and famed wit, he had lived in Europe for seventeen years, serving as the minister to Algiers in 1796. He and his wife, Ruth Baldwin Barlow, moved to Washington City in 1804, where, upon James's election, he nursed the hope of being made secretary of state. The ministry to France, however, seemed to fit his talents best.

The assumption that Dolley obtained this post for Joel Barlow may have stemmed from her efforts to use the mission for her own patronage. She succeeded in securing the job of Joel's secretary for her improvident brother, John, at the impressive salary of $2,000 a year. When, owing to his profligacy and unreliability, John never took up the post, Dolley tried to secure it for Isaac A. Coles, Edward Coles's older brother.[24]

Joel Barlow's appointment preceded a tricky moment in the domino game of U.S. foreign relations. The Barlows were still in America in late June, when James received the bad news from Great Britain that the Orders in Council and other restrictions on trade would be upheld until Napoleon withdrew his decrees; in essence, France had to blink first.

The news of France's release of long-held American ships in July, however, brought hope that Napoleon, indeed, might be the first to crack. Joel's mission, then, was to do whatever he could to encourage the emperor along those lines, with the goal of obtaining reparations for ship seizures and to seek an end to French decrees against commerce. A new, harmonious relationship with France might quell the quarrelsome Federalists and secure the election of 1812 for James. Even more significantly, if Joel Barlow could convince Napoleon to repeal anticommerce decrees and lift trade restrictions, James could force Great Britain to respond in kind, possibly averting war.

Joel sailed for France in July 1811 with his wife and her sister, Clara Baldwin, and his staff. There they were to join William Lee, the U.S. commercial agent. This, too, seemed a good fit; Joel and William had been friends and colleagues for almost twenty years.

The letters between the Barlow household and Dolley were caring and affectionate. Dolley sent gossip and news, many inquiries as to health and happiness, a report of their house left behind, including "the health of your little Dog." But the letters between the women also addressed the political stakes. As the mission unfolded, Dolley expressed support and encouragement; at times, Ruth was apologetic and defensive. After asking about their "progress on the Water," Dolley "confess[ed]" that she cared about their personal happiness much more than "all the success of our Mission." Following this disclaimer, she added, however, that "few have a doubt" of its success, "even the Enemies of *our* Minister admit his talents & Virtue, how then, can any of *them* doubt?"

Along with this rather roundabout compliment (even Joel's enemies—or, more likely, James's—thought he would succeed) Dolley passed on news of successful negotiations with the British in response to the firing on the American ship *Chesapeake*, and of the downfall of Robert Smith. Dolley also complained of the "oppressive" entertaining necessitated by Congress: "Oh! I wish I was in France with you, for a little relaxation."[25]

Though Dolley communicated with the whole party, she had a special relationship with Ruth Barlow, a political wife par excellence and a kindred spirit. A long campaigner in the business of diplomacy, Ruth understood the nuances of her job. She wanted to construct a U.S. presence in France, and twice requested a portrait of the president for their official residence—"if I dare, would ask for yours the same size to hang beside it." Ruth, too, touched upon "feminine" topics in her letters, inquiring about Lucy and the great theater fire in Richmond, while adding that she hoped "things will yet go right here & that good may come out of evil . . . if we can serve our country & do any thing which may add to the honor & prosperity of the present Administration we shall deem ourselves most happy."[26]

As it turned out, Joel Barlow was not succeeding as he and the Madisons had hoped. Probably no one could have; Napoleon had no intention of giving way and even delighted in making trouble by seeming to repeal decrees, throwing U.S. foreign policy into havoc. Welcome news would come of the repeal of the Berlin and Milan decrees—for instance, lifting French restrictions on American shipping—only to be followed by a list of conditions, hidden clauses, and downright prevarications. Indeed, one of Joel's primary missions was to clarify these "repeals." If the emperor would confirm an unequivocal repeal, James would reimpose more stringent trade sanctions on Great Britain.[27] The Barlows were mortified. They feared James's disappointment, and worried that they and their mission might become a political liability, drawing all kinds of fire down upon their heads as well as his. The job of conveying emotion and setting tone belonged to women, and while Ruth and her sister Clara expressed chagrin, Dolley provided reassurance, useful information, and, occasionally, a gentle reprimand.

The off-the-record nature of the women's letters allowed for admissions, appeals to mercy and kindness, and even revelations of process absent from an official report. On occasion, men adopted those models as well. Early in his mission, Joel wrote to Dolley, beginning playfully: "I send you the oddest present that you will receive from France if not of the least value." It was a fourteen-and-a-half-pound beetroot, which he advised she put to seed for animal feed. After a brisk "Our girls will write you about courts & fashions & finery," he got down to business. "I have been here three months at work very hard for our blessed country yet I am afraid I shall have produced but little effect, & the president may think I have been idle." Seeking reassurance, Joel fished, "If he should approve my conduct I wish you would let me know it. For you cannot realize how much I am attached to him & his administration. It is therefore natural that I should be anxious to merit his approbation."

Like other men, Joel did not hesitate to affirm his "attachment" (and to present himself as a sympathetic figure) using women's language of emotion and vulnerability: "Good affections to you & to our beloved Mr. Madison." The connection he felt transcended the "mere" official business of men: "I will not say president, for that name has not so much to do with the heart."[28]

One of Joel's most agonizing tasks was deciding when to send information to the United States via ship. The administration needed as much intelligence as soon as possible, but Joel worried about sending ships off too promptly, only to have some crucial piece of information arrive just after they had departed. However, the longer he kept them, the longer James stayed in the dark. It did not help that the French seemed to delight in toying with the American legate, making him wait for information that never came and feeding him false intelligence.

In his position as a government official, Joel relayed the situation in an official letter to Secretary of State Monroe. He felt so bad, however, that, in addition to his official report, he wrote a private letter to James.[29] Apparently, he also felt the need to explain himself separately to Dolley, sensing that he could describe the ins and outs of the unfortunate situation more freely to her than he could to James.

In December 1811, Joel apologized to Dolley for "his greatest Sin . . . detaining the frigate." He launched into a long and detailed explanation of how the French emperor had kept him waiting by promising an "answer" to American demands. Joel thought this was worth waiting for, especially since Napoleon "assured me with his own mouth" that the answer would be "satisfactory." Moreover, a duke and "every one else that came near the emperor" encouraged Joel by affirming "that he [Napoleon] was very much struck with my note & was probably changing his system relative to the United States."[30] It was not his fault that Bonaparte never gave him an answer.

Though Joel wrote to both halves of the Madison team, Ruth went straight to Dolley to explain the heart of the issue. "I fear my husband will be blamed for having so long detained the *Corvette*," Ruth said, but "he thought it was best, hoping every week & almost every day, the business would be finished as they promised." She expressed her hope that if "they"—the Congress, the newspapers, or the American public—did censure Joel, that "they will not extend it to the president on his account, if not, we shall be content with consciousness of having tried to do the best, to promote the interest & prosperity of the country, the honor & glory of the administration."[31]

Like a Virginia reel, the correspondence between political couples permitted all combinations of partners, switching back and forth with each new call. But perhaps a masked ball supplies a better metaphor: sometimes Ruth spoke as herself to Dolley; at other times, she spoke for Joel. Both Joel and Ruth spoke to James through Dolley, and, in turn, James spoke through Dolley to them.

As the mission continued, Joel's situation grew more awkward. At one point, buoyed by the prospect of obtaining a successful commercial treaty with France, he wrote to a friend and fellow Eli sharing his optimism, with details of his negotiations. James and his administration, however, did not want a commercial treaty at this point, suspecting that Napoleon would use such a development as an excuse to wipe the slate clean, ignoring past American grievances, and wiggling out of a clarification of the repeals. But Joel, a confirmed Francophile, may have thought such a treaty would restore harmonious relations with France.

Unfortunately, he put his trust in someone who lived to persecute the Madisons: the U.S. postmaster general, Gideon Granger. Though seemingly that most rare of political commodities—a Republican from Connecticut—Granger had earlier spread scandals about Dolley and Anna under the guise of refuting them. Since the election of 1808, he had allied himself with the Invisibles and their mission to take James down. In the spring of 1812, Granger leaked Joel's account to the newspapers, simultaneously imparting a false impression of promise (which, if unfulfilled, would cast the French as slippery and dishonest), and the idea that Joel Barlow operated as a loose cannon or independent agent. Indirect damnation was Granger's specialty. In response, Secretary of State Monroe wrote Joel an official letter warning him not to exceed his instructions and make deals with Napoleon that the United States could not support.[32]

James Madison chose to buffer his reaction through his wife's correspondence. Dolley added another layer between the two men, writing to Ruth to "prepare" Joel for the vociferous public reaction. Within a letter in the usual style of news and good wishes, Dolley turned serious. "[A]s I *promised* to write you things, you aught to know you will pardon me when I say *aught,* that gives you pain—I am preparing you, for the disapprobation, expressed at Mr Barlow's having *told* the state of his *Negociation,* to *Mr. Granger* who directly gave it circulation & a place in the N. Papers."

With the blow thus softened, Dolley addressed specifics (James may well have dictated this passage, though Dolley was perfectly cognizant of the affair and its implications): "In the *detail* of objections to *this* communication is—'that you may yet be disappointed'—that 'the *anticipation of such a treaty, might cause improper speculations*—That Mr. G. was not a proper chanel.'" Using the executive branch as a code for the president and the "people" for the House, Dolley comforted both Barlows. "All this is from the *people,* not from the Cabinet—yet you know every thing *vibrates* there." She closed her letter with expressions of love and family ties—"you know that I love you as my sister"—even more effusive than usual.[33]

The story of the Barlow mission once again revealed a government milieu where personalities and personal connections provided the most reliable form of structure.[34] The mission to France would end not only unsuccessfully but sorrowfully. On his way to meet with Napoleon (then in Russia) in order to make the long-desired commercial treaty that would have ensured peace with France, Joel Barlow died from pneumonia, in Vilna, Poland. Sadly, even his death provided political fodder for Madison enemies. The Federalist *Alexandria Gazette* gleefully presented Joel's demise as divine retribution against him and attempts for a separate peace with France.

✤

By 1812, the country's inclination had turned more definitely to war, on the grounds of national "honor," and it was not clear that James could be reelected without a declaration of war. Since the 1810 congressional elections, in which almost half of the older members of the House (most antiwar) lost their seats to prowar candidates, the shift in the country had been evident.[35]

Prominent among the "freshmen" were a group of new legislators who quickly acquired the nickname War Hawks. These young Republicans signaled the rehabilitation of the word "Democratic" by proudly adding it to their party affiliation. This group of articulate and influential "Democratic-Republicans" came from the South and West and included, among others, such future leaders as Henry Clay of Kentucky, who, in 1811, got himself elected Speaker of the House, a post he would hold longer than anyone else in the nineteenth century; John C. Calhoun of South Carolina; and Felix Grundy of Tennessee. They made their case for war on the usual issues of impressment of sailors, the blockading of American ports, and violations of American neutrality, though these concerns had little impact on their home communities.

More fundamentally, it was their vision of an expanding America that fueled their passionate advocacy for war. With the nations of Europe finally expelled from the North American continent, these southern and western members eagerly anticipated the acquisition of Canada, Florida, and Texas. Moreover, the frontier communities that sent the War Hawks to Washington had real-life experience with British "pretensions," as the British incited Native Americans to violence along the edges of the western lands. While the War Hawks' vision ultimately did not inspire the decision to declare war, it did inspire the rhetoric that spurred Congress to action.[36]

From the moment of their arrival in the capital, the War Hawks offered James an opportunity, albeit a double-edged one. Carefully controlled, the Hawks' passion for war could prove useful to James in the future, if he finally decided to resort to armed hostility and needed to persuade his party, his Congress, and his country to support him. On the other hand, the cultivation of such a violent and vociferous minority could backfire if, as he hoped, war proved unnecessary. James needed to keep this growing clique of powerful men close, but he had to avoid an open alliance, which would send a united, yet bellicose, message to the country and the world.

Sharp-eyed Washingtonians soon noted Dolley's adoption of these young men as her protégés. War supporters got the message that war remained a possibility, and James's detractors criticized and caviled. In particular, Henry Clay and Dolley became very close. They shared a taste for snuff; one observer described how she "offered him a pinch from her splendid box, which the gentleman accepted with the grace for which he was distinguished." Snuff could make one sneeze, and Dolley mopped her nose with a "bandana," saying "Mr. Clay, this is for rough work." With a flourish, she then produced "a fine lace handkerchief " as "my polisher," dabbing at her nose in ladylike fashion.[37]

Several of these public encounters with Henry Clay and the snuffbox exist in the Dolley lore, usually mentioned to show Dolley's charming lack of affectation. The politically savvy on the scene, however, read deeper meanings into them. As Sarah Gales Seaton remarked, though snuff taking was felt to be a bad habit, "in her hands the snuff-box seems only a gracious implement with which to charm." Margaret Bayard Smith claimed "a most magical influence" for the snuffbox, delineating its political function: "As perfect a security from hostility, as participation of bread and salt is among savage tribes. For who could partake of its contents offered them in a manner so cordial and gracious and retain a feeling inimical to the interest of the bestower[?]"[38]

Who, indeed? As Washingtonians saw it, the sharing of snuff publicly displayed an alliance between the two families, an alliance that extended into the political realm. Snuff was not the only connection between Dolley and Henry Clay. At times, Dolley seemed remarkably well informed about happenings in the House, perhaps having obtained information from the man she called her "highly valued friend."[39] For the sake of political expediency, too, it made sense for Dolley to ally herself with Clay and his colleagues, who pointed the way to the future.

But the two shared a more profound political synchronicity, as members of the same cohort, the generation whose task it was to translate the abstractions of the founders into political reality. Though neither Dolley nor her "highly valued friend" quite realized it, they were setting the stage for the new democratic system, one that depended not only on popular participation but also on the presence of a powerful federal government and institutionalized political parties. For his part, Clay played a crucial role in preventing the Senate from going the way of the House of Lords, transforming it into a powerful democratic institution. While he could be as noisily male as any of his colleagues (he would even duel with John Randolph in 1825 and weep "with vexation" when he missed), Henry Clay represented the first wave in the development of professional politicians. He would not have understood his work in that way; neither would Dolley. Still, their mutual emphasis on cooperation and compromise distinguished them as modern politicians. Indeed, later in his career, Henry's nickname became the Great Compromiser. In a metaphor for savagery giving way to modernity and professionalization, in December 1811 he even successfully banished John Randolph's dogs from the House.[40]

As it turned out, James did need his hawkish colleagues. As early as December 1811, six months before the declaration of war, Dolley worried to Anna: "I believe there will be War as M sees no end to our perplexities without it—they are going on with the preparations to [g]reat extent."[41] Five months later, she provided her sister with an update: "John Randolph has been firing away at the House, this morning against the declaration of War, but we suppose it will have little effect."

The spring of 1812 brought rapidly deteriorating relations with both England and France. Any headway that Joel Barlow had made with Napoleon died with him; French frigates were burning American ships at sea to prevent shipments of grain to Spain. Though rumor had it that Britain was yielding on the matter of the Orders in Council, British minister Foster informed the congressmen crowded into the State Department to hear the latest dispatches from England that, to the contrary, the Crown had hardened its stance. Moreover, the British government openly threatened the United States with war if the

Madison administration responded in any way, either with anti-British trade restrictions or the arming of American vessels. James felt that the British had left him no choice but war, so "we have nothing left . . . but to make ready for it." Indeed, on June 1, 1812, James sent his War Message to the House. Behind doors closed to the public, the House received the declaration in its usual fashion, with the Federalists moving to quash it through their version of a filibuster. The Republicans responded by throwing spittoons, a surprisingly effective move. The sudden clang of metal stopped the speaker in mid-sentence, allowing the Republicans to declare the delaying tactic ended.[42]

On June 9, the House voted for war, 79–49, with all the Federalists and 15 Republicans dissenting. The message then proceeded to the Senate, where the vote initially stalled at 16–16. On June 17, the tie was broken, and the Senate voted for war, 19–13. War was officially declared on June 18, 1812. At the drawing room the evening before the declaration, the British minister remarked that James looked as though he "very naturally felt all the responsibility he would incur." Many thought that James could not be reelected without a declaration, but the month before, the congressional caucus voted to support James for president, with Elbridge Gerry as vice president. (Upon Gerry's death, in November 1814, James Monroe would become an informal substitute.) New York–based Republicans, determined to break the back of the Virginia dynasty, nominated DeWitt Clinton, nephew of the deceased vice president. Rather than put forth their own candidate, the Federalists backed Clinton as well.[43]

During election season, Dolley's drawing room flourished once again, serving as the nerve center of the process in Washington City. It remained the only place in town where the business of canvassing for office took place, in both subtle and obvious ways. No event better captures the contradictions of a political system built on republicanism than an election, especially a presidential one. With no institutional party system, and with the republican fear of accusations of cronyism, no one could seem openly partisan. James Madison stood as a paragon of republican virtue; as Charles J. Ingersoll marveled, "While a candidate for presidency, no one, however intimate, ever heard him open his lips or say one word of the subject." Just as a man could not run for president, no man could "endorse" a candidate for political reasons. Instead, a candidate had to seem the unequivocal choice of the people's will through no effort of his own. A candidate's "friends" had to justify their support as a reflection of the candidate's inner worth, rather than for any reasons of politics.[44]

In such a system, personality and social attitudes emerged as a basis for rating a man's political prospects.[45] As she had before, Dolley stood in for James as the personification of the candidate. She put herself forward freely as her husband could not, being friendly and intimate, projecting benevolent emotions and inducing them in others. Admirers and enemies alike understood that she acted for her husband, and they complimented and castigated her accordingly. Even as they described Dolley's physical presence and personality using personal language, everyone understood the political implications. For most, the possession of "such a wife!" spoke well for James.

In public, Dolley appeared cheerfully nonpartisan, giving a show of confident good spirits. But she worried about the outcome of the election. She confided her fears to her sister Lucy, who consoled her: "You despair too soon about our ticket. . . . I have great expectations from it yet, no doubt 'twill come out [a] thumping prize." On one occasion, Dolley's fears made her a bit incautious. In December 1811, DeWitt Clinton came to Washington, ostensibly to lobby Congress for funds for a New York canal project but really to feel out support for his presidential bid. As the Federalist Abijah Bigelow reported: "It is said the Queen at the Palace was heard to ask, what that fellow wanted here." Bigelow found this demonstration of petticoat politicking so alarming that he added nervously: "These are things not to be spoken of publicly."[46]

Dolley had reason to worry. Rosalie Stier Calvert reported that James was becoming "poor," "los[ing] supporters every day." Indeed, when the votes came in and the results were declared on December 3, 1812, James had won the election, but by the smallest margin of any election since the Republican Party came to power. The alliance with the War Hawks had made the difference: the five new western states, which had sent them to Congress, gave all of their electoral votes to James. Those states aside, James received only 90 electoral votes from the original states; DeWitt Clinton had 89. In his analysis of the election, James G. Blaine, future congressman, secretary of state, and historian, handed Dolley the credit for securing a second term for her husband. "She saved the administration of her husband, held him back from the extreme of Jeffersonianism and enabled him to escape the terrible dilemma of the war. But for her Dewitt Clinton would have been chosen president in 1812."[47]

Such government bureaucracy as existed during the Madison administration could not handle the issues that faced it: war, election, and a growing, quarrelsome Congress, to say nothing of a renegade secretary of state, dueling congressmen, and an international spy and a con man with letters to sell. At crucial moments, Dolley's social scene supplied an extraofficial political structure, one that fostered a freewheeling atmosphere where all politicked. When a diplomat threatened to stray from approved paths, it was through Dolley's correspondence with his wife that the administration reined him in. Her political work focused on circumventing the presidential weakness dictated by the Constitution. To this end, she fostered an atmosphere of coalition and connection making. She not only expanded the power of the presidency through the unofficial sphere, but also (unintentionally) strengthened Congress during this crucial period in the institution's growth.

Dolley's work expands our definition of the political. Shifting the point of view away from voting broadens the definition of politics to include any action taken that affects affairs of state, the government, or the community. Politics can maintain the status quo or change it; to accomplish either end, people will use both formal and informal channels. The effectiveness of the unofficial sphere lies in its half-hidden quality. Some historians characterize social connections as facilitated by women at social events as "alternative circuits for power to circulate."[48] These circuits are concealed, cleverly disguised, but no less real. The cover of "society," as well as the unofficial sphere's emphasis on process over product, makes it hard to quantify results. At times, however, the results are discernible, with clear wins and losses.

Dolley undoubtedly cut short one cycle of male violence around the business of government when she stopped the Randolph-Eppes duel, but she did not disarm John Randolph for good. Her social strategy failed to stop Robert Smith's pamphlet, though had the Smiths decided to participate in the opportunity she offered, they could have saved his reputation and career. At many specific times, Dolley stepped in with the short-term goal of lowering the pitch and potential unpleasantness of a situation. In the end, these efforts did not stop war nor did they deter the Federalist Party. But her accomplishments amount to more than a mere scorecard of successes and failures in particular incidents. By definition, successful quid pro quo deals in the unofficial sphere remain hidden; only failures are visible, and not in every case. Seen more broadly, Dolley's work answered immediate political needs by building extraofficial structures and shaping a workable political culture. In addition, Dolley, as the administration's charismatic figure, also served longer-term symbolic functions.

Symbolic processes, with their emphasis on emotions, aesthetics, and deep psychological needs, demonstrate that politics is a fundamental human activity. It encompasses all kinds of human behaviors, from the greatest altruism to the basest selfishness. Under Dolley's watchful eye, the members of the quarrelsome Congress, and, more important, the members' families, came to know each other as people.

Dolley did not rely entirely on social conventions to guarantee that political guests would be on their best behavior. She took the political culture and the social sphere of Washington City to a new level by consciously fostering a policy of noncontention and harmony. By example and direct intervention, she forced people to behave well, while exerting a great deal of control over her own emotions. Dolley provided politicians with an alternative to the macho, violent, all-or-nothing official male political structure. With their emphasis on defusing tension and encouraging cooperation, Dolley's feminine forms modeled a modern politics, one that transcended confrontation and coercion. Her understanding of the dynamics that a democracy needs marks her as not only a master politician, but also one of the few modern politicians of her era.

FOURTEEN

"Mr. Madison's War"

*U*nbeknownst to the Americans, two days before America's declaration of war on June 18, 1812, the British government repealed the Orders in Council that had restricted neutral trade, one of the main issues that motivated prowar advocater. Word of the repeal came too late to stop the martial momentum. It was hardly auspicious that the young nation took on the world's premier military power because of slow mail.

When war was finally declared, the usually reserved John C. Calhoun had hugged Henry Clay around the neck and joined the other War Hawks in their version of a Shawnee war dance around the boardinghouse table. Such enthusiasm did not last long.[1] The seemingly unanimous "war fever" that congressmen and other Americans felt in the first weeks arose partly from the relief of finally ending the long, agonizing buildup. But the fever soon broke and all the old troubles asserted themselves. Only months after the declaration, Virginia representative William Burwell dryly remarked to his wife, Letitia, that "Party sentiment runs higher than war." He feared that the United States would "be disgraced by its baneful influence" in the eyes of the world. Burwell also feared for James—"the difficulties of his situation have increased in a great degree." It would become even harder for James to get things done after the next congressional elections, which would send new political enemies from the Federalist camp to Washington. His only hope lay in "influenc[ing] public sentiment by [some] brilliant achievement."[2] New Hampshire representative Jeremiah Kilburn also correctly pinpointed the crux of the "alarming crisis." He called it "alarming not on account of any foreign dangers but internal dangers which threaten destruction to our happy union and nat'l prosperity."

Underlying the anger and dissension was anxiety, another byproduct of the protracted process that had led to war. Though the arguments had lasted for years, the actual declaration caught the nation off guard. Even advocates of war believed that more preparations should have been made before the official start of hostilities. Congressmen were not the only Washingtonians who buckled under pressure. A well-known Washington lady drove to the White House, stood up in her carriage, took down her hair, "celebrated for its length," and declared that "she would gladly part with it to hang Mr. Madison!" Understandably, "Mrs. Madison found it difficult to forgive this insult to her husband."[3]

Rumors abounded. Newspapers warned of plots to "seiz[e] the President and Secretaries . . . making this nation a laughing stock." Of particular concern to Dolley were stories of spies who came to the White House disguised as women, bent on stealing James's papers. Anonymous letters, some threatening, some friendly, warned of attempts to threaten his life with "dagger or poison."[4]

After the declaration, James paid a personal visit to the offices of the war and navy departments, something that he had never done before. Taking a cue from his wife, James donned a "huge cockade" on a little round hat "in a manner worthy of a little commander in chief."[5] But such a brave show could not compensate for the many problems that beset the war effort from the start.

The nation received the declaration in ways that made visible the deep party divisions. Republican strongholds greeted the "glorious" news with parades and cannon fire, and celebratory illuminations lit the night sky. In the Northeast, the Federalists hung flags at half mast, closed shops, and tolled church bells, mourning the "overwhelming calamity." Cities with significant proportions of both parties saw conflicts. Most clashes were symbolic, as in Providence, Rhode Island, where, in a cacophonous competition, the Republican cannons tried to drown out the Federalist church bells. In a Philadelphia coffeehouse, the reading of the declaration of war was greeted by "huzzas and acclimations"; Federalist customers who hissed were informed that they were in "an American Coffee house" and that they should go elsewhere if they wanted to drink British coffee.[6]

Republicans fully expected that, after the first shock, the Federalists would rally to the cause. As the days and weeks passed, these expectations proved unfounded. From the moment of the declaration until the peace treaty, the Federalists openly criticized what they considered to be, in the words of the Massachusetts House of Representatives, an act of "inconceivable folly and desperation." Indeed, to not oppose the war in the New England states was considered "heresy."[7]

The conflict between pro- and antiwar forces ran highest and most deadly in Baltimore. The third largest city in the nation, and a prominent port, it housed a large proportion of single men working its many maritime industries, and they had firsthand experiences of British arrogance. The rowdy populace did not take kindly to Federalists, so when Alexander Contee Hanson and Jacob Wagner, editors of the *Federal Republican,* published antiwar diatribes two days after the declaration, a group of lower-class men decided to attack the newspaper offices. On June 21, 1812, the mob broke into the offices, destroying the presses and scattering type. As a coup de grâce, they pulled the entire building down. Fortunately for Hanson and Wagner, they had left town. Baltimore officials, war supporters almost to a man, decided to ignore the incident.

On July 25, 1812, Hanson and his supporters returned to Baltimore from Georgetown. Two days later, another antiwar edition of the

Federal Republican appeared, which also denounced the mob action and the official indifference. In an act of bravado, Hanson published the newspaper's new address on the masthead. That evening the "boys" gathered again—four hundred strong—and proceeded to stone the house. The standoff that followed lasted through the night. Finally, Baltimore officials intervened, persuading Hanson and his supporters, as well as the crowd, that taking the newspaper's editor to jail was the best solution. Though the mob let the procession pass, later that night they pulled the jail down, and went after the prisoners.

At least two men died in the attack; many more were hurt, and though Hanson escaped by playing dead, he suffered severe internal injuries and damage to his spinal cord. He would die seven years later, at the age of thirty-three. Another casualty, ironically, was a hero of the Revolution, "Light Horse" Harry Lee. The men who attacked him did not care that he was a decorated patriot and that he had eulogized General Washington. Lee, too, suffered from internal injuries; his head wounds were so severe that his speech was affected and his face remained swollen for months. Like Hanson, he never fully recovered, and he died eight years later.[8]

News of this civil unrest must have been daunting for James and Dolley. The war was a month old, and the only blood spilled was American. None of the protests against the Alien and Sedition Acts, with their curtailment of a free press, had been so violent as this stand for censorship.

Prowar advocates might decry the opposition as traitorous, but one of the Federalists' objections proved irrefutable: this was the first time the federal government had tried to organize and wage a war, and it was ill prepared. From the leaders at the top to the men on the ground, the chain of command suffered innumerable weak links. The secretary of war, William Eustis, had no experience in overseeing such a massive operation, and he compensated by focusing on details, such as the price of shoes, while losing touch with his commanders in the field. The senior officers were either old (leftovers from the Revolution) or incompetent, having achieved their rank through political favors. None had experience in evaluating battle strategy and not a single regular soldier met European standards. Promising junior officers, such as Winfield

Scott and Zachary Taylor, would not occupy positions of authority until later.

The structural inadequacies went from top to bottom. Enlistment was low, as was morale, but even the most enthusiastic of volunteers were woefully inexperienced. Desertion became so widespread so quickly that less than four months into the fighting, James had to issue a blanket pardon in order to lure his soldiers back. The government offered enlistees the highest bounty of any army in the world—$124 and 320 acres of land for five years of service. Still, it would not be until the last year of the war that the U.S. Army would perform maximally.[9]

And here was where Federalist resistance proved most damaging. Contrary to the expectations of their elders, young men in the Northeast signed up in respectable numbers, but the governors of Massachusetts and Connecticut would not put the nation's best militias to federal service. Asserting their sovereignty over the state militia, they argued that war with Great Britain did not justify emergency measures. New York's militia relied too heavily on the poor for participation, and it was not until 1814, with a restructured, more equitable system, that the state could offer a well-trained militia.[10]

Personnel was not the only problem. Under Jefferson, the republican fear of standing armies had resulted in reductions in the army's size and scope; in 1802, Congress had dismantled the quartermaster and commissary corps for reasons of economy. The navy was in better shape. In spite of dubious leadership (Paul Hamilton, an acknowledged alcoholic, was said to be useless by noon), the Quasi War with France and the Barbary Wars had underscored the need for American sea power and so budget cuts had been relatively few. Still, it was hardly ready to take on the most powerful navy in the western world. Only in the area of weaponry did the United States stand secure. The congressionally created department was from its inception a well-oiled machine. More important, the nation already possessed thriving armories in Springfield, Massachusetts, and Harpers Ferry, Virginia, which kept the troops well supplied with ammunition, small arms, and test ordnance.[11]

Underlying all the logistical difficulties, of course, was money. The U.S. Treasury was almost bankrupt, and the pool of potential lenders pitifully small. New England bankers lent very little money to the war effort, though the region would prosper through illegal trade with the enemy and manufacturing. Crisis was averted only by John Jacob Astor's $12 million intervention.[12]

Long before war was declared against Great Britain, James had determined that Canada would be the focus of the United States' strategy. At first glance, this seemed to make sense. Canada was the closest British possession, with only about 500,000 white people (at this time the U.S. population was 7.5 million). Moreover, the country posed a tangible threat to the United States, as the British continued to arm northern Native Americans and encourage movement against the settlers across the border.

However sound this logic, it struck many as puzzling that a war over maritime issues would be fought so far inland. The Federalists considered Canada guilty only by association. Many saw more sinister implications in the focus on Canada, suspecting the Republicans of using war as an excuse to annex it. Though James never issued a statement of intentions, the Federalists figured that James intended to capture Canada and hold it hostage, forcing the British to accede to American demands for free trade and the end of impressment. The logic behind this scenario seemed shaky at best: if England refused to negotiate, would the United States find itself, like the kidnappers of Red Chief, saddled with a large and troublesome territory that would undermine national stability? To be fair to the Federalist naysayers, the Republicans had not made it clear how a land war in Canada would earn British concessions on the high seas. But James had no doubts. The capture of Canada would surely bring the British to their knees because they needed the vast natural resources that the territory offered. The loss of the United States and the more recent cessation of trade with France and her possessions made Britain more dependent than ever on Canada's wood, fish, fur, and manufactures.[13]

However Americans felt on the issue of Canada, all agreed that the conquest could be easily achieved. Not only did the United States have a larger army—12,000 troops to Canada's 7,000—but Americans assumed that a significant proportion of Canada's population could be persuaded to join the U.S. cause. Many people in lower Canada were of French origin, and in upper Canada, a third or more of the population was American by birth or descent. At the very least, the Americans fully expected to be welcomed into Canada with cheers. Jefferson was not alone when from his mountaintop he pronounced the conquest of Canada "a mere matter of marching."[14]

James chose his targets with care. He eliminated heavily fortified Quebec, partly because success there would depend on help from unreliable New England. Montreal per se he deemed too far east to seem advantageous to western Americans plagued by Native American depredations. In the end, James and his generals planned a three-pronged attack on Montreal and the Niagara and Detroit frontiers. A great deal of time and effort would be expended to recapture the fort at Michilimackinac, part of the island of Mackinac, off the coast of the present-day cities of the Midwest. Though it was of no discernible strategic importance, men at the top in both the army and the navy repeatedly stressed the need to secure the minor fort. Surely the fact that Michilimackinac was part of John Jacob Astor's empire and that on July 17, 1812, the British had seized furs and goods belonging to Astor, had something to do with their focus.[15]

The western campaign—the attack on Detroit—started promptly enough in July 1812, led by General William Hull, who had a record of distinguished Revolutionary War service, but was fifty-nine, and, as subsequent events would prove, emotionally unstable. Even before the official declaration, Hull had had orders to march on Fort Detroit, located on the Detroit River that linked Lakes Erie and Huron. He had encountered an unexpected obstacle from his own troops, however: some of them refused to cross the border. They would fight *for* their country but only *in* their country. Successfully reaching and occupying Fort Detroit on July 5, Hull next planned to attack Fort Malden, to the south. Though commanding an army twice as large as the British force guarding Fort Malden, Hull suffered setback after setback: he lost his supply lines to the British, while fierce and unexpected attacks by

Native Americans unnerved him to the extent that he decided to abandon his plan and retreat to Fort Detroit.

The British commander, Sir Isaac Brock, mounted a siege of Fort Detroit and spooked Hull with rumors of a large Indian attack. Terrified at the thought of massacre (there were women and children in the fort), Hull fell apart. Over the next few weeks, he developed a tremor in his voice; he began chewing tobacco compulsively and crouching in corners at loud noises. On August 16, 1812, he surrendered to the British, giving up the fort and his whole army. This capitulation, coupled with his earlier evacuation of Fort Dearborn, rendered the northwestern territories of the United States vulnerable.[16]

Two months later, the eastern prong of the Canadian invasion was launched. A forty-eight-year-old Federalist, Major General Stephen Van Rensselaer, a man with no professional military experience, led the assault on Niagara. A militiaman, Van Rensselaer shared the command with Brigadier General Alexander Smyth of the regular army. Though Van Rensselaer had 6,000 troops on the banks of the Niagara River—three times the number of British and Native American combatants—the operation quickly stalled. He had intended to attack in two locations—Queensland Heights and at Fort George—but Smyth refused to take orders from a mere militia commander. Van Rensselaer managed to get an estimated 600 men across the river, led by young, ambitious General Winfield Scott, but when he tried to cross the others, they balked, like Hull's men refusing to leave American soil. Scott's small force could not hold out without reinforcements and surrendered. Van Rensselaer was relieved of his duties, and the command given to Smyth, who readied for an attack on Fort Erie. In this case, not only did the Pennsylvania militia also refuse to cross the border, but Smyth inspired so little confidence that his own officers voted him down.[17]

The third, and most important, target was Montreal. For this action, another former Revolutionary War soldier took command. At sixty-one, Henry Dearborn, secretary of war under Jefferson, was known as Old Granny. In November 1812, with 6,000 to 8,000 men under his command, he managed to infiltrate the area with a small detachment, which actually engaged with the enemy. When darkness fell, however, they began firing on each other. Once again, the militia refused to follow their fellows. Though they had constitutional grounds for doing so—they were *state* militia, not a federal force—probably the sight of the bodies being brought back from the fields had more to do with their decision. Contemporaries regarded the campaign as a "miscarriage, without even [the] heroism of disaster."[18]

The Canadian front, the one aspect of the war that all assumed would succeed (John Randolph called it "a holiday campaign"), brought nothing but what newspapers characterized as "an unbroken series of disaster, defeat, disgrace, and ruin and death." In contrast, the sea campaign was going surprisingly well. In part, this was a matter of the difference in personnel: highly skilled professionals staffed the navy. America had enjoyed a mercantile maritime tradition since its colonial days, and in addition to superb sailors, the navy had men with war experience in the earlier clashes with France and Tripoli. Supplies were also top notch: seventeen ships, of which seven were frigates, warships smaller and faster than battleships. Three of those were "super frigates," bigger and stronger than ordinary ships, carrying forty-four guns apiece.[19]

The Royal Navy, of course, was unparalleled, boasting over a thousand ships, with half deployed at any given time. But Great Britain was preoccupied with Napoleon's rebuilding of the fleet in the Mediterranean and did not dedicate much of its impressive fleet to the comparatively small troubles in North America. In addition, although the repeal of the Orders in Council had arrived too late to avert the U.S. declaration of war, the British hoped that it would end the hostilities.[20]

Americans needed a boost in morale after the disheartening failures on land; in the late summer of 1812, they got one. On August 19, one of the super frigates, the USS *Constitution*, under the command of Isaac Hull (nephew of the less-than-stable William Hull), met the British ship *Guerrière* about 750 miles east of Halifax. The *Constitution* dispatched the enemy ship in about thirty minutes, with only seven U.S. dead and seven wounded. The *Guerrière* counted fifteen dead and sixty-three wounded; the ship itself suffered so much damage that Hull was forced to sink her rather than claim her as a prize. During this battle, the American ship acquired her famous nickname: one of the *Constitution*'s sailors saw a shot bounce off her hull, and exclaimed, "Huzza, her sides are made of iron." In the United States, the story of "Old Ironsides" and Hull's victory was celebrated border to border.[21]

October 1812 brought multiple victories when the American brig *Wasp* seized the British *Frolic*, killing or wounding almost 80 percent of the crew. A more spectacular feat occurred a week later, on October 15, when Stephen Decatur, commanding the USS *United States*, took the British frigate *Macedonian*, bringing her into Newport, the first and only time that a British frigate had been brought in as a prize of war. The Americans lost only about a dozen men; the British lost more than a hundred. And in December 1812, Old Ironsides so devastated the enemy ship *Java* off the coast of Brazil, that, like the *Guerrière*, she had to be burned and sunk. The American commander William Bainbridge lost thirty-four seamen, a small loss compared to the British death toll of 122.[22]

All the while American ships were also serving the nation in less dramatic but nonetheless crucial functions. In first two, and then three squadrons, they escorted American merchant ships returning from Europe safely into port. American ships came in with goods that boosted the national economy, and with them came more experienced sailors who would join the fight on the seas.

Lacking the taste or instinct for war and the decisive, even heavy-handed, leadership it requires, James was at best a middling commander-in-chief. And his commitment to the constitutional separation of powers prevented him from expanding the capacity of the executive to direct and control Congress, as future presidents would do in wartime.

He had little chance for the kind of "brilliant achievement" that William Burwell had prescribed. That achievement would be Dolley's. Hers would not be the dramatic, easily visible acts of battlefield heroism. In the way of women's work, Dolley achieved a subtler, more sustained success. At each stage of James's career, she had taken the work of the political wife to new levels. When James became president, Dolley created the de facto office of First Lady; during wartime, she intensified and focused the First Lady's power as social leader and as the charismatic figure of the Madison administration and the United States.

As always, most of her work took place at social events, where her "course" was to "destroy rancorous feeling—then so bitter between Federalists and Republicans," as Mary Cutts characterized the situation. Following the declaration of war, the Madisons spent only one week at Montpelier, returning quickly to Washington City, according to Dolley, "in the midst of business & anxiety—anxious for the fate of the War, *only*." The congressional season began in October that year, and Dolley got down to the business of society immediately, with her first drawing room on the twenty-seventh. She gave more parties during the war than she had previously, arranging for special treats at table and more music to be performed during her wartime drawing rooms.[23] As it became increasingly difficult for members of Congress to work out their troubles in the official houses, the social space in the president's house assumed greater importance. At work, legislators challenged one another, the government, and even the union. Under Dolley's eye, the mandate of sociability ensured that legislators check their differences at the door and treat each other well, as though they were all one nation.

For the rest of the country, Dolley's events were assurance that the government was functional and continuing on a clear path. Women remained her greatest allies, and in her mission to keep everyone calm and optimistic, according to Mary Cutts, "the Ladies as usual participated strongly." Anna and Lucy joined her in the hostess duties, and, though married ladies have their charms, Dolley also enlisted "a multitude of Beauties" to attract visitors. "Miss Mayo," "Miss Caton," "Miss Hay," and the always bewitching Elizabeth Patterson Bonaparte supplied the White House with a wellspring of allure and gaiety. Dolley likened her social campaign to a military one (albeit humorously), calling up her female allies as a general would his troops. Urging Sarah Gales Seaton to attend her "Wednesday nights," she implored her "not to desert the standard altogether."[24]

As both cause and consequence of Dolley's strategy, the level of social activity in Washington City reached an unprecedented pitch. With much business curtailed by first the embargo and then the war, visitors and travelers had begun coming to the capital in increased numbers to while away their enforced "leasure." Increasing numbers of political families came, too, especially after the declaration; locals noted the presence of more members' wives than ever before during the 1812–13 congressional season. During the wartime crush, that seasoned social veteran Margaret Bayard Smith confessed herself a poor caller, visiting only fifty families in one week. Dolley no doubt visited that many and more.[25]

"Mrs. Madison's Wednesday nights" had always drawn crowds of two and three hundred. During the war, five hundred guests regularly "squeezed" at her drawing rooms. Dolley felt the strain of it; the phrase that she used to describe the social season—"routine of gaiety"—hints at the labor and calculation behind these "brilliant scenes." To make things even more hectic, that first month of the 1812–13 congressional season, Dolley's butler left for France. As she confessed to Edward Coles: "I am acting in his Dept. & that the city is more *than ever* crouded with strangers!! My head is *dizy*."[26]

Beyond the social demands, there were plenty of reasons to be anxious. Dolley followed the war closely, as she passed on news of "the disgraceful conduct of Hull . . . & the brave Harrison" to Edward Coles. She castigated the general who had given over the Northwest Army: "Genl. Hull had surrender'd Detroit, *himself* & the whole Army to the British! Do you not tremble with resentment, at this treacherous act?" But her famed tolerance—or perhaps her political caution—as always asserted itself. "Yet, we must not judge the Man until we are in possesion of his reasons—they have not arrived, but all we *have* hear'd is unfavorable to his honor."[27]

Dolley's role as the personification of the Madison team continued and intensified as the war limped along. No matter the news, Dolley demonstrated, in the words of one observer, "remorseless equanimity."[28] The fighting belonged in the field, not at her drawing room. James represented one side of an unpopular and divisive war; in contrast, Dolley could transcend sides, assuming the mantle of disinterested patriotism, and present the one thing everyone could agree on (at least in public): the United States of America.

She made herself visible everywhere, never neglecting the local community. With Marcia Burnes Van Ness she organized "fringe parties," reminiscent of the "Spinning bees" of the American Revolution; instead of producing homespun, the ladies braided white cotton trim for the epaulets of the militia. Dolley had always been held in high regard by the military; when James was the secretary of state, troops had paraded past the Madison house, rather than the president's house, to be addressed by her. During wartime, she remained a focus for the troops, reviewing them like a general. When soldiers marched by the White House, she invited them inside and served them refreshments, "giving liberally of the best of the house."[29]

Dolley well understood that visibility was vital to both military and national morale. She publicly touted and celebrated every meager success of the American forces. After General William Henry Harrison, fresh off a victory, reported to James at the White House, the president ordered him back to the field. Dolley, however, rightly intuited that the public would want to see him and honor him, and, contravening James's orders, brought him to her drawing room.[30]

When the American forces captured the British ships *Guerrière* and *Macedonian* during the 1812 naval campaign, officers presented Dolley with their colors in ceremonious fashion at balls and parties. Edward Coles instigated the first of these presentations, no doubt apprehending their worth to a public starved for good news. Federalists such as the Massachusetts congressman Samuel Taggert did their best to taint these tableaux of triumph with stories of Dolley defiantly stamping on the colors. "An Englishman in the city hearing this report basely observed that Charlotte, meaning the Queen of Great Britain, would not have done so with the American colours." Always sensitive to slander, Dolley maintained that on the occasion in question, the men had been carrying the flag to her by the corners, when "Commodore Stuart let his end fall, either by accident or design (the motive has been much questioned. . . .)." According to Dolley's version, it was another lady who "said instantly, 'trample on it trample on it!'" Dolley drew back, saying, "'Oh! not so!' while the Lady advanced and put her foot upon it!"[31]

For all her conciliatory political style and her personal preference for noncontention, Dolley was a fierce, at times rabid, patriot. She supported "Mr. Madison's War" unquestioningly, and not just because it was her husband's doing. Dolley believed in the honor culture; six months before the declaration of war, she reported to Anna of the United States' "determination to fight for our rights." At the presentation of the *Macedonian*'s standard, Sarah Gales Seaton remarked on Dolley's spontaneous reaction: "I saw her color come and go."[32] The deep flush of pride and emotion at this display of American victory in war came from her heart.

Still, as a woman, and a woman who stood for the United States as a whole, Dolley had to avoid displays of aggressiveness. With the country so divided, a prowar stance became a partisan stand. As so often, Dolley had to walk a fine line—this time between patriotism and the "natural" passivity of women—and she mostly succeeded. When the Quaker preachers Rebecca Crispin Hubbs and Sarah Scull met with her in July 1813 as part of their mission to persuade James to end the war, they left assured that "the adulation she received, could not corrupt her *pure and pacific disposition*." Even in wartime, according to her cousin Sally Coles, "you are ever the same benevolent being, always attentive to the happiness of others." But Dolley's tack combined peacefulness with principle; she would not have "peace at any price." The "pacific" Dolley played strictly to type when she forgave the lady who offered her hair to hang James; "she did not [forgive], however, before the Lady changed her politics."[33]

❧

In January 1813, William Burwell began the new year by observing to his wife: "Mr. Madison is in a most perilous situation unless he can impress more energy into the Army than heretofore . . . disgust will prevail everywhere."[34] James needed to make some changes, and, if the *New England Palladium* was to be believed, he employed Dolley to soften the blow. It reported that a few days before he asked Secretary of Navy Paul Hamilton to resign, his wife began to suspect such an eventuality.

Her proof? "The great attention paid her by Mrs. Madison." It was common knowledge that "whenever any of the *great state dependents* are to be sacrificed" Dolley, "who knows everything going on—and indeed moves many things—" treated the female family members with "more than common attention and civility." James replaced Hamilton with William Jones and Secretary of War William Eustis with John Armstrong that month.

Once again, the navy achieved significant victories. In February 1813, the USS *Hornet* defeated the British *Peacock,* and in August, the *Essex,* a small American frigate, not only overmastered HMS *Alert* but also captured a troop transport with 160 soldiers. The American strategy still centered on Canada, but shifted to attacking the principal naval base at Kingston, Ontario, a secondary naval base at York, and Forts Erie and George. Since water travel proved the only way to move through the dense Canadian wilderness, control of the Great Lakes, especially Ontario and Erie, was crucial. Indeed, British control of the lakes had contributed to the earlier American defeats.[35]

Captain Isaac Chauncey commanded the American naval forces on Lakes Ontario and Erie. Aside from skirmishes with the British fleet under the command of Sir James Yeo, Chauncey launched his most significant action against the town of York.[36] A secondary base at the western end of Lake Ontario, with only about six hundred residents, York was primarily valuable as a symbol: it was the capital of upper Canada. In late April 1813, Chauncey quickly overpowered the seven hundred British and Native American defenders of the city. The Americans gained one British ship; the British had to destroy another, along with some supplies, to avoid American capture. The British suffered 150 casualties; however, the Americans lost 320 men when a magazine exploded. Rattled by this calamity, the Americans needed little pretext for mayhem. They found it when they supposedly discovered a scalp in one of the government buildings. On the ill-founded theory that this indicated that the British had encouraged Indian atrocities, the American forces proceeded to loot the town.[37]

Chauncey did not gain Lake Ontario, but the victory over "little York" enabled the Americans to maintain parity on the water. And the

British and Canadians felt very keenly the humiliation of having their capital looted. On Lake Erie, victory was more decisive. In October 1812, in a surprise attack, Lieutenant Jesse Elliot had captured two British ships, the *Detroit* and the *Caledonia*. Almost a year later, on September 10, 1813, the new commodore, twenty-eight-year-old Oliver H. Perry, commanding the *Lawrence,* met with two British ships, the *Detroit* (named after the lost vessel) and the *Queen Charlotte*. Perry was ready for a fight—he had spread the decks with sand so that his men would not slip on seawater or blood—but after two hours of combat he had to abandon his floating husk, fleeing in a small boat. He returned with the *Niagara,* fought off six British ships, and captured the ill-fated *Detroit*. Scribbling on the back of an old letter, he reported back to Harrison: "We have met the enemy and they are ours." The line and the story quickly became the cause of national rejoicing and passed almost immediately into legend.[38]

Perry's securing of Lake Erie led to more success. From his days as the governor of the Indiana territory, Harrison had both martial and diplomatic experience with the area's Native Americans. In 1811, he had marched on a confederation of Native American tribes led by the Shawnee chief Tecumseh. The ensuing battle of Tippecanoe settled no issue definitively, but it broke up the confederation. In late September 1813, Harrison met his old nemesis, now fighting with the British, at the battle of the Thames, a Canadian river about 350 miles east of Detroit. The assembled British troops, five hundred Native Americans and eight hundred regulars, gave way easily to Harrison's three thousand men. The Native American fighters lasted longer, but lost heart and fled when they learned that Tecumseh had been killed. In a grisly display, American soldiers plundered the Shawnee chief's body for souvenirs—clothes, hair, and even skin. Perry and Harrison had turned the tide in their theater of war, as was evident eighteen months later, when, in the Second Treaty of Grenville, Harrison secured a pledge from the remaining tribes to switch sides and fight against the British.[39]

Even in the face of such good news, the Federalists sulked. In June, the victories at sea inspired celebration in the capital in the form of "a splendid dinner." Two hundred people attended, but not one Federalist, though they had been invited. The joke that made the rounds was that the famously French-hating Federalists were "reserving themselves to celebrate the Russian victories over Napoleon."[40]

Phoebe Morris reported on Philadelphia's reaction to the war news, describing the city as: "So animated . . . that I can scarcely suppose myself in sober Philadelphia." Not one, but "two general illuminations" fanned the "patriotic Spirit." Both public and private buildings sported the names and pictures of Perry and Harrison and indeed, their images "have been introduced in every form that Fancy could devise to celebrate their fame." At the theater, colored lamps, "intertwined with the laurel of Victory," spelled out Perry's name.[41]

In spite of these initial victories, by the second half of the year the scales had tipped. If the British had been slow to apprehend the challenge from American ships in 1812, they quickly caught up. Their weapon of choice was the blockade. Whereas in the autumn of 1812, the British had blockaded the coast from Spanish Florida up to Charleston, South Carolina, by early 1813, the blockade extended to the Chesapeake and Delaware Bays. By late that year, they had obstructed the entire coast south of New England. As a reward for the region's antiwar stance, the British fleet kept the northern New England coast free, which also served the purpose of allowing supplies to keep flowing from Canada and the British West Indies.

Foreign trade dried up, but the British presence interfered with domestic coastal trade as well. Deprived of water transport, American merchants clogged the inadequate roads. The mercantile traffic jam caused both gluts and shortages, as well as trebling the price of commodities such as coffee, tea, flour, sugar, and molasses.[42]

⚜

In the spring of 1813, a prospect for peace appeared and from an unlikely source. Russia had its own part to play in the European hostilities. In 1806, Napoleon had declared a "continental blockade" against trade with England. When in 1812 he discovered that Russia was indeed conducting commerce with its ally, he invaded. Tsar Alexander I decided that the Americans needed to make peace with Great Britain, an outcome that would benefit both Russia and the United States. Obviously, Russia wanted all the great or potentially great powers behind it against France; peace with America would allow Great Britain to concentrate on defeating Napoleon. And perhaps a grateful America would join its new benefactor. Accordingly, through his representative in Washington City, Andrei Dashkov, the tsar issued an offer to mediate. For James, this proposal, first made at a White House dinner on January 28, 1813, represented a chance to bring the feckless conflict to an end—as well as an opportunity to ally the United States with a superpower besides the troublesome twosome. Moreover, if Russia did Great Britain's job and quelled France, additional British land armies might be freed up to travel across the Atlantic. That winter, in light of the hostilities, Dolley had decided not to visit the houses of foreign ministers, but she signaled the administration's appreciation of the tsar's offer by attending Daschoff's imperial ball on March 5, where she "feasted and stayed late."[43]

The peace commission for the Russian mediation would have to be first-rate. With ex-Federalist John Quincy Adams already in place in Russia, it only made sense to send the multilingual Albert Gallatin as well. To give the commission a unified cast, the sympathetic Federalist James A. Bayard joined the team. In addition, James assembled three attachés—Payne Todd, now twenty-one and the nearest thing America had to a prince, and two other young men, George M. Dallas and Christopher Hughes. The Gallatins also decided to send their seventeen-year-old son, James, to accompany his father. Daschoff kept the wheels moving by suggesting that the chancellor of the Russian Empire, Count Romanzoff, send presents to Dolley, decorate the young men with military honors, and cover the expenses of the American delegation.

In order to arrive before the Russian winter set in, the party sailed as soon as Congress approved the mission, which it did on May 9, though the commission members still had to be approved. In early June, Albert Gallatin's enemies in the Senate saw their chance and rejected his nomination to the peace commission. Federalist and Invisible senators pointed out that Albert could not hold two positions—as peace envoy and secretary of the treasury—at once. They insisted that James replace Albert at the treasury and then come to them with the peace nomination. At which point, they could exclude Albert from government altogether.

Albert himself had foreseen that "my going to Russia will probably terminate in the appointment of another Secretary of the Treasury, and thus a return to private life." Left behind at home, Hannah would have welcomed this; in fact, she hoped that the news of his rejection would reach him in time for a summer return.[44]

James and Albert had been colleagues for years, and respected and liked each other. For his country's good, as well as on account of his own preference, James wanted to keep such a talented man in the government. At the same time, Albert constituted an enormous political liability, being the focus of hate groups like the Invisibles. (Robert Smith's downfall had only shifted, rather than ended, this animus.) More than once, an exasperated Albert had threatened to tender his resignation. James refused to accept it; but also, more than once, he had had to find ways of appeasing him. He was not free to favor Albert as he wished; for instance, he did not risk antagonizing his enemies by appointing him secretary of state.

As surrogates for their husbands, Dolley and Hannah had delicate work to do, and not for the first time. During the tense early months of the war, Dolley honored Hannah by inviting her to preside at one of her drawing rooms. New York's own Washington Irving reported that "she filled Mrs. Madison's chair to a miracle." Hannah's sartorial style, while not as splashy as some, had "more splendor than any other of the nobles."[45]

But for James, there was more than Albert Gallatin's position(s) at stake; a gauntlet had been thrown down and he must assert his executive power. And at the same time, he had to keep both Gallatins soothed, reassured, and indignant enough to hang on. Once again, James and Dolley entered into a minuet of the personal and political, played out in correspondence between women.

By 1812, Dolley and Hannah had enjoyed a long relationship. They even shared an important ally, John Jacob Astor, who danced attendance on both ladies like a French dandy. The chief difference between them, aside from Dolley's inordinate charm, was Hannah's willingness to talk politics. She was not afraid of contention; her writing was full of emphatic underlines and confident, decided opinions. Hannah and Albert conducted detailed political discussions in their letters to each other. On occasion, taking the role of a good wife, the circumspect Albert advised her to temper her political enthusiasm, "for it may tend to inflame the passions of your friends and lead to consequences you would forever regret."[46]

Given Hannah's forthrightness, contemporaries focused on her as an extension of her husband. Throughout the prewar period, people besieged her for information from Albert's letters, especially about the possibility of invasion. At times, Albert directed her on how to answer the inevitable questions. In turn, with her characteristic confidence of conviction, Hannah passed on the "public mind," as she did when war was declared: "There seems but one sentiment. We cannot submit to be degraded."[47]

Hannah's directness did not always work to her advantage, or to the administration's. The "public mind" took seriously any rumor that could be linked to her. Only a few weeks before the invasion of Washington in 1814, Dolley would use their favorite go-between to send Hannah a not-so-subtle warning: "I desired Mr. Astor to tell you the strange story they [the general public] made, about your haveing reccd. a letter from Mr. G. [i.e., Gallatin] full of alarming information." And the public believed it: "It had a distressing effect on our Loan [for the war, a loan Astor was overseeing] & threw many into consternation for a while but we ware able to contradict & soften consequences." In truth, the story was not so "strange." Albert had indeed written Hannah a pessimistic letter, with evacuation instructions should the British invade New York.[48] Hannah had told one or two people, enough to give the story wings. The ever-subtle Dolley no doubt knew Hannah herself was the source, but chose to cloak admonition obliquely.

Now, with Albert deep in his journey and out of touch for weeks if not months, Dolley and James turned to Hannah as deputy husband. In deciding whether to keep Albert as treasury secretary or as a peace envoy, James wanted to take his colleague's wishes into account, but no one knew for sure which position he would prefer, if it came to that. In July, Dolley and the ubiquitous John Jacob Astor had "a very long conversation . . . in confidence." Astor then passed on to Hannah Dolley's inquiry "whether I thought Mr. Gallatin would prefer a confirmation of the nomination or remain in the department."[49]

Negotiations with the Senate over Albert's nomination dragged on, and the business was stalled further when in early June 1813, James fell seriously ill with bilious fever, a condition very similar to yellow fever, but characterized by extreme gastrointestinal turbulence. By mid-month, he and Dolley were still in Washington, but he was canceling appointments. His condition was dire enough to be a matter of diplomatic speculation. Sérurier reported to another French official that "his death, in the circumstances in which the Republic is placed, would be a veritable national calamity. . . . All good Americans pray for the recovery of Mr. Madison." As word of his illness spread, his detractors tried to take advantage of the grave circumstances. When Daniel Webster related that James was too sick to read the tax resolutions that he delivered, the *New York Evening Post* opined that current politics were "rather too much for the delicate nerves of our Chief Magistrate."[50]

Dolley was frantic, in "dispair"; for five weeks, she barely left her husband's side. By early July, she reported with relief to Edward Coles that James was in recovery. Still, she did not relax her vigilance, watching over him "as I would an infant, so precarious is his convalessence." Dolley also saw political dimensions to James's condition, blaming "disappointments & vexations, heaped upon him by party spirit" for making him sicker. James's illnesses always took their toll on Dolley; with her patient nearly out of the woods, she confessed that "now that I see he will get well I feel as if I should die myself, with fatigue."[51]

The Senate rejected Albert again on July 19, and Dolley and James finally set off for Montpelier in August. Even in the midst of moving back and caring for her husband, Dolley wrote to Hannah, sending the letter via the conveniently on-hand John Jacob Astor. She addressed Hannah as her "beloved friend," tied to her by mutual concern for "our dear Voagers," then informed Hannah of James's illness, both "its extent" and "the dispair, in which I attended his bed for nearly five

weeks!" While she directly connected James's condition to political discord, "nothing however has borne so hard, as the conduct of the Senate
in regard to Mr Gallatin." Dolley relied on Astor to "tell you many particulars, that *I aught not* to *write,* of the desertion of some whose support we had a right to expect: & of the *maneauvering* of others, allways
hostile to superior merit." She united the families in righteous indignation in a way that James could not, either in an official document or
even a private letter, since an official man's correspondence might easily
become public property.

Dolley continued to support Albert in the face of this second veto,
and she signaled that the fight was not over: "We console ourselves with
the hope of *its* terminating both in the Public good, and M. Gallatins
honorable triumph." Hannah Gallatin wrote back from New York
promptly. Expressing great concern and sympathy for James in his illness, she dismissed the triumph of his enemies as a mere "trifle" to Albert, a man with "self approving conscience and his peace . . . within
his own breast." The only significance of all this trouble to her, Hannah
assured Dolley, "is that the Presidents feelings have been so tortured at
a time too when it was necessary for him to enjoy repose. I hope our
country will not suffer by their wickedness." She closed her letter with a
phrase that expressed the Gallatin family's loyalty and sense of
obligation—"your sincere & grateful friend."[52]

Dolley also wrote back at once, though she had a "croud of company," including Anna and her brood, and James was still such a worry
that she had to apologize: "I have made a sad letter of this my darling, but
have no time to copy or correct it." In discussing "their" travelers, Dolley
mixed personal sentiment with political assessment: "I am constantly
cheared with the sweet hope of their safe & early return, when you will
find your dear Husband standing higher than ever in his countrys estimation & attatchment." And, she assured Hannah, this was not only her
opinion: "[F]or Mr. Madison says, that tho his Enimies immagin they
have prevailed in a *degree* against him, their machinations will trouble
his friends & show him to the world as he really is, one of the best, as
well as one of the greatest men." In her postscript, Dolley bade Hannah
to convey "My love to Mr. Astor."[53]

As summer turned to fall and then to the winter of 1814, letters flew between the two women. Mail from the "Voagers," on the other hand, was slow and irregular, and letters arrived randomly, sometimes months after they were written and not necessarily in chronological order. If a letter did not specifically mention it, Dolley and Hannah did not know if their own correspondence had been received or if other letters from the party had been lost. In fact, Albert had not learned that the Senate had rejected his nomination until October, when he was already in Russia. This extinguished any hope Hannah had that her husband would return home quickly. The frozen rivers of wintertime Russia prevented travel, and therefore mail, until the thaw.

Dolley and Hannah shared whatever letters each received, anxiously looking for reassurances that, at least at the writing of a particular letter, Albert and Payne were well. Though anxiety and love dominated their own correspondence, the women also exchanged a variety of information and news. Following a familiar pattern, not all Hannah's information came just from her, nor was it intended exclusively for Dolley. At times, the choreography became complicated. In a letter to Dolley, Hannah included a long extract from Albert's letter to *her*, but meant for *James*, concerning the comings and goings of various delegations across Europe. Both women understood that the information and insight contained in their correspondence should not fall into the wrong hands. On more than one occasion, Dolley sent along the same kinds of admonitions that she included in letters to her sisters— "burn this scrall."[54]

Dolley trod carefully with her friend, always sharing her hopes that her husband, who was, after all, a free agent at this point, would come home, while reconciling her to circumstance and political necessity. James had plans for Albert. During the winter of 1813–14, the attempts at Russian mediation fell apart, and the delegation left Russia, preparing to sail home from Great Britain. James had no intention of squandering the opportunity of having his best men already in Europe should a chance for peace emerge. On February 8, 1814, he appointed Albert, along with the rest of the party, as peace commissioners to Great Britain, with negotiation to take place in Ghent. Dolley let her friend down gently: "It may be, that your good Husband, will have sailed for America before Mr Ms letters could reach him—still it is not probable." But in any case, "the Negotiations will not last more than a month," and they would all be home in the spring.[55]

Dolley also shared her anxiety about her Payne, who, once the party had reached Paris en route to Ghent, had dropped out of sight. When she had not heard from him in a while, she hoped that it was for good, even edifying, reasons. "I am consoled for your absence & your silence by the impression that you are engrossed by the variety of objects in Europe which are to enlighten and benefit you the rest of your life." When it became clear that Payne had truly abandoned Albert and the others, Dolley fretted: "What could have led him to do so? [N]othing but anxiety to get home I hope."[56] Unfortunately, that was not the case; Paris held distinctly un-homelike attractions for Payne, who had fallen into his uncle John's pattern of disappearance and dissipation.

Dolley did her best to soothe Hannah's impatience and worry. Only days before the invasion of Washington City, she wrote to assure Hannah of the security of the family's possessions in storage. She also wanted her friend to know that James had just received a "short Official letter" from Albert, but wondered if Hannah had received a more personal one. Dolley was looking not only for word of the errant Payne, but for a fuller account of the process of peace not present in the official document. And she wondered: "In case of peace would you like to be in Europe, as *Minister*?" Dolley was playing, dangling a plum appointment in a conflation of the political partners.[57] But this was no joke: a ministerial post was a serious office, one of the few at the president's disposal. Surely, Dolley would not even hint at the possibility without James's knowledge, if not his instigation.

The feeler would have been his; he no doubt wanted to know how Hannah felt before he made the offer official. His caution stemmed from her obvious desire that Albert not be so far from her, but how would she feel about being with him in a glamorous capital city? Hannah replied with equal caution. She had not heard from Payne since Paris, and as for the idea of such an appointment: "The question you put to me about going to Europe, I can only answer for myself, as far as I can judge thus hastily I think it would not be disagreeable to me, but I cannot answer for my husband." Message received.

In February 1815, James would make the appointment, with Dolley following up in a letter in early March. "I trust you are pleased with Mr. G——s appointment to France. You know I enquired of you long ago how *you* would like it, since which many circumstances have occured to render more agreable to your Husband, a residence at that Coart."[58]

But before the Gallatins could reunite, Dolley and Washington City had to endure their greatest trial.

FIFTEEN

Potomac Phoenix

*S*ince the declaration, Washington City had been gripped by the "melancholy business" of war, as Dolley called it. During the business day, the conduct of the various campaigns, and the surrounding logistical and financial issues, set the legislative and executive agenda. At Dolley's drawing rooms, everyone talked about strategy, tactics, victories, and defeats. Indeed, sometimes the war itself came to the party, as when military heroes attended and when the festivities were interrupted with events such as a presentation of colors.

But of course, in that first year, Washingtonians did not experience the actual fighting, which took place far from the city, in the northwest, and increasingly along the Atlantic coast. By the start of 1813, however, with British ships raiding nearby seacoasts along the Chesapeake, the war came closer to home, and Washingtonians harbored a quiet and sometimes-not-so-quiet fear: invasion.

The British had been raiding the coast as early as December 1812, but mostly as a diversionary tactic intended to wreak havoc on both naval and private ships and to interrupt trade. However, even then the British displayed an inordinate interest in terrorizing the civilian population.

The Americans considered this focus on civilian intimidation to be "barbaric" and dishonorable. The leader of the naval operations, Sir George Cockburn, became the most hated British officer of the war. American animus intensified when he attacked Havre de Grace, a Maryland harbor, in May 1813. Stories of pillage and destruction spread. Perhaps of particular interest to Dolley were the tales of women who confronted the British forces, and even Cockburn himself, pleading for their homes. Surprisingly, the "Beast of Havre de Grace" acquiesced.

Dolley's Virginia neighbors did not fare as well. In late June, Cockburn and his forces attacked Craney Island in Norfolk; not only did the soldiers destroy and pillage property, but they raped women. The discreet newspaper language—"abused in the most shameful manner," "indignity on the persons"—could not disguise the shocking events. Most appalling of all, some white women were rumored to have been attacked by black slaves and freedmen who had joined with the British or who otherwise took advantage of war's chaos.

It seemed, by the summer of 1813, that the barbarians were at Washington City's gates. As early as May, rumors of just that had begun to circulate. To Cousin Edward Coles, in Philadelphia recovering from hemorrhoid surgery, Dolley could confide her anxieties: "If I could, I would describe to you the fears & alarms, that circulate around me. For the last week all the City & G. Toun [Georgetown] (except the Cabinet) have expected a visit from the Enimy, & ware not lacking in their expressions of terror & *reproach*." The reproach, of course, focused on the men in charge, particularly James. Dolley countered that "we are makeing considerable efforts for defence. The Fort is repairing, & 500 Militia, with perhaps as many regulars are; & *to be*, stationd on the green near the *Wind Mill*, or rather, near Majr. Tayloes." She took comfort in the sight of "the 20 Tents, [they] allready look well, in My eyes as I have allways been an advocate for fighting when *assailed*, tho *a Quaker* I therefore keep the old Tunesian Sabre within my reach."

Washingtonians were caught off guard. "Until the late alarm," Margaret Bayard Smith confessed to her sister Jane, "I have never been able to realize our being in a state of war." But even with the enemy so near at hand, she reassured her sister, "there is so little apprehension of danger in the city, that not a single removal of person or goods has taken place."

On July 21, William Burwell, too, wrote soothingly to Letitia: "I assure you, upon my honor, I do not believe there is the smallest cause for alarm." He, too, took his reassurance from the state of the city. "I do not perceive the least alarm among the women; they perceive the ample means taken to defend them and are well aware of their safety."[1]

These attempts at denial crumbled in the face of a citywide panic. Contrary to its usual measured tone, the *National Intelligencer* printed sensational tales of British atrocities, the local theater produced patriotic plays, and the populace began to complain about the lack of any plans (twenty tents notwithstanding) to defend the city.

Once again, Dolley paid the price for serving as the leading figure of the administration and her husband's proxy. Cockburn framed an 1813 boast of invasion in reference to her; while relating to Edward Coles the plot, which had "*Rogues*" landing at Alexandria and setting fire to the president's house under cover of night, Dolley admitted: "I do not tremble at this, but feel *affronted* that the Admiral . . . should send me notis that he would make his bow at my Drawing room *soon*."[2] Dolley could be forgiven if she did "tremble," even if she would not admit it; after all, Cockburn had already subjected Marylanders to what she called a "savage stile of warfare."

Early in her husband's administration, Dolley had made herself a visible presence, thus leaving herself open to the diatribes of men such as John Randolph. But as vicious as his assaults were, Randolph's vindictiveness brought with it no physical threat, at least not to Dolley.

By taking that presence into the men's game of war, Dolley raised the stakes and the risks.

But the British did not invade in 1813. Still, Washingtonians would not forget the specter of interracial rape and assaults on white women, but as the hostilities continued into 1814, they found it easier to regard the 1813 threat as a false alarm. Though the menace of an enemy attack was never far from anyone's mind, most adopted a pose of day-to-day denial. They could present numerous good reasons why the British could not or would not march on the capital, and they clung to their logic even as, by 1814, the possibility became more real. Almost two years into the war, the Americans found themselves in a desperate situation. Money was pouring out of the Treasury, and enlistments had declined further, necessitating increased dependence on expensive and inefficient state militias. In April, as James had long feared, Napoleon abdicated, and the end of hostilities between France and England freed more British troops for the North American operations. In 1814, the British turned their full attention to their former colonies, determined to swat the fly once and for all.[3]

They began by bottling up the entire East Coast, even occupying parts of Maine and Massachusetts. The Royal Navy stepped up their raids on the coast at its leisure, sending parties of 150 or so into coastal towns to pillage and plunder. The British forces also intensified their operations on the Gulf Coast, and, most worryingly, began a major operation on the Chesapeake. In planning what they hoped would be a decisive and crushing victory over the United States, Major General Robert Ross and Vice Admiral Sir Alexander Cochrane eyed the long, undefended coast of the Chesapeake, and the added enticement of Washington City and Baltimore. As before, a campaign on the Chesapeake could push the United States to shift forces from the Canadian campaigns. But now, the two cities offered the chance for a "measure of retaliation" for wartime defeats and particularly for the looting of York. Both British commanders understood very well the psychological implications of taking the U.S. capital.[4]

Calling an emergency cabinet meeting on July 1, 1814, James

outlined his plans to strategically locate 2,000 or 3,000 armed men between the coast and capital, with 10,000 to 12,000 militia and other volunteers on standby in the District and in nearby states. The participation of the citizenry was critical, since the regular army was far away, serving from Canada to New Orleans. Accordingly, James formed the 10th Military District, with a thirty-nine-year-old political appointee, Brigadier General William Winder, in charge. Dolley's old friend John P. Van Ness assumed responsibility for the District militia, while Winder commanded the militias from Maryland, Virginia, and Pennsylvania. James's precautions and preparations made sense if invasion loomed; as it happened, much of his planning, especially as it regarded troop formation, came to naught.[5]

In the practical preparations to defend the capital, as always, the presence of the federal government complicated matters. Unfortunately for Washington City, Secretary of War General John Armstrong shared his neighbors' penchant for denial. Both Van Ness and Winder deferred to Armstrong, who refused to believe that the British would try to capture the seat of government, even after they landed in Maryland in July 1814. When Van Ness suggested that British leaders might in fact aim for Washington City in retaliation for York, Armstrong disagreed emphatically, asserting, "Baltimore is the place, sir; that is of so much more consequence."[6]

Ironically, the long-standing inferiority complex that Washingtonians had about their upstart capital blinded some of their leaders to the need to defend it. The British understood better the significance of the capital city. Armstrong was correct: Washington City had no *practical* strategic importance. But the British commander-in-chief in North America, Admiral Sir Alexander Cochrane, had promised "a complete drubbing" to the former colonists and knew that seizure of their capital would humiliate and demoralize them. So, in late July and early August, under the pretext of hunting down an American flotilla that had been raiding their ships, the British began sending increasing numbers of men into the Patuxent River. This had the effect of placing forces even closer to Washington City, which did not escape local notice.[7]

Still, most of the capital's occupants persisted in their belief that Washington City was not what Armstrong called "the place"; they reassured faraway relatives and friends that they were in no danger. It is hard to blame local Washingtonians for their lack of foresight when there was so little agreement among the people who were supposed to protect them. Even their newspaper, the *National Intelligencer,* often mixed invasion concerns with reassurances that all was well. This contradictory editorial position stemmed in part from the Madisons' express request that the paper not print rumors.[8]

Dolley's job had always been to reassure the nation and the world that the government had full control of the situation, and accordingly her entertaining had become more purposeful in the months leading up to the invasion. In the summer of 1814, she focused on reassuring the Washington community in particular. Only a few weeks before the invasion, she reported to Payne in Paris. Ever mindful of leaks, she no doubt tailored her comments for the European public eye, blending bravado with propaganda: "The British on our shore's are stealing & destroying private property, rarely comeing to battle but when they do, are allways beaten. . . . If the War should last 6 months longer the U. S. will conquer her Enimies." Dolley succeeded so well in reassuring her fellow residents that many were taken quite unawares when the British arrived. Indeed, some Washingtonians, white and black, continued to evince disbelief even as the British army marched into the capital.[9]

While Dolley may have been certain, at least on paper, that the British would not get within twenty miles of Washington City, by late July she harbored doubts. To Hannah Nicholson Gallatin in Philadelphia, she admitted: "We have been in a state of purturbation here, for a long time—The depredations of the Enemy approaching within 20 miles of the City & the disaffected, makeing incessant difficulties for the Government." Feeling the tension, Dolley burst forth with a lamentation usually confined to the family circle: "Such a place as this has become I can not discribe it—I wish (for my own part) *we ware* at Phila. The people here do not deserve that *I* should prefer it— among other exclamations & threats they say if Mr. M. attempts to move from *this House,* in case of an attack, they will *stop him* & that he shall *fall with it*—I am not the least alarmed at these things, but entirely disgusted, & determined to stay with him."[10] Still, even as late as August 6, Dolley told Hannah, "We are still without an idea of going from hence."[11]

The long-dreaded invasion began in the early hours of August 19, as the British, four thousand strong, landed at Benedict, Maryland, the main port of the Patuxent. Couriers racing to Washington conveyed Admiral Cockburn's declaration that he intended to dine in Washington City in two days. Secretary of the Navy William Jones was still not entirely convinced that the British were aiming for the capital, interpreting the threat as "a feint . . . mask[ing] a real design on Baltimore." Still, he, along with Winder, Van Ness, and Secretary of State James Monroe, began preparations to defend the city.[12]

Dolley continued to serve as a particular target for the boastful Admiral Cockburn. Shortly before the British landing, he "sent word to Mrs. Madison that unless she left, the house would be burned over her head": he did not mention James's. He also threatened to take Dolley hostage and parade her through the London streets.[13] Though inwardly worried about the state of preparations, outwardly Dolley proceeded as usual. Even after James had left for the field to review the troops on August 23, she prepared a dinner party for the usual mix of government and local families. That day, however, the *National Intelligencer* broke its pledge and reported the rumor that five or six thousand British troops had joined the force already in Maryland. Washington City fell into a panic, triggering a mass exodus.

Dolley's dinner party could not calm the hysteria. A masterfully understated note of regret arrived from William Jones's wife, Eleanor: "In the present state of alarm and bustle of preparation, for the worst that may happen, I imagine it will be mutually convenient, to dispense with the enjoyment of your hospitality today and therefore pray you to admit this as an excuse for Mr. Jones, Lucy and myself." Mrs. Jones concluded tersely: "Mr. Jones is deeply engaged in dispatching the Marines. . . . Lucy and myself are busy packing."[14]

That evening, Dolley began her famous letter to sister Lucy, continuing it all the next day. Sunrise on August 24 found her on the top floor of the president's house with her spyglass, "watching with unwearied anxiety hoping to discern the approach of my dear husband and his friends." It was not clear whether she, too, would have to evacuate, as had nine tenths of the city, but if Dolley had to leave, she wanted to do so with James. Of course, she knew that he might not be able to reach her in time, and she might have to decide herself to abandon the executive mansion to the British. She received little guidance in making this important decision. The blustering General Armstrong had once again assured her that there was no danger, while the mayor of Washington, Dr. James Blake, came twice to plead with her to flee.

Dolley nonetheless continued with her dinner preparations, set for later that afternoon, pausing every so often to write a bit more to Lucy. As Dolley was deciding whether to stay in the White House or flee, her previous knowledge of Cockburn may have played a part on both sides. After all, the women of Havre de Grace had pleaded successfully for their homes; Dolley may have considered doing the same. Still, the image of the "outraged" women of Craney Island must have haunted her as well. She also returned to the spyglass on the roof throughout the day. James was not to be seen. Rather, Dolley noted with alarm the "military wanderings" of the troops. Her reading of their postures as indicating "a lack of arms or of spirit to fight for their own firesides!" proved distressingly apt: the British routed the American army in a skirmish that lasted less than half an hour. The retreating Americans went "flying t[h]rough the City," justifying the derisive title the "Bladensburg Races."[15]

From her own house only blocks away, Anna sent Dolley a note by a slave pleading, "tell me for gods sake where you are and what [you are] going to do. . . . We can hear nothing but what is horrible here—I know not who to send this to—and will say but little."[16] Dolley waited for James all that long afternoon. French John Sioussat stayed by her side, as did fifteen-year-old Paul Jennings and the "most efficient" Sukey. With his "usual activity and resolution," John Sioussat "offered to spike the cannon at the gate and lay a train of powder which would blow up the British should they enter the house." Dolley vetoed that plan. John Sioussat's idea was not outlandish, but, again, Dolley might have feared unleashing further havoc from an unpredictable enemy with a track record of terrorizing civilian populations.

Transport was scarce, but Dolley managed to send out a good amount of silver, cabinet papers, books, and a small clock from the White House. She was very conscious that she was abandoning items that belonged to the public, but she justified her actions by also sacrificing personal items, such as clothes and all the Madisons' "valuable stores" of food and necessaries. Perhaps in a moment of sentiment, she also pressed into a trunk the red velvet curtains that had come to characterize her "blazing" drawing rooms.[17]

Several men had been urging her to go for hours, including the local landowner Charles Carroll. Though Carroll's family would later insist that he had saved the famous portrait of George Washington, Dolley remembered that after he left her to join James in the field, she "directed my servants in what manner to remove it from the wall, remaining with them until it was done." Seeing "two gentlemen of New York," Robert G. L. De Peyster and Jacob Barker, passing by, she bade them to secure the precious portrait under a "humble but safe roof."

Dolley explained her insistence on saving this particular piece out of "my respect for General Washington." Did she suspect that the British would have the temerity to burn the executive mansion? Perhaps, but she was reasonably certain that the invading forces would gleefully seize the portrait as a prize of war. John Sioussat and Paul Jennings had different memories of how the picture was preserved. Paul Jennings insisted that "she had no time for doing it": he mistakenly remembered that the incident took place as Dolley left, rather than hours before. Traditional accounts have Dolley, carving knife in hand, with John and a gardener wrestling with the heavy gilt frame. John himself recalled cutting the canvas with a penknife, but the portrait reveals no marks of cutting.[18]

Meanwhile, out in the field with the army in retreat, James realized that American forces could not stop the invasion and sent his messenger, James Smith, to Dolley. The freeman rode to the White House, shouting, "'Clear out, clear out! General Armstrong has ordered a retreat!'"[19] Dolley's worst fears were realized; she would have to leave without James. So, two hours before the enemy's capture of the capital, as Dolley later wrote to Mary Hazelhurst Latrobe, "I left the house where Mr. Latrobe's elegant taste had been justly admired, and where you and I had so often wandered together." She crammed as much silverware as possible into her reticule, and walking out of the front door for the last time, took her seat in the carriage with the impatient Charles Carroll, who had returned for her, Anna, Richard Cutts, and Sukey. The Madisons' coachman, Joe Bolen, drove the party across Rock Creek to Georgetown. Stopping first at Navy Secretary Jones's house, they then made their way to Charles Carroll's home, Belle Vue.[20]

John Sioussat and Paul Jennings were the last to leave the White House. French John locked the front door, then carried Dolley's beloved pet macaw over to the Octagon House. Owned by Dolley's friends the Tayloes, the elegant mansion had become, for this occasion, the temporary headquarters of the French ministry, protected by diplomatic privilege.[21]

Not long after Dolley departed the White House, the long-awaited James did arrive. Along with Attorney General Richard Rush and General John Mason, he took some refreshment at the mansion, while sending several messages to Dolley at Belle Vue. Finally, he decided that they should rendezvous across the Potomac the next day, at Wiley's Inn, near Great Falls, Virginia. Then James, too, left the house for the last time, riding "proudly" off with his friends, crossing the river by bridge or ferry into Virginia. Dolley also made it to Virginia in the late afternoon, taking refuge with her friend Matilda Lee Love at Rokeby Plantation.

The White House hosted one last public event. John Sioussat returned to the house in time to encounter William Simmons, who had ridden with James from Bladensburg, and who ordered him to give out brandy to the passing troops. As afternoon turned to evening, Jennings, who had stayed behind in the city, saw with dismay that "rabble" were looting the executive mansion, stealing silver and anything else they could carry.[22]

Meanwhile, the American forces in the city continued to fall apart. As the troops drifted toward Capitol Hill, there was some talk of launching a defense from there, but as Colonel Winder studied the troops, he realized that his soldiers were too depleted to fend off the enemy. In the worst case, the American army might find itself trapped and under siege if they attacked from inside the government buildings. Reluctantly, he ordered the troops to the higher ground of George-town, reckoning that if any counterattack was possible, the heights afforded the most advantageous location.

At sundown, the British forces, led by Vice Admiral Sir George Cockburn and Major General Robert Ross, marched into Washington City. An eyewitness, the freeman Michael Shiner, remembered them as the living embodiments of the destruction they brought: "They look like flames of fier all red Coats and the Stoks of ther guns painted With red ver Milon and the iron Work shind like a Spanish dollar."[23]

The British headed for the deserted Capitol, and upon reaching the Senate and House of Representatives, were awed by the magnificence of the "Houses of Parliament." Some of the officers were even reluctant to desecrate this architectural achievement. But in the end they did. At first, British soldiers tried to use rockets to burn the roof, but, covered with sheet iron, it did not ignite. The men then made a bonfire with furniture in the chamber of the House of Representatives and lit that with rockets. This proved more successful. The imported mahogany burned like so much tinder, and the fluted columns that had drawn such great admiration during James's inauguration dried and cracked. Glass melted in the intense heat, but some of Latrobe's masonry vaults acted as firebreaks, thus preserving parts of the structure. The Library of Congress had no stone vaults; and with its timbers and a shingle roof, it burned easily. Three thousand volumes were destroyed.

The White House was next, and by the time the troops arrived, it was evening, and they were tired and hungry. Dolley's table beckoned. A British soldier described the "elegant and substantial repast" that the soldiers discovered, complete with "several kinds of wine," a fully set table, down to the plate holders, joints of meat on the fire, and full saucepans on the stove. Though some feared that the food might be poisoned, the soldiers dug in, toasting the king with James's wine. One soldier put James's tricorn hat, a symbol of the Revolution, on the tip of his bayonet, boasting that if they could not capture "the little president," they would parade his hat through the streets of London. Dolley's friends had feared that she would be taken as a valuable hostage; Cockburn had to settle for capturing her portrait, to "keep Dolley safe and exhibit her in London." He also took her seat cushion, remarking that he wished to "warmly recall Mrs. Madison's seat." Cockburn continued in this vein, "adding pleasantries too vulgar to repeat."[24]

After dinner, the destruction began. At first, men raced through the rooms starting fires at random; the British had a more systematic way to guarantee the building's total destruction, however. Fifty men marched on the mansion, each armed with a pole topped with what an eyewitness described as "a machine of wild-fire." These "machines" were spheres about the size of a dinner plate that held fiery coals pilfered from a nearby saloon. The men stood by windows outside the executive mansion, and on command, broke them, flinging the "wild-fire" in, starting "an instantaneous conflagration." Everyone watching "stood in awful silence." The fire burned so intensely that the "city was light and the heavens redden'd with the blaze."[25]

The invaders moved on to torch the Treasury, next door. Almost simultaneously, the American commander of the Navy Yard, Captain Thomas Tingey, ordered the buildings, the stores, and the new warships burned, so that the enemy would not take them. To many, it appeared at this point that all of Washington—"our poor undefended & devoted city" in the words of Anna Maria Brodeau Thornton—was aflame. After leaving the White House, Paul Jennings had met up briefly with James and his guard at the Georgetown ferry, then went on to stay with a Methodist minister. "In the evening," Paul recalled, "while he was at prayer, I heard a tremendous explosion, and rushing out, saw the public buildings, navy yard and, ropewalks, & c. were on fire."[26]

The blazes filled a black night sky. Dolley could see them from

Rokeby Plantation, ten miles away. James spent most of that night on horseback, riding around the countryside, and every time he and his party came to a rise or a hill, they looked back upon the burning city. The next day, though James had told Dolley to meet him at Wiley's Tavern, he first sought her out at a local plantation, Salona, where he assumed she had spent the night. Arriving at Wiley's tavern with Sukey, Dolley discovered that not every local family was an ally. She walked upstairs, only to have the lady of the house shout: "Mrs. Madison! If that's you, come down and go out! Your husband has got mine out fighting, and damn you, you shan't stay in my house; so get out!" Only an impending storm convinced the landlady to allow Dolley to wait for her husband.[27]

On that second day, the British determined to continue their destructive work. The Departments of State and War were their next targets, and while key paperwork had been removed earlier, the remaining books, paper, and furniture guaranteed a sizable blaze. The British army would have also destroyed the Patent Office had it not been for the personal pleas of Dr. William Thornton, who compared destroying it to the Saracens' burning of the famous Alexandria library "for which the Turks have been ever since condemned by all enlightened nations." Admiral Cockburn took especial delight in sacking the offices of the *National Intelligencer*, whose editor, Joseph Gales, had, in his estimation, long slandered him. Though he and his troops burned paper and scattered type, he held off from destroying the building when told that it was private property, not owned by Gales.

For the most part, the invasion force left private property alone, burning only houses from which they were fired upon. Unfortunately, one of those was the Gallatins', which housed, in the estimation of local gentrywoman Martha Custis Peter, "[a] worthless hairdresser," who shot General Ross's horse out from under him. The enraged troops wanted to kill him, but Ross stopped them, dismissing the culprit with yet another disparaging remark about Washington City: though "he was certainly too worthless to live . . . he might [as well] live there."[28]

That second day saw two incidents, one caused by humans, one natural, that put an end to the rampage. While destroying munitions at the arsenal on Greenleaf's Point, about two miles from the Capitol, British troops accidentally ignited 130 barrels of gunpowder. The explosion was enormous, leaving a crater twenty feet deep and forty feet across. Thirty men died at once, some buried alive. The remaining forty-five or so suffered severe injuries. The grisly scene shook even men who had seen battle.[29]

Between the deliberate burnings and explosion, the entire city might have gone up in the general inferno, but early that afternoon, hurricane-force rain and winds swept the city. The freak storm put out much of the fire, spooking the British solders in the process. Witnesses described it as "tremendous," the sky alternately as black as night with "heaving black clouds of rain," then brilliantly illuminated with lightning flashes. The storm lasted for two hours, the wind so fierce at times that buildings were torn from their foundations and put down again. The Americans saw the torrents as providential, putting out the fires; superstitious British soldiers viewed the display of lightning and thunder as a manifestation of God's wrath.[30]

Demoralized by the carnage at Greenleaf's Point and the daunting weather, Cockburn ordered the troops out of the city that night. Under cover of darkness, the British marched back to regroup at Benedict and continued their rampage elsewhere. The British forces followed up their success by taking nearby Fort Washington and Alexandria, Virginia, but suffered defeats in the Niagara Peninsula, Vermont, and upstate New York campaigns. In September, the enemy also made an unsuccessful attempt to take Baltimore. On September 13 and 14, the British laid siege to Fort McHenry, where they fired 1,500 rounds over twenty-five hours, but to no avail. During the fierce fighting, Georgetown resident and volunteer soldier Francis Scott Key was on board a British ship to negotiate the return of Marylander Dr. William Beanes. Inspired by the sight of the American flag still flying at the end of the siege, Key penned a poem, "The Star-Spangled Banner," which he put to an old eighteenth-century drinking song. By Saturday, September 17, copies of the song were in the hands of everyone stationed at Fort McHenry, and the publication of the text in the *Baltimore Patriot* made it accessible to all Americans. Over the next few months, the British turned southeast, heading for the troublemaking U.S. troops on the Gulf of Mexico.

As for the capital that they had left behind, though their plundering had been cut short, the British soldiers and their commander could be satisfied that they had wrought a sufficient amount of devastation. And so they had. No one put it better than Michael Shiner: "The commander of the British squadron in 1814 that came up the potomac River dident act no Ways like a gentelman Wher ever he landid. [F]or the Worst of hetheans wouldent of acted anny More hetheanly."[31]

*

Four days after Dolley had fled the White House, she and James returned to the capital city, stopping at their old house on F Street, now the home of the Cuttses. As soon as they could, the couple went to see the White House wreckage. Nothing remained "but its cracked and blackened walls." Tellingly using a language of vulnerability, people poignantly described the walls as "unroofed," "naked," "cracked," and "defaced." The lawyer William Wirt, who would later serve as James Monroe's attorney general, tried to describe the ruins to his wife, Elizabeth Gamble Wirt, but words failed him: "I cannot tell you what I felt as I walked amongst them."[32] The sight of the official residence that had been both her home and the site of her most celebrated efforts so distressed Dolley that she could not speak of it afterward without emotion. According to Anna Maria, seeing American soldiers marching by, Dolley railed violently against the English, wishing that "we had ten thousand such men as were passing *to sink our enemy to the bottomless pit.*"[33]

William Wirt called on the president, whom he found "miserably shattered and woebegone. In short, he looks heart-broken." Bad enough that the capital city, consigned to his care, lay in ruins; he also felt betrayed by his incompetent, sometimes even perfidious, commanders and fellow Americans. James's mind, deduced Wirt, was "full of the New England sedition." James introduced the topic and continued to "press it—painful as it obviously was to him." To cheer his leader, William Wirt dismissed the possibility that the New Englanders would go over to the British, then attempted to shift the topic of conversation. But James returned to the theme of betrayal, convincing Wirt "that his heart and mind were painfully full of the subject."[34]

Dolley was equally inconsolable. Margaret Bayard Smith saw her shortly after the fire, and found her friend "much depressed, she could scarcely speak without tears." Months later, Dolley would relate to Mary Hazelhurst Latrobe the depth of her feelings of anger and betrayal: "I confess that I was so unfeminine as to be free from fear, and willing to remain in the Castle! If I could have had a cannon through every window; but alas! those who should have placed them there fled before me, and my whole heart mourned for my country!" However, she did not waste time in lamentation. The woman who once declared, "I would rather fight with my hands than my tongue," and who kept "the old Tunesian Sabre within reach" in spite of her Quaker background, could not be kept down for long.[35] Dolley knew that the city, the American people, and the whole world were watching with varying degrees of anxiety to see what effect the British invasion would have on the new republic.

The Madisons were not the only people confused and shaken upon their return to the city. As the days passed and refugees slowly made their way back, the sight of the public buildings in ruins was demoralizing. They mourned for "those beautiful pillars" in the House Chamber, "that noble dome, painted and carved with such beauty and skill," still smoking amongst the debris. Though few private houses had suffered British depredations, the storm had wrought its own damage, and bodies from the arsenal explosion strewed the landscape, and the ones buried at the arsenal were not to be excavated for weeks. For a few days after the British retreat, the populace feared that the invader would return. When that danger had clearly passed, the finger pointing and accusations started.[36]

Everyone cried cabal and faction; rumors and accusations sped from house to house, reflecting Washingtonians' feelings of betrayal. The "public voice" attributed the fall of the capital to General Armstrong. The accusation appeared at least partly true, since the general had refused to prepare for the possibility of invasion. But many

Washingtonians read implications darker than mere incompetence. Rumor surmised that Armstrong "intentionally neglected" his duties because "it is well-known that he was very desirous of a removal of the seat of government. This consideration among others," according to the young visitor Richard Cranch Norton, "has induced a very strong suspicion that he intentionally neglected the means necessary for the security of this district."[37]

Armstrong quickly resigned, with James Monroe taking over as temporary secretary of war. But Armstrong was not the only target of public disgust: Mayor Blake also received his share of blame for the District's lack of readiness, as did General Winder, and, of course, the president. But even as residents were casting about for a scapegoat, a profound shift was taking place in the rest of the country. In targeting the nation's capital, the British had aimed to demoralize a population that had shown little enthusiasm for what was derisively titled "Mr. Madison's War." Instead, they unwittingly rallied the nation. Thanks to Dolley, by 1814, many Americans identified with their capital and their White House, and its desecration transformed apathy and antipathy toward the war into anger and outrage. As a prestigious national newsweekly, *Niles's Register*, declared: "The Spirit of the nation is roused. If the barbarian warfare of an inflated enemy would not have roused it, our liberties had perished forever." Even DeWitt Clinton, who had opposed James and the war, asserted that "the questions are not now whether the war was just or unjust in its commencement; whether the execution of it was politic or expedient," or any number of other hypotheticals. The only question, Clinton asked, was whether Americans were going to fight; the answer resounded: "Yes!" The burning of the capital may not have turned the tide of the war in a military sense, but it won the battle for public support that Dolley and James had been waging even before its declaration.[38]

With the British gone, Washington City's troubles were just beginning. As in the suspicions about General Armstrong, the larger crisis that loomed involved relocating the capital, a subject that gripped Washington City almost before the last fires died down. Older cities enticed the federal government with invitations to move; on August 27, the "select and common councils of the city of Philadelphia" promised, among other advantages, the one thing Washington City did not currently have—buildings.[39]

Much discussion and energy surrounded the issue of adjournment and relocation; Washingtonians quickly realized that their city might not ever be the capital again and that, as Margaret Bayard Smith mourned, "in one night, have hundreds of our citizens been reduced from affluence to poverty." Some, having never warmed to the federal city, anticipated from the first year of government habitation that the Congress would remove to Baltimore or Philadelphia; for them, the invasion had just hastened the inevitable.[40]

James called Congress back early to decide this question. On September 19, they gathered in Blodgett's Hotel. Expected to last only several days, the debates took four and a half months in the House and Senate to reach a resolution. Congress's first step was to decide whether removal was even an issue. The initial vote recorded 79 for considering removal, with only 37 dissenting. All of the votes to reconsider the capital location came from northern states (and Kentucky), with all of the southern states (and Pennsylvania) voting to simply keep the capital in Washington.[41]

It was tempting to abandon the project of recreating a capital city from the ground up and to move back to Philadelphia or New York. The government could pick up where it had left off, while those who constituted it could also enjoy the delights of one of the most sophisticated metropolises in the western world. And yet, even allowing for the availability of a built environment in another city, such a move would effectively put the federal government on hold for months. And what would it mean to Americans, and to the rest of the world, if the national government seemed to retreat as the vanquished party? As the *Intelligencer* framed the issue, "It would be kissing the rod an enemy had wielded: it would be deserting the seat of government at the dictation of any enemy!"[42] If it was apparent to some people at the time that the new U.S. capital needed to stay put, hindsight and history would prove them correct. In a few months, the New England Federalists would press for increased powers for their states over taxes and commerce; a months-long reorganization would only have strengthened their case for the ineffectiveness of the federal government.

Logistical and symbolic concerns did not pass unnoticed among those concerned. Some legislators might not like the climate or the condition of Washington City (old arguments that proponents for relocation revived); as Barnabas Bidwell, representative from Massachusetts, wrote to his wife, Mary: "This city is an unpleasant and unhealthy place." However, Bidwell continued, "I am afraid to think of a removal . . . lest the attempt should agitate and disturb the nation."[43]

Feelings ran high on both sides. Some argued that the government should not betray the locals who had invested heavily in the capital, as "Washington City" would wither and die without the governmental presence. Others replied that the general good of the nation must not be sacrificed to the private interest of a few citizens. Through the autumn of 1814, rumors and "certainties" flew. William Lowndes, representative from South Carolina, took a positive stance: "There is no probability of our leaving Washington." Representative John Forsyth, writing to a colleague back home in Georgia, hedged his bets: "We are still quarreling about removal. I still think we shall not stir. If we do go, Philadelphia will be the resting place of the political ark." No possibility was out of the question, though. The city father and land developer Thomas Law gloomily opined to his son: "He [Governor Claiborne of Louisiana] says that he expects that the United States will obtain West Florida this winter and then the capital will be removed to Baton Rouge."[44]

❧

While Congress debated, Dolley and her allies sprang into action. Differences with local Federalist families were put aside. Residents of all political stripes had always feared the removal of government and the consequent loss of their investments. On the eve of the attack, they, not Congress, paid for the defense of Washington City, and the first rebuilding funds came from local banks, not the federal government. Thomas Law, John P. Van Ness, Daniel Carroll of Duddington, and Richard Lee, among others, raised money to build a substitute for the

Capitol on the site of the present-day Supreme Court—the "Brick Capitol"—as well as additional public buildings. Having met under Dolley's roof, the local men and pro-Washington government officials knew one another and, in this crisis, the two groups worked together as they had on previous projects. As they had done during the capital's infancy, the Van Nesses expressed their commitment to the city through architecture. Just a few months after Washington burned, they began construction on one of the finest private homes in America, a Latrobe-designed combination of an Italian villa and southern plantation on "Mansion Square" facing C Street.[45]

Though heavily invested in real estate, Thomas Law was no mere entrepreneur. A former British nabob who came to Washington City in the mid-1790s, Law marshaled his pen as well as his purse in support of the rebuilding. He wrote poems inspired by "the scenes of conflagration." He also wrote letters to the president and legislators urging them to not only keep the government in Washington but also make efforts to improve it. He pointed out that Congress's neglect of the city had foreign policy implications: "I have also long apprehended that parsimony and neglect exhibited in this city would tend to deceive foreign governments into contempt of the national spirit, productive of insults and injuries . . . and that foreign ministers . . . must convey unfavorable intimations from what daily could not escape their notice."[46]

In the past, Law had worked with the ladies of Washington City on various civic projects, as in 1809, when he asked Dolley, Hannah, and Margaret Bayard Smith to support his real estate development—"a row of Houses" in a desirable neighborhood. Now, in the city's time of trouble, they pulled together once again. Dolley also enlisted her own female networks to fight Congress's bias against Washington and its residents. If Washington lacked the usual city amenities, it had few equals in one area of urban life: poverty. Lured by the promise of a building boom that never happened, male laborers and their families had flocked to the city in the 1790s and early 1800s, and found themselves unemployed and desperate. Families broke up as men died or deserted their wives and children. The invasion, especially the destruction of the Navy Yard, increased unemployment and the pool of orphaned and abandoned children.[47]

Dolley had long been involved in private charity efforts, including visits to the poor as well "the cause of general literature" [literacy]. But at this precise moment, when Washington City needed to assert its identity as a viable town, and when the locals, still feeling betrayed and abandoned by their leaders, needed to feel part of the federal enterprise, Dolley turned to Marcia Burnes Van Ness and Margaret Bayard Smith to help the local population.

The most concrete manifestation of their efforts did not make its debut until the next congressional season, but it played its part in healing the city. The Washington Female Orphan Asylum was conceived on October 10, 1815. As "First Directress," Dolley contributed $20 and a cow; she also stitched clothes for orphans. Marcia Burnes Van Ness oversaw the actual running of the asylum; Margaret Bayard Smith contributed her time and talents as well, auctioning off copies of her book, *What Is Gentility?*, to raise money. From the very start, the project received publicity of a kind not usually associated with female endeavors. The first announcement in the *National Intelligencer* made the seriousness of the business clear by the location of the meeting: "The Ladies of the county of Washington and neighborhood are requested to meet in the Hall of Representatives [the "Brick Capitol"], this day, at 11 o'clock, A.M. for the purpose of joining an association to provide asylum for the destitute orphans." The fund-raising and opening ceremonies—at which Marcia Burnes Van Ness gave a speech and two little girls presented her with flowers—received press coverage as well.

The *Intelligencer* praised the project as a specifically womanly effort: "A nobler object cannot engage the sympathy of our females— when we reflect, too, how uncertain are all human possessions, we know not, but that we may be providing a respectable and comfortable asylum for our own descendants. 'Cast your bread upon the waters, and after many days, it shall return to you.'" The Orphan Asylum became a long-established city institution—"the glory of Washington City."[48] Its success was twofold: as a charity, it was effective; on a political level, the project made a statement about the city's stability, as well as knitting the city and the government more closely together.

The House debates over the capital's removal raged on. A temporary relocation was mooted; pro-Washington forces recognized this for what it was, a sneaky maneuver to make a "temporary" location permanent. A congressman from North Carolina put it best when he hazarded that once "on wheels, there was no saying where [the government] would stop."[49]

One factor that the virtuous republican representatives eschewed with horror was "personal considerations," that is, trying to obtain the capital city for the personal profit of one's own region. A Federalist representative from New York, Thomas P. Grosvenor, exemplified this principled stand for the official record: "Whoever voted from personal motivations on this question, whether for or against it, deserves condemnation."[50] But official records do not tell the whole story. Some congressmen tried their best to bring this prize home to their constituents, even as they couched their case in ways that stressed their disinterest. But "personal motivations" went both ways. Legislators had good reasons to stay in Washington City.

For almost fifteen years, Dolley had worked hard to make the capital a viable city and center of power. It helped the pro-Washington case that the city was as developed as it was, a consequence of efforts by local boosters and Dolley, who used the power of politics wrapped in the allure of society to attract investors. To be sure, Washington was still no Philadelphia or New York, but some recognized that if the capital moved to a more established city, one with a more layered and complicated social, economic, and political milieu, they might find themselves out in the cold. But their commitment to Washington encompassed more than just a desire not to be somewhere else. Dolley had created political opportunities that had no parallel in any American city. Even with the federal government at its center, a city like Philadelphia would always be *about* many other things. In contrast, this town centered around politics, and everything in it existed in the service of that single purpose.

Doubtless, Dolley had direct conversations with congressmen about the capital. Doubtless, she tried to influence their votes and in some cases succeeded. But her greatest influence lay in the cumulative effect of her work of the past years. On a concrete level, the intangible effects of attachment, connection, and loyalty that she fostered in the official community had a significant impact in the way legislators felt, thought, and voted. The psychological effect was of paramount importance: the very existence—to say nothing of the growth—of the federal government and the union depended on a stable capital.

On October 17, 1814, the resolution for the capital to stay in Washington City passed in the House. The majority vote came from the Democratic-Republicans—a not unexpected outcome, as they stood as the chief beneficiaries of Dolley's social policies. However, in the final vote in the House, 30 Democrat-Republicans had voted for removal, obviously ready to abandon whatever attachments they had to the capital city. But Dolley's vision of Washington had always been bipartisan, accommodating other politics even as she and James tried to change them. Surprisingly, though 44 Federalists stood for removing the capital to another location, 9 voted "pro–Washington City."[51] In the days of all-or-nothing political rhetoric, and given the close margins, it was a particularly significant number: the bill that kept the capital in Washington City passed by 9 votes.

There would be months of agonized waiting for Washingtonians and Americans across the country as the Senate delayed its vote pending the long investigation of the feasibility of rebuilding. Finally, on February 4, 1815, the Senate sent a resolution passing an act for "making appropriations for repairing or rebuilding the public buildings within the City of Washington" to the House. The House passed the bill on February 9, with 78 yeas to 63 nays.[52] Benjamin Henry Latrobe was immediately brought in to supervise the reconstruction of the Capitol, while the original designer, James Hoban, took over the White House.

The Madisons had their own private rebuilding projects. Dolley needed a house in which she could reestablish the Madison administration's power and legitimacy, a house that showed the world that the

Americans might be licked but they weren't beaten. The three-story brick Octagon House still stood, its high-style Federal design making a dramatic statement, on Eighteenth Street and New York Avenue. Designed by William Thornton and owned by John Tayloe III, an "outrageous" Federalist who strongly disapproved of President Madison, it now offered the largest entertaining space in the city. John and Ann Ogle Tayloe were part of Dolley's circle, which also included their mutual friends the Thorntons; in spite of their political differences, the Tayloes lent the Madisons their home. At the Octagon House, Dolley opened the 1814 social season on September 21, two days after the return of Congress, and enjoyed a record attendance. The *Washington City Gazette* expressed disappointment in such resiliency. The editors had hoped that the destruction of the White House would "put an end to drawing-rooms and levees; the resort of the idle, and the encouragers of spies and traitors."[53]

While the Octagon remained the only private residence large and elegant enough to enable Dolley to entertain in the style to which Washington City had grown accustomed, it could not rival Dolley's White House. Dolley mourned the loss of her "piano, book cases and other handsome furniture," as well as "presentation gifts . . . busts and cases of medals," all "consumed by the devouring element." To her friends, she confessed to finding herself "nearly *bereft* of furniture & cloaths." She bought some pieces from the American legation in France, and as Hannah Nicholson Gallatin was moving to France, Dolley asked if she intended on selling her Washington furniture— specifically, "2 or 3 beds, *the* 2 *Eustis* Chairs, & some other articles." Hannah, writing from Philadelphia, promptly replied: "You may have what you may want of my furniture, at the same time I wish it could suit you to take all that is in the house at Washington." Dolley also asked Hannah to look around Philadelphia before she left for "any easy french Chairs . . . for a reasonable price," as well as "second hand Sophas Carpits—or in short any handsome furniture that would answer for us."[54]

Lacking expensive furniture and elaborate architectural additions, Dolley did her best to compensate with visual effects. Deprived of her large dazzling silver pieces and glamorous lighting fixtures, at one notable party she flooded the house with light by stationing enslaved men from cellar to attic to hold pine torches aloft.[55]

Later, in August 1815, the Madisons moved from the Octagon to a set of rooms in the "Seven Buildings," at the corner of Pennsylvania Avenue and Nineteenth Street. Mary Boardman Crowninshield couldn't help but think back to better days when she visited Dolley there. Cambric curtains, stamped to look like damask, stood in for Dolley's famous crimson velvet. In lieu of luxurious carpet, "a dark gray cloth" covered the floor. Gone were the satin "sophas" and chairs, the immense sideboard, covered with decorative pieces; they had been replaced by "two little couches covered with blue patch, [and] a small sideboard with I don't recollect what on it." Still, Dolley transcended her setting: Mary added, "You could not but feel at your ease in her company."[56]

During the rest of her tenure as the president's wife, Dolley would be almost overwhelmed by "company." In 1816, she reported to Edward Coles that "we count one hundred young ladies in the city—not 10 of them belong to the place." Looking back on the last years of the Madison administration, Margaret Bayard Smith would remark that "the parties became so frequent that our social intercourse degenerated into downright disipation."[57]

⚜

Dolley's flight from the White House had captured the public imagination, building on her already larger-than-life image. Among the stories that circulated included the tale that the British had offered to escort her to a safe place, an offer scornfully rebuffed. Supposedly, it was Dolley who urged James to give Francis Scott Key the authority to rescue Dr. William Beanes, thus inadvertently providing the opportunity for Key's inspiration. The truth of these stories matters less than the larger message they carried. Another story that made the rounds had her insisting that the "Founding Fathers" had chosen the seat of the capital, and there it should stay, proclaiming, "We shall rebuild . . . the enemy cannot frighten a free people." To emphasize the effect of this statement, some even depicted her making this declaration amidst the smoking ruins of the White House. Just as Dolley's persona had changed with the declaration of war, her role as the charismatic figure shifted again as she became the symbol of the rebuilding effort.[58]

Dolley became an active symbol of the renewed patriotism that Americans felt as well. Thomas Law wrote a poem, "The Dream," to inspire the rebuilding of Washington. Ostensibly about a man's dream after seeing the ruins of the White House, Law's poem cast women as the central figures. In this, Law worked within the classical tradition, though the goddesses and other females of classical literature were women in name only, displaying fierce, unfeminine attributes. In contrast, Law endowed his female symbols "Columbia," "Liberty," and "Justice" with conspicuously Dolley-like characteristics. Columbia symbolized Washington City and the spirit of America in a particularly feminine style, with "hope, joy, and kindness beaming on her face." Columbia's sighs and tears were feminine expressions; one might have expected a more martial tone, especially as part of the poem's purpose was to urge men to war. But "Justice," delivering the news of the eventual downfall of the British straight from God, also speaks with a voice "though solemn soft with love."

In another version of this poem, the second character is "Liberty who comes with heav'nly grace." Though Liberty had long been depicted as a woman, this Liberty seemed a particularly feminine goddess who, with a comforting smile "quick with ardor presses downcast Columbia to her panting breast." Again, the feminine style and manners that Dolley personified prevailed, dispensing freedom, justice, and victory. As Law urged in another poem: "Let love succeed to war & make them blest."[59]

While Law may not have been referring to Dolley directly when he rendered a poem about war, justice, and rebuilding in feminine terms, he may subconsciously have been responding to the strong association in the public mind. At the very least, he was playing to his audience, using female values and the female language of emotions to appeal to the influential ladies. Law was not the only artist who made the feminine association. A broadside that gloried "Peace on Honorable terms" portrayed "Liberty" and "stern Justice" not just as women, but, again, as buxom Dolley look-alikes.[60]

Law's symbolic choices may also have reflected the longing for peace that the country felt after the invasion. As long as war fever raged, Americans wanted strong men to lead and fight; when their desires turned to peace, more feminine symbols and values could emerge. Through the fall of 1814, as the Americans and British fought for Louisiana, everyone anxiously awaited news of peace. Dolley and Hannah were better informed than anyone except James Madison. The American public and the newspapers might be in "painful suspence," but Dolley told Hannah that commissioners will not sign a "disadvantagious Treaty . . . tho *I* apprehend there is not much room to hope for a happy settlement of the question of *Impressment*." Dolley added, "The existence of this Negotiation was not made public here. It is best, therefore, not to mention it until one of our Ministers shall write."[61]

As it turned out, a final military effort would make as much difference to the outcome of the war as a peace treaty. After their success on the Chesapeake, the British had focused further south. On November 7, 1814, the commander of the U.S. Gulf Coast army, Andrew Jackson, attacked and subdued Pensacola, Florida, on his own initiative. The national government had little interest in this "conquest," since the area was dominated by Spain; indeed, the Spanish governor did not even mount a defense. Jackson marched in, and then out again, heading for what he assumed would be a more attractive target to the British—New Orleans. He reached that city by December 1, to find an uncooperative population. Although the city belonged to the United States, most residents gave their allegiance to France or Spain and "absolutely refused to be marched" by an American general. Jackson swept into town, imposing martial law and, according to one observer, "electrif[ying] all hearts." In assembling his forces to resist an expected attack by the British, Jackson used not only the usual white militia, including 850 Tennessee riflemen, but also free black men, including special corps of black troops. Though he despised pirates, he took them, including the infamous Jean Laffite, up on their offer to fight.

Throughout December, the British steadily moved toward New

Orleans. Having decided to attack by sea, they found themselves delayed by American naval forces led by Thomas Ap Catesby Jones, but finally got within eight miles of New Orleans late in the month and then proceeded overland. Determined to seize the advantage of surprise, Jackson attacked the encamped troops on the night of December 23 with the aid of two American ships, the USS *Carolina* and the *Louisiana*. The fighting continued into January as Jackson constructed defensive lines in the Louisiana swamps, and the Tennessee riflemen picked off British soldiers one by one.

On January 8, 1815, the real battle for New Orleans took place. Two thousand British soldiers were killed or captured, while the United States lost approximately 70 men. The British held on for ten more days, but eventually retreated. In all, the entire Gulf Coast campaign had been a disaster for the British: almost 2,500 men were dead, wounded, or captured, compared to only 350 men on the U.S. side.[62]

By early February, Washingtonians were at the edge of their seats, awaiting news of the battle's outcome—or, alternatively, of peace. News of either event would have to come via the New Orleans mails (held up by the flooded Tennessee River) or by transatlantic ship. The tension was hard on everybody, but some showed the strain more than others. "Mr. Madison looks very thin and infirm," wrote William Ward to his son, but "Mrs. Madison as blooming as a country lass."[63] More than ever, Dolley had come to symbolize not just the rebuilding but peace itself.

Unbeknownst to the Americans, the war had ended even while Jackson's men were killing British soldiers in the Louisiana bayou. On December 24, 1814, the American peace commission—Albert Gallatin, John Quincy Adams, Henry Clay, Jonathan Russell, and James Bayard—had signed the peace treaty in Ghent. The treaty was promptly sent to England by ship for His Majesty's ratification.

On February 13, 1815, a messenger rode into Washington City, carrying the news that a British sloop-of-war had arrived in New York City, bearing the document. By noon the following day, the town was abuzz. In the late afternoon of February 14, 1815, the Treaty of Ghent arrived, carried by Henry Carroll, a secretary to the peace commission.

Without knowing the terms, the crowds cheered as Carroll rode to the Octagon House. The cabinet joined James, and they all retired to an upstairs room. While they studied the document behind closed doors, Dolley, with her unerring instinct for the right gesture, opened the front door of the Octagon House, welcoming all.

By early evening, her drawing room was filled, with guests crowded to the walls, and Dolley "doing the honors of the occasion. And what a happy scene it was!" according to a reporter for the *Intelligencer*. Members of both houses of congress were there, as well as "gentlemen of the most opposite politics" who had been pitted "against one another in continual conflict and fierce debate." With Dolley presiding "with a grace all her own," these men now had "elated spirits" and "softened hearts," and they circulated through the room, "thanking God" and "cordially felicitating one another."

In this throng, the reporter assured readers, "the most conspicuous object in the room, the observed of all observers was Mrs. Madison herself." Dolley dominated the room not merely because she was a "queenly beauty" "in the meridian of life." No, the reporter emphasized; "*she* was, in her person for the moment, the representative of the feelings of him who was, at this moment, in grave consultation with his official advisers."

Like a good hostess, Dolley moved among the crowds, exchanging congratulations and dispensing refreshment. But her primary function was symbolic. Dolley exuded serenity and confidence. "No one could doubt, who beheld the radiance of joy which lighted up her countenance and diffused its beams around, that all uncertainty was at an end." More than just uncertainty: "the government of the country had in very truth . . . 'passed from gloom to glory.'"[64]

Dolley's triumph that day was all the more impressive considering what was going on behind closed doors at the Octagon. The Treaty of Ghent basically conceded nothing; James was "in grave consultation with his official advisers" on how to convince the American public that they had won anything. With respect to territory and boundary issues, the two nations were in exactly the same positions as before the war. Americans had to relinquish their dreams of acquiring Canada once and for all. The English did not even promise to end impressment; that practice would die out on its own, since, with the conclusion of the Napoleonic Wars, the need for British sailors would diminish. And of course, the hated Orders in Council, which had forbidden trade with the United States and had served as a primary impetus to the hostilities, had been repealed before the war started. The only "victory" was psychological, and this became clearer in the next few weeks as the treaty's terms became public.

But the public mind was Dolley's specialty, and Washingtonians, according to Paul Jennings, "were crazy with joy" from the moment Dolley's cousin Sally Coles, who had been waiting outside James's door upstairs at the Octagon House, came to the head of the stairs, crying out, "Peace! peace!" The butler, John Freeman, passed out wine to everyone, including servants, and Paul Jennings played "The President's March" on the violin as French John and other servants began a two-day bender. Paul Jennings wryly observed that "Mr. Madison and all his Cabinet were as pleased as any, but did not show their joy in this manner." Nonetheless, the event took on a decidedly Dolley-like cast in the public eye. One newspaper illustrated the coming of peace as an event where "social hearts and cheerful glee warm the rapt bosoms of the free."[65]

With the arrival of "our glorious Peace," Dolley had one final piece of news for the stalwart Hannah Nicholson Gallatin. Deliberately or otherwise, James did not send Albert notification of his new appointment as minister to France while he was still in London, thus not "sav[ing] him the voage home." For Hannah, however, James's omission meant that "about the 10 or 15th. of may you will embrace your estimable Husband & son."[66] This was news Dolley was happy to share.

As the news of the peace traveled to the rest of the country, so did the joyful response. Federalists could grumble as much as they wanted, but if the entry into the war had been a grievous error, the conclusion of hostilities represented victory for the Madisons. Spitefully, Harrison Gray Otis depicted the presidential couple as crude—"Madison and Dolley chuckle heartily at the event of peace"—ostentatious, and shallow. "She sent to the Secy of State's office as I heard, for several former treaties, to see in what mode the Seal had been affixed, so as to trick off her husbands with decorations of ribbands, and to compare the hand-writing of the different Kings and Princes of Europe." The Boston Brahmin sighed at the southern bumpkins: "What a Satire upon grandeur!"[67]

Otis may have found such sniping comforting in the face of his fellow New Englanders' failed bid to negotiate more state power and regional autonomy (they had discussed, though finally rejected, secession) at the infamous Hartford Convention.[68] The Federalists had never been accurate readers of the public mind, but no one could have predicted the public relations miscalculation when in late January 1815, they set off to Washington City to present their proposals. News of the triumph at the battle of New Orleans reached Washington City by February 4, beating the Federalists to the punch and rendering their position irrelevant. No matter that the battle occurred *after* the signing of the peace—slow mail again—the United States was still at war, since the Senate and president had yet to ratify the treaty (which they would on February 18, 1815). The American people eagerly embraced Jackson's stunning success as a national vindication.

The news of Jackson's triumph of militiamen over His Majesty's forces went a long way to softening the disappointing treaty terms. The first substantial account of the battle came to Dolley in early February from one of her most troublesome patronage candidates—Louisa Catherine Johnson Adams's brother, who had gained his position as postmaster of New Orleans through Dolley's efforts. After asserting that "the American Army in Louisiana has gained immortal glory," Thomas Johnson sent along the first details of troop movements and casualties. So up-to-the-minute was his letter that he even interrupted himself in the middle to announce that "the British have evacuated the country."

Johnson ended his account: "The country is saved, the enemy vanquished and hardly a widow or orphan whose tears damp the general joy. All is exultation and jubalee." He wondered rhetorically: "What do we not owe a protecting Providence for this manifestation of his favor?"[69] Only Providence could answer that question, but for achieving the psychological "vanquishing" of enemies foreign and domestic, some of that victory belonged to Dolley. She had become, in effect, everyone's Dolley, the Queen of America, and when the troops demobilized, they marched past the temporary President's House and cheered for her.

⊛

Though contemporaneous Republicans and most later historians tried to dress it up as a second War for Independence, the War of 1812 resolved no practical issues. Ironically, if any group could have been said to have won the war that nobody won, it was the Federalists. They had warned that the Republicans would not achieve their goals and that failure would come at a great cost. The experience of war *did* change the direction of the government, but in ways that Federalists had long argued for: increased military expenditures, the implementation of internal taxes, the founding of a national bank.[70]

Still, many agreed that the war had given Americans a new sense of self. "The war has renewed and reinstated the national feelings and character which the Revolution had given, and which were daily lessening," Albert Gallatin wrote to a colleague in May 1816. The war, he observed, imparted to the American people "more general objects of attachment, with which their pride and political opinions are connected." As a result, "they are more Americans; they feel and act more as a nation, and I hope that the permanency of the Union is thereby better secured." (Since Albert was still in Europe, this characterization may have been Hannah's.)[71]

The assault on Washington City proved crucial to the "connection" and the "attachments" to "general objects" that begin the processes so crucial to nationalism. Contemporaries observed that the burning of the White House aroused indignation that not only garnered support for the war but also prepared the Americans for the taxes that would be needed to pay for it.[72] And what was true for America was doubly true for Washington City. With the relocation issue decided and the rebuilding begun, fresh optimism and energy swept the town. Anthony Baker, the chargé d'affaires who ferried the final Treaty of Ghent from Europe, noted a new attitude of confidence in the capital. Even the Federalist Rosalie Stier Calvert admitted that "the burning of the public buildings of Washington is the best thing that has happened in a long time, as far as we are concerned, since this has finally settled the question of whether the seat of government would stay here." Though it must have chagrined her to admit it, Rosalie bravely and accurately predicted: "In the future they will no longer keep trying to change it and as long as the union stands, the government will remain in Washington, despite the jealousy of Philadelphia, New York and Baltimore."[73]

Indeed, Washington was here to stay. The question of relocation had been on the table since the government had moved to the capital on the Potomac; after 1814, it never resurfaced. By 1816, in spite of the slow pace of rebuilding, Americans perceived the new Washington as having become a real capital overnight. The secretary of the new Board of Navy Commissioners wrote to a friend in New York of the changed atmosphere: "All of Washington is now jumping alive. Strangers and members of Congress and gentlemen are daily arriving and the tavern keepers and boardinghouse people laugh for joy. . . . [E]verybody and everything seems to hang upon the government."[74]

For some months, Dolley had held the city, and by extension the country, together in a delicate balance, until the arrival of the Treaty of Ghent and the news of New Orleans tipped the scales toward victory. Clearly, now everyone regarded Washington City as a power center; attracted to the new opportunities, people arrived in droves. Taking a page from Thomas Law, newspapers began to demand that the planners do more than merely replace the buildings—which, in any case, had not been finished in 1814, but rather, seemed "elegant skeletons, half-finished, half-dilapidated structures." The people of the newly affirmed United States of America deserved "the most splendid public edifices in the world," a circumstance "in no way incompatible with the purest principles of republican government." The Capitol and the White House had emerged as truly national symbols, a process that had begun in earnest with Dolley's work and that war had accelerated.[75]

Nineteenth-century Americans were becoming participants in a modern democracy, and if the war produced nothing concrete, it nurtured a national faith, one represented by symbols and mottos supplied by its military encounters: "We have met the enemy and they are ours";

"Don't give up the ship"; and "Our country—right or wrong." It was during this conflict that America acquired a national anthem, "The Star-Spangled Banner." The national symbols of the White House and the Capitol joined with other representations of the federal government; this era marked the arrival of "Uncle Sam." But the most enduring image of all was Dolley Madison saving the portrait of George Washington as she fled the burning White House.[76] By saving the cabinet papers, Dolley ensured James's place in history, but in preserving the portrait, she guaranteed her own posterity.

Dolley Payne Todd
Madison in 1794—
newly widowed
and newly wed

Eliza Collins Lee,
Dolley's friend from
her Philadelphia
girlhood

Philadelphia as it appeared during the Paynes' residence there in the 1790s

James and Dolley Madison in 1796. The dress shows Dolley's shift
from Quaker matron to Virginia gentlewoman. On the eve of his first
"retirement," James plays the country gentleman.

Thomas Jefferson, from his time as ambassador to France

Benjamin Henry Latrobe, Dolley's collaborator on the White House project

The White House, setting for Dolley's most dramatic work

A view of early Washington City, at its most pristine and promising

Future president James Monroe, minister to England under Jefferson and secretary of state in the Madison administration

Albert Gallatin, secretary of treasury for both the Jefferson and Madison administrations, as well as James's close colleague and most problematic political liability

Anna Payne, Dolley's "daughter-sister," just before her 1804 marriage to Richard Cutts

The paired portraits rendered
by Gilbert Stuart during his
whirlwind tour of the new
capital city

Margaret Bayard Smith, both
"sister" and "spy" to Dolley

Samuel Latham Mitchill,
the "Stalking Library" and
husband to Catharine
Akerly Mitchill

John Jacob Astor, who danced
attendance on Dolley and
Hannah Nicholson Gallatin

America's prince, John Payne Todd, in his prime. During Payne's Montpelier years, Edward Coles called him "a veritable serpent in the Garden of Eden."

John Quincy Adams, a powerful man connected to the Madisons through Dolley's patronage and networking

Louisa Catherine Johnson Adams, who modeled her own role as "campaign manager" on the work of "dear Dolley"

In this imaginative re-creation of the business of government, Dolley is featured below the chandelier in the gallery.

"The Republican Queen"

John C. Calhoun,
a future Congressional
leader who got his first
taste of national politics
under Dolley's tutelage

TOP LEFT: John Randolph of Roanoke, who hated the Madisons and took every chance he could to bedevil them

TOP RIGHT: Henry Clay, Dolley's "valued" friend and fellow snuff addict

The painting of George Washington, modeled after Stuart, that Dolley rescued from the doomed White House

A British reaction to "Mad-ass-son's" insanity

The sight of the gutted White House devastated all of Washington

The Madisons at
the height of their
popularity—and
on the eve of their
retirement

Montpelier

Dolley as Elder Stateswoman. Note that in pictures and photographs from her last years, Dolley had a "standard" costume that hearkened back to the early republic. The elements of the ensemble were not just evocations; Dolley was so impoverished by that time that she wore clothes from her presidential wardrobe.

President James and Sarah Childress Polk, with James Buchanan, Harriet Lane, General Cave Johnson, Robert Walker, and Dolley Madison, circa 1845-46. When a daguerreotypist working at the White House learned that Dolley was visiting, he made this spur-of-the moment attempt to record the political line of succession.

Dolley with the niece who made her later life possible, Annie Payne Cutts, her "sterling girl," in Matthew Brady's 1848 daguerreotype

The Last of the Founders in another Brady daguerreotype

SIXTEEN

To Home and History

*T*he election of James Monroe to the presidency in 1816 seemed a right and fitting end to the Madison administration. As the last of the Virginia dynasty, Monroe was James's appointed successor. The country was in a celebratory mood; not only had it successfully concluded a war, but even the old bitter party feuds seemed to have run their course. The Hartford Secession had dealt the Federalists a deadly blow, and their candidate, Rufus King, had garnered only 34 electoral votes to Monroe's 183.

The war with Great Britain, however mitigated and ultimately useless, continued to elicit nationalism and pride, which spilled over onto the Madisons. When Dolley and James departed Washington for Montpelier and retirement, they did so triumphantly, and it seemed the whole country was sad to see them go. They attended so many "balls

public and private" that they stayed on until April 1817, a full month after Monroe's inauguration. They were showered with tributes—both
prose and verse—as well as gifts. (At one Georgetown event, the encomiums took the form of "richly framed" transparencies, paintings,
and poetry etched on white velvet that covered the walls; these were
sent on to Montpelier as souvenirs.) Yet even as Dolley packed up
the Madisons' furniture and belongings for the journey home, wrote
farewell letters, and made and received last visits, political watchers and
pundits began constructing the legacy of the Madison administration.[1]

Dolley came in for a fair share of acclaim of her own. The Georgetown ball was held in her honor; one of the verses that decorated the
hall compared her to the sun in her power to illumine, cheer, and to be
"admired by all." Politicians of all persuasions lauded the way her manners "encourage[d] the diffident [and] tempted the morose," and how
she "suffered no one to turn from [her] without an emotion of gratitude." Dolley had launched many young women and men into society,
marriages, and careers, and they, too, remembered their benefactress.[2]

Personal friends and the press alike evaluated Dolley's legacy to her
country. Some of the praise was formulaic, emphasizing the qualities
that made her an exemplar of American womanhood—she was "handsome," "graceful," and "gracious," "loved alike by rich and poor"—but
most also acknowledged the political value of her work. As always,
members of the diplomatic corps were the most astute in their praise.
Lucia Alice von Kantzow, the wife of the Swedish minister, declared
that no future experience in another country would "open more our
eyes, enlarge our ideas, experience more the delight of natural, easy
kind deeds, and kind ways, than what charmed us, in your flourishing,
prosperous and fortunate country." Like other diplomats before her,
Lucia conflated Dolley with the United States, so that in the same
breath she admired both Dolley's "many virtues" and "the gigantic
strides your Republic makes to rival the best parts of Europe." Lucia
recognized James's high-minded and idealistic stewardship of government, but extolled Dolley's mastery of the political game. In Lucia's
metaphor, with cards "so well delt" and "well played," Dolley made
"friends among both parties," and became "loved by all your country

men and country women." In her role as the president's wife, Dolley "honored his elevated post," garnering respect "for your judicious conduct, and affable kind manners."[3]

While the noted Philadelphia magazine *The Port Folio* highlighted Dolley's traditionally feminine accomplishment of creating a social circle that "was at once the model of the polished life and the dwelling of cheerfulness," they also explicitly praised her political achievements. "At a time when the restless spirit of party covered every path with thorns," proclaimed the publication, "this lady held the branch of conciliation and she well deserves a place among those who endeavor to promote peace and good will." Thomas Jefferson may have uttered the famous words, "We are all federalists, we are all republicans," but "in her intercourse with society, Mrs. Madison reduced this liberal sentiment to practice." Once again, Dolley inspired solar metaphors, as *The Port Folio* unintentionally echoed the Georgetown verse: "Like a summer's sun she rose in our political horizon, gloriously, and she sunk, benignly."[4]

Some of Dolley's tributes acknowledged her contributions to the war effort. Commodore John Rodgers sent his respects to her, along with a "Mat . . . composed of pieces taken from the flags of all the vessels . . . captured by the President while under his command."

As she had upon Dolley's ascension to high office eight years earlier, Eliza Collins Lee acknowledged the passing of a milestone moment, the doffing of the "robe of state." She recalled that inaugural letter and how she had predicted Dolley's success in filling the station in which Fortune had placed her. "How much greater cause have I to congratulate you, at this period for having so filled it as to render yourself more enviable this day," noting how much more difficult it is to achieve "gratitude and thanks" for a job well done than merely to receive congratulations. Eliza assured Dolley that she wrote not just as a loving friend, but also as a "citizen." She framed her praise of Dolley's political effectiveness in high-flown language, designed to veil even as it lauded, but not all of her political allusions were subtle: she also asked Dolley to convey her regards and thanks to James, who had recently appointed Eliza's husband, Richard Bland Lee, as commissioner of claims, thus relieving the Lees of substantial financial worries.[5]

At times Dolley seemed a bit overwhelmed by the attention. Even with Congress adjourned, "still our house is crouded with company—in truth ever since the peace my brain has been turn'd with noise & bustle. Such over flowing rooms I never saw before—I sigh for repose." With the arrival of peace and with Washington City's status as the capital affirmed, all flocked to the seat of power. To Edward Coles, Dolley marveled at the "unusual numr. of young men from every direction—in short, we never had so busy a winter because the city was never before so full of respectable strangers." At the drawing rooms, "we have such throngs, *you never saw.*"[6]

<hr />

Later historians, not on the scene to be blinded by the light, would tot up the list of James's failures, especially concerning the near catastrophic war, and deem his presidency an exercise in bad leadership. At worst, detractors would charge James with betraying his own ideals and the country; at best, more sympathetic chroniclers would wonder how such a brilliant man could have gone so wrong.[7]

The general opinion of the time, however, found the Madison presidency an overwhelming success. No less an expert—and a judgmental one at that—than John Adams declared that James's administration had "acquired more glory, and established more Union, than . . . Washington Adams and Jefferson, put together." Without doubt, the country was in a euphoric mood, but the gratitude and admiration did not stem from a misplaced and mistaken assessment of James as a powerful leader. Quite the opposite was true: the public praised James for his restraint in war, his refusal to sacrifice "civil or political liberties" for "power and national glory," as one committee of citizens phrased it. In republican theory, war bred corruption, but James had not used the excuse of a national emergency to grab power or crush supporters—no Alien and Sedition Acts for him.[8]

Once the war ended, then, the country saw no barriers to unity. With the cessation of hostilities, Americans and their government were able to resume business as usual, free from the treason trials, libel actions, or the general hard feelings that would characterize future major American conflicts. In 1817, the legacy of James Madison seemed to be that he had held the country together in time of war, guiding the ship of state through the dangerous shoals of international politics and domestic discord. After the storms, the ship emerged still sound, ready to sail into the sunrise of a clearing sky and a new era of unity.[9]

This happy state of affairs, all agreed, stemmed not from specific actions but from James's sterling character. His "philosophic mind," moderate temper, and purity of spirit ensured that even so violent an event as war would proceed wisely and temperately. While conceding the preeminence of James's intelligence, those closest to him insisted that his personal qualities were paramount, rendering him the perfect statesman. In a cutthroat capital city, surrounded by treacheries foreign and domestic, he remained unruffled. He did not seem motivated by revenge, nor did he indulge in the character assassination that distinguished contemporary political discourse.[10] Indeed, James's greatest political achievement—the transcendence of partisanship—was only made possible by his character. By not indulging his vanity with petty shows of anger and selfishness, he had truly served his country.[11]

In the eyes of his assessors, these characteristics stood him and the country in particularly good stead through the greatest trial of the war, the burning of Washington. Though some observers, including Edward Coles, compared James to the great George Washington in his steady leadership and self-control, the character traits admired by all—modesty and restraint, especially self-restraint—belonged to a more feminine ideal. Like those of a perfect lady, James's accomplishments were passive; it was what he didn't do that garnered admiration.[12]

Dolley, of course, best exemplified this model. She came to prominence as the very symbol of conciliation in a world of men who liked their politics rough and ready. She had acted when James could not. Her dramatic act of bravery during the invasion became the most memorable moment of the war, and her quieter, quotidian efforts during the relocation debates played a large part in securing Washington City as the capital. Dolley had often served as a lightning rod for James, reflecting and deflecting criticisms of him. Now, at the end of the administration, her persona performed an opposite service, as people projected her qualities and achievements onto James. In their political partnership, Dolley had always taken charge of the psychological and emotional aspects of politics, and her work paid off. Ultimately, the victories in this realm—a united country, a secure capital, and an enhanced and optimistic sense of nationality—emerged as James's gift to the nation. And this proved a highly significant bequest to the future United States. The public's focus on psychological and emotional successes was not just a way to avoid discussing military errors. In praising James's (and implicitly Dolley's) steady command, contemporaries recognized that the task of unifying a fractious government and citizenry could be harder than the more dramatic job of winning a war with an external enemy.[13]

The presence of Dolley in a leading role in the drama of federal politics also ensured that other accomplishments, good and bad, passed undetected by those eager to cast the administration for "History." Political observers noted approvingly that James had refrained from taking advantage of wartime circumstances to expand the power of his office, most notably through the dreaded monarchical practice of patronage. But of course, Dolley ran the Madison patronage machine; it was through her letters that she and James issued rebukes and assurances, building bridges and strengthening barricades as they expanded, at least temporarily, the power of this president.

But perhaps, in the end, it is fruitless to attempt to separate the strands of the complex weave of Dolley and James that made up the Madison political partnership. James was indeed the restrained and sober presence that Edward Coles and others described. No doubt, the secret of the Madisons's professional and personal success was that James and Dolley were both people who valued harmony and thoughtful consideration above all. Nonetheless, Dolley was the one who personified theory, who rendered it concrete and palpable to the public. If in the final laudatory verdict, observers, historians, and the American people considered the Madison administration a success and believed that character counted, then the achievement belonged to both husband and wife.

On April 6, 1817, as Dolley and James and their retinue, complete with Dolley's macaw, Polly, boarded a steamboat on the Potomac River and set out for Montpelier, James Monroe was traveling as well. Shortly after his inauguration, he, like the revered Washington, embarked upon a months-long goodwill tour across the country. He even traveled to the Detroit frontier, the farthest west a president had ever been. The power shift made clear by his election was further underscored when his tour took him to Boston. There, in the heart of Federalism, crowds cheered him and newspapers printed acclamations and praises.

As America moved through the 1820s and 1830s, the nature and limits of the Madisons' accomplishment became clearer. It seemed that the Republicans had achieved their goals. With the Federalists down, faction had been abolished, and they were finally free to realize Jefferson's original vision of a pure, republican dreamworld. From that perspective, it was no wonder that Dolley and James were so celebrated. If America had had to fight Great Britain once again, so be it. James's unwavering vision of the ideals of republicanism and liberty, and his commitment to them, kept the nation on its course, even as circumstances threatened confusion and chaos. For her part, Dolley made the Revolution real, securing the republic by anchoring her husband's ideas to the everyday. Their utter triumph was reflected in the nickname bestowed upon the first years of Monroe's term: the Era of Good Feeling. With the republic secured, at least on paper, the story of America could have ended right there.

But of course, it did not. As applied to the low temperature of partisanship, the label "Good Feeling" may well have fit, but the years of Monroe's administration and afterward were some of the most disruptive in American history. In 1819 came the worst financial panic experienced by America up to that date, as shippers and manufacturers suffered from the resumption of British prewar shipping, and farmers lost their land in a frenzy of speculation. In 1820, the debate over the place of slavery in the nation reached a fever pitch with the decision whether to admit Missouri as a slave state. The 1823 Monroe Doctrine, which sanctioned unfettered geographic expansion as the United States' "destiny," seemed a far cry from George Washington's warnings against "entangling alliances" with other nations.

Two major slave rebellions—Denmark Vesey's conspiracy in Charleston, South Carolina, in 1822, and Nat Turner's 1831 rebellion in Southampton County, Virginia—marked an era of growing African-American unrest. Throughout the 1820s and 1830s, the very fabric of the social order seemed under threat as all kinds of people would begin clamoring for rights—poor white men, free black men, and women of all races. There were culture-wide discussions not only about states' rights, but also about the relationship between government and the individual. American arts and letters were entering a period of efflorescence, even as Americans and Europeans debated the very possibility of "American" art. Change was rife in the most profound arenas of American life. New religious ideas, which emphasized the individual's relationship to God, took hold, fostering new valuations of human worth that would fuel slave resistance and reform movements.

In addition to being an "Era of Good Feeling," the 1820s and 1830s emerged as an age of "individualism," a term coined by the French observer Alexis de Tocqueville during his travels to America in the thirties. While noting the tendency of Americans to join organizations in droves, Tocqueville was struck by their sense of individuality, especially among white men. All of this change and turbulence mostly passed by the Madisons on their quiet Virginia farm. James and Dolley had presided over an essentially eighteenth-century world; private interests were to be subsumed to the public good, and "purely republican" citizens would join with republican wives and mothers (and the occasional queen) to create a social order that ran like clockwork. The "individual" was viewed as a selfish being, inimical to the good society.

The world of nineteenth-century America was indisputably different in ways incomprehensible to people of earlier eras. No wonder that Thomas Jefferson, John Adams, and other founders who lived into the 1820s expressed shock, and even horror, at the way their experiment was evolving. They had intended to create a republic but were ending up with a democracy.

"Different times, different manners," however, could not fully explain the rates and qualities of change. America was not just becoming different; she was becoming modern. All of the crises of the age could be traced to this growing modernity. The "Panic of 1819" occurred because the financial infrastructure was converting to a purely cash economy, and people had not yet caught up to the complicated concepts of speculation and investment. Slaves rebelled precisely because of the new ideas of human life that accompanied modern religion and philosophies. Innovative technologies, such as steamships, railroads, telegraphs, and revolutionary methods of manufacture, fueled the exploding capitalist culture.

New archetypes also emerged from this era, American "selves" created directly in response to the market. The growing world of business and commerce demanded a segregation of human activities into spheres. The Self-Made Man, all energy and initiative, populated the public sphere of business and politics. His female correlate, the True Woman, guarded the private sphere of home, as an angel of the hearth. Her job was not only to create a "haven in a heartless world," from which her man could return, refreshed, to the cutthroat world of the market, but to use the home as a repository of values incompatible with the business of making money—love, truth, and emotion.

Dolley and James had little part to play in this new world, though in his 1815 message to Congress, James had outlined a plan of economic development, first proposed by Alexander Hamilton and long endorsed by James's Federalist enemies. It was a sign of things to come that the last of the Republican fathers espoused a national bank, internal taxes, and a national system of roads and canals. And although, throughout his retirement years, politicians and journalists would turn to James for his thoughts on particular political questions, they turned to him as a repository of Original Intentions, rather than a generator of current, original ideas. Having achieved their goals of securing the union and realizing (to whatever extent) the republican dream, Dolley and James would cease to serve their country in active ways; instead, they reigned as symbols of living history. They realized this as well, and would spend significant portions of their retirement positioning themselves for posterity. But they could not escape the problems of the modern world entirely. The increasingly complicated dilemma of slavery appeared as irresolvable to the Madisons as it seemed to the United States at large.

⁓⁓⁓

Boarding the boat for Montpelier that April morning in 1817, James must have felt the weight of office lift off his shoulders, talking and joking with all, as "giddy as a schoolboy on summer vacation.[14] The steamboat took the Madison party down the Potomac to Aquia Creek, where they disembarked and took a carriage the rest of the way home. Like an earlier momentous carriage ride, the end of this journey signaled new lives for the pair. In 1801, the Madisons had bumped along a rutted Pennsylvania Avenue, approaching the prospect of a high-powered political life in Washington City with excitement and no doubt some anxiety. Now, as they rode up the long drive of the Madison plantation, waiting for the house to come into view, they looked toward a less exciting but more contented existence.

Dolley and James intended to fully retire, remaining at Montpelier for the rest of their lives, and, at least while James lived, they did stay put. Over the next nineteen years, they left the plantation for a prolonged period only once—to spend the winter in Richmond in order to attend the Constitutional Convention in 1829. They visited their old friend Thomas Jefferson at Monticello each year, and as an officer of Mr. Jefferson's university, the University of Virginia, James made an annual trip to Charlottesville, sometimes accompanied by Dolley, sometimes not. He never saw Washington City again.

When he arrived at his birthplace in 1817, James Madison was sixty-six years old, his always delicate constitution taxed by the stress of public life. In contrast, Dolley "retired" at just shy of forty-nine, an age her era considered still the prime of life. Though she experienced her share of illnesses over the years, she arrived at Montpelier strong and vigorous. Public life had taxed her, too, sometimes to the point of exasperation, but she also thrived on people, society, and high-stakes politics.

Certainly, everyone expected unalloyed happiness for Dolley at Montpelier, a long rest after a crowning career. Eliza Collins Lee thought Dolley's position "more enviable—more exalted—and more bless'd" than ever, since "now indeed you are at *Home.*" Eliza expressed her gratification at learning from one report that Dolley's "soul is as big as ever and her boddy has not decreased Mr. M—— is the picture of happiness." But life at Montpelier was not without obligations. Her hostess duties were considerable, though Dolley declared she would rather entertain one hundred at Montpelier than twenty-five in Washington. (On one memorable Fourth of July, she did in fact seat ninety people, mostly local gentlemen, for dinner.) In good weather, the Madisons rarely dined alone, regularly hosting a dozen or so guests at table. Dolley often found the company "a great disadvantage," and like many women of her time complained that her time was not her own. "House full of company—I have scarcely a moment to breathe."[15]

But when the Madisons were not overwhelmed with guests, life was slow and quiet, even isolated. Certainly, Dolley was accustomed to that; she had grown up in the Virginia countryside and had spent a great deal of time at Montpelier since her marriage to James. But she felt the dullness of country living more keenly than did James. She was a woman of the world, used to moving within the highest circles of the nation, and she had enjoyed the gratification of praise and approbation as people admired her, explicitly as an exemplary woman, and implicitly as a power in her right. And Washington had always been *her* town. All that changed as she settled down in the Virginia countryside. "Two years absence from Washington has not deminished my attachment to it," she sighed to Eliza. She fantasized about being "*oblidged* to visit W-n *before long,*" but she would or could not go.[16]

Themes of isolation, loneliness, and constraint ran through Dolley's letters during the almost twenty years of retirement with James at Montpelier. She tended toward the melodramatic in voicing her complaints, accusing her kin of "forgetting" her and playing on their guilt by invoking her "disappointment" if they would not visit. As exhausting as the troops of company could be, the winter became the hardest time for Dolley, as it was "not the season for visiting." Rather, "our amusements in this region, are confined to books and rural occupations," a limited set of activities indeed for a woman used to crowds, color, and change. The "Norwegian Winter," as Dolley styled it, proved often too bitter for her and brought colds and influenzas that lasted for weeks and even months. Though she knew people in the neighborhood, to her old, real friends in Washington, she tellingly characterized "our society" as "strangers all, to you."[17]

The issues that had occupied the Madisons during their public life—family, finances, politics—remained their chief concerns, but it was money that now assumed paramount importance. After years in the public service, often expending his own funds, James determined to secure his family's fortune as a farmer. But farming was, as always, a precarious way to make a living, and he would struggle over money for the rest of his life, as his widow would do for hers.

⁂

The country isolation sharpened Dolley's longing for her family. Though James's mother, Nelly Conway Madison, was still alive, presiding in her own wing of the house, it was not the same as having sisters nearby. Lucy was surprisingly absent from the scene. Ensconced at her husband's estate in Kentucky, "engrossed with her children & grandchildren," she was forever promising to visit, but seldom did; at one point, Dolley did not see Lucy for seven years. Anna and her young family, however, spent long stretches of time in the summer at Montpelier. Dolley was thrilled when she had her "daughter-sister" by her side, with her nieces and nephews filling the house with life and noise. But it was a letdown when they returned to the capital, where Richard Cutts served in the Treasury as second comptroller until 1829. Dolley wrote wistfully of the "round of pleasant society" that Anna enjoyed in the metropolis, mixing longing and envy in her letters.[18]

A busy mother and political hostess, Anna tried to keep in touch with her sister, but Dolley sometimes wanted more than she could give. She couched her desire for communication in self-pity: "If I could allways know you & yours ware well I should not be so unreasonable as to ask you to give your time or attention to writeing to me." When Anna did not write often enough, Dolley "excused" her by acknowledging the trouble she caused: "I see plainly by the little of late that it is a task."

Not that she blamed Anna for her reluctance, "for I am . . . [a] poor dull creature, & at such a distance that I must submit & live along as well as I can detached from others."[19]

To be fair, Dolley did not only complain. Her letters to Anna were as wide-ranging as they ever had been, laced with charm and humor, always her saving grace. She sent "a thousand kisses," as well as produce and articles of clothing, to her friends and family in Washington City. She could even joke about her own clinging tendencies, remarking to her sister, "I've kept cherries & flowers for you until they wither on the stem—like me."[20] But everyone went to Washington except Dolley, or so it must have seemed. Payne Todd had no use for the charms of country life, preferring the racier amusements of an urban setting. Dolley entertained a different idea of how her son spent his time in the capital, and she longed "to be with you to witness . . . the respect and love shewn my son would be the highest gratification the world could bestow."[21]

As she grew older, Dolley wanted to depend on Payne, but would have settled for his independence. According to family lore, James had a favorite saying which fit her son: "Errors like straws upon the surface flow / Those who would duck for pearls must dive below." Apparently, however, no one was able to dive deep enough to find Payne's pearls. He lived by his uncle's pattern, dropping out of sight for weeks at a time, his travels up and down the Eastern Seaboard discernable only by the trail of debt. At a time of increasing financial strain for James and Dolley, James paid about $40,000 to cover Payne's shortfalls. Dolley was under the impression it was half that amount; James tried to spare her, quietly paying Payne's creditors "to ensure her tranquility by concealing from her the ruinous extravagance of her son." Even so, she knew enough "to make her wretched" during the times of his silence and absence. His neglect was a constant source of heartache, as when she sadly reported that Payne "comes not—nor do I hear from him, which covers me with sadness in the midst of pleasantness."[22] When he did show up, Payne shamelessly appealed to his mother for help, and she supplied him with whatever money she could get her hands on, only for him to spend it on drink, gambling, or worse.

Regardless, Dolley's letters to Payne overflowed with love and an almost romantic sensibility. He remained her "dearest," "my beloved"; she even quoted a love poem, Thomas Moore's "Love's Young Dream," in a plea for him to visit her. Spring had come, she reported, the world was "bathed in sun-shine," and "such would be the case, even with me, if you ware with me—and *happy at being so,* The freshness of spring would rest upon my spirits in your presence, now, 'tis odour fled as soon as shed; Tis mornings winged dream.'" In marked contrast, Payne's letters to his mother were all business.[23]

In 1829, he landed in debtor's prison in Philadelphia, one of two such stays in his "strange and distressing" career. As always, Dolley poured out her heart to Anna. "I enquired of you if you had heared from or of my dear Child—you say nothing & since that letter, I recd. one from him in which he tells me that he was boarding within Prison bounds! [F]or a debt of 2—or 300$ he has submitted to this horrid— horrid situation. It almost breaks my heart to think of it." Dolley could hardly bring herself to speak of it: "I don't know that I shall send you this letter—in truth I feel as if I could not write a letter—My pride— my sensibility, & every feeling of my Soul is wounded." No matter the pain her son caused, in the next breath, Dolley declared: "Yet *we* shall do something—what or when, depends on Mr M-s health, & strength, to do business—his anxiety, & wish to aid, & benefit P. is as great as a Father's."[24] Indeed, if Dolley read James's anxiety correctly, he showed an amazing patience with his erring stepson. Sadly, that indulgence of both Dolley and Payne benefited no one and hurt him.

Dolley's political genius lay in her ability to combine traditional female passivity with a strong will and desire to advance. In her public life she made her submissiveness work for her, turning the ability to acquiesce into an active tool of her ambition. But what served her in public life let her down in some of her personal relationships. Many in her wide circle of family and friends appreciated Dolley's seemingly infinite capacity to accommodate and nurture; the dynamic benefited both parties, with Dolley getting something back, whether it was love, respect, emotional support, or practical care. With Payne, however, she gave her all and received little in return but grief. Dolley understood her son's fundamental weakness, yet still she found excuses for him. When he did not answer her letters, she quickly blamed the new postmaster in Philadelphia. Whether she actually believed the man had failed to deliver her letters, or whether she presented the scenario to help Payne save face (or maintain her own denial), her wistful neediness clearly emerged: "The Mail of this day may chear me by your own good acct. of yourself."[25] It did not.

Dolley's willful blindness did her son no good; it endangered the Madisons' financial welfare, and it set her up for continual disappointment. For a while, she set her sights on marrying Payne to one of her "adopted daughters," Phoebe Morris. Perhaps hoping, as in the plots of the novels she read, that the love of a good woman would reform the rake, Dolley seemed oblivious to the fact that she was taking the chance of ruining Phoebe's life. At a time when marriage was an irrevocable step, every woman's nightmare was to discover she had married a wastrel. It is not clear who vetoed the plan—perhaps the pupil surpassed the teacher in her judgment and prudence—but in any event, Phoebe did not marry Payne.[26]

Payne's transgressions became a source of public embarrassment. In 1824, after relating how his "old acquaintance" asked about him, Dolley ventured: "But my dear son it seems to be the wonder of them all that you shd. stay so long from us! & now I am ashamed to tell, when asked, how long my only child has been absent from the home of his mother!" Why would he not avail himself of their guidance? "Your Papa & myself entreat you to come to us—to arrange your business with those concern'd to return to them when necessary, & let us see you here, as soon as possible." At the very least, Payne should play the dutiful son. "Your Papa thinks as I do, that it would be best for your reputation & happiness as well as ours, that you shd have the appearance of consulting your parents, on subjects of deep acct. to you." This was as close to reproach as Dolley got, but she ended her letter wishing him in "our arms, who love with inexpressible tenderness & constancy."[27]

⚜

Dolley's world of women grew with the happy addition of Anna's two oldest daughters—her namesake, Dolley Payne, and Mary Estelle

Elizabeth. She had always loved her nieces, but during the 1830s she drew even closer to the two Cutts girls, young women in their teens and twenties, unmarried, and enjoying life in Washington. Indeed, they may have been having too good a time to marry; Dolley described them as "well educated sensible girls, full of gaiety and fashion."[28] Without husbands and children, the Cutts girls relished the social scene and the many distinguished people whom they met. Mary even circulated an autograph book, enlisting her aunt to help collect signatures and verses from her famous friends. With Anna, Dolley acted as part mother, part big sister. With the Cutts girls, she was mother and best friend.

She took it upon herself to teach them the ways of the world. When they went to Richmond, she approved: "I think it will be an advantage to them to see other characters, than those they are confined to, in W[ashi]n[gton]—You know it expands the minds of Men & women to look into the varieties of this world, to a certain degree."[29] When they neglected their social duties, Dolley chided them. Upon learning that they had failed to pay the first call on a diplomat's wife, she asserted her credentials as the Queen of Washington City to gently reprimand and advise: "[S]urely Dolley and yourself know better the etiquette near courts." She reminded her two nieces that "I lived sixteen years in the midst of ceremonies," as well as "four years in Philadelphia, where Mrs. Washington presided, and intimate with the heads of Departments and Minister[s]" and "in my humble opinion they were in the right—When they or you take a journey the first call must be made by you."[30]

Concern for her nieces also brought out the savvy side of Dolley, who always acted in such a way as to appeal to people's better nature while always being aware of their darker instincts. She helped her protégées reconcile many issues, from the pressure to conform ("It is best for us my dear, to beware of 'most everybody'") to conversation with a boor ("Mr. —— is an elegant and accomplished person, but—be perfectly respectful to him and ready to receive the instruction which lurks forever in his conversation").[31] About a new addition to their "sett," Dolley advised: "It is in her power to be kind and perhaps useful to you, but if she is ever offended in any way she is *bitter*."

Neither Mary nor young Dolley escaped their aunt's deep neediness—"You never answer half my letters"—and she could be petulant and demanding, as when she reproached Mary for letting a Virginia family leave Washington for Orange without sending along anything for her. At times, her tone was wistful: "You have all the world with you now & will soon be gay." But Dolley sincerely enjoyed the two young people, and she also expressed her love and appreciation freely, encouraging their confidence, as when she wrote to Mary: "[E]xpress yourself freely to me, my darling, and if you tell me all the secrets of the nation, they shall be sacred."[32]

Her affection for them inspired her prose, as when she wrote to "Dolché," her extravagant nickname for her namesake: "We have had two weeks of spring like weather, when the birds came out with their summer song and I went to gardening." Dolley even dressed up everyday annoyances in a way designed to amuse: "Imagine if you can, a greater trial of patience than seeing the destruction of a *radiant patch* of green peas, by frost! It came last night on the skirts of a storm, and while I was lamenting that our dear midshipman [her nephew Walter Cutts], should ever be exposed in such wailing winds, my young adventurers were wrecked off their moorings! But away with complaints, other patches will arise, and I will mourn no longer, over a mess of peas or of pottage."[33]

Unlike Payne, Mary and Dolley acted properly filial—as, in Dolley's words, "dutiful daughters"—and they reciprocated her love. Like their celebrated aunt, the Cutts girls understood that little things meant a lot. "Yours of the 2d. my beloved Mary," enthused Dolley, "gave me more than common pleasure, because it express'd love, & care for me, as well as for your Unkle M." From Washington they sent gloves, books, a bead ring for "Unkle M.," and a "prized" music box. Mary and young Dolley also passed along the news that Dolley craved, and so they kept her connections alive.[34]

The Cutts girls could not write often enough for Dolley, but she was easier on them than on Anna. She admitted: "*I asked too* many questions in my last—did I no[t]? Yes—but you are very good & amiable my dear to write me as much as you do, & I value you accordingly tho' I may complain a little now and then at your not answering questions." Nothing was more flattering than being asked for advice and Dolley responded to appeals to her wisdom. "I have no idea of the new dance or its motions but approve of your declining to learn it, if disapproved of by society—*Our sex* are ever loosers, when they stem the torrent of public opinion."[35]

Perhaps Mary and Dolley provided James, too, some compensation for Payne. He wore the bead ring Mary "placed on his finger [and] look[ed] at it every now and then." Of course, Dolley loved her nephews as well: "I long to hear good news from my favorite Walter and hope to see him a good man and a great captain—Tell Madison [Cutts] that I hope he is quite well, that his Uncle John [C. Payne] talks of writing to him for new books &c."[36] But with her nieces, she could express her affections with perfect freedom. When the Cutts boys began showing uncomfortable signs of their male relations' fecklessness, Dolley may have held back from them.

In terms of her own family dynamic, at least, she operated on a double standard. As unmarried women, Mary and Dolley had no particular responsibilities and did not have to make their way in the world. Things were harder for the men in Dolley's life; as her nephew J. Madison Cutts lamented: "Young & old, it almost seems we cannot get a start." On many occasions, Dolley had seen young men make much of a "start," often one provided by her. In contrast, she watched a host of lost opportunities pass generation after generation of her menfolk by. On occasion, Dolley showed her acerbic side. While her targets remain unidentified, her attitude is clear in a letter to Mary: "The persons you enquire after are well & good for nothing."[37]

Complaints about country living and melodramatic letters to Anna aside, Dolley often acknowledged Montpelier's charms, especially when spring transformed the countryside: "We have had three dishes of Asparagus and Lalacks are in bud!" Still, Dolly missed her sisters, and the "happy scenes" of her past. "The flowers are blooming—the trees changeing to green & yet my heart is solitary." She thought her "stationary" life was not good for her health.[38] While Washington City might possess gaiety, old friends, and Anna, however, Montpelier had

James. They had always been a close couple, but in retirement at Montpelier, their relationship became almost symbiotic. Even Mary Cutts's prim prose could not disguise the intensity of their connection: "She was his solace and comfort, he could not bear her to leave his presence, and she gratified him by being absent only when duty required." Even when "agreeably employed," Dolley seemed to know by instinct when James needed her. She would interrupt a conversation mid-sentence, rising and saying, "I must go to Madison."[39]

James did not travel, and Dolley would not travel without him. His health and well-being remained her chief concern. Throughout his retirement, James suffered from rheumatism, "bilious fever," and innumerable colds and flus; at one point, he had an "Eruption all over him," with itching and burning that lasted over three weeks. Dolley loved playing caretaker, and James's health brought out her protective instincts. She complained to Anna that those who wrote and visited James during his illnesses did not know how sick he was, which she found exasperating. "He rec[eives] letters, & visitors as if he was made of Iron—to his great disadvantage & mine," as she had to double her nursing efforts to compensate for the extra strain.[40]

Dolley was right. Remaining "stationary," being so assiduous a nurse, proved deleterious to her. She was herself quite unwell during the Montpelier years. She suffered her own bouts of rheumatism in the ankle, but for the most part her illnesses were the kinds caused by or acerbated by stress. An active, outgoing woman who thrived on the energy of others, Dolley did not do well in her "anxious, and confined" situation. By her late fifties, she wore glasses (which she shared with James) for close work. Most likely this loss of vision had more to do with age than with her old eye troubles, which also continued to plague her, preventing her from reading and writing the letters that kept her connected to her family and to the larger world.[41] In her own words, her eyes were "weak" or "half-closed," at times, unable to bear light or strain. Even a brilliant snow could dazzle her. "From the feeling of heat and itching," Dolley reckoned that the insides of her lids were probably inflamed. She tried to alleviate the inflammation "by the application of milk and water or cream, and sometimes with fresh butter." Dolley also reported a discharge, though that might have stemmed from some of the more noxious treatments, such as an ointment mixed up with "fresh lard."[42]

❧

Retirement offered Dolley few opportunities to exercise her political muscle, though she continued to obtain jobs for likely candidates and to exchange political information with a wide circle of correspondents. She fought her rural seclusion by keeping up with the *Globe* and the *Intelligencer,* the best sources for national and international news. Like a movie fan who passes on star gossip as personal news, she reported secondhand accounts of Washington society, "splendid parties," and the "fashion of dissipation" to far-flung correspondents. Sometimes she got frustrated with being out of the know, as evidenced by her underscores: "I can tell *you nothing new.*"[43]

Her Washington friends played their part in keeping Dolley connected. A young protégée, Judith Walker Rives, wrote long, detailed letters full of descriptions of drawing rooms and weddings. She hoped that Dolley would not think her disrespectful for writing of "'trifles light as air,'" but those trifles were sustenance to Dolley. Like a dutiful student, Judith also kept her eyes open for any signs of "party spirit." People knew of her connection to Dolley, and personages such as the British minister asked her to transmit good wishes and remembrances. Phoebe Morris also delighted to report on the details of Washington life, including the social event of the 1823–1824 congressional season, the Jackson ball, hosted by one of Dolley's successors, Louisa Catherine Adams, the wife of the secretary of state.[44]

Dolley was especially sensitive to issues of party discord and its effect on social life. Like many others of her generation, she was fascinated and shocked by the emergence of political parties. She solicited news from her niece with the usual assurance of confidentiality regarding female political talk. "I confess I do not admire the contention of parties, political or civil, tho' in my quiet retreat I am anxious to know all the manoeuverings of both, the one and the other, so, be not timid in laying their claims before me, no one shall see statements but myself."[45]

If Dolley could not come to Washington, Washington came to her. In 1829, her correspondents kept her abreast of a new scandal. The so-called Eaton Affair centered on Margaret O'Neale Timberlake Eaton, the wife of President Andrew Jackson's secretary of war. Because Jackson was a widower, Margaret became the de facto leading woman of Washington, but the ladies of Washington, both official and local, were having none of it. "Peggy" Eaton had grown up as a Washington City boardinghouse keeper's daughter, but, more gravely, she had earned a scandalous sexual reputation. She had met the man she would eventually marry, Jackson's good friend John Eaton, while married to someone else. Margaret's first husband went to sea, and Margaret and John soon were seen together in public. After Margaret's first husband died, John tried to redeem her reputation through matrimony, but it was too late.

While the ladies of Washington City might maintain that they resented having Margaret foisted on them by virtue of mere political office, in fact their concerns ran much deeper: Margaret's escalation to the top of society tapped into deep fears about democracy in general and Jackson in particular, as well as the usual anxiety about women, sexuality, and political power.[46]

Dolley had actually encountered the leading lady of the drama, when she had presented a teenaged Margaret with a crown after a dancing demonstration. (In her old age, Margaret Eaton even claimed that Dolley had attended her wedding to John Eaton in 1816, but Margaret possessed a colorful and not always reliable memory.) Now Dolley avidly followed the unfolding contretemps, aided by her old correspondents, such as a Madison cousin, James Taylor, in Washington on business. To her horror, both pro- and anti-Margaret factions used social events—parties, balls, and calling—to issue snubs, make declarations, and lodge protests. Male politicians and political families tried to use the affair to their own various ends, and repercussions kept multiplying. Since one's attendance or absence from a particular social event was considered a political statement, both men and women stopped socializing altogether.[47]

Eventually President Jackson found himself at loggerheads with his vice president, Dolley's old colleague, John C. Calhoun, and then with his whole cabinet, as he tried to "force," as they saw it, the cabinet families to call on Margaret. Some Washingtonians dismissed the situation as a tempest not even worthy of a teacup; others merely laughed. Dolley, who understood the delicate balance of society and politics, knew to take the scandal seriously. She predicted: "The conduct of the P[resident]. & his Cabinet, is indeed astonishing, & exhibits a melancholy perspective, as well as re-trospect to our country—but I doubt not of—*impeachments,* by & by, if they go on in this *lawless,* & unfeeling manner."[48] She was right. With social circles at a standstill, political business lurched to a halt. Something had to give, and the scandal culminated with the dissolution of the entire cabinet, some by resignation, some by dismissal. The occurrence set off alarm bells across the country, and newspapers dubbed "Peggy" Eaton "The Doom of the Republic."[49]

As always, Dolley had her opinions, and, out of the political spotlight, she was confident enough to share them, albeit prefaced by the self-deprecation customary for political women. She conveyed her low assessment of party contention to the diplomat Christopher Hughes: "In politicks you know, I was never an Adept—I therefore will only observe, that our Country seems now to be entirely of Mr. Laws opinion that 'Agitation and excitement are happiness.'" This was a disgraceful situation, to any thinking person. "I hope some, of the Scenes got up in the House of Representatives, *never* reach you as in that case, they would exite even more regret among the considerate here, than they now do."[50]

Her own past experience made Dolley particularly sensitive to the political use of sexual slander that characterized the Eaton Affair, especially its corrosive effect on public virtue. Writing from rural Montpelier, she worried to Anna: "I'm affraid the licence people take with their tongues & pens, will blast the good of the country—& display all sorts of evil traits of character that can mark a selfish & Savage Race."[51]

❧❦❧

The gardens and vistas of the Blue Ridge Mountains may have lulled visitors into Edenic fantasies, but Montpelier *was* a working plantation.

Actually, the estate was divided into four farms, each with a cluster of slave cabins. James cultivated tobacco and wheat for profit, and grew corn and other vegetables and raised livestock to feed the workforce and the Madison family. Pork was a mainstay of the southern diet, but James also stocked cattle and sheep. Skilled artisan slaves, among them weavers, carpenters, and blacksmiths, also ensured Montpelier's self-sufficiency.

Running the plantation household, Dolley was at least as busy as when she had served as the nation's hostess. In some ways, she was even more occupied than James. Managing the farm did not demand daily, year-round, labor-intensive concentration. In contrast, Dolley arranged for three daily meals for more than one hundred people working in as many as five locations, including the house. Merely monitoring and apportioning the "stores," the food and other raw materials, was a constant job. And unlike their menfolk, the mistresses of southern plantations often performed some of the same kind of labor as the slaves, whether it was overseeing a special dish in the kitchen or making clothes for both the slaves and the family. As Dolley joked to James: "I am too busy a House keeper to become a poetess in my solitude."[52]

As part of the regular routine at Montpelier, members of the Madison household used the telescope on the front portico "to spy the road where carriages and large parties were seen almost daily winding their way from afar to this harbor of hospitality."[53] Anyone with business at the Orange County courthouse, on their way to the capital or to the famed Virginia Springs spas, or in the neighborhood visiting Monticello found their way up the winding drive. In this era of great "public houses," even strangers felt comfortable treating Montpelier and the Madisons as a requisite stop on a sightseeing tour, and, also according to the customs of the day, the Madisons entertained all. And they did so lavishly, no matter the state of their finances. The Madisons' standards in food and wine remained unchanged from their Washington days, and this bounty, along with Dolley's gracious presence, worked its effect on guests.

The details of everyday life at the Madisons' home enchanted observers. They noted how in rainy weather, James took his daily walk under the shelter of the gracious portico. Father of the Constitution he might be, but, like any good farmer, he kept track of the rain via a large cup in the center of the gravel walk. Dolley came in for her own share of picturesque description. A French gardener, M. Bizet, whose name Dolley spelled "Beazee," oversaw the more formal gardens. Madame B. created a "hideous" but effective sun hat for Dolley, who wore it on her morning "rambles." Guests expressed delight in seeing the erstwhile "Queen of Washington City" and fashion leader walking with her self-styled "Beazee bonnet."[54]

Visitors vied for superlatives to describe the two-thousand-acre estate, with its lavish green lawns and many varieties of trees—among them tulip trees, silver poplars, weeping willows, walnut trees, cedars of Lebanon, and groves of aspen—as well as varieties of fruits and "esteemed flowers." They also marveled at the house itself, admiring its Persian carpets and extensive art, including portraits of the founders and "beautifully chiseled" sculptures. Still, all agreed the time spent with Montpelier's inhabitants constituted the high point of any visit. Visitors were conscious that they were in the presence of history, the last remnant of an ideal age rapidly disappearing in the face of modernity.[55]

James never seemed too tired to entertain his guests; perhaps he, too, found country life a bit slow. Though increasingly frail in appearance—balding, with his remaining hair "nicely powdered" in the old style—when he spoke "his brow loses its wrinkles, his face brightens." His conversation, as "sprightly" as it was solid, gleamed with intellect and good humor, though it often appeared more monologue or lecture than dialogue. If recollections are correct, he seems almost compulsively verbose, as if eager to pass on his knowledge.[56]

He talked to both men and women, though some of these marathon sessions took place after the ladies left the gentlemen at the dinner table. A single conversation could touch upon a wide variety of many topics, including the savage nature of man, Indian life, Christianity, great events in which James had played a part, constitutional history, colonial trade, ancient and modern literature, witticisms, and celebrity stories. Mostly visitors seemed more than content to let James direct the conversation and ramble over whatever ground interested him at the moment, and many tried to record these monologues verbatim. James's wisdom rendered all charms peripheral. One young man, Henry D. Gilpin, son of a Quaker friend of Dolley's, proved himself "a poor beau" to the dozen or so pretty girls he met on a visit to Montpelier: "The truth is pretty girls I can find plenty of, I c[oul]d see but one Mr. Madison, and him probably never again."[57]

Visitors praised Dolley for the same qualities that had made her famous, her "handsome form," her "nobleness," her "gracious" bearing, her "gentle" speech, and a presence "fresh and full of sweetness."[58] These descriptions differed from the appraisals during her White House years in one significant aspect. Her houseguests did not read into Dolley, projecting their hopes and fears upon her, as they had done when she reigned as the social leader of Washington City. Having left the public eye, Dolley ceased to appear larger than life, being transformed into a private person, just another Virginia gentry wife, albeit an exceptional one.

Not that she had no audiences. While men sat respectfully with James, Dolley entertained all. She had always delighted children, and if the smallest visitors to Montpelier found James "a worn feeble old man," Dolley won them over, cutting a dashing figure in her turban. Girls and boys responded to her gracious manner as she took them through the house, displaying her treasures. For good or ill, Dolley's macaw, Polly, made a big impression on youthful visitors as well. Her colorful feathers and ability to talk fascinated them, but the tendency of this "object of terror" to dive-bomb intruders, screaming and pecking, terrified children and grownups. On one occasion, James, attempting to save a female guest from Polly's beak and claws, had his finger bitten to the bone. To the guest's amazement, James merely chuckled indulgently. (Polly eventually got her just desserts; in her old age, she became a hawk's prey.)[59]

Political protégés made up one of the most important categories of visitors to Montpelier. James continued as a political force to be reckoned with, offering practical help and guidance. Moreover, as the 1820s went on, he became increasingly valued as a symbol of an earlier era.

Much as Dolley had functioned symbolically through the war, James figured as the touchstone of power for men eager for a career in politics.

Chief among the rising politicians who sought not only James's aid but also his imprimatur was William Cabell Rives, a well-born but not wealthy young man, who secured his position in the ruling class in 1823 by marrying a clever, moneyed, well-connected Virginia gentlewoman, Judith Walker. The appointment of a Walker family friend as minister to Spain left a seat in Congress vacant, and the powerful men of the area "invited" young Mr. Rives to assume it. This was William's first foray into public life; on the way to Washington City, he and Judith stopped to pay their allegiance to the Madisons.[60]

At one point in the visit, Dolley drew Judith aside and gave her "a necklace of great beauty" and a diamond cross. "'I have a special fancy,' she said, 'that you should wear these during your campaign in Washington. If my friends there should happen to recognize them, they will be as sure a passport to their hearts as the letters of introduction I have given you.'" Judith hesitated to accept so costly a gift, but Dolley insisted, and "the compact was sealed with a warm embrace." Embraces and references to hearts aside, Dolley was clearly taking pains to ready her own candidate for the coming "campaign."[61]

Any person or family of note considered a visit to the former president de rigueur. In 1824, an aging hero of the Revolution, General Marie Joseph Paul Yves Roch Gilbert du Motier Lafayette, made a triumphal tour of the United States, accompanied by a party that included a Scottish woman "friend," the young Frances Wright, who went on to make her own brand of scandal and history. As Dolley described it to John G. Jackson: "We have lately had a visit from Genl. LaFayette & family of a few days—the former, you know, was an old friend of Mr M——s I was charmed with his society—& never witnessed so much enthusiasm as his appearance occationed here and at our court house, where hundreds of both sexes collected together, to hail & welcome him." Indeed, the town of Orange was abuzz, with the men of the university "doing all their possible . . . to do him honor." According to Dolley, the general found his stay so delightful that "he has promised to spend some time with us again, before he leaves this country."[62]

For his part, James enjoyed a warm embrace from his old friend, noting that Lafayette "is in fine health & spirits but so much increased in bulk & changed in aspect that I should not have known him." As with other visitors, James conducted long talks with Lafayette, who, as it turned out, had an agenda. Slavery was the topic on his mind. As the party traveled through the countryside, the presence of the young Miss Wright gave rise to salacious whispers. However, Lafayette's alliance with her proved even more shocking than the gossips could imagine. Frances Wright was an abolitionist, and, as she explained to James and Dolley, she wished to seek support for her proposed sexually and racially experimental community. She very much desired James's "testimony under his own hand" as to the worthiness of her project, in order to make the enterprise more acceptable to southerners. In the tradition of political women, she sought his support through a later letter to Dolley. Frances Wright went on to found her community in Nashoba, Tennessee, and to become one of America's great radical reformers, but she did it without the Madisons' blessing.[63]

In March 1835, Dolley happily reported to her niece, "We have lately had the pleasure of a visit, of two or three days from Miss Martineau, whose character and writings you are familiar with no doubt."[64] Unlike other lady "scribblers," Martineau excelled in the male fields of economics and social philosophy. Her celebrated *Illustrations of Political Economy* made the doctrines of Adam Smith, Thomas Malthus, and others accessible to the public. From 1834 to 1836, she traveled around the United States researching a future book; when she arrived at Montpelier, she subjected the Madisons, as she did all things American, to her ruthless eye and incisive mind.

Among many other observations and stories that she related in her landmark *Retrospect of Western Travel* (1838), Harriet presented an idyllic picture of Dolley and James presiding over their Virginia kingdom. She described Dolley as "celebrated throughout the country for the grace and dignity with which she discharged the arduous duties which devolve upon the president's lady." Harriet recognized the "discretion, partiality, and kindliness" with which Dolley performed her role. But it was also clear to her that Dolley was "a strong minded woman, fully capable of entering into her husband's occupations and cares; and there is little doubt that he owed much to her intellectual companionship, as well as to her ability in sustaining the outward dignity of his office."

James was pleased to have such a distinguished and intelligent guest. According to Harriet, his "relish of conversation could never have been keener." She enjoyed the experience, as did other Madison audiences, though the descriptions of her conversational encounters suggest the compulsive nature of James's desire to communicate. On occasion, fearing that their long sessions were exhausting him, Harriet changed her position in the room, moving over to the sofa next to Dolley, hoping to break the flow of conversation. James would not be deterred and followed her, seating himself between the two women. Finally, Harriet capitulated and settled down to her "station," by the arm of his chair, "and never left it but for food and sleep; glad enough to make the most of my means of intercourse with one whose political philosophy I deeply venerated."[65]

A social and economic radical, Harriet Martineau was also an abolitionist. The topic of slavery haunted the eighty-three-year-old James as well. In their sittings, "he talked more on the subject of slavery than on any other," and "he found himself to be almost in despair." In 1816, a Presbyterian minister, Robert Finley, had founded the American Colonization Society, which aimed to buy slaves from their masters and send them "back" to Africa, along with members of the growing free black population who could be persuaded to join them. Finley sought support for his organization among prominent politicians. James was a founding member, as were Francis Scott Key, Henry Clay, and Bushrod Washington (nephew of the late president). Aside from the society's role in establishing Liberia, it was a pie-in-the-sky scheme and never took off, partly for financial reasons (the sheer cost of the buy-back aspect) and partly (not surprisingly) because free blacks, as deeply American and at home as any member of the Virginia gentry, proved reluctant to leave their country for a foreign land.

But James believed in the society and clung to the hope of its success, an intellectual lapse that Martineau found baffling: "How such a mind as his could derive any alleviation to its anxiety from that source is surprising." Kindly, she attributed the delusion to his "inexhaustible faith" in the "well-founded commonwealth" rather than to the tortured twists of a guilty conscience.[66]

Only dinner broke up these hours-long sessions, and, according to Harriet, James began talking immediately upon rising from the table. The originality of his ideas made these long monologues worthwhile. He unfailingly shaped his conversation to his audience; indeed, though the topic of slavery undoubtedly consumed him, he may have dwelt on it because it was a subject that interested Harriet. Because Harriet was an economist, he talked to her of Malthus. Because she was an English writer, he declaimed on the "security of literary property across the world." Perhaps in acknowledgment of her sex, James also talked to her about women. According to Harriet, he declared that when it came to education and training—"the brains and the hands . . . trained together"—"no distinction in this respect should be made between men and women."[67] Harriet's sex also ensured that Dolley could be present for James's discourses, as she might not have been during the men-only sessions.

Harriet possessed an eye for contradiction, especially for the untenable position of slavery in a land of freedom. Life at Montpelier embodied those contradictions, and Harriet related the odd juxtaposition of words and actions, as when James talked of slavery as an abstract problem, while surrounded by actual slaves, "two or three . . . loung[ing]" in each room of the house. At regular intervals, careful not to disturb the disquisitions of the master, slaves came to Dolley for the keys necessary to run the house. Harriet's visit to the Madisons affected both parties. Dolley told a friend that she and James found Harriet "so interesting that we hastened to procure her books, and are now reading her Political Economy, so handsomely Illustrated."[68] For her part, Harriet left Montpelier even more certain that it was folly to base a modern civilized nation on a practice as barbaric as slavery.

Unlike James, Dolley left no official statement of her views on the intractable problem of slavery; no inquiring observer solicited her opinion.

As always, her attitudes and assumptions were revealed not in philosophical disquisitions, but rather, in her everyday life. In 1824, in one of
her playful and delightful letters to her seven-year-old nephew, Richard
D. Cutts, Dolley thanked him for sending along a sample of his own
homegrown tobacco as well as a letter. "Your Unkle has reccd. Your Elegant & lerned Epistle, & his finger being a little sore at present he desires me to answer it for him." She congratulated the young planter on
his accomplishment, even addressing the letter "Richard Cutts Tobaco
planter Washington." Dolley also passed on news of Montpelier,
adding, "All your friends White Yellow & black send complmts. to
you." On more than one occasion, Dolley assured Richard "of the love
of all here . . . even the black faces."[69]

Life in a slave state rendered the appalling ordinary. In her casual
use of the adjective "yellow" to describe some of the friends who
wished young Richard well, Dolley unwittingly acknowledged one of
the more horrifying aspects of the system: the sexual exploitation of
enslaved black women. The more scrupulous members of the southern
gentry did not view the issue in that modern way; they based their objections on grounds of religion and morality. James even made a reference, albeit an oblique one, to this great crime. According to Harriet
Martineau, during one of their long talks, James "spoke with deep feeling of the sufferings of white ladies under the system, declaring that he
pitied them even more than their negroes." He talked at length about
the difficulty of superintending the "negroes," especially in the presence
of free blacks, who tried to incite the slaves to violence. With dangers
both internal and external, the ladies lived "in a state of perpetual suspicion, fear, and anger." But surely this would be true for both white
women and men. It seems most likely that, though James would not
speak of blatantly sexual matters in front of Harriet (though he did allude to early motherhood among slave girls), they were on his mind
when he referred to the "saddest slavery of all" for "conscientious
Southern women."[70]

Dolley was, not surprisingly, silent on the widespread issue of mu-
latto children born to exploited female slaves; it is not clear what effect
it had on her world. Oral tradition in one African-American family had

it that James fathered a child with an enslaved woman during his marriage to Dolley.[71] More likely, given some of the details of the story, the child's father was another one of the many white Madisons in the state. Still, James had a long bachelorhood before his marriage to Dolley, and it would not have been unusual for a young master to take advantage of the sexual opportunities offered by an enslaved workforce. Indeed, it would have been more singular had he not. What Dolley knew or thought about any of this is lost to us.

Dolley was well aware, however, of the increasing volatility of the slave system. In 1831, the greatest slave insurrection in American history, led by Nat Turner, took place in nearby Southampton County. Fifty-one white people were killed. Again, in her brief mentions of the incident, Dolley appeared unable to empathize with the rebels. Like many Americans, and more than most, Dolley possessed a ready grasp of the vocabulary and ideas of revolution, but she made no connection between the desires for "natural liberty" that drove the American Revolution and the natural rights of enslaved men and women. Instead, she saw the violence only in relation to herself: "I am quiet, knowing little about it and that I cannot help myself if I am in danger." The lesson to be learned from the rebellion? "I hope all will be on guard ever after this."

Dolley's reaction might appear complacent, but like many of her class, she felt trapped by slavery; men and women of slaveowning families perceived themselves as helpless, downplaying their fear so as not to let it overtake them. The Madison family had its own personal experience with slave violence: three slaves who had belonged to James's grandfather Ambrose Madison had been convicted of poisoning their master.[72] As Jefferson famously phrased it, the planter class had the wolf by the ears, with no choice (as they saw it) but to ride it out, holding on for dear life.

❦

It was perhaps only natural that in retirement, James became part pundit, part seer, advising on contemporary constitutional issues. Much political debate in the 1820s and 1830s focused on the definitions,

boundaries, and limitations of states' rights and the relationship between state and federal governments. Whatever the specific issue under
examination—for instance, the right of a state to nullify a federal
tariff—slavery always drove the discussion. Southern states were reluctant to concede sovereignty on any issue, even ones that had nothing to
do with slavery, lest the federal government use the precedent to abol-
ish their peculiar institution.

James's chief interest lay not just in current politics, but also in
those of the past. During his retirement, he was positioning himself as
a man of history, much as Adams and Jefferson had done. After the
death of his mentor and colleague Thomas Jefferson in 1826, James became the caretaker of his old friend's fame as well and sometimes
found himself in the position of having to answer for him. Unlike his
illustrious colleagues, however, he expressed more concern with the
facts themselves, than with placing himself at their center. Indeed, his
need to preserve and disseminate the history of the nation lay at the
heart of James's compulsive conversation. When he had as his audience
someone like the famous writer and historian Jared Sparks, he covered
topics like a walking textbook—discursions on the origins of the First
Bank of the United States, observations of George Washington, John
Jay, and Alexander Hamilton, analyses of his own work in the War of
1812, thoughts about Congress. James even shared his letters from
George Washington and his notes on the Constitutional Convention
for a book Sparks was writing about the first president.[73]

He spent an enormous amount of time readying his papers for publication. While concerned with his own legacy, he possessed very specific and exalted ideas about the role of history in the formation of the
nation: republics were held together not by consolidated power, but by
the psychological force of attachment. Though many Americans might
never leave their own state or town, they had to imagine themselves as
part of a larger enterprise. History, the sense of a long, shared past or, as
James put it, "antiquity," stabilized a nation. He also believed it inspired
attachment and loyalty in the populace, what he called "veneration."

The new United States enjoyed a glorious, but brief history, and
James was determined to make the most of it. Indeed, one of the reasons

he had delayed the publication of the proceedings of the Constitutional Convention of 1787 was to add to their "antiquity." In addition to this theoretical and abstract commitment to the role of history in a republic, a more immediate worry drove James. He feared for the union. The bitter process that led to the Missouri Compromise, as well as the debates about states' rights, alarmed him, especially as proponents on both sides used his words to make their cases. It was important to James to leave this world with the record set straight.[74]

The task of editing James's papers proved overwhelming, and since it was James's occupation, it became Dolley's as well. She joined in assembling, transcribing, filing, and editing the papers. In an age before there were professional male historians and archivists, let alone female ones, Dolley was a woman making history. Working from ten in the morning until three o'clock in the afternoon, she acted as part editor, part secretary, and part collector. Dolley enlisted her own networks of friends to ferret out documents in other people's possession, for instance importuning her cousin Sarah Coles Stevenson to obtain James's papers from the Randolph family.[75] The workload grew so intense that they enlisted Dolley's brother John, now living nearby, to help with the transcription and copyediting.

Like many historians before and since, Dolley and James underestimated the time their project would take. As the years passed, it served as one more reason for the two to stay at home. As early as 1820, she confessed to Sarah Coles Stevenson that they were "fixed" at Montpelier. "This is the third winter in which he has been engaged in the arrangement of papers, and the [business] appears to accumulate as he proceeds—so that I calculate its out-lasting my patience and yet I cannot press him to forsake a duty so important, or find it in my heart to leave him during its fulfillment."[76] Perhaps she figured that one way to live with the project was to embrace it, for she found her patience as she became more involved in the editing and transcription process. The work reached a peak in 1823. By that time she identified so much with it that not even illness prevented her from going forward. If a bad cold meant that she could not write, at least, in her view, she could still copy.[77]

Though Dolley considered James's words to be "Sacred and no more to be infringed or altered than his last will," she also confessed to a certain editorial license. She was careful to explain that it was "consonant to his wishes and direction," but also as well with her "concurrence," when she made any changes. Upon her reading, "if any letter—line—or word struck me as being calculated to injure the feelings of any one or wrong in themselves that I would withdraw them or it."[78] To the end, Dolley was her husband's partner. His final document, "Advice to My Country," was written in her hand.

Dolley had saved James's words and the history of the country once before, during the invasion of Washington, and she continued to serve as a devoted caretaker. No doubt there existed a deeper, more emotional reason for her commitment. As James aged, she knew that the day was coming when his words would be all that was left, and she was determined that they would live.

SEVENTEEN

Legacies

hrough the 1830s, visitors still flocked to Montpelier, partaking of the Madisons' generous hospitality, even as they remarked on the deterioration of the house, and the fragility of the ex-president. In 1836, one of the many who made the pilgrimage was a former congressman and longtime supporter, Charles J. Ingersoll. He pronounced the edifice of "good design, but decayed and in need of inconsiderable repairs, which, at a trifling expense, would make a great difference in favor of the first impression." Inside, the walls were still brave with portraits, engravings, and prints, but the interiors showed their age as well.[1] Bad harvests and falling commodity prices, combined with the Madisons' habit of living beyond their means, dug them deeper and deeper into debt. Dolley expressed a farmer's frustration with weather and international markets, bitterly remarking on the folly of "depend[ing] on a plantation for *pin* money."

James tried his best to stem the flow. He sold off some land in Kentucky, mortgaged part of Montpelier, and in 1834 sold a parcel of slaves. It was not enough, and he increasingly pinned his hopes on the proceeds from the publication of his papers, though his failing health slowed the project considerably.

James's "rheumatic" attacks had begun in earnest after 1830. He failed a great deal of the time, and because she would not leave his side, Dolley in effect shared his invalid existence. Sometimes she would not go beyond her yard for weeks at a time; at one point, she had not left the grounds for eight months. For the last four years of James's life, she did not ride a horse. Dolley recognized the extremity of her devotion and could even joke about it. At one point, she told Payne that though James had been sick he was now recovered enough for Dolley to leave him for an "expedition to the Court house." She wryly added, "It would be quite an event, for me to go there—5 miles from home!" During one desperate winter, she tended James through "disabling Rheumatism" and a bilious fever that left him so depleted he could "only walk from one bed to another." In her first years at Montpelier, Dolley had written of books and visitors, even as she complained about her uneventful existence. Near the end of James's life, when asked how she spent her time, she replied: "*My days* are devoted to nursing and comforting my *patient*." She confessed that she had "never left him half an hour, for the last two years—so deep is the interest, & sympathy, I feel for him!"[2]

Originally settled in Louisa County, Virginia, John C. Payne and his wife, Clary Wilcox, were now neighbors of the Madisons. If he never became the strong male support that Dolley wished, at least he had set aside his profligate ways. The couple had produced eight children; and in the 1830s, John C. Payne's daughters came to Montpelier to help with the nursing.[3] Dolley characterized the young Payne women as "very amiable girls, rather pretty, & so far, have good plain educations." As was her wont, Dolley all but adopted his third daughter, Anna, born in 1819. Though most called her Annie, Dolley referred to her niece as Anna or Anne, a conscious or unconscious tribute to her own sister (Anna Payne Cutts was actually christened Anne). Dolley reported that Annie "lives entirely with me & the others are much with me also." Annie was a teenager when she came to Montpelier, and Dolley praised her as "a sterling girl [who] stays much at home with me and sleeps beside my bed ever since the illness of Mr. Madison."[4]

Of course, no one could take the place of the original Anna. As she aged, Anna Payne Cutts had developed an unspecified "nervous condition," over which Dolley's anxieties escalated. She had always felt protective of her sister; now she grew positively frantic with worry: "That you, who have been since your birth, the darling—the friend & the Sister that lived most in my thoughts & affections should be sick & unhappy—I at a distance unable to sooth, nurse or comfort you! Alass I cant bear it much longer, & if you come not—I will see you where ever you are." Her concerns even led to (for her) an extreme suggestion. "I will leave my husband & run all risks to see you."[5]

Half anxiously, half playfully, she next threatened abduction. "So let me hear from you directly—that you'l come or you shall see me bounce in upon you some night from the boat, to force you all on board next day for Montpelier, as I could not stay from my Husband." Instead, she enlisted friends, such as Frances Dandridge Lear, to watch over her darling. Eliza Collins Lee sent long reports monitoring the situation, assuring Dolley that she was tending to Anna like a sister.[6]

Apart from her son, Dolley cherished two great loves in her life: Anna and James. That she enjoyed a large circle of loved ones only testified to the depth and passion of her connection with the woman she took care of and the man who took care of her. Such connections can be enormously fulfilling, as they were for Dolley, but they also result in the loss of a certain amount of individuation, as when Dolley identified so closely with James that she could not leave him to ride a horse or even go for a walk. And, rewarding as these relationships were, the payment for such love was the pain of loss. In late 1830, the fifty-one-year-old Anna suffered from what Anna Maria Brodeau Thornton called a "dropsy of the heart," from which she recovered slowly. In August 1832, she was ill again, possibly with heart ailments, and on August 4, Dolley posted a letter to her hoping that "the last attack was the crisis of your disorder and that good spirits and a quiet mind will soon restore you to us." She added, "What should we do without you!"[7] Unbeknownst to Dolley, Anna died that day.

When the news reached Dolley a few days later, she was composed enough to write a loving, though formal, note to Richard Cutts: "The heart of your miserable Sister mourns with you, with your precious daughters, with your Sons! Come to us as soon as you can, & bring them with you." Dolley asked Richard for information, expressing her interest "in all that concerned my sister & her children," including "her Will, & where you have deposited her remains!" But Dolley could not sustain the effort: unable to write another line, not even to her pets, she begged Richard: "Shew this to Dolley and Mary as, I cannot write to them at this moment."[8]

With her beloved sister gone, Dolley's circle of attention narrowed to her patient. In 1836, Annie reported that "she [was] incessantly engaged as Uncle's deputy morning, noon, & night." By late June 1836, physicians were offering to prolong James's life with stimulants so that, like Adams and Jefferson, he too could die on the Fourth of July. Always the least flamboyant of the founders, to the end, James eschewed such shows of ego. He preferred to die "in the full possession of all his noble faculties," and he did, on June 28, 1836.[9]

Fittingly for a person whose existence was made possible by enslaved labor, James drew his last breath in the presence of Paul Jennings and Sukey. Paul had lived by James's side, "shav[ing] him every other day for sixteen years." According to Paul, for the last six months of his life, James could not walk and spent his days lying on a couch. But "his mind was bright, and with his numerous visitors he talked with as much animation and strength of voice as I ever heard him in his best days." On the last morning, Sukey brought him breakfast, but he could not swallow. His niece Nelly Conway Madison Willis asked him, " 'What is the matter, Uncle James?' 'Nothing more than a change of *mind,* my dear.' His head instantly dropped, and he ceased breathing as quietly as the snuff of a candle goes out."[10] James was eighty-five and had been married to Dolley nearly forty-two years. At sixty-eight, she was again a widow.

James was buried at his beloved Montpelier, eulogized by his neighbor Governor James Barbour. The letters of condolence that poured in from all around the country tended toward the formal, framing James's death as the country's tragedy as well as a personal one. President Andrew Jackson wrote to Dolley on behalf of himself and Congress on "the loss [sustai]ned by yourself and the nation," casting James not only as her "[be]loved companion" but as "one of the [country's] most [valu]ed citizens," and "the illustrious man" who lived a "glorious and [patriot]ic life." Even a close family friend, Louisa Catherine Johnson Adams, characterized the mourning period as "a moment of deep interest to the whole American Nation." She offered Dolley "the sentiment of respect, and veneration . . . for . . . one of the *greatest men*; whose name will adorn the annals of his Country, in the proudest days of her existence, and deck the page of history with an honoured fame."[11]

To Richard Cutts and Eliza Collins Lee, Dolley revealed her broken self. "I would write more, dear Richard, but have no power over my confused and oppressed mind to speak fully of the enduring goodness of my beloved husband. He left me many pledges of his confidence and love. Especially do I value all his writings." To Eliza, Dolley confessed that "I had not the power to tell you how highly I valued your kind sympathy, and how much I needed it! Indeed, I have been as one in a troubled dream since my irreparable loss of him, for whom my affection was perfect, as was his character and conduct thro' life."[12]

To the best of her abilities, Dolley answered all the letters that she received, deeming it "not proper to answer in the pen of an amanuensis." Fortunately, just after James's death, Jackson granted her free lifetime postage, a privilege hitherto accorded only to sitting members of Congress and ex-presidents. For the more formal notes, Dolley rallied, writing to the president of the United States: "I received, Sir, in due time, the communication from Congress, made more grateful to me by the kind expression of your sympathy, which accompanied it." James's passing was so much a national event that newspapers reprinted the correspondence between Dolley and Jackson.[13]

But answering the mountain of letters proved a daunting task, made even more so by the onset of illness which "reduced" Dolley, and the continuing "rheumatism" (probably arthritis) in her right arm and hand. She leaned on her family and friends, enlisting help from Annie and John C. Payne in her personal correspondence. She wrote to Anthony Morris, inviting him to come to Montpelier in the month after James's death. As always, she craved company and personal connection. By mid-July, Annie Payne reported, "She no longer gives way to the grief and dejected spirit which could not at first be restrained. Such a loss as was hers! but she is even now striving to be composed, if not cheerful as Uncle Madison, begged and entreated her to be."[14]

James had left Dolley everything—land, slaves, and the responsibility for his legacy. He bequeathed to her "all my manuscript papers, having entire confidence in her discreet and proper use of them." The publication of his papers, especially those pertaining to the Constitutional Convention, "will be particularly gratifying to the people of the United States, and to all who take an interest in the progress of political science and the cause of true liberty." Confident that the papers would generate a significant income, James not only willed the proceeds to Dolley, he also tied several bequests—to the University of Virginia, the American Colonization Society, and family members, among others—to those proceeds. (Dolley decided to disengage the legacies from the papers' profits, and paid them in advance from her own funds, leaving herself very little cash.) He also stipulated that no slaves were to be sold without their consent, except for misbehavior.[15]

Dolley's statement to Richard, "Especially do I value all his writings," proved more than an understatement. Almost from the moment of James's passing, she made publication her major goal. No existing reply to a condolence letter fails to mention the importance of the project directly alongside her expressions of sorrow. Even as she confided to Eliza about her powerlessness in the face of grief, she also wrote: "Accordingly I strive to give my mind to business, as far as my anxious friends will allow me." Dolley echoed the same sentiment in her reply to President Jackson: "I am now preparing to execute the trust his confidence reposed in me—that of placing before Congress and the World, what his pen had prepared for their use, and with the importance of his

Legacy, I am deeply impressed." Again, Dolley considered anything to
do with James's papers to be so much a matter of public interest that
she published her letter to Jackson as well as those portions of James's
will that pertained to his writings.[16]

Within a month after his death, Annie reported on "three clerks
finishing copies [triplicates] of Uncle M.'s manuscripts," under the supervision of her father, John C. Payne. The first three volumes would
contain James's notes made during the Constitutional Convention of
1787 and his notes on the debates of the Confederation Congresses of
1782, 1783, and 1787, with pertinent "selections" from his letters. It took
the remaining thirteen years of Dolley's life to publish even part of the
collection; the rest would appear after her death. While Dolley wisely
enlisted the help of the famous writer James K. Paulding and the historian and editor Jared Sparks, as well as of Henry Clay and Edward
Coles, she also gave over much of the work to Payne. Everyone, except
Dolley, agreed he was "the last man in the world to compass such a
business."[17]

No doubt Payne's participation turned a complicated process into a
convoluted mess. In important ways, he was neither his mother's son
nor a reflection of either of his fathers. Not only was he incompetent,
but his arrogant treatment of other people cut off many publishing opportunities. He left a trail of hard feelings, as well as debts, in his wake.
Of course, his actions reflected badly on Dolley, and Edward had to
convince publishers that she did not want to "jew, screw, or make a hard
bargain."[18] It did not help matters that Payne disappeared at crucial
points in the process.

After all the letters back and forth, the accusations of double-
dealing and treachery, followed by fence-mending from all sides, in the
end Congress paid $30,000 for the first three volumes, which appeared
in 1840. In 1848, Congress paid Dolley $25,000 for the last four volumes,
which included two volumes of James's letters before 1801, one volume
of papers from the Washington years, and a volume of documents relating to constitutional topics. The combined sum was far less than the
$100,000 that James had hoped for. The first cash payment went largely

to Dolley's creditors and to Payne's extravagances; for the second set of volumes, Congress paid Dolley $5,000 outright, with $20,000 in a trust specifically set up to keep the money out of her son's hands.

❧

With James gone, it was almost inevitable that Dolley would not stay in the countryside. In 1837, she continued to press for publication, only setting aside time "for packing, & arranging for my absence." She took possession of the Cutts house on Lafayette Square in November 1837, and after a little remodeling—"[t]he colour of the walls was chosen by Payne for the sake of my eyes & I like it of course"—Dolley moved in, beginning her second reign. She intended to replicate the schedule that she had enjoyed with James—winters in Washington, summers in Orange.[19]

Everyone wanted to visit, and from the moment of her arrival, she embarked on a social merry-go-round. No Washington event could take place without her; she attended inaugurations and other White House parties. Her engagements proved so numerous that she bought a congressional directory, using it as a ledger sheet in order to keep track of her visiting "debts."[20]

Unable to afford new clothes, Dolley adapted old ones and wore them over and over again, which only enhanced her emblematic status. One such ensemble consisted of a black velvet gown with leg-of-mutton sleeves and a very low neckline. White "illusion" filled the décolletage; her white satin turban, trimmed in tulle, concealed the thinning of her hair, as did the false black curls peeking out from the cap. Long, richly colored shawls had been the fashion in her day, and Dolley retained the look. There was nothing out-of-date about her spirit, however. At one dinner party, a fellow guest characterized Dolley as "a very hearty, good looking woman," though he added four years to her age. Seated together, "we became on the most friendly terms & I paid her the same attentions I would have done a girl of 15—which seems to suit her fancy very well."[21]

Public adulation notwithstanding, Dolley's troubles continued. The year 1838 saw the loss of two of Anna's children. First Lieutenant Thomas Cutts died in September at Fort Jesup, Louisiana, and in

December, Dolley relayed the sad news that "poor dear Niece Dolley Cutts extremely ill with pleurisy which terminated her life yesterday, about 8 O'clock in the morning—leaving her family especially her only sister Mary, inconsolable." Annie and she found themselves "both much occupied at this time with the afflicted!"[22]

Dolley had left Montpelier in the hands of Payne, and both he and the estate suffered under the burden of responsibility. He was a middle-aged man now; whatever pleasure he had derived from his vices in his youth, now they only fueled his decline and his personal anguish. The mental instability and self-loathing of a full-blown alcoholic came to the fore in his rural retreat. To his credit, he loved his mother and believed that he would be the one to care for her in her old age. He spent his time at Montpelier struggling to reform himself by the induction of "regular habits" (such as brushing his teeth), and by constructing a housing compound on Madison land.[23] Dubbed "Toddsberthe," this fantastical edifice stood as the most obvious sign of his mental deterioration, though he designed it according to what he imagined would be his mother's preferences; he even included a ballroom.

At James's funeral in 1836, mourners had been moved when "the hundred slaves gave vent to their lamentations in one violent burst that rent the air." The white mourners saw this demonstration as proof of James's kindness as a master.[24] Any sincere grief aside, the enslaved workers had other reasons to lament. The death of the master meant an uncertain future, perhaps the exchange of a kind owner for a cruel one, or even sale and separation.

As it turned out, the slaves had been right to cry. Immediately following the funeral, rumors began circulating that Dolley intended to sell slaves. Edward Coles stayed with her the August after James's death, and he reported with disgust that "every day or two . . . a Negro trader would make his appearance. . . . It was," he concluded, "like the hawk among the pigeons." There must have been some truth to the rumors. Dolley permitted traders to examine her "black family," and she did sell some of them to neighbors and friends, including "a woman and 2 children to her Nephew Ambrose Madison who lives near her." Edward

Coles sadly noted that the sale contravened James's will: the woman did not want to be sold and thereby separated from her husband.[25]

The threat of sale hung over the heads of the African-Americans at Montpelier, with periodic scares keeping the anxiety level high. In October 1839, Senator George Waggaman of Louisiana, after talking with Payne, inquired of Dolley if "you would be willing to dispose of the negroes on your estate," This was a serious offer in several ways. It would mean a substantial profit, but also a complete change of life for Dolley if Waggaman meant to take her whole workforce. Of course, the lives most changed would be those belonging to the unlucky men, women, and children on the bill of sale. Besides family separation, enslaved Americans most feared being sold to the Deep South. With its swamps, fevers, and backbreaking labor in the sugarcane and rice fields, a Louisiana exile was an almost certain death sentence for most.

Fortunately, Dolley refused Waggaman's offer. Though she did not say so, she might have apprehended what it would mean for Virginia slaves to go "down south." In any case, her expressed reasons were both altruistic and self-interested. She told Waggaman that, though she had wanted to part with twenty-five or so—about a quarter of the community—she had decided against it "owing to their reluctance to leave this place or its neighborhood." But, she added, the workers were also needed to process "a large and tedious crop of Tobacco" and other crops. Dolley had another plan: while retaining the house and surrounding grounds for herself, she hoped to rent the fields and the slaves. This, too, failed to materialize. The dilemma would only increase with time. Before his death, James had already begun selling off pieces of the estate, which Dolley would also do, leaving an ever-smaller parcel of land from which to support an enslaved community that only increased in size through birth. And, of course, with each passing year, more and more elderly enslaved women and men could no longer work, detracting from production and constituting a serious liability.[26]

When Dolley was at Montpelier, she took her responsibilities for "her people" seriously; here again, she was driven by both kindness and selfishness. In 1842, during a disease outbreak among the African-Americans, Dolley "nursed, and attended" a slave family, "following the

Physician's advice with great anxiety and fatigue." This picture of a maternal mistress is somewhat mitigated by Dolley's characterization of one of her patients who died as "a woman Cook of great value to me." To her credit, she maintained James's stand against physical correction. In 1842, she approved Payne's decision not to employ as overseers two men who had a reputation for violence. In an unconscious echo of the revolutionary rhetoric of her youth, she noted that "no whipper of Negroes shd ever have our people or any others, to tirenize [tyrannize] over."[27]

In Washington, she maintained a regular correspondence with her "ole servants" (as Paul Jennings styled them) back in Montpelier. Except for the inelegant penmanship and nonstandard spelling, in tone, the letters from Madison slaves such as Jennings and Sarah Steward could have been from any of Dolley's wide circle of white correspondents. Paul not only felt comfortable enough to report of the health of "mas Payne"—"witch is good"—but also to scold Payne for not writing to his mother. Confronted by Paul, Payne felt defensive enough to offer an excuse—he was "to bisey." Sarah Steward, too, wrote letters filled with news of her own health, effusive wishes for the health of Dolley and Annie, gossip about the weddings of white people, as well as general news of "people in the naibourhood." She also charged Dolley with passing on news and love to and from the black people she owned.[28]

For the enslaved people "lucky" enough to stay at the only home they knew, with an unstable master at the helm, life at Montpelier must have been hellish. (Indeed, under Payne's management, an overseer enriched himself mightily, no doubt abusing slaves as he did so.) Payne had become obsessed with his family's debts, and dunned and sued debtors, even as his own creditors hounded him. While Dolley played Queen Mother in Washington City, Payne used Montpelier as his own personal bank account and garage sale, selling pieces of the furniture and even some of his stepfather's papers to raise money.[29]

Of her "family white and black," without question it was the dependent workforce that suffered most from Dolley's financial insecurity. Though James's will had stipulated that no slave be sold without his or her consent, a suit brought by a Madison relative raised the specter of a sheriff's sale. To avoid seizure, Dolley deeded forty slaves to Payne. Desperate, Sarah Steward enlisted the help of a "young lady" to write a note to Dolley, one more formal than her usual chatty missives. In the letter to "My Misstress," Sarah played on Dolley's feelings, invoking the helplessness of the enslaved community, skillfully using guilt and tact. "I don't like to send you bad news but the condition of all of us your servants is very bad, and we do not know whether you are acquainted with it." With the sheriff threatening to sell them all to satisfy the suit, Sarah feared "negro buyers" would separate families. She suggested that if Dolley had to sell slaves then perhaps she could sell them to neighbors as to "save us some misery."

Cannily, Sarah appealed to Dolley's vanity, lamenting the prospect of being separated "from you as well as from one & another." Like her famous mistress, Sarah prefaced the strongest part of her case with a ritual apology. "We are very sure you are sorry for this state of things and we do not like to trouble you with it but think dear mistress what our sorrow must be." For additional emphasis, Sarah reminded Dolley that "[t]he husband of Caty is with you what is to be done with her and her children."[30]

Something needed to be done to salvage the Madison finances. In 1839, Dolley once more left Washington City for Montpelier, both to generate some income by renting out the house on Lafayette Square and to turn a profit by farming. After metropolitan life, Dolley found rusticity trying, especially the degree to which weather restricted her movements. In 1842, she obtained a new mortgage from her old friend, financier John Jacob Astor, but that kept the sinking ship aloft for only a short time, and she struggled to pay it back. The next year, after selling off parts of the property to a Virginia merchant, Henry Moncure, she moved back to Washington City for good, and in 1844, she finally sold her husband's entire estate to Moncure, including the slaves, who at least had a chance of staying together.[31] Naturally, she felt the decision to sell the family seat keenly; James had entrusted her with his precious Montpelier, but she could not save it. The details of the sale are unknown, but Dolley's financial trials continued, so apparently the transaction provided little monetary relief.

Dolley's old age was not just a whirlwind of family troubles, health and money worries, interspersed with social events. She experienced an inner efflorescence, too. The long years of editing and transcribing her husband's papers provided Dolley a kind of advanced education in writing and expression; her later letters exhibit more confidence and "voice." This intellectual process, not to mention the involved fight for publication, may have turned Dolley's mind to her own legacy.

If a man was not supposed to show much ambition or concern with his own place in history, that a woman should desire historical renown was unthinkable. But just as Jefferson, Adams, and their compatriots quietly ensured at significant moments that History would have their side of the story, so did Dolley. She possessed ambition of her own, though it was muted and convoluted, expressed through feminine models of thought and behavior. Dolley took pride in her femininity, though its strictures denied her other needs. Like other respectable political women, she expressed herself in ways more subtle than the publication of an "Anas" or a straightforward statement in a diary.

Poetry was one of the most acceptable forms of expression for a well-born white woman. It was even a safe enough skill for a woman to pursue professionally, though most middle- and upper-class women never intended their verses for the public eye. Female poetry was an appropriately small art, as compared with published essays or public speeches, and the lofty topics of most poetry, such as religion and nature, made it suitably ladylike.

The indifferent quality of much of this verse hardly mattered. Whether the poetry expressed what Emily Dickinson called "dimity convictions," or clothed strong convictions in dimity, for women of intellect and feeling, poetry provided an outlet, part therapy, part artistic release. Some of Dolley's contemporaries, such as Louisa Catherine Adams, wrote like fiends.

The world may have seen Dolley as a symbol, a muse, or a dynamic person of practical action, but Dolley had a different idea of herself, one that she occasionally revealed (as when she joked that she continued too busy to be a "poetess"). She once casually mentioned to Anna that she was "allways a dreamer you know." The more reflective side of Dolley emerged in the poetry of her later years. As a poet, she followed the conventions of her time, including allusions to the classical age. Poems invoking Greece and Rome were not merely exercises in erudition. One of Dolley's efforts centered on the mythological figure of Nysa, stepmother of Bacchus, the god of wine. The poem goes on to warn young men about the dangers of drunkenness: "I tremble for thee! Ah! Be wise! / Nor gaze too long on Nysa's eyes / fond youth, beware!" Dolley surely knew something of the "endless chain" of alcoholism that she depicted and of its result, "a bleeding heart." Only once did she attempt to enter the public realm with her poetry. Inspired by the Washington Monument project in 1848, Dolley decided to celebrate Washington's relationship with General Lafayette, "*Europe's noblest son.*" She wrote out a beautiful fair copy of a poem she had written earlier, and circulated it.[32]

Epigrams offered yet another ladylike way to be a sage. Like poetry, they expressed elevated thoughts in a modestly small form. The autograph book was much in vogue among women of all ages, allowing them a way to "publish" their sentiments. Dolley had a trademark epigram that she used on several occasions: "Habit and hope are the crutches which support us through the vicissitudes of life." With its eschewal of the "grand sweep" in favor of the quotidian, emphasizing contained control and cautious optimism, no wonder this phrase became known as her standard offering. A longer passage that began "The passions are like sounds of nature only heard in solitude!" was also a favorite. The meditation included warnings against "vanity" and being "enamour[ed]" with "rank."[33]

For Dolley, the epigram craze fit in nicely with her lifelong occupation of giving advice, especially to young people. Her nieces became the recipients of her most elegantly expressed thoughts. Longer than the usual one- or two-line epigram, these little mini-essays addressed the most exalted issues, as when she advised Mary Cutts on destiny: "We have all, a great hand in the formation of our own destiny. We must press on, that intricate path, leading to perfection and happiness, by doing all that is good and handsome before we can be taken under the silver wing of our rewarding angel." Dolley had no doubt that Mary would take hold of her fate. "This, I cannot doubt you will aim at and succeed in. I need not re-capitulate all the virtues necessary to render us worthy and deserving of good fortune, because, you know them 'at your fingers ends.'"[34]

She had advised Dolley Payne Cutts to always "appear in a feminine and more congenial character": "If I could see to express myself with these eyes of mine, I might fill a volume in favor of *always sustaining* a sweet and gentle character."[35] Niece Mary remembered her famous remark on party spirit: "I confess I do not admire contention in any form, either political or civil. I would rather fight with my hands than my tongue." Like a professional writer, Dolley refined a repeated phrase, testing its fit, as in this request for political information from her young niece: "But I confess I do not admire the contention of parties, political or civil, tho' in my quiet retreat I am anxious to know all the manoeuverings of both."[36]

Serious meditations on God and religion play only a small part in Dolley's extant writing, though she composed a poem to Him who "sent redemption onto his people; he hath commanded his covenant forever; holy and reverend is his name." A lifelong, albeit sporadic, churchgoer, Dolley was not baptized until quite late. On July 15, 1845, both she and Annie were "churched" at St. John's Episcopal Church in Washington. Denomination mattered little to Dolley, and her choice of institution reflected class consciousness and convenience as much as doctrinal bent. St. John's was the church of Washington's elite—and it was across the street from Dolley's house on Lafayette Square.[37]

In these small, quietly feminine ways, Dolley constructed her legacy. While she could not overtly acknowledge her desire to be remembered and revered, she could cast her historical, political, and philosophical observations as mere life lessons shared among loved ones. But epigrams and poetry would not suffice: Dolley led a life larger than most women, and she had spent years shaping her husband's legacy. Inspired by this example, and her own sense of self, she took an active part in shaping her own.

Dolley was conscious of her position as the steward of the first White House and, like a good historian, answered queries about it, as when the diplomat Christopher Hughes inquired about the paintings in the old president's house while trying to track the provenance of paintings he saw abroad. She also felt keenly the responsibility of representing her late husband to the world and had no qualms about asserting his place in the pantheon, to the extent that she sometimes capitalized pronouns that referred to James, as one would do for a deity.[38] When it came to actively promoting herself, however, she was cautious. In her old age, she attracted more biographical attention than any other American woman. In 1830, Margaret Bayard Smith had expressed an interest in immortalizing James in a manuscript volume ostensibly for her son; four years later, her focus turned to Dolley. (Actually, Margaret probably had been documenting the Madisons for years. Her 1826–27 commonplace book includes several transcriptions of letters between the couple, though they are not in her hand.) In 1834, while Dolley was still nursing James at Montpelier, Margaret contacted her with the news that she had been commissioned to write Dolley's biographical sketch for the four-volume *National Portrait Gallery of Distinguished Americans,* and accordingly needed information on Dolley's background. This was a great honor and opportunity for both women. Margaret was one of only a few women writers asked to participate, and Dolley was the only woman slated for Volume III. Dolley agreed enthusiastically, at the same time managing to deprecate herself, flatter Margaret, and inadvertently reveal some trepidation. "If a Biographical Sketch must be taken, its accomplishment by your pen, would be more agreeable to me than by any other to which such a task could be committed." Not only could she be confident of "its competency," but, Dolley was sure, it would be friendly and complimentary, by virtue "of the just dispositions by which it would be guided."[39]

When the claims of history got closer to home, Dolley exhibited the same conflicted feelings as her male contemporaries. On the one hand, she wished to be remembered by her country and to receive proper credit for her accomplishments. On the other, she was terrified of being thought "egoistical." In addition, she expressed concerns about what Margaret might discover, a matter over which she had no control. Initially, Dolley appeared very cooperative. In her first reply to Margaret, she assured her biographer that had her nieces been in Washington City and not with her in Orange, she would have bade them to show Dolley's correspondence with them, as well as with their mother, to Margaret. Full of wise saws and sayings, these were letters Dolley clearly had earmarked for posterity.

Not that the more recent correspondence could "have thrown light on the early occurrences of my life," admitted Dolley, "but that they contain my unvarnished opinions and feelings on different subjects." Dolley promised Margaret that "as it is I will have them sent here [to Montpelier], when the Girls return to the city, in order that I may select those at all worthy of your attention."[40]

It seems hard to believe that Dolley wanted to present anything "unvarnished" to the world, however, when in the next paragraph, she lied. Dolley declared that "my family are all Virginians except myself, who was born in N. Carolina," turning the abortive frontier experience into "a visit of one year, to an Uncle." She affirmed her sterling Virginia pedigree and presented the radical and unsettling move to Philadelphia in glowing terms: "Their [her parents'] families on both sides, were among the most respectable and they, becoming members of the society of friends soon after their Marriage—manumitted their Slaves, and left this state for that of Pennsylvania, bearing with them their children to be educated in their religion." Dolley also misdated her age at the time of the move, reckoning herself to be "11. or 12 years," though she was fifteen at the time.

She then quickly encapsulated some of her most controversial and complicated years in a way calculated to reveal nothing and ending with a flattering diversion. "I was educated in Philadelphia where I was married to Mr Todd in 1790, and to Mr. Madison in 94, when I returned with him to the soil of my Father, and to Washington, where you have already traced me with the kindness of a Sister." In response to Margaret's questions, Dolley also described the whereabouts of her mother during the 1790s and beyond, reassuring Margaret that "Should any particular information be desired, I will endeavor to furnish it."[41]

That stated willingness to share information stands as perhaps the biggest lie of all. From this initial exchange on, Dolley proved extraordinarily, if graciously, uncooperative. The prospect of putting her life in Margaret's hands unleashed a variety of anxieties, some quite contradictory. She worried about putting Margaret off, even as she stood in her way. She feared that her life was not going to be sufficiently noteworthy, confessing to Mary Cutts: "Dear good Mrs. Smith will have so few incidents to make her Biography interesting that I ought to *tremble* for it (between you and I)."[42] But she also balked at giving Margaret free rein to discover anything "interesting."

There is something ominous about Dolley's "where you have already traced me with the kindness of a sister." Or, one might conjecture, like a spy. Dolley and Margaret had known each other for a long time, but their relationship probably had as much to do with the business of politics as with friendship. Dolley expressed gratitude that it was an old friend who undertook the task of presenting her to the public, but she may have felt the opposite. Margaret may have known too much; not only had she known the Madisons for years but also she was a reporter and a writer, always a tricky personage to include in one's circle. Dolley had expressed concern about Margaret's interest years earlier, when her sister was still alive. Congratulating Anna on a "properly" cautious reply to one of Margaret's enquiries, Dolley warned that Margaret was "a *curious* body—& tho she appears affectinate & frank, I think she is *dangerious*."[43]

Over the course of the two-year project, Dolley edited letters, coached informants, and generally obstructed the biographical process, all the while maintaining a pleasant and cooperative façade. "Give my kind love to Mrs. Smith & tell her It wd. give me pleasure to do what she recommends, & that I hope it will not be long before I make the effort, tho' I can not promise much, as I cannot give her anything of importance *in my own Eyes*."[44] One almost has to feel sorry for Margaret. Like any properly raised southerner, Dolley was a master at avoiding the direct confrontation of a no, and fighting shadows is the hardest battle of all.

That Dolley did crave recognition and honor complicated the situation. She could have deterred Margaret easily, but she did not want the equivalent of "no comment" on the historical record. Accordingly, she apologized on a regular basis. "My delinquency has not proceeded from want of love, and confidence in your friendship," she assuaged her would-be biographer, "nor am I without explanations, which will at least mitigate."[45]

Dolley had legitimate reasons for "delinquency," including some bad spells with her eyes as well as concerns for an increasingly frail James. She also offered a plethora of other excuses for not producing the letters that Margaret requested. "My letters to my Sister Todd at the closing scenes of the War, happen to be with her in Kentucky, and I was unwilling to have them exposed in the Mail, if I had been sure of their arrival in time, and that they contained any thing worthy of being extracted." In uncharacteristically tortured prose, she offered a veritable laundry list of additional explanations: "I might plead also my constant engagements of different sorts at home, which have not permitted me to search over papers, and bring my mind to the revisal of scenes or circumstances that might possibly throw a faint interest over a recital of them, and lastly I must in candour say, that I have felt more than a mere reluctance in being a Judge and witness, of incidents if existing, that might be worthy of the use to be made of them." Even as she dithered, though, Dolley also sent along the "good picture" of her, an engraving from the Stuart portrait, as a "better likeness than Mr Wood's [this was the artist Joseph Wood, well known for portraits and miniatures]."[46]

Though Dolley expressed reluctance to expose her letters either to the mail or to Margaret (between Dolley's ambivalence and her nieces' dilly-dallying, it is not clear whether Margaret ever saw any), one document existed that she was willing, even eager, to share. It was within the context of Margaret's project that Dolley's most famous letter came to light, the one written over two days, supposedly addressed to Lucy, detailing the last hours of the White House. Dolley did not give Margaret the original document. Instead, she offered a copy or an extract, which Margaret reproduced for the entry. Some confusion exists in Dolley's account of the fate of the actual letter. While she told Mary Cutts that mice had "torn [it] to bits," she also cited it as among the inaccessible letters in Kentucky. Of course, both things might have been true, though it is unlikely that Dolley would know the condition of a paper so far away.[47] Even the identity of the addressee remains a mystery. Addressed to "my Sister," the letter could have been meant for Anna or Lucy. According to Dolley's memory, she was writing to her "Sister Todd," and there is no cause to doubt her, though no easy explanation exists for Lucy's letter being in the possession of Anna's daughters.[48]

None of which is to say that Dolley did not write the letter, or one very similar to it. Other authenticated documents that Dolley wrote after the invasion agree with the account in the famous White House letter. More likely, Dolley may have edited or embellished the one slated for publication. In contrast to her typically slapdash style, this letter unfolds like a novel, in language more formal and flowery than her usual vocabulary. The text also includes details unnecessary in a letter between sisters, though useful to general readers.

Without casting aspersions on the overall truth relayed, the letter can be seen as a "performance." A similar letter that can be authenticated as written in 1814 to Mary Hazelhurst Latrobe appears much more consonant with Dolley's epistolary style and interests. In her letter to Mary Latrobe, Dolley bemoans the loss of her beautiful things and even indulges in a little self-pity. To be fair, Dolley might have made consumer goods the focus of that letter since Mary had bought many of them during the restructuring of the presidential mansion; still, the contrast between the Latrobe letter and the more famous one is striking. In the latter, Dolley loftily notes that "our private property must be sacrificed." The tone rings noble and defiant, designed to arouse patriotism and pride around a rather inglorious event. If Dolley edited and rewrote the letter for publication, she was following a time-honored custom among nineteenth-century historians and men of letters, just as when she exercised editorial control of James's papers.[49]

Whatever else, she wanted the White House letter to be part of her record, along with the "varnished" letters of good advice to her nieces. Over a year after Margaret's initial request, Dolley began a long letter to Mary Cutts in her usual chatty tone, but quickly turned businesslike, listing her instructions by number. "In the first place—I *fear* that you have not given Mrs. Smith the extract of a letter I wrote my sister, finished, the day of the destruction of the Ps. House. If you have lost it, or omitted to give it to her, it *will be* much to my injury, as the original is nearly torn to *bits* by the mice with several others, describing what followed—2d. did you rece. the residue of my letters to you & Dolley & lend them to Mrs. Smith for her perusal? I *pray* you to do these things."[50]

Though she continued on in a more familiar vein of news and good wishes, in closing she returned to the subject clearly on her mind: "You will hasten to write me abt. the *letters for Mrs. S. & what she says*. I am miserable to think that I have not written to her, & know not when I can do so—love to her & dr. Mrs. Lear." As always, discretion was a priority, so Dolley added: "Now burn this."[51]

Dolley counted on Mary to manage both the situation and Margaret Bayard Smith. She informed her niece that "I have other letters beside the one the extract was taken from—which continues the *little* history of the War times; & *my especial difficulties*; but egotism is so repugnant to my nature that I *shrink* from recording my own feelings, acts or doings." To ensure that her properly feminine fear of "egotism" was duly noted, Dolley directed Mary: "You can *repeat this* to Mrs. S." She also added another "message" for Mary to convey, in a way that seemed like dictation: "whom I consider a kind friend, & amiable lady."[52]

If Dolley's nieces seem confused about what their aunt wanted, it would be hard to blame them. For years, they had received instructions such as "Take care of all my letters to your mother until she is able to read them, hide them from every eye under lock and key." Now, with veiled eagerness, Dolley pressed her niece. "I must ask the favor of yo[u] to allow our friend Mrs. S. H Smith to peruse" her letters. Dolley sweepingly insisted: "They contain nothing she may not see."[53]

The *Portrait Gallery* piece finally appeared in 1836, and Dolley had won: the White House letter formed the centerpiece of the entry. Given the dearth of personal information from her subject, Margaret had filled in with her own recollections during their seventeen years together in Washington. While Dolley had had good cause for unease, in fact she should have trusted Margaret's loyalty and discretion. As Margaret remarked to her sister, "In the last Portrait gallery—you will see my memoir of Mrs. Madison—all I say is true—but I have not of course told the whole truth."[54]

As ambivalent as she may have been about her personal history, Dolley was crystal clear on the facts when it came to matters of public record. In 1848, Robert De Peyster, one of the "gentlemen of New York" who ferried the George Washington portrait to safety in 1814, contacted Dolley, then aged eighty, asking her to confirm to the public the parts that he and Jacob Barker played. The family of Charles Carroll, the man who had tried to hurry Dolley out of harm's way and who left before the painting was secured, had claimed in print that he had rescued the portrait. A sense of history impelled Dolley into the public eye.

Dolley had never entered the newspaper fray before to defend herself, even in the face of the most scurrilous of slander. But in this case, she saw fit to issue her own correction.[55] True to form, she played down the story in which she played a central role as a "little narrative," but she insisted that "[t]he impression that Mr. Carroll saved Stuart's portrait of Washington is erroneous." "On the contrary," Dolley insisted pointedly, "Mr. Carroll had left me to join Mr. Madison." She underscored the authority of her account with specifics: "I directed my servants in what manner to remove it from the wall, remaining with them until it was done." In addressing the issue of her presence, she also confirmed that De Peyster and Barker had been the "passing" gentlemen who transported the portrait to shelter.

Of course, Dolley's concern with setting the record straight was not completely selfless. In the straightforward style she rarely used outside her own family circle, she concluded with a touch of asperity: "I acted thus because of my respect for General Washington—not that I felt a desire to gain laurels; but, should there be a merit in remaining an hour in danger of life and liberty to save the likeness of anything, the merit in this case belongs to me. Accept my best wishes."[56]

During these later years, Dolley may have taken more active steps to preserve her legacy. Shortly after Dolley's death, Mary Cutts produced a memoir of her beloved aunt. She ended up with two versions; since the combined documents cover Dolley's entire life, and Mary was not born until 1814, it is not illogical to assume that Dolley herself was the source of the information. Still, it is hard to discern the extent of her participation, and, though the obvious aim of the documents was to preserve Dolley's memory in the best light possible, the final result only adds to the questions. Direct testimony was never Dolley's forte, however, and, as was true in her life, the case for her historical significance would be made by the testimony of others, especially their testimony about her actions.

When Dolley returned to Washington City in 1844, she entered the iconic stage of her life. If she was a significant presence in the capital before, she now became a personage for the ages. She knew all twelve presidents, having taken tea with George Washington, attended the 1845 inauguration of James Polk, and met with Zachary Taylor. In her final years, she performed her most symbolic acts and received her highest honors: sending the first private telegraph message, accepting her own seat in the House, receiving a version of a medal commemorating the War of 1812 specially cast for her in silver, presiding over the laying of the cornerstone of the Washington Monument. At that 1848 event, as at many others, Americans read her presence as a sign that the "executive part of the government was still influenced to some extent by ideals and practices of an earlier day," a message no doubt exploited by some in the executive branch. A "Relict" of James Madison and of the republic itself, Dolley seemed even to transcend personhood in her symbolic value; an 1846 correspondent for the *Boston Cultivator* assured its readers that Dolley "may be justly regarded as one of [Virginia's] monuments." The photographer Matthew Brady, who would go on to fame for his work during the Civil War, made a conscious effort to capture the likenesses of the last of the founding generation, and Dolley made his list. Like the earlier Stuart depiction, the Brady daguerreotype showed an iconic Dolley—an elder stateswoman, wise and serene as Minerva, goddess of, among other things, wisdom, defense of the state, and civilized society. In both renderings—the idealistic Stuart and the realistic Brady—Dolley's essential kindness shines through.

Dolley maintained and enlarged the role of an ideal woman, appearing even in a 1831 plea for organized labor. Dolley modestly accepted all these tributes "as a token of their remembrance, collectively and individually, of One who has gone before us."[57] The capitalized deity was, of course, James.

She was even given another chance to save James's papers (at least secondhand), and in a manner reminiscent of her rescue of the Washington portrait. At four in the morning on May 1848, the fire alarm sounded and her slave, Ralph, woke up Dolley and Annie, imploring them to get out of the house. They left by the stairs, made their way through the fire, and took refuge in the garden. Standing on the wet grass, Dolley sent Ralph back in to retrieve the trunks of papers. The fire was later determined to be arson, though the perpetrator was never caught.[58]

She continued to suffer losses, some inevitable to anyone who reaches a great age. Sister Lucy died in 1846 of an "apoplexy," probably a stroke. In spite of the sale of James's papers and Montpelier, financial troubles continued to plague her. She had sold the invaluable Paul Jennings to her neighbor, Senator Daniel Webster, in order to allow him to earn his freedom. Paul regularly came by her house with food from Webster, often adding small sums of money from his own pocket.[59]

Dolley experienced one of the sad ironies of slaveholding life: with her husband and sisters gone, the people closest to her, who knew her best, were her former or present property. And yet, in 1848, Dolley felt compelled to sell one of her few remaining slaves, Ellen, for $400, for, according to James's instructions, bad behavior. On April 18, 1848, seventy-six African-Americans, enslaved and freed, hijacked the schooner *Pearl* and attempted to sail for freedom from Washington to New York. They were captured, jailed, and sold south. Ellen was a participant. (Paul Jennings was one of the chief instigators of the *Pearl* rebellion, but Dolley evidently did not know that.)[60]

During the months before her death, she became noticeably frail. Her letters were no longer long and gossip-filled, but rather short and even elegant. It was as though age and time had distilled her to her essence. To her old friend Frances Dandridge Lear, she wrote: "You have sent me the first rose of your garden dear friend, which in the old fashion I shall wear in my bosom during its life—but it is even less sweet to me than the fragrance—of your friendship so long reciprocated and which brightens as we advance together thro' the season of flowers." But she always kept her sense of humor. In the same letter to Frances, she added: "I rose this morning with the sun, and felt as if I could fly with the aid of a sweet breeze then blowing, but now, at 10 O'clock I am so ready for a *nap* that I may not sign my name to this."[61]

Sadly, her last known letter to Payne is yet another plea for his attention, coupled with financial concerns: "I ardently hoped that you would have written me about our affairs before this, and that I should have some guide to lead from whelming darkness—but it is in vain to wait! I wish to tell you all that concerns us, but you are silent about your being at home or absent from it." She went on to ask Payne for his estimation about items that she wished to raffle. "I wrote you a week ago but no answer has come to me tho' twas important I should have one."[62]

For most, the best death is a quiet one, when one is ready to leave a world whose charms have ceased to beguile. In her prime, Dolley was a woman of the world, involved in its many cares and joys. But by 1849, she was indeed ready to depart. On July 8, she took to her bed. As family members read to her from her favorite gospel of St. John, Dolley slipped in and out of a coma, a state her doctors described as "a sleep," stemming from a "slow apoplexy." She lingered for several more days, seemingly without suffering, only waking when aroused to momentary consciousness, at which point she would, in the words of Eliza Collins Lee, "smile her loving smile, put out her arms to embrace those whom she loved and who were near her, and gently relapse in that rest which was peace."

In her day, deathbed utterances and last words were of paramount importance. Dolley's oft-repeated and official "last words" were recorded a few days before her lapse into unconsciousness. In Mary Cutts's telling, when "a niece" (who may have been herself) came to Dolley with a problem, she replied: "My dear, do not trouble yourself about it, there is nothing in this world worth caring for." Her niece wondered, "'Aunt, you who have lived so long, do you think so?' 'Yes!' she again said, with emphasis, 'believe me, I who have lived in it so long, repeat to you that there is nothing in it worth caring for.'"[63]

But she did speak again, during her decline, and in some ways, those words proved more emblematic. At her deathbed, she was attended, as she had been through her life, by Eliza Collins Lee, who reported with relief that "when not disturbed by the frequent attacks of the disease appeared to suffer no pain and conscious when spoken to tho' she spoke but faintly." Dolley's niece and companion Annie Payne asked her to open her eyes and look at "the Ladies around her Bed." She caught the gaze of Eliza, who asked if Dolley knew her. She replied distinctly and with "a sweet smile"—'Do I *know* you, my dear Betsey—Yes, and I love you." Dolley reached out her arms and "this greatful recognition of an Old Friend reverting to our early days when she ever call'd me *Betsey* is to me at least a greatful and conclusive evidence of her being in sound mind."[64] To the end, Dolley knew what to say to connect and comfort.

Dolley Payne Todd Madison died the night of Thursday, July 12, 1849, at the age of eighty-one. Loving hands prepared her body at home, laying her out in the Lafayette Square house, where mourners paid their respects. On Monday, July 16, her body was moved, and she lay in state in St. John's Episcopal Church. Hundreds of admirers came to say good-bye to the woman whom they called both "Queen" and "Dolley."

Washington City gave Dolley a state funeral, acknowledging to the last her importance to the government and the capital city. All government business was canceled so that officials, including the president, the cabinet, and members of both houses of Congress, as well as the Supreme Court justices, could participate. Dolley's was the largest funeral that had ever been held in Washington. Its formal nature may have signaled her official status; the size of the crowd was a testament to the place she had held in their hearts.

No doubt the throngs of mourners would have pleased Dolley. Of the many who accompanied her to the grave, however, two had special claims to her love. Anthony Morris and Eliza Collins Lee had known Dolley from her Philadelphia days, when she had come "upon our comparatively cold hearts . . . suddenly and unexpectedly with all the delightful influences of a summer sun."[65] The two had stood with her at her first wedding and stood by her through grief, new love, and all the tumults of public life. Now at the end, they took one final journey with their friend.

Payne chose to bury his mother in the Congressional Cemetery, but almost ten years later, family members moved her remains back to Montpelier to rest with James. A simple, soaring white obelisk marks her grave.

Epilogue

olley Madison wrote her last will on July 9, 1849, three days before her death. She had been roused from a comatose condition by her worried female relatives and friends, who saw that the end was near. Dolley's previous wills had been detailed documents, outlining various bequests of small sums of money and personal items, but they had one thing in common: they left all of her property and cash to John Payne Todd.

In contrast, this final will addressed only the disposal of the $20,000 that Congress had put in trust for her upon purchasing the second set of James's papers. With Montpelier gone, the trust was her only real asset. In this final will, Dolley divided the sum between Payne Todd and her niece and companion, Annie Payne. When the world learned of the details of her bequest, it approved. Annie had given her youth to care for her aunt, passing up opportunities to have a family of her own. Few could question that Annie's energy and strength not only made Dolley's last years more comfortable, but also probably prolonged her life. Payne on the other hand had inflicted only griefs, not to mention decades of financial hardship, on his mother in later years. While acknowledging that Dolley would never disinherit her beloved son, some felt that he should receive nothing at all.

But Payne cried foul. He could not see the justice of the new arrangement, pointing out that not only did his mother's previous wills make him the sole heir (though in the 1841 version Dolley had had the sense to appoint trustees so that Payne would not squander his inheritance), but that she had already drawn up a will the previous month, once again giving him everything. This final will, prepared by Dolley's nephew J. Madison Cutts, must have been the product of coercion.

Payne, who never got anything right, might have been correct this time—though he, too, may have been guilty of manipulating his mother. When he approached her in mid-June, Dolley was not in full possession of her faculties. Those around her had been noticing her slow decline for months. That the June version of her will lacked the trustee clause hints at either her mental state or Payne's deception. Still, although one would like to imagine that in the end Dolley finally stood up to her son and did the right thing by Annie, she was clearly only partly conscious when she signed the final will. That was the day the doctors had begun giving her opium.

Throughout her death vigil, Dolley was attended, as she had always been, by her female friends and kin, including Annie Cutts and Eliza Collins Lee and her daughter. According to later testimony by Eliza Collins Lee, at one point on July 9, "the ladies said let her have a will." J. Madison Cutts obliged, and asked Dolley if she wanted to give something to both Payne and Annie "and she gave consent," though Eliza does not say exactly how. Perhaps the ambiguous wording disguised something less than legal; perhaps, simply, in the end "the ladies" guided her to the right decision. J. Madison drew up the will, and Dolley signed it then and there.

Nothing would have distressed Dolley more than for Payne to

contest the will, dragging the family name through the courts of law and public opinion. This, of course, was what Payne did. He took the will to court; J. Madison Cutts assured that public opinion was on Annie's side, enlisting the endorsement of prominent men, including Secretary of State James Buchanan, Senator Henry Clay, and Governor John J. Crittenden, of Kentucky (who was also a former and future U.S. attorney general). Justice was on Annie's side as well, and in February 1851, the will was settled in her favor.

In his later years, Payne's mental instability had manifested itself in a mania for clearing the family debt. He had been disposing of Dolley's personal effects even before she died, and he did not wait for the court's decision to make arrangements to auction everything, including some three thousand James Madison letters that were part of the second congressional purchase, and some small items that Dolley had promised to Annie. Engaged to Dr. James H. Causten, whom she married during this time, Annie battled Payne for what she considered her property over the next two years.

She also did not wait for the courts to render a decision concerning Dolley's papers. Her final will did not mention them, but Annie pointed out that in her last full will, Dolley had bequeathed Annie her "private papers to *burn*." But of course, Dolley did not want all of her papers burned. According to Annie, Dolley had instructed her to examine the whole private correspondence and "what she thought essential for her own use she should retain, and the rest should be destroyed." Accordingly, Annie and Mary Cutts stormed into the house of one of Payne's agents with a carpetbag and confiscated all of Dolley's letters. Ironically, considering all the waste and theft committed by Payne, one wishes that he had retained these letters and that they had reached the auction block, however unjustly. Though Annie and Mary no doubt felt righteously victorious over the perfidious Payne, in their zeal they burned reams of valuable material.

All this family squabbling came to naught. Legal fees had diminished Dolley's estate, so that, in the end, Payne and Annie only received about $5,000 each. Nor did either much outlive the court battles. John Payne Todd died on January 16, 1852, of complications from typhoid fever, at the age of fifty-nine. Thirty-three-year-old Annie, too, died before that year was out, on November 9, leaving behind a fifteen-month-old girl, Mary. With her money dissipated, Montpelier in the hands of strangers, and her possessions scattered to the winds, Dolley's estate would seem to amount to nothing. But her legacy was never to be measured in material possessions, and her worth would compound over the years.

Mary Cutts understood Dolley's elliptically worded instruction about her papers, that those "essential for her own use" were to be retained. These letters were for history, and at some point after Dolley's death, Mary embarked on her "memoir"—really a biography—of her aunt. In fifty-seven handwritten pages, Mary covered Dolley's life from birth to the invasion and rebuilding of Washington City, mixing narrative with transcribed letters. Mary was clearly interested in publication; she even wrote a second version, after editorial feedback encouraged her to make the memoir more conventional, adding material on battles and politics, and even excerpts from James Madison's speeches. Unfortunately, in the second version, Mary lost sight of Dolley; the ninety-five-page piece starts Dolley's story only in 1801 and is larded with listless accounts of "real history."

Initially, Jared Sparks was willing to publish the piece, as long as Mary included the important men and masculine subjects that would ensure that the work would be taken seriously. But he seemed to lose interest, and Mary turned to another family friend, Henry D. Gilpin, who had published James's first set of manuscript volumes. Perhaps the final form of Mary's memorial to her aunt would have added back the material on Dolley, but fate intervened before she had the chance to complete the project. Mary Estelle Elizabeth Cutts died in 1856, at age forty-two, in Nahant, Massachusetts. Later, her own niece, Lucia Cutts, used bits of both memoirs to create the first biography and collected letters of Dolley Madison, which would remain the standard text until 2003. Annie Payne may have received the money and the silver forks, but Mary Cutts had that most valuable of commodities, the last word.

Just as slavery shaped Dolley's life, so it shaped her posterity, at least initially. She has come down in history on the right side: the popular notion is that she sold Montpelier rather than break up slave families. Though it is clear that human considerations played a part in many of Dolley's dealings with her slaves, the reasons behind the sale of Montpelier were more complicated, as had been the living Dolley's relationships with enslaved people. Edward Coles, among others, was shocked when Dolley did not free the remaining Madison slaves at her death. (The majority, of course, had been sold with Montpelier, but Dolley had between three and five slaves in her household.) This outrage stemmed from a long-held belief that James had wanted to free his one hundred slaves upon his death as a statement of principle, but was reluctant to impoverish his widow. However, so the story went, he made Dolley promise to do so at her death. When Dolley's will passed her slaves on to Payne, Edward Coles was so incensed that he gathered a few informal depositions from friends who testified to James's intentions. Henry Clay even volunteered that "Mrs. Madison had mentioned to him that her Husband expected her to free his slaves at her death."

Assuming the story was true, and even though Dolley was unquestionably a loyal wife, perhaps it was not surprising that Dolley did not keep her final promise. After all, James's will explicitly bade her to refrain from selling slaves without their consent, except for bad behavior. Only a month or so after his death, however, she had sold a woman and child against their will, and throughout her widowhood, she sold slaves as she needed. In her 1841 will, made before the Montpelier sale, slaves were passed to legatees as "Marks of my affection." Indeed, for a woman not known for her business sense, Dolley was careful to ensure that she did not accidentally endow her slaves with freedom. After her final move to Washington, she inquired of her nephew, Richard D. Cutts, whether her previous failure to register Katy as a slave in the District would enable Katy to sue for freedom. According to District law, after twelve months of permanent residence, an unregistered slave could do so. Richard assured his aunt that her previous time spent in Washington would not count, as her permanent home had been in Orange, Virginia. However, now that she was a full-time District resident,

Richard advised her to register Katy in order to prevent "evil-designed person's" from persuading Katy to seek freedom.

Dolley's failure to act on her slaves' behalf, either on her own or in accordance with James's wishes, sullied her reputation. As she had in life, Dolley deflected criticism of her husband. Coles and others who had been disappointed at James's failure could now blame her for not carrying out James's secret abolitionist wishes. In her last years, the foremost periodical of the growing abolition movement, William Lloyd Garrison's *The Liberator,* reported on her treatment of her slaves, including tales of backdoor sales of young and old. *The Liberator* disputed her poverty, mentioning the sums that Congress had given her, sums that seemed astronomical to the average American. But even conceding her penury, the editors were blunt and censorious: "It is said she has not cash to go to market with from day to day. The members of her family, therefore, one after one, she disposed of to furnish her with the means of living."

Why did Dolley not free her slaves upon her death? Perhaps, following James's motivation, she did not want to impoverish Payne. Ironically, the only member of her immediate family to fulfill the highest ideals of the American Revolution *was* Payne. The posthumous criticism of his mother may have sensitized him, for he did free his slaves when he died, bequeathing $200.00 to each, with the residue to go to the American Colonization Society. But Payne was doomed to fail, even in his finest hour. He died in so much debt that it is doubtful any of his high-minded bequests were carried out.

But any indictment of Dolley on the issue of slavery soon faded from the public mind. Instead, Dolley Madison became most famous as a heroine: her saving the portrait of George Washington and escaping from the White House in 1814 emerged as the most enduring image of the War of 1812. It continues so through modern times, and not only because the Washington portrait is one of the very few items left from the original White House. It deserves this honor because—pure Dolley—the image strikes such a precise psychological note, now as then. Even if modern Americans do not know the whole story or understand the full context of Dolley's work, they remember the story of the First Lady and the portrait. This strong association is not accidental nor a random quirk of the public mind. It stands as a tribute to the power of memory.

Dolley left behind that which eighteenth-century public men valued most: a reputation. While her culture could not openly acknowledge her political power, her association with charm, femininity, sociability, and Americanness proved so powerful and enduring that her image and name became a commodity for many businesses, corporations, and organizations. And, like other public images, hers was mutable. Dolley might have recognized herself, depicted in cap and curls, as the symbol for products such as "Dolly Madison Ice Cream," or "Dolly Madison Cakes and Pies." But no doubt she would have been horrified by the picture of a sultry, sexy brunette advertising "Dolly Madison Cigars." Of course, she became a special icon for women, and in the late nineteenth century, the Daughters of the American Revolution adopted her as a symbol of their essentially conservative, anti-immigration stance. They, too, became caretakers of her legacy, assiduously combing the country for Dolley's letters and material possessions hidden away in private hands. A 1912 "Harmony Breakfast" used her birthday as an excuse to celebrate the successful Democratic elections. The fascination with the Quaker maid who became First Lady still holds; even today, many American women treasure the memory of a childhood biography of Dolley, and she remains one of the most popular subjects for young people's nonfiction.

But, of course, Dolley's true gift to the nation lies far beyond dessert and a rags-to-riches story. When she departed from Washington in 1817, she left behind a thriving, secure capital city and a rudimentary political machine that would ease the transition of the United States into democracy and the status of a nation-state. Dolley's most lasting contribution to the formation of American politics lay in her creation of the "unofficial office" of First Lady, setting parameters that made her the First Lady to whom all others would be compared. The First Lady answers the crucial need for the ceremonial in American politics; quite deliberately, the Constitution downplays the role of the ceremonial in its formula for a weak central government, ruled by law and not by personality. While in other modern governments, the functions are divided (as in Great Britain, where the prime minister rules as the head of government, while the head of the royal family reigns as the head of state) the American president both presides over ceremonial functions, such as they are, and serves as the head of government, making major appointments and playing a decisive role in legislation. Moreover, that the president lives where he works blurs the line between the ceremonial and the executive. In addition to the official and the unofficial spheres, however, politics requires the ceremonial. Democracies characteristically are short on ceremony, but they need it more than almost any other kind of governance.[1]

Ceremonial symbolism, which operates on emotional and psychological levels, unites people. In ordinary times, Dolley's performance supplied a kind of structure that allowed the government to function, unifying (or at least gathering) the branches of government and the individuals within those branches. Dolley also held the nation together in a time of crisis, and, by her ceremonial symbolism, allowed Americans, many of whom might never leave the town of their birth, to imagine themselves as part of a larger entity—as citizens of the United States of America.

Margaret Truman, a presidential daughter who closely observed her mother's work, asserts that the First Lady greatly influences how people feel about a president's performance, demonstrating that politics is always about winning hearts and minds. Certainly, Dolley's example, if it did not begin that association, solidified it. Dolley's First Lady was a bridge between presidential dignity and democratic accessibility. According to Truman, love, the purest of emotions, is part of the First Lady's role—"she speaks to the nation's heart." Just as Dolley's niece observed that "You like yourself more when you are with her," so, too, did the fractious young republic "like" itself more when she was with them. Dolley took that even further, demonstrating that "love," and other "soft" emotions, could be put to effective political use, thus offering modern Americans a model beyond the bluff and bluster of coercive realpolitik. In the early republic, and indeed for most of American history, she has stood as one of the few national figures whose prominence was not based on battlefield accomplishments, but on the profound and enlarging human capacity of love.[2] Dolley's answer to Henry Clay's compliment—"Mrs. Madison loves everybody"—speaks to the power of that projection. On a national level, Dolley *did* love everybody, and they loved her right back.

Notes

The heart of the historical enterprise is the primary sources—the papers and material culture of past lives. The almost two thousand extant letters of Dolley Payne Todd Madison supply the core of this story. Until recently, only a small portion of her letters had been published, albeit in heavily edited forms. While the papers of her male contemporaries had long been identified, cataloged, and gathered together for official documentary editions, Dolley's letters remained scattered in archival collections large and small and even in private hands. Because she was a woman—albeit a famous woman—her letters suffered the fate of much other female correspondence, relegated to folders of "Private" or "Family" letters. A private individual, who would conscientiously donate a letter from James Madison to a historical venue, making it available to the public, might keep a letter from Dolley as a family treasure.

In the 1990s, David B. Mattern, senior associate editor of the Papers of James Madison, and Holly C. Shulman, research associate professor, Studies in Women and Gender, at the suggestion of J. C. A. Stagg, the editor in chief of the Papers of James Madison, set about collecting and copying every letter to, from, and about Dolley that they could find. Luckily, they were not starting from scratch. Famed James Madison biographer Ralph Ketcham had long appreciated Dolley's historical significance, and had begun collecting and cataloging her letters, as he did James's. In 2003, Mattern and Shulman published a representative sample of her papers in a familiar form, a handsome, rigorously edited and annotated volume, *The Selected Letters of Dolley Payne Madison* (Charlottesville: University of Virginia Press). The three hundred letters featured, interspersed with essays that offer striking insights about Dolley as well as her historical context, cover her whole life. But, fittingly for a woman who prepared the American government for modernity, Dolley's historical renaissance was not limited to the old-fashioned form of ink on paper. Working with Rotunda, the electronic imprint of the University of Virginia Press, and the Virginia Center for Digital History (VCDH), Shulman created and maintains the Dolley Madison Digital Edition, a fully digitized edition of transcripts of all the letters written until James's death in 1836. Eventually, all of Dolley's papers will be in the DMDE; the nature of the digital genre means that the collection can be easily expanded to cover her whole life span, and letters may be added as they are found. The DMDE, along with the Dolley Madison Project, which Shulman created as a prototype, are truly the latest word on all things Dolley. (And, as Dolley pointed the way of the future for American politics, the DMDE is the nexus of another VCDH project, a larger digital archive, the Women of the Founding Era.) The DMDE's capacity searching, as well as the supporting annotating features that identify every person, place, and book title in the papers, has made this present undertaking possible. Consequently, in *A Perfect Union*, all correspondence to and from Dolley Payne Todd Madison before 1836 will be cited from the digital edition as DMDE. Letters after 1836 will be identified by collection or from Mattern and Shulman's *Selected Letters* (as *SL*). While some of the text has been modified for reasons of style and flow (upper- and lowercase letters have been changed and final ellipses eliminated to accommodate sentence structure, for instance) the transcriptions and proofing conventions follow Mattern and Shulman. I am deeply grateful to J. C. A.

Stagg, David B. Mattern, and Holly C. Shulman for their generosity and help with my project, even as they readied their own.

Finally, a word on the letters themselves, especially as regards the topic under discussion—politics. Like all bodies of letters, Dolley's corpus presents some challenges. The first is a rather common one—the problem of conflagration. Like many of her time, Dolley requested that her surviving relatives burn her letters at her death. She entrusted her two nieces, Annie Payne and Mary Estelle Elizabeth Cutts, with that task. Intriguingly, however, she did not want all her letters burned, only those that they would deem "not essential." I am arguing that Annie and Mary understood this elliptical language as veiled permission to use some of Dolley's letters to secure her legacy. And in the years following her aunt's death, Mary Cutts would go on to write not one but two memoirs of Dolley, using her letters. Indeed, we have a significant number of Dolley's letters available only because Mary Cutts transcribed them.

Still, ample evidence exists that Annie and Mary did carry out their Aunt Dolley's wishes and destroyed much of her correspondence—to the extent that they would hunt down and confiscate letters in the possession of others. Which letters did Dolley wish to be destroyed? A clue may lie in the fact that the First Lady years contain the fewest letters of all in the existing collection. Perhaps Dolley was just too busy to write, but perhaps not. Allowing for a certain percentage of private matters, family scandal, or love letters contained in the numerous destroyed papers, logically, the frank discussion of political matters seems the most likely target for two loving nieces who wished to present Dolley as a perfect, apolitical lady.

Strikingly, Dolley's letters to her sisters, brothers-in-law, and other family members that remain do not discuss the aspects of her life that made her famous; there are no long discussions of political strategy, deep analysis of personalities, political debates, or projected outcomes for her. She did not even discuss in any great detail the acceptable "feminine" topics that went into the creation of her political persona—clothing, decoration, menus, parties. Those letters may have been lost or burned, or, as Shulman surmises, Dolley may have consciously refrained from commenting on her public role, keeping it in the realm of cere-mony and not in the written record.

As stated above, Mary Estelle Elizabeth Cutts, Dolley's niece, wrote two "memoirs" of her aunt. Problematic, inaccurate, and troubling, these are the closest we can get to Dolley's voice and so have a place of honor in any examination of Dolley Payne Todd Madison. What was most probably the first version is owned by the Schlesinger Library at the Radcliffe Institute for Advanced Study. It is cited as CM I, with pagina-tion supplied by the archivists. The second, rewritten version, CM II, is part of the Cutts Family Papers at the Library of Congress, Manuscript Division, District Branch. The transcription and pagination used (with gratitude for her permission) are by Lee Langston-Harrison, curator, James Madison's Montpelier.

Key to Abbreviations

Proper Names

DPT(M)—Dolley Payne Todd (Madison)
JM—James Madison
APC—Anna Payne Cutts
LPWT—Lucy Payne Washington (Todd)
MEEC—Mary Elizabeth Estelle Cutts
DPMC—Dolley Payne Madison Cutts
MBS—Margaret Bayard Smith
JBK—Jane Bayard Kirkpatrick
MB(B)—Maria Bayard Boyd
CAM—Catharine Akerly Mitchill
SLM—Samuel Latham Mitchill
MAM—Margaretta Akerly Miller
ECL—Eliza Collins Lee
EC—Edward Coles
JGJ—John G. Jackson
TJ—Thomas Jefferson
MJR—Martha Jefferson Randolph
JPT—John Payne Todd
AG—Albert Gallatin
HNG—Hannah Nicholson Gallatin
BHL—Benjamin Henry Latrobe
AJF—Augustus John Foster
AM—Anthony Morris
PPM—Phoebe Pemberton Morris
RSC—Rosalie Stier Calvert
HJS—Henri Joseph Stier
IVH—Isabelle Van Havre
SGS—Sarah Gales Seaton
LCJA—Louisa Catherine Johnson Adams
AA—Abigail Adams
JQA—John Quincy Adams
JWR—Judith Walker Rives
MBC—Mary Boardman Crowninshield
MHB—Mary Hodges Boardman
FDL—Frances Dandridge Lear
SC(S)—Sarah "Salley" Coles Stevenson

Manuscript Archives

History lives, and is kept alive, in the many archives and libraries across the nation. I have been privileged to work at several premier historical institutions. Often supported by partial government funding and institutional support, these repositories of our past are very dependent on the generosity of private citizens as well. They are cited in the text as below.

AAS—American Antiquarian Society, Worcester, Mass.
DLC—Library of Congress, Manuscript Division, District Branch, Washington, D.C.
MDHS—Maryland Historical Society, Baltimore, Md.
MHS—Massachusetts Historical Society, Boston, Mass.
NYHS—New-York Historical Society, New York, N.Y.
SCHL—Schlesinger Library, Radcliffe Institute for Advanced Study, Harvard University, Cambridge, Mass.

Documentary Editions

Documentary editors, such as Mattern and Shulman, make biographies and other scholarship possible. In particular, studies of the founding era would be sadly wanting without the benefit of the various papers projects, dedicated to producing documentary editions of the era's leading players. Many began their work decades ago and have long years of work ahead of them. Funded by institutions, private donations, and taxpayer dollars, these projects are truly America's treasures. Full cites and abbreviations appear below.

The Papers of James Madison (*PJM*) was established in 1956 and is housed in the Alderman Library at the University of Virginia. The University of Chicago Press published the first ten volumes of the Congressional Series, edited by William T. Hutchinson and William M. E. Rachal. The University of Virginia Press published the final seven volumes of the Congressional Series, along with seven volumes of the Secretary of State Series (of a projected sixteen) and five volumes of the Presidential Series (of a projected twelve). Preliminary work has begun on the Retirement Series. At present, J. C. A. Stagg is the editor-in-chief; over the years, the *PJM* has been guided by many editors, including Robert Allen Rutland, David B. Mattern, Robert J. Brugger, and Mary A. Hackett.

The Papers of Thomas Jefferson (*PTJ*) is located at the Firestone Library, Princeton University. Princeton University Press published volumes 1–21, which cover the years 1760–1791 and were edited by Julian P. Boyd. Charles T. Cullen edited volumes 22, 23 (1791–1792) and John Catanzariti edited volumes 24–28 (1792–1796). The series continues under Barbara B. Oberg with volußmes 29–32 (1796–1801). Recently, the Retirement Series moved to the Robert H. Smith International Center for Jefferson Studies at Monticello, where volumes 1–2 (1809–1810), edited by J. Jefferson Looney and published by the Princeton University Press, have appeared.

The Adams Family Papers (*APM*) are housed at the Massachusetts Historical Society. Though the project has produced thirty-six volumes, published by Harvard University Press, the letters cited here are from the microfilm collection, cataloged and filmed by Lyman H. Butterfield and Celeste Walker. The project is currently guided by C. James Taylor.

The Hamilton Papers (*PAH*), complete in twenty-seven volumes that cover the years 1768–1804, were edited by Harold C. Syrett and Jacob E. Cooke (New York: Columbia University Press).

A Further Thought on Names

The use of "Dolley" for the subject of this biography is apt from both the writerly and historical perspectives. Though hers was not a world in which first names were used casually when referring to white people, Dolley, as was often true, was an exception to her time. In her political work, she became a public person, and, though generally designated as "Mrs. Madison," members of the public often referred to her as "Dolley," as a mark of affection and a sign of her popularity. In an age when men referred quite formally to their spouses—"Mrs. Washington"—even in letters to their wives' families, James Madison called his Dolley by her first name.

There is also some justice in restoring Dolley's name to the official record. Well into the twentieth century, biographers have insisted that her name was "Dorothy" or "Dorothea," and that she was named for an illustrious relation, Dorothea Dandridge. However, Dorothea Dandridge, being only ten years old at the time of Dolley's birth, would have had little opportunity to acquire much luster. Dolley's own niece started the story, perhaps for the same reason that biographers perpetuated it, from an inability to accept such a "frivolous" name for a lady so famous and held in such high regard. But "Dolley" appears on her birth certificate and in the few, full signatures we have of Dolley's, most notably on her marriage certificates and wills. So Dolley she is. (For the best summation of this historical confusion, see Ethel Stephens Arnett, *Mrs. James Madison: The Incomparable Dolley* [Greensboro: Piedmont Press, 1972], 9–12.)

PROLOGUE

1. Anthony S. Pitch, "The Burning of Washington," *White House History* 4 (Fall 1998): 9; Anthony S. Pitch, *The Burning of Washington: The British Invasion of 1814* (Annapolis, Md.: Naval Institute Press, 1998), 41–42.
2. DPTM to LPWT, 23 Aug. 1814, DMDE.
3. JM to DPTM, 23 Aug. [1814]; DPTM to LPWT, 23 Aug. 1814, DMDE.
4. DPTM to LPWT, 23 Aug. 1814, DMDE; Pitch, "Burning," 9.
5. DPTM to JPT, 6 Aug. [18]14, DMDE; Reginald Horsman, "War of 1812," in Eric Foner and John A. Garraty, eds., *The Reader's Companion to American History* (Boston: Houghton Mifflin, 1991), 1130; Pitch, *Burning*, 17–18, 22–23.
6. DPTM to LPWT, 23 Aug. 1814, DMDE; Paul A. Jennings, *A Colored Man's Reminiscences of James Madison*, www.whitehousehistory.org.
7. DPTM to LPWT, 23 Aug. 1814, DMDE; CM I, 55.
8. Jennings, *Reminiscences*; DPTM to LPWT, 23 Aug. 1814, DMDE; Lieutenant James Scott, cited in "Eyewitness Accounts of the Burning of the White House: They Were There," *White House History* 4 (Fall 1998): 56–57.
9. Charles J. Ingersoll, *Historical Sketch of the Second War Between the United States of American and Great Britain* (Philadelphia: Lea and Blanchard, 1849), vol. 2, 206–207.
10. See: David B. Mattern, "Dolley Madison Has the Last Word: The Famous Letter," *White House History* 4 (Fall 1998): 38–41. David B. Mattern and Holly C. Shulman, *The Selected Letters of Dolley Payne Madison* (Charlottesville: University of Virginia, 2003), 3–5.
11. John Adams to TJ, 2 February 1817, cited in Lester J. Cappon, ed., *The*

Adams-Jefferson Letters: The Complete Correspondence between Thomas Jefferson and Abigail and John Adams (Chapel Hill: University of North Carolina Press, 1959), vol. 2, 508.

12. Joanne B. Freeman, *Affairs of Honor: National Politics in the New Republic* (New Haven: Yale University Press, 2001), 213–23.

13. On Abigail Adams's role as political partner, see Edith B. Gelles, *Abigail Adams: A Writing Life* (New York: Routledge, 2002). Pinpointing exactly when the president's wife acquired the appellation is a matter of some scholarly dispute, but it was not in use in Dolley's time. Like the other spouses of upper-class men, president's wives had been called "Lady" from the start; in an era of erratic capitalization, the title was almost always capitalized when applied to this larger group of elite women. (It also appeared as a noun, as in "Mr. Madison's Lady.") A widespread popular notion, which has made its way into First Lady scholarship, was that "First Lady" was first used at Dolley's funeral by Zachary Taylor: "She will never be forgotten, because she was truly our First Lady for a half-century," but this cannot be documented. Edith P. Mayo, curator emeritus of the Division of Political History, National Museum of American History, Smithsonian Institution, and the historian responsible for the stunning reconceptualization of the popular First Ladies exhibit, connects the popularization of the term with a shift in the meaning of the word "lady," from an aristocratic address to a description of a proper, mannerly woman. She, along with Carl Sferrazza Anthony, point to a May 8, 1858, article in *Harper's Weekly*, that called Harriet Lane "Our Lady of the White House." Two years later, on March 31, 1860, *Frank Leslie's Illustrated Magazine* called her "First Lady." Oddly enough, Harriet was not the wife of President James Buchanan, but his niece and official hostess.

Certainly, by Lincoln's administration, the term was in use. The *New York Herald* and *Sacramento Union* dubbed Mary Todd Lincoln "First Lady." Carl Sferrazza Anthony has found such a reference in a letter from a German immigrant to his wife. According to Betty Boyd Caroli, a British journalist referred to Varina Davis as the "first lady of the Confederacy." By 1870, with the popular Julia Dent Grant, "First Lady" had entered the American lexicon, though Caroli and Margaret Truman did not find its first appearance in a dictionary until Merriam-Webster's second edition (1934). Edith P. Mayo, general editor, *The Smithsonian Book of the First Ladies* (New York: Henry Holt and Company, 1996), 34; Carl Sferrazza Anthony, *First Ladies: The Saga of the President's Wives and Their Power, 1789–1961* (New York: William Morrow and Company, 1990), 164, 618; Betty Boyd Caroli,

First Ladies (New York: Oxford University Press, 1987), xv; Margaret Truman, *First Ladies* (New York: Random House, 1995), 17–18.

14. *Daily National Intelligencer,* 14 July 1849, DM Papers, DLC.

I: MRS. MADISON GOES TO WASHINGTON

1. Irving Brant, *James Madison: Secretary of State* (Indianapolis: Bobbs-Merrill, 1953), 41; TJ to JM, 30 Apr. 1801, in *PJM-SS,* I, 126–27.

2. Brant, *SS,* 41–42; James Sterling Young, *The Washington Community, 1800–1828* (New York: Columbia University Press, 1966), 44, 46; MBS to JBK, 5 Oct. 1800, MBS Papers, DLC.

3. Christian Hines, *Early Recollections of Washington City* (originally published Washington, D.C., 1866; reprint, Washington, D.C.: Junior League of Washington, 1981), 17, 20–21.

4. EC to Hugh Blair Grigsby, 23 Dec. 1854, cited in Ralph Ketcham, *James Madison: A Biography* (Charlottesville: University of Virginia Press, 1990), 407. Edward may have had political reasons to exaggerate his mentor's size; some sources put James at five feet, four inches, and only 100 pounds.

5. SLM to CAM, 3 Jan. 1802, cited in "Dr. Mitchill's Letters From Washington," *Harper's New Monthly Magazine* 58 (Dec. 1878–May 1879): 743. Dolley's hair is most popularly described as black, but the sample of her hair, collected by her niece, Mary E. E. Cutts, and archived at the Massachusetts Historical Society, is a dark brown. Dolley's sister Mary Payne Jackson described her daughter, Lucy, as having "beautiful brown curls as much as Dolley's did." Mary Payne Jackson to APC, 20 July [1804], Cutts Microfilm, SCHL.

6. JM to TJ, 10 Jan. and 28 Feb. 1801, cited in Ketcham, *JM,* 405–406.

7. Kenneth R. Bowling, *Creating the Federal City, 1774–1800: Potomac Fever* (Washington, D.C.: American Institute of Architects Press, 1988), 23–37.

8. Joseph J. Ellis, *Founding Brothers: The Revolutionary Generation* (New York: Knopf, 2000), 48–50, 55–58; Constance McLaughlin Green, *Washington: Village and Capital, 1800–1878* (Princeton: Princeton University Press, 1972), 8–9; Stanley Elkins and Eric McKitrick, *The Age of Federalism: The Early American Republic* (New York: Oxford University Press, 1993); Elaine C. Everly and Howard H. Wehmann, "'Then Let Us to the Woods Repair': Moving the Federal Government and Its Records to Washington in 1800," in *Establishing Congress: The Removal to Washington, D.C., and the Election of 1800,* ed. Kenneth R. Bowling and Donald R. Kennon (Athens: Ohio University Press, 2005), 56–71.

9. Bob Arnebeck, *Through a Fiery Trial: Building Washington, 1790–1800*

(Lanham, Md.: Madison Books, 1991), 549–63; John Rhodehamel, "Washington's City," *White House History* 6 (fall 1999): 4–13.

10. On the standing of the Payne family, see: Virginia Historical Society, "The Payne Family of Goochland," *Virginia Magazine of History and Biography*, vols. 6, 7 (June, July 1899).

11. Frederick B. Tolles, *Quakers and the Atlantic Culture* (New York: Macmillan, 1960), 1–2; Margaret H. Bacon, *As the Way Opens: The Story of Quaker Women* (Richmond, Ind.: Friends United Press, 1980), 2–3; Carol and John Stoneburner, *The Influence of Quaker Women on American Society: Biographical Studies* (Lewiston, N.Y.: Edwin Mellen Press, 1887), 4.

12. Bacon, *Way,* 3–4; Frederick B. Tolles, *Meeting House and Counting House: The Quaker Merchants of Colonial Philadelphia, 1682–1763* (Chapel Hill: University of North Carolina Press, 1948), 8. Carol and John Stoneburner assert that the "quaking" was a reaction to the introspective process, which might "expos[e] a considerable amount of distressing self-knowledge." *Influence,* 8.

13. William Wade Hinshaw, ed., Encyclopedia of American Quaker Genealogy (Ann Arbor, Mich.: Edwards Brothers, Inc., 1950), 262; William Wade Hinshaw, Encyclopedia of American Quaker Genealogy (Baltimore, Md.: Genealogical Publishing, 1978), vol. 1, 565; "New Garden Monthly Minutes" (Men's), 30 Nov. 1765, Guilford College Library.

14. J. Hector John DeCrevecoeur, *Letters from an American Farmer,* cited in Ethel Stephens Arnett, *Mrs. James Madison: The Incomparable Dolley* (Greensboro, N.C.: Piedmont Press, 1972), 3; Hinshaw, *Genealogy,* vol. 1, 512; New Garden Monthly Minutes, 1: 29, Guilford College Library. For a discussion of the log cabin and its subsequent history, see Arnett, *Incomparable,* 7–8.

15. New Garden Monthly Minutes (Men's), 25 Feb. 1769, Guilford College Library; Arnett, *Incomparable,* 15–16; David B. Mattern and Holly C. Shulman, *The Selected Letters of Dolley Payne Madison* (Charlottesville: University of Virginia Press, 2003), 10–11; DPTM to MBS, 31 Aug. 1834, DMDE. Mary Cutts repeated the obfuscations as well; see CM I, 5.

16. Arnett, *Incomparable,* 17–20; CM I, 5.

17. Mary Payne may have had as many as three children who died in infancy. Ella Kent Barnard, *Dorothy Payne, Quakeress: A Side-Light Upon the Career of "Dolly" Madison* (Philadelphia: Ferris & Leach, 1909), 33.

18. For Quakers and slavery, see chapter 7 in Jay Worrall, *The Friendly Virginians: America's First Quakers* (Athens, Ga.: Iberian Publishing, 1994); Hiram H. Hilty, *By Land and by Sea: Quakers Confront Slavery and Its Aftermath in North Carolina* (Greensboro: North Carolina Friends Historical Society, 1993). For Philadelphia in this era, see Susan Branson, *These Fiery Frenchified*

Dames: Women and Political Culture in Early National Philadelphia (Philadelphia: University of Pennsylvania Press, 2001) and Daniel Kilbride, "Philadelphia and the Southern Elite: Class, Kinship, and Culture in Antebellum America," Ph.D. diss., University of Florida, 1997.

19. Mattern and Shulman, *SL*, 13–14.
20. Anthony Morris to Annie Payne, 26 June 1837, *Records of the Columbia Historical Society,* 44–45 (1942–43): 217–20.
21. W. Jay Mills, *Historic Houses of New Jersey* (Philadelphia: J. B. Lippincott, 1902), 328.
22. Later in life, Dolley would say that she was "educated in Philadelphia," but did not supply details. DPTM to MBS, 31 Aug. 1834, DMDE.
23. Anonymous, "Hammond memoir," n.d., n.p., *PJM,* UVA.
24. CM I, 6–7.
25. CM I, 8.
26. CM I, 8–9.
27. Barnard, *Quakeress,* 65–66.
28. Allen C. Clark, *The Life and Letters of Dolly Madison* (Washington, D.C.: W. F. Roberts, 1914), 14.
29. Todd House Furnishing Plan, Independence National Historical Park, Philadelphia, Office of History Collection, Box 26; Conover Hunt-Jones, *Dolley and the "Great Little Madison"* (Washington, D.C.: American Institute of Architects Foundation, 1977), 10.
30. Mattern and Shulman, *SL,* 14.
31. John Todd, Jr., to DPT, 30 July 1793, DMDE.
32. www.sas.upenn.edu~yehchrisyellowfever.html. For the Yellow Fever Plague of 1793, see J. Worth Estes and Billy G. Smith, eds., *A Melancholy Scene of Devastation: The Public Response to the 1793 Philadelphia Yellow Fever Epidemic* (Canton, Mass.: Science History Publications, 1997); Paul G. Sifton, "'What a Dread Prospect . . .': Dolley Madison's Plague Year," *Pennsylvania Magazine of History and Biography* 87 (1963): 182–88. See also: J. H. Powell, *Bring Out Your Dead: The Great Plague of Yellow Fever in 1793* (Philadelphia: University of Pennsylvania Press, 1993).
33. CM I, 10; James Todd to William Linn, 9 Dec. 1793, cited in Sifton, "Dread," 183–85; Mattern and Shulman, *SL,* 15.
34. Mary Coles Payne to Amey, c. 25 Oct. 1794, W. Parsons Todd Collection, Independence National Historical Park.
35. CM I, 13; Mattern and Shulman, *SL,* 16; Ketcham, *JM,* 378.
36. www.sas.upenn.edu~yehchrisyellowfever.html.
37. John Todd, Jr.'s will, cited in Arnett, *Incomparable,* 53.
38. DPTM to James Todd, [28, 31 Oct. 1793, 7 Feb. 1794], DMDE.

2: MEETING MADISON

1. CM I, 13–14; Catharine Coles to DPT, 1 June 1794, DMDE.
2. CM I, 14.
3. CM I, 14; Ralph Ketcham, *James Madison: A Biography* (Charlottesville: University of Virginia Press, 1990), 108–111; Ethel Stephens Arnett, *Mrs. James Madison: The Incomparable Dolley* (Greensboro, N.C.: Piedmont Press, 1972), 56.
4. SLM to CAM, 3 Jan. 1802, cited in "Dr. Mitchill's Letters From Washington," *Harper's New Monthly Magazine* 58 (Dec. 1878–May 1879), 743; Irving Brant, *James Madison: Father of the Constitution, 1787–1800* (Indianapolis: Bobbs-Merrill, 1950), 343.
5. Catharine Coles to DPT, 1 June 1794. Thanks to Holly C. Shulman for her thoughts on James's "Campaign."
6. The literature on republicanism is extensive. For a sampling, see Lance Banning, *The Jeffersonian Persuasion: Evolution of a Party Ideology* (Ithaca: Cornell University Press, 1978); Richard Buel, Jr., *Securing the Revolution: Ideology in American Politics, 1789–1815* (Ithaca: Cornell University Press, 1972); Stanley Elkins and Eric McKitrick, *The Age of Federalism: The Early American Republic* (New York: Oxford University Press, 1993); Joseph J. Ellis, *Founding Brothers: The Revolutionary Generation* (New York: Knopf, 2000); Gordon S. Wood, *The Radicalism of the American Revolution* (New York: Knopf, 1992).
7. CM I, 15–16.
8. Maude Wilder Goodwin, *Dolly Madison* (New York: Scribner's, 1896), 14.
9. JM to DPTM, 18 Aug. 1794, DMDE.
10. Ketcham, *JM*, 381–82; DPTM to Eliza Collins Lee, 16 Sept. 1794. The rest of the letter is torn, so we don't know what, if anything, Dolley added to clarify the "Alass!"
11. Brother Isaac had also been expelled for immorality, as had William Temple for joining the army.
12. Drew R. McCoy, *The Last of the Fathers: James Madison and the Republican Legacy* (Cambridge, U.K.: Cambridge University Press, 1989), 20–22; Paul A. Jennings, *A Colored Man's Reminiscences of James Madison*, www.whitehousehistory.org.
13. JM to James Todd, 17 Jan. 1795, *PJM*, 15: 457. Isaac was shot during an altercation; the cause of William Temple's death is unknown.
14. Judith Apter Klinghoffer and Lois Elkins, "'The Petticoat Electors': Women's Suffrage in New Jersey, 1776–1807," *Journal of the Early Republic* 12:2 (summer 1992): 159–93; Linda K. Kerber, "The Paradox of Women's Citizenship in the Early Republic: The Case of *Martin vs. Massachusetts,*

1805," *American Historical Review* (April 1992), 25; Jan Lewis, "The Republican Wife," *William and Mary Quarterly* 44 (Oct. 1987), 689, 701–2, 710; Ruth Bloch, "The Gendered Meanings of Virtue in Revolutionary America," *Signs* 13 (Autumn 1987), 46.

15. Rosemarie Zagarri, "Morals, Manners, and the Republican Mother," *American Quarterly* 44 (June 1992): 195, 199, 201–2, 204–5. See also Zagarri, "American Women's Rights Before Seneca Falls," in *Feminism and the Enlightenment*, ed. Barbara Taylor and Sarah Knott (New York: Palgrave, forthcoming); and Zagarri, "Women and Party Conflict in the Early Republic," in *Beyond the Founders: Essays in the New Political History of the Early Republic*, ed. Jeffrey L. Pasley, David Waldstreicher, and Andrew Robertson (Chapel Hill: University of North Carolina Press, forthcoming).

16. Fredrika J. Teute and David S. Shields, "Jefferson in Washington: Domesticating Manners in the Republican Court," Institute of Early American History and Culture Third Annual Conference, 1997, 11–17; Susan Branson, *These Fiery Frenchified Dames: Women and Political Culture in Early National Philadelphia* (Philadelphia: University of Pennsylvania Press, 2001), 133–40.

17. Elkins and McKitrick, *Federalism*, 513–28; Joanne B. Freeman, *Affairs of Honor: National Politics in the New Republic* (New Haven: Yale University Press, 2001), 213–15. Until the passage of the Twelfth Amendment in 1804, the man who received the second highest number of votes—whether in the state elections or in the House—became vice president. The rule changed after the election of 1800, when Thomas Jefferson and Aaron Burr were tied for president.

18. On the collaboration, see Ellis, *Brothers*, 171–74. On Montpelier, see Montpelier Visitors Guide, www.montpelier.org.

19. Freeman, *Affairs*, 230.

3: LADY ABOUT TOWN

1. AG to HNG, 15, 22 Jan. 1801, AG Papers, NYHS; Henry Adams, *Life of Albert Gallatin* (Philadelphia: J. B. Lippincott, 1879), 252–53. According to Earman, the term "mess" to refer to an eating group dates from the fifteenth century; it also came to include military dining groups. Cynthia Diane Earman, "Boardinghouses, Parties and the Creation of a Political Society: Washington City, 1800–1830," M.A. thesis, Louisiana State University and Agricultural and Mechanical College, 1992, 19.

2. TJ to MJR, 28 May 1801, Edwin Morris Betts and James A. Bear, eds., *The Family Letters of Thomas Jefferson* (Charlottesville: University of Virginia Press, 1986), 202.

3. Now Washington Circle. Ralph Ketcham, *James Madison: A Biography* (Charlottesville: University of Virginia Press, 1990), 409; William Thornton to JM, 16 March 1801, *PJM-SS*.

4. TJ to Martha Jefferson Randolph, 28 May, and TJ to Mary Jefferson Eppes, 28 May 1801, Betts and Bear, *Family Letters,* 202–203.

5. MBS to MBB, 28 May 1801, MBS Papers, DLC.

6. Ketcham, *JM,* 415, 409; Conover Hunt-Jones, *Dolley and the "Great Little Madison"* (Washington, D.C.: American Institute of Architects Foundation, 1977), 22; JM to William Thornton, 8 August 1801; William Thornton to JM, 15 August 1801, *PJM-SS*.

7. Barbara Carson, *Ambitious Appetites: Dining, Behavior, and Patterns of Consumption in Federal Washington* (Washington, D.C.: American Institute of Architects Press, 1990), 2; Earman, "Boardinghouses," 6, 7; James Sterling Young, *The Washington Community, 1800–1828* (New York: Columbia University Press, 1966), 2, 8–9, 78–82; Joseph J. Ellis, *American Sphinx: The Character of Thomas Jefferson* (New York: Knopf, 1993), 171–73; Howard Gillette, Jr., "Introduction," in *Southern City, National Ambition: The Growth of Early Washington, D.C.,* ed. Howard Gillette, Jr. (Washington, D.C.: American Institute of Architects Press, 1995), iii–v; Sarah Luria, *Capital Speculations: Writing and Building Washington, D.C.* (Durham: University of New Hampshire Press, 2005), 3–37.

8. Constance McLaughlin Green, *Washington: Village and Capital, 1800–1878* (Princeton: Princeton University Press, 1972), 21; Kathryn Allamong Jacob, "High Society in Washington During the Gilded Age: Three Distinct Aristocracies," Ph.D. diss., Johns Hopkins University, 1986, 8; Carson, *Appetites,* 3–4.

9. Carson, *Appetites,* 2; Earman, "Boardinghouses," 9–11; Christian Hines, *Early Recollections of Washington City* (originally published Washington, D.C., 1866; reprint, Washington, D.C.: Junior League of Washington, 1981), 20–21. On early housing among the elite, see Bernard L. Herman, "Southern City, National Ambition: Early Town Houses," in *Southern City,* 21–46; Elaine C. Everly and Howard H. Wehmann, "'Then Let Us to the Woods Repair': Moving the Federal Government and Its Records to Washington in 1800," in *Establishing Congress: The Removal to Washington, D.C., and the Election of 1800,* ed. Kenneth R. Bowling and Donald R. Kennon (Athens: Ohio University Press, 2005), 66.

10. Ebenezer Mattoon to Thomas Dwight, Dwight-Howard Collection, MHS; AJF, *Jeffersonian America: Notes on the United States of America,* ed. Richard Beale Davis (San Marino, Calif.: Huntingdon Library, 1954), 120.

11. Lady Emmeline Stuart Wortley, *Travels in the United States during 1849*

and 1850 (New York: Harper & Brothers, 1851), 82; Job Pierson to Sarah Pierson, 1 Dec. 1831, Job Pierson Papers, DLC.

12. Gillette, "Introduction," iii; Green, *Washington*, vii. "Permanent seat of empire" comes from an 1810 House of Representatives committee report on a petition for banking charters. Cited in Green, *Washington*, 33–34. Henry Adams, *History of the United States During the Administration of Thomas Jefferson* (New York: Albert and Charles Boni, 1930), vol. 1, 23–24; Kathryn Allamong Jacob, *Capital Elites: High Society in Washington, D.C., After the Civil War* (Washington, D.C.: Smithsonian Institution Press, 1995), 2–3; Young, *WC*, 26–27; "Temple of Liberty," catalog for the exhibit "Building the Capital for a New Nation," Library of Congress, Madison Gallery, 24 February–24 June 1995, 2–3. Contrary to popular notions, and though undoubtedly semitropical, especially in the summer, Washington, D.C., is *not* located in a swamp. See Kenneth R. Bowling, *The Creation of Washington, D.C.* (Fairfax, VA: George Mason University Press, 1991), 237–38.

13. Abigail Smith Adams to Mary Smith Cranch, 21 Nov. 1800, APM, MHS.

14. LCJA to JQA, 16 and 22 Sept. 1801, APM, MHS.

15. MBS, "National Portrait Gallery," 20; JQA, "Diary," 11 Jan. 1805, 13 Feb. 1806, APM, MHS; Washington Irving to H. Brevoort, 13 Jan. 1811, cited in Irving Brant, *James Madison: The President, 1809–1812* (Indianapolis: Bobbs-Merrill, 1959), 239.

16. CM II, 3.

17. See Sarah Luria, *Capital Speculations: Writing and Building Washington, D.C.* (Lebanon, N.H.: University of New England Press, 2005), 32; Mary Beth Corrigan, "The Ties That Bind: The Pursuit of Community and Freedom Among Slaves and Free Blacks in the District of Columbia, 1800–1860," in *Southern City*, 69–90.

18. Carson, *Appetites*, 7–9; Elizabeth Ellet, *Court Circles of the Republic* (Hartford: Hartford Publishing Co., 1869), 80–81; Fredric Cople Jaher, *The Urban Establishment: Upper Strata in Boston, New York, Charleston, Chicago, and Los Angeles* (Urbana: University of Illinois Press, 1982), 9; Jacob, *Elites*, 3, 8–9. For a good discussion of the "we"s and "they"s of Washington City, see Jacob, *Elites*, 29–33.

19. Holly Shulman describes Washington's social and political circles as "layers of intensity . . . and concentric rings of inclusiveness." David B. Mattern and Holly C. Shulman, *The Selected Letters of Dolley Payne Madison* (Charlottesville: University of Virginia Press, 2003), 42.

20. Marshal Smelser, *The Democratic Republic, 1810–1815* (New York: Harper & Row, 1968), 125; CM II, 12.

21. Jacob, *Elites*, 3, 5, 8–9.

22. Green, *Washington*, 28–39; Jacob, *Elites*, 8. For a good account of the governance relationship, see: William C. diGiacomantonio, "'To Make Hay while the Sun Shines': D.C. Governance as an Episode in the Revolution of 1800," in *Establishing Congress: The Removal to Washington, D.C., and the Election of 1800*, ed. Kenneth R. Bowling and Donald R. Kennon (Athens: Ohio University Press, 2005), 29–55.

23. Susan L. Klaus, "'Some of the Smartest Folks Here': The Van Nesses and Community Building in Early Washington," *Washington History*, vol. 3, no. 2 (Fall/Winter 1991–1992): 24, 31–32, 37.

24. For more on the Thorntons, see Allen C. Clark, "Dr. and Mrs. William Thornton," *Records of the Columbia Historical Society* 18 (1915): 144–208; C. M. Harris and Daniel Preston, *Papers of William Thornton: 1781–1802* (Charlottesville: University of Virginia Press, 1995); C. M. Harris, "The Politics of Public Building: William Thornton and President's Square," *White House History* 3 (spring 1998): 46–59.

25. Ethel Stephens Arnett, *Mrs. James Madison: The Incomparable Dolley* (Greensboro, N.C.: Piedmont Press, 1972), 148.

26. Anna Maria Brodeau Thornton to DPTM, 24 Aug. 1802, DMDE. The portrait Stuart repudiated was, of course, the one that Dolley would risk her life to save in 1814.

27. Aaron Burr to James Monroe, 10 Mar. 1796, TJ to Benjamin Hawkins, 14 Mar. 1801, cited in Ketcham, *JM*, 387.

28. Much of what historians know about early Washington comes from her pen. Margaret Bayard Smith is receiving long-deserved scholarly attention from scholars such as independent scholar Rose Barquist, Fredrika J. Teute, editor of publications, Omohundro Institute of Early American History and Culture, and Susan H. Perdue, associate editor, *Papers of Thomas Jefferson: Retirement Series.*

29. MBS to JBK, 23 April 1820, MBS Papers, DLC.

30. Klaus, "'Smartest ,'" 23, 45.

31. Earman, "Boardinghouses," 6–7, 33–34, 36, 45–48; Young, *WC*, xii, 2, 9. See also: George Thacher to Sarah Thacher, Thacher Family Papers, April–Dec. 1800, MHS.

32. Young, *WC*, 75; Carson, *Appetites*, 2. For a good account of boardinghouse life, see Cynthia D. Earman, "Messing Around: Entertaining and Accommodating Congress, 1800–1830," in *Establishing Congress: The Removal to Washington, D.C., and the Election of 1800*, ed. Kenneth R. Bowling and Donald R. Kennon (Athens: Ohio University Press, 2005), 128–47.

33. Young, *WC*, 49–64. For the best depictions of the political culture, see

Joseph L. Ellis, *Founding Brothers: The Revolutionary Generation* (New York: Knopf, 2000), and Joanne B. Freeman, *Affairs of Honor: National Politics in the New Republic* (New Haven: Yale University Press, 2001).

34. Thomas Dwight to Hannah Dwight, Dec. 1804, Dwight-Howard Collection, MHS.

35. Legislators and government officials had brought wives to the previous capitals. For an absorbing account of one such relationship, see: William C. diGiacomantonio, "A Congressional Wife at Home: The Case of Sarah Thatcher, 1787–1792" in *Congress at Philadelphia. 1791–1800*, ed. Donald R. Kennon (Athens: Ohio University Press, forthcoming). William Plumer, *William Plumer's Memorandum of Proceedings in the United States Senate, 1803–1807*, ed. Everett S. Brown (New York: Da Capo Press, 1969), 634.

36. Young, *WC*, 219.

37. Jacob, *Elites*, 24–25; AJF, *Jeffersonian America: Notes on the United States of America*, ed. Richard Beale Davis (San Marino, Calif.: Huntington Library, 1954), 47; RSC to HJS (father), 21 June 1805, cited in Rosalie Stier Calvert, *Mistress of Riversdale: The Plantation Letters of Rosalie Stier Calvert*, ed. and trans. Margaret Law Callcott (Baltimore: Johns Hopkins University Press, 1991), 122–23.

38. MBS to JBK, 28 June 1801, MBS Papers, DLC.

39. AJF, *Notes*, 155; Peder Blicherolsen to JM, 21 June 1803, *PJM-SS*.

40. DPTM to AC, 22 May 1805, DMDE.

41. DPTM to AC, 4 June 1805, DMDE.

42. DPTM to APC, 26 April 1804, DMDE; Brant, *SS*, 205–206. Many thanks to J. C. A. Stagg and David B. Mattern for their insights on this episode.

4: SOCIAL WORK

1. AA to Abigail Adams Smith, 27 Nov. 1800, APM; Elizabeth Ellet, *Court Circles of the Republic* (Hartford: Hartford Publishing Company, 1869), 63–64; Fredrika J. Teute and David S. Shields, "Jefferson in Washington: Domesticating Manners in the Republican Court," Institute of Early American History and Culture 3rd Annual Conference, 1997, 19.

2. "Alien and Sedition Acts" in Eric Foner and John A. Garraty, eds., *The Readers Companion to American History* (Boston: Houghton Mifflin, 1991), 26–27; Stanley Elkins and Eric McKitrick, *The Age of Federalism: The Early American Republic, 1788–1800* (New York: Oxford University Press, 1993) 590–93, 700–01. Also see James Morton Smith, *Freedom's Fetters: The Alien and Sedition Laws and American Civil Liberties* (Ithaca: Cornell University Press, 1966).

3. Joseph J. Ellis, *American Sphinx: The Character of Thomas Jefferson* (New

York: Knopf, 1993), 178–81; *Connecticut Courant*, 20 Sept. 1800, cited in Charles O. Lerche, "Jefferson and the Election of 1800: A Case Study in the Political Smear," *William and Mary Quarterly*, vol. 5, no. 4 (October 1948): 480. For the latest scholarship on the election of 1800, see Bruce Ackerman, *The Failure of the Founding Fathers: Jefferson, Marshall, and the Rise of Presidential Democracy* (Cambridge, Mass.: Belknap Press, 2005); Cal Jillson, "Fighting for Control of the American Dream," in *Establishing Congress: The Removal to Washington, D.C., and the Election of 1800*, ed. Kenneth R. Bowling and Donald R. Kennon (Athens: Ohio University Press, 2005), 17–20; John H. Aldrich, "The Election of 1800: The Consequences of the First Change in Party Control," in Bowling and Kennon, *Establishing*, 23–38; Elkins and McKitrick, *Federalism*, 741–54.

4. Ellis, *Sphinx*, 182. Under Jefferson, prosecution under the Alien and Sedition Acts ceased, though the laws remained on the books and were sporadically enforced in the future.

5. Ellis, *Sphinx*, 198–200.

6. AJF, *Jeffersonian America: Notes on the United States of America*, ed. Richard Beale Davis (San Marino, Calif.: Huntingdon Library, 1954), 155; Ellis, *Sphinx*, 136–37; Joseph J. Ellis, *Founding Brothers: The Revolutionary Generation* (New York: Knopf, 2003), 139–43.

7. Richard L. Bushman, *The Refinement of America: Persons, Houses, Cities* (New York: Knopf, 1992), xiv, 52–58.

8. See Jan Lewis, "'The Blessings of Domestic Society': Thomas Jefferson's Family and the Transformation of American Politics," in Peter S. Onuf, ed., *Jeffersonian Legacies* (Charlottesville: University of Virginia Press, 1993), 109–46.

9. Ellis, *Sphinx*, 178–80, 184–86, 198–99.

10. See Linda Kerber, *Women of the Republic: Intellect and Ideology in Revolutionary America* (Chapel Hill: University of North Carolina Press, 1980); Mary Beth Norton, *Liberty's Daughters: The Revolutionary Experience of American Women, 1750–1800* (Boston: Little, Brown, 1980); Ruth Bloch, "The Gendered Meanings of Virtue in Revolutionary America," *Signs* 13 (Autumn 1987), 37–59; Jan Lewis, "The Republican Wife," *William and Mary Quarterly* 44 (Oct. 1987), 689–721; Carole Pateman, "The Disorder of Women," *Ethics* 91 (October 1980): 20–34.

11. AA to JA, 31 March 1776; JA to AA, 14 Apr. 1776, APM. Though John seemed to dismiss Abigail's concern, the contradiction worried him and he discussed his concern with James Sullivan. JA to James Sullivan, 26 May 1776, APM, MHS.

12. TJ to George Washington, 4 November 1788, *PTJ*.

13. TJ to Anne Willing Bingham, 11 May 1788, *PTJ*. See also TJ to Anne Willing Bingham, 7 Feb. 1781, TJ to Angelica Church, 21 Sept. 1788, *PTJ*.

14. Ellis, *Sphinx*, 170–71. On the interdependence of style and substance in republican theory, see: Lance Banning, *The Jeffersonian Persuasion: Evolution of a Party Ideology* (Ithaca: Cornell University Press, 1978), 59, 83, 117–18, 121, 183, 227.

15. Dumas Malone, *Jefferson the President: First Term, 1801–1805* (Boston: Little, Brown, 1970), 374–76; Henry Adams, *History of the United States During the Administration of Thomas Jefferson* (New York: Albert and Charles Boni, 1930), vol. 2, 363–64; Merrill D. Peterson, *Thomas Jefferson and the New Nation: A Biography* (New York: Oxford University Press, 1970), 725–30; James Sterling Young, *The Washington Community, 1800–1828* (New York: Columbia University Press, 1966), 167–69.

16. Marshall Smelser, *The Democratic Republic, 1810–1815* (New York: Harper & Row, 1968), 3; Ellis, *Sphinx*, 190–91; Young, *WC*, 168–70, 190–91; Joanne B. Freeman, *Affairs of Honor: National Politics in the New Republic* (New Haven: Yale University Press, 2001), 63–66, 86–87; Teute and Shields, "Manners," 20–24; John Trumbull, *The Autobiography of Colonel John Trumbull, Patriot-Artist, 1756–1843*, ed. Theodore Sizer (New Haven: Yale University Press, 1953), 173–75; Young, *WC*, 169. Special thanks to Joanne B. Freeman.

17. William Plumer, 1 Jan. 1806, cited in William Plumer, *William Plumer's Memorandum of Proceedings in the United States Senate, 1803–1807*, ed. Everett S. Brown (New York: Da Capo Press, 1969), 363; Teute and Shields, "Manners," 20–21; William Plumer to Sally Fowler Plumer, cited in William Plumer, Jr., *Life of William Plumer* (Boston: Phillips, Sampson and Co., 1856), 246.

18. William Plumer, cited in Teute and Shields, "Manners," 22–23; James Roger Sharp, *American Politics in the Early Republic: The New Nation in Crisis* (New Haven: Yale University Press, 1993), 279–83.

19. CM II, 2; MBS, "Mrs. Madison," in *The National Portrait Gallery of Distinguished Americans*, James B. Longacre and James Herring, eds., vol. 3 (New York: Hermon Bancroft, 1836), 21.

20. JQA, "Diary," 11 Jan. 1805, 13 Feb. 1806, APM. See also Shields and Teute, "Manners," 24–25. For a favorable account of a Jefferson dinner, but with women, see MBS to MB, 28 May 1801, MBS Papers, DLC.

21. Samuel Harrison Smith to MBS, 26 April 1803, MBS Papers, DLC.

22. William Parker Cutler and Julia Perkins Cutler, *Life Journals and Correspondence of Rev. Manasseh Cutler, LL.D.* (Athens, Oh.: Ohio University Press, 1987), 154.

23. CAM to MAM, 8 April 1806, CAM Papers, DLC.

24. AJF, *Notes*, 88; SHS to MBS, 5 July 1803, MBS Papers. DLC. Thanks to Sarah Hagan for explaining loo.

25. DPTM to AC, May–June 1804, DMDE.

26. CM II, 10.

27. In regard to politics, according to Henry Adams, Jefferson "shrank from whatever was rough or coarse, and his yearning for sympathy was almost feminine." Henry Adams, *History*, vol. 1, 144; II: 439. See also Ellis, *Sphinx*, 89–90, 120, 136, 146–47, 226–27.

28. See also Shields and Teute, "Manners," 28.

29. DPTM to ECL, 6 Jan. 1803, DMDE; Harrison Gray Otis to Sally Foster Otis, 10 March 1801, Harrison Gray Otis Papers, MHS.

5: THE MERRY AFFAIR

1. Elizabeth Merry to Thomas Moore, n.d. [after 26 November 1803], in Thomas Moore, *Memoirs, Journal, and Correspondence*, ed. Lord John Russell (London: Longman, Brown, Green, and Longman, 1853–56), vol. 8, 50–52; Anthony Merry to George Hammond, 7 December 1803, cited in Malcolm Lester, *Anthony Merry Redivivus: A Reappraisal of the British Minister to the United States, 1803–6* (Charlottesville: University of Virginia Press, 1978), 18.

2. Interestingly, Mary Cutts wrote that Jefferson had decided on this course of action upon hearing Elizabeth Merry's intention of teaching the Americans some manners. He "secured Mrs. Madison's promise to dine with him the next day at a State Dinner." But even from this account, it is not clear that Dolley knew what he would do, while Jefferson's premeditated focus on Elizabeth, not Anthony, Merry is clear. CM II, 9. Lester, *Redivivus*, 25.

3. Ibid., 24–25; Philadelphia *Aurora*, 25 Nov. 1802, cited in ibid., 24.

4. TJ to William Short, 23 Jan. 1804, *PTJ*.

5. AJF to Elizabeth Foster, 30 Dec. 1804, AJF Papers, DLC; Anthony Merry to Lord Hawkesbury, 6 Dec. 1804, Foreign Office communication cited in Lester, *Redivivus*, 33.

6. Anthony Merry to Lord Hawkesbury, 6 Dec. 1804, Foreign Office communication cited in Lester, *Redivivus*, 34; Benjamin Ogle Tayloe, *Our Neighbors on La Fayette Square* (originally published Washington, D.C., 1872; reprint, Washington, D.C.: Junior League of Washington, 1982), 73; AJF, *Jeffersonian America: Notes on the United States of America*, ed. Richard Beale Davis (San Marino, Calif.: Huntingdon Library, 1954), 52; CM II, 9.

7. Louis André Pichon to Charles Maurice Talleyrand-Périgord, 5 February 1804, cited in Henry Adams, *History of the United States During the Administration of Thomas Jefferson* (New York: Albert and Charles Boni,

1930), vol. 2, 552. Since the chargé of Denmark had not been invited, this was not a full diplomatic dinner, to which the whole corps would have been invited. Jefferson did not invent the *pêle-mêle* style; it was a social option used by courts in certain specific situations.

8. Anthony Merry to George Hammond, 7 December 1803, cited in Adams, *History*, vol. 2, 547; Louis André Pichon to Charles Maurice Talleyrand-Périgord, 5 February 1804, cited in Adams, *History*, vol. 2, 552; TJ to William Short, 23 Jan. 1804, *PTJ*.

9. Anthony Merry to George Hammond, 7 December 1803, cited in Adams, *History*, vol. 2, 547; Dumas Malone, *Jefferson the President: First Term, 1801-1805* (Boston: Little, Brown and Co., 1970), 379-80; ASF, *Notes*, 52.

10. Irving Brant, *James Madison: Secretary of State* (Indianapolis: Bobbs-Merrill, 1953), 164-65.

11. TJ to AA, 22 Feb. 1787; TJ to William Smith, 13 Nov. 1787, *PTJ*. JM to Nicholas Trist, May 1832, cited in Drew R. McCoy, *Last of the Fathers: James Madison and the Republican Legacy* (Cambridge: Cambridge University Press, 1989), 144.

12. JM to Rufus King, 18 Dec. 1803, *PJM-SS*, 6: 186-87.

13. Ibid.; Rufus King to JM, 22 Dec. 1803, *PJM-SS*, 6: 197-99.

14. "Cannons of Etiquette," in *The Writings of Thomas Jefferson*, ed. Paul Leister Ford (New York: G. P. Putnam's Sons, 1892-99), vol. 10, 47-48; Lester, *Redivivus*, 39.

15. TJ to William Short, cited in Lester, *Redivivus*, 41.

16. MBS to JBK, 23 Jan. 1804, MBS Papers, DLC, 46-47; Malone, *First Term*, 383-84.

17. JM to James Monroe, 19 Jan. 1804, cited in David B. Mattern and Holly C. Shulman, *The Selected Letters of Dolley Payne Madison* (Charlottesville: University of Virginia Press, 2003), 44; JM to James Monroe, 26 Dec. 1803, *PJM-SS*; Brant, *SS*, 167-68.

18. JM to James Monroe, 16 Feb. 1804, *PJM-SS*; Anthony Merry to George Hammond, 7 Dec. 1804, cited in Lester, *Redivivus*, 36.

19. JM to James Monroe, 16 Feb. 1804, *PJM-SS*; Lester, *Redivivus*, 43-44.

20. On the first republican court, see Fredrika J. Teute and David S. Shields, "The Republican Court and the Historiography of a Woman's Domain in the Public Sphere," paper presented at SHEAR Annual Meeting, 1993; on Anne Willing Bingham, see Fredrika J. Teute and David S. Shields, "Jefferson in Washington: Domesticating Manners in the Republican Court," Institute of Early American History and Culture Third Annual Conference, 1997, 11-14.

21. Lester, *Redivivus*, 10.

22. MBS to JBK, 23 Jan. 1804, MBS Papers, DLC.

23. Ibid.

24. TJ to James Monroe, 8 January 1804, in Ford, *Writings,* vol. 8, 290–91.

25. Linda Colley, "The Female Elite in Unreformed Britain," Paper presented at Brown University, April 1995, 2.

26. *Philadelphia Gazette of the U.S.,* 17 Jan. 1801, cited in Lester, *Redivivus,* 40; Pichon to Talleyrand, 5 February 1804, cited in Malone, *First Term,* 381.

27. Lester, *Redivivus,* 40–41, 46–47; Augustus John Foster to Elizabeth Foster, 20 July 1806, AJF Papers, DLC.

28. *Washington Federalist,* 1 Feb. 1804, AAS. For more on the role of newspapers of the era, see Jeffrey L. Pasley, *"The Tyranny of Printers": Newspaper Politics in the Early American Republic* (Charlottesville: University of Virginia Press, 2001).

29. TJ to Martha Jefferson Randolph, 23 Jan. 1804 in Edwin Morris Betts and James A. Bear, eds., *The Family Letters of Thomas Jefferson* (Charlottesville: University of Virginia Press, 1986), 254–55.

30. Ethel Stephens Arnett, *Mrs. James Madison: The Incomparable Dolley* (Greensboro, NC: Piedmont Press, 1972), 95–96; Thomas Fleming, *The Man from Monticello* (New York: William Morrow, 1969), 279; Irving Brant, *James Madison: The President, 1809–1812* (Indianapolis: Bobbs-Merrill, 1959), 168; Brant, *SS,* 243.

31. Amanda Foreman, *Georgiana: Duchess of Devonshire* (New York: Modern Library, 2001), 140–47.

32. Lester, *Redivivus,* 46, 98–112.

33. Ibid., 50, 74, 87, 99–103; AJF, *Notes,* 281–82.

34. Lester, *Redivivus,* 38–39, 92.

35. Ibid., 96.

36. Ibid., 86–90.

37. Ibid., 82, 90, 97.

38. MBS, "Mrs. Madison," 20. Holly C. Shulman sees the hand of MBS in this famous quote.

39. DPTM to AC, 25 May 1804, DMDE.

40. DPTM to APC, 4 June 1805, DMDE; Edward Thornton to DPTM, ca. 1803–1804, Item #839, Alexander Autographs Auction Catalog. See also DPTM to APC, 27 Mar. 1807, DMDE.

41. On women, diplomacy, and foreign relations, see Cynthia Enloe, *Bananas, Beaches and Bases: Making Feminist Sense of International Politics* (Berkeley: University of California Press, 1990), 97; Rosemary Foot, "Where Are the Women? The Gender Dimension in the Study of International Relations," *Diplomatic History* 14 (Fall 1990): 621.

42. On the informal public, see Mary Beth Norton, *Founding Mothers and Fathers: Gendered Power and the Forming of American Society* (New York: Knopf, 1996), and Laurel Thatcher Ulrich, *Goodwives: Image and Reality in the Lives of Women in Northern New England, 1650–1750* (New York: Vintage, 1991). For more on female alternatives to traditional civil space, see: Kathleen M. Brown, "Tea Table Discourses and Slanderous Tongues: The Domestic Choreography of Female Identities" in *Good Wives, Nasty Wenches, and Anxious Patriarchs: Gender, Race, and Power in Colonial Virginia* (Chapel Hill: University of North Carolina Press, 1996); Karen V. Hansen, *A Very Social Time: Crafting Community in Antebellum New England* (Los Angeles: University of California Press, 1994); Cynthia A. Kierner, *Beyond the Household: Women's Place in the Early South, 1700–1835* (New York: Cornell University Press, 1998).

43. On the softening effect of women, see Jan Lewis, "'The Blessings of Domestic Society': Thomas Jefferson's Family and the Transformation of American Politics," in Peter S. Onuf, ed., *Jeffersonian Legacies* (Charlottesville: University of Virginia Press, 1993), 109–146; and Teute and Shields, "Manners."

6: PORTRAIT OF A LADY

1. DPTM to APC, 20 [ca. 8] May [1804], DMDE.

2. The account of Stuart comes from a letter to APC, found in the Cutts Family Papers, DLC. Since it is a transcription, Dolley herself may have written it. Emily Christine Burns, "Portraits of a First Lady: Images of Dolley Madison," M.A. thesis, George Washington University, 2005, 41–45; William Kloss, *Art in the White House: A Nation's Pride*, suppl.: *Acquisitions 1992–2002* (Washington, D.C.: DC WHHA, 2002), 6–7; Carrie Rebora Barratt and Ellen Miles, *Gilbert Stuart*, New York Metropolitan Museum of Art Catalog (New Haven: Yale University Press, 2004), 258–59; DPTM to AC, [ca. 8 May 1804], DMDE; Richard L. Bushman, *The Refinement of America: Persons, Houses, Cities* (New York: Knopf, 1992), 64; Fredrika J. Teute, "The Spectacle of Washington: Creating Public Celebrity in the New Nation," paper presented at Omohundro Institute of Early American History and Culture Annual Meeting, 2005. Dolley and James were lucky to have finished Stuart portraits. Stuart was a notorious procrastinator: the Adamses waited fifteen years for their finished product, Jefferson over twenty.

3. Bushman, *Refinement*, 57–60, 319–35.

4. MBS to JBK, 10 Dec. 1803, MBS Papers, DLC.

5. CM II, 19.

6. DPTM to APC, 18 May 1804, DMDE.

7. DPTM to APC, 20 May 1804, DMDE.

8. Carroll Smith-Rosenberg, "The Female World of Love and Ritual: Relations Between Women in Nineteenth-Century America," in *Disorderly Conduct: Visions of Gender in Victorian America* (New York: Oxford University Press, 1985), 64–66.

9. DPTM to APC, 26 Apr. 1804, DMDE.

10. DPTM to APC, 25, 8, 18, 20 May 1804; 26 April 1804, DMDE.

11. DPTM to APC, 26 Apr., 18 May 1804, DPTM to APC, [ca. 8 May 1804], DMDE.

12. DPTM to APC, 26 Apr. 1804, DMDE.

13. DPTM to APC, 4 June [1805], DMDE.

14. DPTM to APC, 8 July [1805], DMDE.

15. DPTM to JM, 23 Nov. [1805]; DPTM to APC, 19 Aug., 31 July, 8 July [1805]; DPTM to JM, 30 Oct. 1805, DMDE.

16. DPTM to APC, 29 July 1805, DMDE.

17. Ibid.

18. DPTM to APC, 19 Aug. [1805], DMDE.

19. DPTM to JM, 23 Oct. 1805; DPTM to JM, October 1793, DMDE.

20. DPTM to JM, 23 Oct. 1805; DPTM to APC, 19 Aug. [1805], DMDE.

21. DPTM to JM, 23, 26, 28, 30 Oct. 1805, DMDE.

22. JM to DPTM, 28, 31 Oct. 1805; DPTM to JM, 23 Oct. 1805, DMDE.

23. DPTM to JM, 1 Nov. 1805; DPTM to JM, 26 Oct. 1805, DMDE.

24. DPTM to JM, 2 Nov. 1805; JM to DM, 19–20 Nov. 1805, DMDE.

25. JM to DPTM, [ca. 2 Nov. 1805]; JM to DPTM, 19–20 Nov. 1805; DPTM to JM, 2 Nov. 1805, DMDE.

26. DPTM to APC, 19 Aug. 1805; DPTM to JM, [3 Nov. 1805], DMDE.

27. DPTM to JM, 1 Nov. 1805, DMDE.

28. JM to DPTM, 19–20 Nov. 1805; DPTM to JM, 23 Nov. [1805], DMDE.

29. JM to DPTM, 15 Nov. 1805, DMDE.

30. DPTM to JM, 12 Nov. 1805, DMDE.

31. Ibid.

32. DPTM to JM, 1 Nov. [1805], DMDE.

33. JM to DPTM, [6 Nov. 1805], DMDE.

34. Joanne B. Freeman, *Affairs of Honor: National Politics in the New Republic* (New Haven: Yale University Press, 2001), 144–45.

35. DPTM to JM, 1 Nov. [1805], DMDE. If a Washington neighbor, "Mrs. L." might have been Eliza Custis Law.

36. DPTM to JM, 15, 23 Nov. [1805], DMDE. See also DPTM to JM, 19–20 Nov. 1805, DMDE.

37. DPTM to Mary Coles Payne, Aug. 4 [1806], DMDE.

38. DPTM to an unidentified correspondent, 7 Nov. 1807, DMDE.

39. Isaac Winston III to DPTM, 30 Jan. 1808, DMDE.

40. DPTM to ECL, 26 Feb. 1808, DMDE.

41. David B. Mattern and Holly C. Shulman, *The Selected Letters of Dolley Payne Madison* (Charlottesville: University of Virginia Press, 2003), 15.

42. DPTM to APC, 3 June [1808], DMDE. See also DPTM to APC, 18 June [1807]; DPTM to APC, 3 June [1808], DMDE.

43. DPTM to APC, 5 May, 28 Aug. [1808], DMDE.

44. DPTM to APC, 28 Aug. [1808], DMDE.

7: SEX, LIES, AND THE ELECTION OF 1808

1. "Dr. Mitchill's Letters From Washington," *Harper's New Monthly Magazine* 58 (Dec. 1878–May 1879): 740–41.

2. SLM to CAM, 23 Nov. 1807, cited in ibid., 752.

3. "Embargo Act of 1807" in Eric Foner and John A. Garraty, eds., *The Reader's Companion to American History* (Boston: Houghton Mifflin, 1991), 352–53.

4. DPTM to APC, 28 Aug. 1808, DMDE.

5. Marshall Smelser, *The Democratic Republic, 1810–1815* (New York: Harper & Row, 1968), 168–69, 177.

6. Ibid., 176; Marshall Smelser, "The Federalist Period as an Age of Passion," *American Quarterly* 10 (Winter 1958), 400, 418.

7. Joseph J. Ellis, *American Sphinx: The Character of Thomas Jefferson* (New York: Knopf, 1993), 237–38.

8. Smelser, *DR*, 182.

9. SLM to CAM, 29 Jan. 1806, cited in Carolyn Hoover Sung, "Catharine Mitchill's Letters from Washington, 1806–1812," *The Quarterly Journal of the Library of Congress*, vol. 34, no. 3 (July 1977), 177.

10. SLM to CAM, 25 Jan. 1808, cited in "Letters," 752; Maria Beckley to Lucy Southall, 8 June 1808, Cutts Family Papers, DLC.

11. This would remain true until the electoral reforms of the Jacksonian Age. On caucuses, see Smelser, *DR*, 182, 318; Margaret Truman, *First Ladies: An Intimate Group Portrait of White House Wives* (New York: Random House, 1995), 21; Joanne B. Freeman, *Affairs of Honor: National Politics in the New Republic* (New Haven: Yale University Press, 2001), 237–41.

12. Freeman, *Affairs*, i–iv. See: Joseph J. Ellis, *Founding Brothers: The Revolutionary Generation* (New York: Knopf, 2000), 123–24.

13. Richard L. Bushman, Presentation at Historic Deerfield, July 1995; Smelser, *DR*, 318.

14. MBS, "Mrs. Madison," in *The National Portrait Gallery of Distinguished*

Americans, James B. Longacre and James Herring, eds., vol. 3 (New York: Hermon Bancroft, 1836), 21.

15. DPTM to Lucy Coles Winston, 9 Apr. [1807], DMDE.

16. Smelser, "Passion," 419; Andrew Burstein, *The Inner Jefferson: Portrait of a Grieving Optimist* (Charlottesville: University of Virginia Press, 1993), 203. For a thorough discussion of the honor culture, see Freeman, *Affairs.* Freeman contends that the fragile new republic was a "government of character striving to become a government of rules" (p. 69).

17. Smelser, "Age," 391–92, 418–19.

18. John G. Jackson to DPTM, 8 Oct. 1808, DMDE.

19. *Federal Republican,* 19 April 1814, AAS.

20. SLM to CAM, 1 Apr. 1808, cited in "Letters," 753; Ralph Ketcham, *James Madison: A Biography* (Charlottesville: University of Virginia Press, 1990), 467. These implications proved to have staying power. When Dolley became First Lady, a federal judge, Richard Peters, of Philadelphia, took delight in discussing "the [sexual] insatiability of democratic women" in discussing political prospects. He referred to Dolley as "the leader of the ceremonious flock . . . [who] carries with her if not the thing itself at least the appetites of the second of the four insatiable things mentioned in the thirtieth chapter of Proverbs, verse 16," that is, "the barren womb." Irving Brant, *James Madison: Secretary of State* (Indianapolis: Bobbs-Merrill, 1953), 243.

21. John Randolph to James Monroe, 16 Sept. 1806, cited in Brant, *SS,* 322.

22. JQA, "Diary," 1 Feb. 1806, APM, MHS; Irving Brant, *James Madison: Commander in Chief, 1812–1836* (Indianapolis: Bobbs-Merrill, 1961), 135.

23. Brant, *SS,* 243–44.

24. Anonymous, "Hammond Memoir," n.d., n.p., *PJM,* UVA.

25. Anna Maria Brodeau Thornton to DPTM, 21 Aug. 1809, DMDE. Other letters between the two women at this time are friendlier, but seem to lack the spontaneity of the earlier correspondence. See, e.g., DPTM to Anna Maria Brodeau Thornton, 26 Aug. [1807], DMDE. William Thornton also noted a "marked distance and coldness." Cited in Allen C. Clark, *Life and Letters of Dolley Madison* (Washington, D.C.: W. F. Roberts Co., 1914), 121.

26. *Intelligencer,* 4 July 1808, AAS; Brant, *SS,* 451; DPTM to APC, 3 June [1808], DMDE; Ketcham, *JM,* 460.

27. Cited in Brant, *SS,* 451.

28. SLM to CAM, 25 Jan. 1808, in "Letters," 752.

29. Carl Sferrazza Anthony, *First Ladies: The Saga of the Presidents' Wives and Their Power, 1789–1961* (New York: William Morrow, 1990), 80–81.

30. Subsequent secretaries of state and their families took advantage of the precedent that Dolley had created. Louisa Catherine Johnson Adams proved Dolley's successor in many ways. When she arrived in Washington City in 1817, she literally built upon Dolley's foundation to help her husband move from the position of secretary of state to that of president. Determined to be the town's leading family in their own right, the Adamses bought the Madison house on F street, making it campaign headquarters for the election of 1824. They immediately renovated the house, particularly the social spaces, allowing them to entertain large groups of legislators and their families. Their success was even more marked: John Quincy's election was decided in the House, where Louisa Catherine's guests made him president on the first ballot. No wonder that the author of *Etiquette at Washington City* declared that an invitation to a party at the house of the secretary of state was so prized, as it "is thought by many to be more honorable to be one of his guests, than to be at the president's levee." E. M. Cooley, *A Description of the Etiquette at Washington City* (Philadelphia: L. B. Clarke, 1829), 30. See Barbara Carson, *Ambitious Appetites: Dining, Behavior, and Patterns of Consumption in Federal Washington* (Washington, D.C.: American Institute of Architects Press, 1990), 151–53.

8: LADY PRESIDENTESS

1. CAM to MAM, 11 Dec. 1808, CAM Papers, DLC.
2. Ralph Ketcham, *James Madison: A Biography* (Charlottesville: University of Virginia Press, 1990), 474–75; Irving Brant, *James Madison: The President, 1809–1812* (Indianapolis: Bobbs-Merrill, 1959), 12–14; MBS to Susan Bayard Smith, 4 Mar. 1809, MBS Papers.
3. MBS, "Inaugurations," *Ladies' Magazine and Literary Gazette,* vol. 4, no. 12 (Dec. 1831): 529, 530.
4. Ibid., 532.
5. Ibid., 533; Sarah Ridg, "Diary," Sarah Ridg Papers, DLC, 8.
6. MBS, "Inaugurations," 533–34; MBS to Susan B. Smith, 4 March 1809, MBS Papers, DLC.
7. MBS, "Inaugurations," 536; MBS to Susan B. Smith, 4 March 1809, MBS Papers, DLC. Historians often credit Dolley with "giving" the first inaugural ball. The "first" claim is problematic—President Washington attended such a ball in New York on May 7, 1789, after his first swearing-in. However, the 1809 ball was the first in Washington City (Jefferson had eliminated them), and, in contrast to the New York event, the president's wife was present. Technically, however, the ball was not *given* by the presidential couple. The most significant aspect of this "first inaugural ball" is

that it was sponsored by the local gentry, and the Madisons' support of it
was part of a continuing pattern of community relations.

8. MBS, "Inaugurations," 536; MBS to Susan B. Smith, 4 March 1809, MBS Papers, DLC.

9. Ibid.; *National Intelligencer,* 4 March 1809, AAS.

10. MBS to Susan B. Smith, 4 March 1809, MBS Papers, DLC; MBS, "Inaugurations," 535. Senator Samuel Latham Mitchill referred to Dolley as both prospective "Presidentess" and "Lady President" in his letters to his wife. SLM to CAM, 25 January 1808 and 23 November 1807, CAM Papers, DLC. Some historians have changed it to "Presidentress." See Carl Sferrazza Anthony, *First Ladies: The Saga of the Presidents' Wives and Their Power, 1789–1961* (New York: Morrow, 1990), 611.

11. Anonymous, "Hammond Memoir," n.d., n.p., *PJM,* UVA.

12. On both women in politics and business as usual as well as the special apolitical status of white women, see Linda Colley, "The Female Elite in Unreformed Britain," Paper presented at Brown University, April 1995; Amanda Foreman, *Georgiana: Duchess of Devonshire* (New York: Modern Library, 2001), 28; Elizabeth R. Varon, *"We Mean to be Counted": White Women and Party Politics in Antebellum Virginia* (Chapel Hill: University of North Carolina Press, 1998); Rosemarie Zagarri, *Petticoat Government: Women and Politics from the American Revolution to the Age of Jackson* (forthcoming, Penguin Press). Janet L. Coryell has coined a term—the "woman politico." See *Neither Heroine Nor Fool: Anna Ella Carroll of Maryland* (Kent, OH: Kent State University Press, 1990).

13. DM to Ruth Barlow, c. 19 April 1812, DMDE. For example, see JM to Richard D. Cutts, 26 Nov. 1817, Madison-Cutts Collection, MHS.

14. For an early specimen of Dolley's secretarial participation, see "1794 Report on Fisheries." The most obvious manifestation of their political partnership would come from the public actions Dolley took on behalf of her husband and the subsequent benefits that James received. But though the couple's reluctance to spend time apart meant that they wrote few letters to each other, their correspondence from the presidential years demonstrates the centrality of politics to their lives.

15. JM to DPTM, 7 Aug. 1809, DMDE.

16. JM to DPTM, [9 Aug. 1809], DMDE.

17. James Sterling Young, *The Washington Community, 1800–1828* (New York: Columbia University Press, 1966), 157–59; AG to JM, cited in Young, *WC,* 181–82.

18. Brant, *President,* 211.

19. For discussions of James's style, see: Ketcham, *JM,* 470–72.

20. Young, *WC*, 74–75, 157–59, 174–78.

21. For Hamilton calling Jefferson "womanish," see Alexander Hamilton to Edward Carrington, 26 May 1792, Syrett and Cooke, *PAH*, 11:439. William Plumer implied the same: "Mr. Jefferson is too timid—too irresolute—too fickle—he wants nerve—he wants firmness and resolution." William Plumer, *William Plumer's Memorandum of Proceedings in the United States Senate, 1803–1807*, ed. Everett S. Brown (New York: Da Capo Press, 1969), 455; *Federal Republican*, 19 April, 3 June 1814, DLC.

22. Cited in Ethel Stephens Arnett, *Mrs. James Madison: The Incomparable Dolley* (Greensboro, NC: Piedmont Press, 1972), 110.

23. Ketcham, *JM*, 498.

24. Norman K. Risjord, "National Honor as the Unifying Force," in Bradford Perkins, ed., *The Causes of the War of 1812: National Honor or National Interest?* (New York: Holt, Rinehart & Winston, 1962), 86, 92.

25. Judith Walker Rives, "Autobiography," William Cabell Rives Papers, DLC, 60; Ketcham, *JM*, 436–37; Dumas Malone, *Jefferson the President: Second Term, 1805–1809* (Boston: Little, Brown, 1974), 105–106; Brant, *President*, 263.

26. Brant, *President*, 263–64; Cynthia A. Kierner, *Scandal at Bizarre: Rumor and Reputation in Jefferson's America* (New York: Palgrave Macmillan, 2004), 92–93.

27. CAM to MAM, 3 Apr. 1806, CAM Papers, DLC. On public women, see Fredrika J. Teute, "'A Wild, Desolate Place': Life in Early Washington" in *Southern City, National Ambition: The Growth of Early Washington, 1800–1860*, ed. Howard Gillette, Jr. (Washington, D.C.: American Institute of Architects Press, 1995), 52.

28. CAM to MAM, 28 Feb. 1809, CAM Papers, DLC. On John Randolph and his family, see Kierner, *Scandal*.

29. CM I, 37.

30. MBS to JBK, 13 March 1814, MBS Papers, DLC.

31. Jan Lewis, "Politics and the Ambivalence of the Private Sphere: Women in Early Washington," in *A Republic for the Ages: The United States Capitol and the Political Culture of the Early Republic*, ed. Donald R. Kennon (Charlottesville: University of Virginia Press, 1999), 134–45.

32. MBS to JBK, 13 March 1814, MBS Papers, DLC.

9: PRESIDING GENIUS

1. William Seale, *The President's House: A History* (Washington, D.C.: White House Historical Association, 1986), vol. 1, 111–18; Conover Hunt-Jones, *Dolley and the "Great Little Madison"* (Washington, D.C.: American Institute of

Architects Foundation, 1977), 29; Margaret Brown Klapthor, "Benjamin Latrobe and Dolley Madison Decorate the White House, 1809–1811," *United States National Museum Bulletin 241: Contributions from the Museum of History and Technology*, paper 49 (Washington: Smithsonian Institution, 1965), 156; Thomas Moore, cited in Hunt-Jones, "*Great,*" 29. See also Michael Fazio and Patrick Snadon, "Benjamin Latrobe and Thomas Jefferson Redesign the President's House," in *White House History*, 8 (fall 2000), 36–53.

2. James Sterling Young, *The Washington Community, 1800–1828* (New York: Columbia University Press, 1966), 5; Jack Shepherd, *Cannibals of the Heart: A Personal Biography of Louisa Catherine and John Quincy Adams* (New York: McGraw-Hill, 1980), 113.

3. Richard L. Bushman, *The Refinement of America: Persons, Houses, Cities* (New York: Knopf, 1992), 96–97, 132, 441–42; Nancy F. Cott, "Giving Character to Our Whole Polity: Marriage and the Public Order in the Late Nineteenth Century," in *U.S. History as Women's History: New Feminist Essays,* eds. Linda Kerber, Alice Kessler-Harris, and Kathryn Kish-Sklar (Chapel Hill: University of North Carolina Press, 1995), 109; John F. Kasson, *Rudeness and Civility: Manners in Nineteenth-Century America* (Chapel Hill: University of North Carolina Press, 1980), 169; Laurel Thatcher Ulrich, *Good Wives: Image and Reality in the Lives of Women in Northern New England 1650–1750* (New York: Vintage Books, 1991), 115–16, 258. For more on the consumer revolution, see: *Of Consuming Interests: The Style of Life in the Eighteenth Century,* ed. Cary Carson, Ronald Hoffman, and Peter J. Albert (Charlottesville: University of Virginia Press, 1994).

4. TJ to JM, 30 Mar. 1809, *PJM-P*; BHL to Christian Latrobe, 4 Dec. 1808, cited in Robert L. Raley, "Interior Designs by Benjamin Henry Latrobe for the President's House," *Antiques* 75 (June 1958): 568.

5. Holly Shulman, "Dolley (Payne Todd) Madison," in *American First Ladies: Their Lives and Their Legacy,* ed. Lewis L. Gould (New York: Garland Publishing, 1996) 53; Hunt-Jones, "*Great,*" 35–36.

6. Hunt-Jones, "*Great,*" 35.

7. Bushman, *Refinement,* 71–73, 122–27; BHL to JM, 10 Mar. 1809, *PJM-P*; Samuel Smith to DPTM, 10 Mar. 1809, DMDE.

8. Hunt-Jones, "*Great,*" 42–44, 88–89; Allison Enos, "Summary of Artwork at Montpelier Finding Aid," James Madison's Montpelier, Orange, Virginia.

9. Mary Hazelhurst Latrobe to DPTM, 12 April [1809]; BHL to DPTM, 29 Mar. 1809, DMDE.

10. BHL to DPTM, 29, 22 March 1809, Mary Hazelhurst Latrobe to DPTM, 12 April [1809], DMDE.

11. BHL to DPTM, 22 March 1809, DMDE.

12. Bushman, *Refinement,* 124–27. For the history of Argand lamps, see www.terrypepper.com.

13. BHL to Bradford and Inskeep, 21 Nov. 1809, cited in Klapthor, "Decorate," 161.

14. Klapthor, "Decorate," 157; Hunt-Jones, *"Great,"* 36–37.

15. Bushman, *Refinement,* 71–72; Klapthor, "Decorate," 157.

16. BHL to DPTM, 22 Mar. 1809, DMDE; Hunt-Jones, *"Great,"* 37.

17. BHL to DPTM, 20, 22, 29 Mar., 21 April 1809, DMDE.

18. BHL to DPTM, 22 Mar., 7 May, 4 July 1809, DMDE.

19. BHL to DPTM, 4 July 1809, DLC.

20. BHL to DPTM, 8 Sept. 1809; BHL to DPTM, 21 April 1809, DMDE.

21. BHL to DPTM, 21 Apr. 1809, DMDE; Klapthor, "Decorate," 160–61.

22. BHL to DPTM, 8 Sept. 1809; Klapthor, "Decorate," 162, 158; Hunt-Jones, *"Great,"* 38; Raley, "Interior," 569.

23. BHL to DPTM, 8 Sept. 1809, DMDE.

24. DPTM to BHL, 12 Sept. 1809, DMDE, Hunt-Jones, *"Great,"* 37.

25. See Washington Irving to H. Brevoort, 13 January 1811, cited in Ethel Stephens Arnett, *Mrs. James Madison: The Incomparable Dolley* (Greensboro, NC: Piedmont Press, 1972), 171–72; Lord Francis Jeffery Diary, *PJM,* UVA.

26. Elbridge Gerry, Jr., *Diary of Elbridge Gerry, Jr.* (New York: Brentano's, 1927), 180–81.

27. Hunt-Jones, *"Great,"* 36; Klapthor, "Decorate," 163.

28. RSC to IVH, 3 Dec. 1808, cited in *Mistress of Riversdale: The Plantation Letters of Rosalie Stier Calvert,* ed. and trans. Margaret Law Callcott (Baltimore: Johns Hopkins University Press, 1991), 194. America's attachment to aristocratic forms can still be found in the present day. The Washington coat of arms, which the general used extensively at Mount Vernon (in bookplates, for instance), still lives—on Washington, D.C., license plates.

29. Kasson, *Rudeness,* 166.

30. For more, see David B. Mattern and Holly C. Shulman, *The Selected Letters of Dolley Payne Madison* (Charlottesville: University of Virginia Press, 2003), 92–93.

31. Bushman, *Refinement,* 39–41.

32. Joanne B. Freeman, *Affairs of Honor: National Politics in the New Republic* (New Haven: Yale University Press, 2001), 45–47; Hunt-Jones, *"Great,"* 26. For more on George Washington's style, see Betty C. Monkman, "The White House Collection: George Washington: Influences and Images," *White House History* 6 (fall 1999): 62–65; Stanley Elkins and Eric McKitrick,

The Age of Federalism: The Early American Republic, 1788–1800 (New York: Oxford University Press, 1993), 49–50.

33. On the use and meaning of the word "lady," see Linda Colley, "The Female Elite in Unreformed Britain," paper presented at Brown University, April 1995, 16. Freeman, *Affairs*, 47–48; Kenneth R. Bowling, *Creating the Federal City, 1774–1800: Potomac Fever* (Washington, DC: American Institute of Architects Press, 1988), 11, 21, 78; Bushman, *Refinement*, 189–91.

34. Baltimore Whig cited in W. B. Bryan, "The Name White House," *Records of the Columbia Historical Society* 33–34 (no date): 306, 307. A British minister used the term in the spring of 1811. One congressman wrote to his wife: "There is much trouble at the white house, as we call it, I mean the president's." Abijah Bigelow to Hannah Gardner Bigelow (wife), 18 March 1812, in "Letters of Abijah Bigelow, Member of Congress to His Wife, 1810–1815," *American Antiquarian Society Proceedings* 40 (October 1930): 331.

35. Arnett, *Incomparable*, 168.

36. Daniel J. Boorstin, "Roles of the President's House," in *The White House: The First Two Hundred Years*, eds. Frank Freidel and William Pencak (Boston: Northeastern University Press, 1994), 3–4.

10: "THE GREAT CENTRE OF ATTRACTION"

1. CAM to MAM, 2, 11 Jan. 1811, CAM Papers, DLC; Washington Irving to H. Brevoort, 13 January 1811, cited in Ethel Stephens Arnett, *Mrs. James Madison: The Incomparable Dolley* (Greensboro, NC: Piedmont Press, 1972), 171–72.

2. CAM to MAM, 2 Jan. 1811, CAM Papers, DLC.

3. Constance McLaughlin Green, *Washington: Village and Capital, 1800–1878* (Princeton: Princeton University Press, 1972), 28.

4. Barbara Carson, *Ambitious Appetites: Dining, Behavior, and Patterns of Consumption in Federal Washington* (Washington, D.C.: American Institute of Architects Press, 1990), 75; Simeon Olcott to Tryphena Olcott, 3, 19 Jan. 1802, Olcott Papers, DLC. He confessed to his homebound wife: "The labors of the day are not half so fatiguing or disagreeable as attending law courts."

5. CAM to MAM, 3 Apr. 1806, CAM Papers, DLC; MBS to JBK, 13 March 1814, MBS Papers, DLC; CAM to MAM, 19 December 1808, CAM Papers, DLC. On the "theatrics" of congressional display, see Jan Lewis, "Politics and the Ambivalence of the Private Sphere: Women in Early Washington," in *A Republic for the Ages: The United States Capitol and the Political Culture of the Early Republic*, ed. Donald R. Kennon (Charlottesville: University of Virginia Press, 1999). Judith Walker Rives also dubbed the

Capitol the "favorite morning lounge." JWR, "Autobiography," 59, William Cabell Rives Papers, DLC. See also CAM to MAM, 28 Feb. 1810, 7 Dec. 1811, DLC.

6. CAM to MAM, 11 Dec. 1808, CAM Papers, DLC; MBS, *Reminiscences,* 1837, MBS Papers, DLC.

7. MBS, *Reminiscences,* 1837, MBS Papers, DLC.

8. MBS to JBK, 20 June 1801, MBS Papers, DLC.

9. MBS to JBK, 20 June 1801, MBS Papers, DLC; Richard L. Bushman, *The Refinement of America: Persons, Houses, Cities* (New York: Knopf, 1992), xix; Fredrika J. Teute and David S. Shields, "The Republican Court and the Historiography of a Woman's Domain in the Public Sphere," Presentation at the SHEAR Annual Meeting, 1993, 3.

10. Cynthia Diane Earman, "Boardinghouses, Parties and the Creation of a Political Society: Washington City, 1800–1830," M.A. thesis, Louisiana State University and Agricultural and Mechanical College, 1992, 34, 74–75.

11. James Sterling Young, *The Washington Community, 1800–1828* (New York: Columbia University Press, 1966), 197–201.

12. MBS to Mary Ann Kirkpatrick, 9 Feb. 1807, MBS Papers, DLC.

13. AJF, *Jeffersonian America: Notes on the United States of America,* ed. Richard Beale Davis (San Marino, Calif.: Huntingdon Library, 1954), 55–57; Elizabeth Ellet, *Court Circles of the Republic* (Hartford: Hartford Publishing Co., 1869), 333–34.

14. Seymour Martin Lipset, *The First New Nation: The United States in Historical and Comparative Perspective* (New York: Basic Books, 1963), 34–35; Joseph J. Ellis, *Founding Brothers: The Revolutionary Generation* (New York: Knopf, 2000), 11–12; Marshall Smelser, "The Federalist Period as an Age of Passion," *American Quarterly* 10 (Winter 1958), 392–93; RSC to HJS, 12 Dec. 1808, cited in *Mistress of Riversdale: The Plantation Letters of Rosalie Stier Calvert,* ed. and trans. Margaret Law Callcott (Baltimore: Johns Hopkins University Press, 1991), 198.

15. Peter Field, review of Elaine K. Swift, "The Making of the American Senate: Reconstructive Change in Congress, 1781–1841," *William and Mary Quarterly* 3rd ser., vol. 55, no. 1 (Jan. 1988), 187. J. C. A. Stagg disagrees with this characterization, pointing out that the Senate's evolution was more gradual, more contingent, and more creative. Personal communication, J. C. A. Stagg.

16. Young, *WC,* 94–97.

17. DPTM to APC, 3 Apr. 1818, DMDE.

18. Charles Hurd, *The White House: A Biography* (New York: Harper & Row, 1940), 50. Kathryn Allamong Jacob, *Capital Elites: High Society in Wash-*

ington, D.C., After the Civil War (Washington, D.C.: Smithsonian Institution Press, 1995), 18. Marianne Means, *The Woman in the White House: The Lives, Times and Influence of Twelve Notable First Ladies* (New York: Random House, 1963), 69.

19. John H. McCormick, "The First Master of Ceremonies of the White House," *Records of the Columbia Historical Society* 7 (1904): 175–77; DPTM to LPWT, 23 Aug. 1814, DMDE; CM I, 42–43.

20. "A gentleman," *The Laws of Etiquette; or, Short Rules and Reflections for Conduct in Society* (Philadelphia: Carey, Leas, and Blanchard, 1839), 139; LCJA, "Miscellany," 1 Mar. 1819, APM, MHS.

21. For a vivid description of JM at his best, see MBS, *What Is Gentility?* (Washington, D.C.: Pishey Thompson, 1828), 153–56, and Benjamin Ogle Tayloe, *Our Neighbors on La Fayette Square* (Originally published Washington: 1872; reprint, Washington, D.C.: Junior League of Washington, 1982), 14; William Campbell Preston, cited in Conover Hunt-Jones, *Dolley and the "Great Little Madison"* (Washington, D.C.: American Institute of Architects Foundation, 1977), 126.

22. Elbridge Gerry to Ann Gerry, 8 June 1813, MHS.

23. Elbridge Gerry to Ann Gerry, 2 June 1813, 29 May 1811, MHS.

24. Bushman, *Refinement*, 58, 83, 89.

25. SGS, 12 Nov. 1812, cited in Josephine Seaton, *William Winston Seaton of the "National Intelligencer:" A Biographical Sketch* (Boston: James Osgood and Company, 1871), 85; Barbara Carson, *Ambitious Appetites: Dining, Behavior, and Patterns of Consumption in Federal Washington* (Washington, D.C.: American Institute of Architects Press, 1990), 111–12; (Russian minister) Baron Tuyl, cited in Tayloe, *Neighbors*, 24; LCJA, "Adventures of A Nobody," Jan. 1804–1805, APM, MHS; AJF, *Notes*, 58: RSC to HJS, 25 Jan. 1805, cited in *Mistress*, 109.

26. Dolley's enduring association with the frozen dessert, and her reputation for introducing it to America (some have even thought, erroneously, that she invented it), may have stemmed from this practice. Personal communication, Judy Frank. For the record, Dolley did not invent ice cream, nor was she the first to serve it in America, nor was she the first First Lady to serve it, nor was she the first to serve it in the White House. Martha Washington and Abigail Adams served it (or some form of it) at executive functions in the capitals of New York and Philadelphia. Thomas Jefferson is most noted for serving it in the new president's house in Washington. Jefferson's account books include wages for someone to turn the ice cream freezer, and several visitors describe an early form of Baked Alaska, "ice cream brought to the table in the form of small balls enclosed

in cases of warm pastry." CAM to MAM, 8 April 1806, CAM Papers, DLC. Technically, then, Dolley was the first president's wife to serve it in the new capital.

27. Mary Douglas, "Deciphering a Meal," *Daedulus* 101 (Winter 1972), 61; Carson, *Appetites*, vi; Peter Farb and George Armelagos, *Consuming Passions: The Anthropology of Eating* (Boston: Houghton Mifflin, 1987), 4, 73; Joanne B. Freeman, *Affairs of Honor: National Politics in the New Republic* (New Haven: Yale University Press, 2001), 52–53; AJF, *Notes*, 57; Joanne B. Freeman, "Slander, Poison, Whispers and Fame: Jefferson's 'Anas' and Political Gossip in the Early Republic," *Journal of the Early Republic* 15:1 (spring 1995), 27.

28. Farb and Armelagos, *Consuming Passions*, 9, 158–59, 161.

29. ECL to DPTM, 2 March 1809, DPTM.

30. Joseph J. Ellis, *Founding Brothers: The Revolutionary Generation* (New York: Knopf, 2000), 17, 211; Young, *WC*, 178.

31. Ellis, *Brothers*, 54, 172–74.

32. Young, *WC*, 151–52.

33. David B. Mattern and Holly C. Shulman, *The Selected Letters of Dolley Payne Madison* (Charlottesville: University of Virginia Press, 2003), 95; Amanda Foreman, *Georgiana: Duchess of Devonshire* (New York: Modern Library, 2001), 23, 27; Elizabeth Ellet, *Court Circles of the Republic* (Hartford: Hartford Publishing Co., 1869), 83.

34. Frances Few, 25 Feb. 1809, "The Diary of Frances Few," ed. Noble Cunningham, Jr., *Journal of Southern History* 29 (Feb.–Nov. 1963): 360; CAM to MAM, 2 Jan. 1811, CAM Papers, DLC.

35. CAM to MAM, 2 Jan. 1811, CAM Papers, DLC.

36. SGS, 2 Jan. 1814, cited in Seaton, 113–14.

37. Foreman, *Georgiana*, 27; SGS, 2 Jan. 1814, cited in Seaton, 113; CAM to MAM, 2 Jan. 1811, CAM Papers, DLC.

38. SGS, 2 Jan. 1814, cited in Seaton, 113.

39. CAM to MAM, 2 Jan. 1811, CAM Papers, DLC.

40. LPWT to APC, 8 Mar. 1812, Cutts microfilm, SCHL; Timothy Pickering to Rebecca Pickering, 4 June 1809, Timothy Pickering Papers, MHS.

41. Jacob, *Elites*, 18.

42. David Truman, *The Governmental Process: Political Interest and Public Opinion* (New York: Knopf, 1971), 322, 324.

43. AJF, *Notes*, 108; Arthur M. Schlesinger, *Learning How to Behave: A Historical Study of American Etiquette Books* (New York: Macmillan, 1947), 7.

44. Ann Hartman and Joan Laird, *Family-Centered Social Work Practice* (New York: The Free Press, 1983), 319–22.

45. Alexander Dick, "Journal," 7 June 1809, cited in Helen Beall Lewis, "Journal of Alexander Dick in America, 1806–1809," M.A. thesis, University of Virginia, 1984.

46. Cited in Irving Brant, *James Madison: The President, 1809–1812* (Indianapolis: Bobbs-Merrill, 1959), 465.

47. AJF, *Notes*, 106–07; RSC to CJS, 10 Mar. 1815, cited in *Mistress*, 278.

48. Holly Cowan Shulman, "Dolley (Payne Todd) Madison," in *American First Ladies: Their Lives and Their Legacy*, ed. Lewis L. Gould (New York: Garland Publishing, 1996), 60; Jonathan Roberts to Matthew Roberts, 2 Dec. 1811, *PJM-PS*.

49. Sophia May, "Diary," 23 April 1812, Sophia May Papers, AAS; DPTM to APC, [ca. 27 March 1812], DMDE.

50. Jonathan Roberts to Matthew Roberts, 21 June 1809, cited in Irving Brant, *James Madison: Commander in Chief, 1812–1836* (Indianapolis: Bobbs-Merrill, 1961), 27.

51. DPTM to Ruth Baldwin Barlow, 15 November 1811; DPTM to James Taylor, 13 March [1811], DMDE.

52. DPTM to PPM, [1811–1812]. 14 Jan. 1813, DMDE.

53. See Freeman, *Affairs*, 62–66.

54. Brant, *CC*, 99.

55. Irving Brant, *The Fourth President: A Life of James Madison* (Indianapolis: Bobbs-Merrill, 1970), 378. On gossip, see Patricia Meyer Spacks, *Gossip* (New York: Knopf, 1985); Freeman, *Affairs*, ch. 2.

56. Brant, *President*, 433, 435.

57. Ibid., 260.

58. Spacks, *Gossip*, 5, 8, 13, 207, 261. Spacks quotes Norbert Elias: "Speech . . . is nothing else but human relations turned into sound" (p. 20). On the use of gossip by the powerless, especially women, see also Jane Kamensky, *Governing the Tongue: The Politics of Speech in Early New England* (New York: Oxford University Press, 1999); Terri L. Snyder, *Babbling Women: Disorderly Speech and the Law in Early Virginia* (Ithaca: Cornell University Press, 2003). On the centrality of gossip to human evolution, see Robin Dunbar, *Grooming, Gossip, and the Evolution of Langauge* (Cambridge, Mass.: Harvard University Press, 1997).

59. The next president who tried to control society in the capital, Andrew Jackson, brought the political and social machine to a halt during the infamous Eaton Affair. He saved his presidency only by firing his whole cabinet.

60. On personalization, see Fredrika J. Teute and David S. Shields, "Jefferson in Washington: Domesticating Manners in the Republican Court,"

Institute of Early American History and Culture Third Annual Conference, 1997, 20.

61. Margaret Truman, *First Ladies: An Intimate Group Portrait of White House Wives* (New York: Random House, 1995), 11, 23; John H. McCormick, "The First Master of Ceremonies of the White House," *Records of the Columbia Historical Society* 7 (1904), 178.

62. CM I, 9.

63. Michael McGerr, "Political Style and Women's Power, 1830–1930," *Journal of American History* 77, no. 3 (Dec. 1990): 865–66.

64. Young, *WC*, 26–28, 32, 34–36.

II: FAMILY MATTERS

1. DPTM to an unidentified correspondent, 3 June 1810, DMDE.

2. Irving Brant, *James Madison: The President, 1809–1812* (Indianapolis: Bobbs-Merrill, 1959), 113, 131.

3. DPTM to JGJ, 10 April 1811, DMDE.

4. DPTM to APC, 20 June [1811], DMDE.

5. DPTM to APC, 18 June [1807], DMDE.

6. DPTM to APC, 18 June 1807; DPTM to APC, 22 Dec. [1811], DMDE.

7. DPTM to APC, 19 Aug. [1811], [8 April 1812], DMDE.

8. DPTM to APC, [8 April 1812], DMDE.

9. CM I, 38.

10. LPWT to DPTM, [July 1811], 18 April 1812, DMDE.

11. Ibid.

12. DPTM to APC, 20 March [1812], DMDE; Leon Friedman and Fred L. Israel, eds., *The Justices of the United States Supreme Court 1789–1969: Their Lives and Major Opinions* (New York: Chelsea House Publishers, 1969), vol. 1, 411; DPTM to APC, [8 April 1812], DMDE.

13. DPTM to APC, 20 March [1812]; DPTM to APC, [8 Apr. 1812], DMDE.

14. LPWT to DPTM, 18 April 1812, DMDE.

15. After Walter set sail for Great Britain in 1784, a family friend, the celebrated diarist Elizabeth Drinker, never mentioned him again. In 1795, Elizabeth wrote in her diary: "I heard this evening of the death of two of Molly Payne's sons, Temple and Isaac: the latter offended a man in Virginia, who sometime after shot him with a pistol." Elaine Forman Crane et al., eds., *The Diary of Elizabeth Drinker* (Boston: Northeastern University Press, 1991), 1:638.

16. DPTM to John C. Payne, 21 Sept. 1809, DMDE.

17. Ibid.

18. EC to DPTM, 10 June 1811; DPTM to APC, 15 July [1811], DMDE.

19. LPT to APC, 20 July 1811, Cutts Microfilm, SCHL.

20. LPWT to DPTM, 18 April 1812; DPTM to APC, 19 Aug. [1811], DMDE.

21. DPTM to APC, 19 Aug. [1811], DMDE.

22. LPWT to DPTM, 18 Apr. 1812, DMDE.

23. DPTM to APC, 22 Dec. [1811], [8 April 1812], DMDE.

24. Drew McCoy, *The Last of the Fathers: James Madison and the Republican Legacy* (Cambridge, U.K.: Cambridge University Press, 1989), 268–69.

25. I. Finch, *Travels in the United States of America and Canada, etc.* (London: Longman, Rees, Orme, Brown, Green, and Longman, 1833), 244.

26. Paul A. Jennings, *A Colored Man's Reminiscences of James Madison*, www.whitehousehistory.org.

27. Joseph J. Ellis, *American Sphinx: The Character of Thomas Jefferson* (New York: Knopf, 1993), 149–52.

28. Sarah Luria, "National Domesticity in the Early Republic: Washington, D.C.," www.common-place.org, 3: 4, 2003; EC, "Autobiography," cited in McCoy, *Last*, 311–12.

29. DPTM to John C. Payne, [4 Dec. 1829], DMDE.

30. JM to DPTM, 27 Aug. 1814, DMDE; LPW to APC, 20 July 1811, Cutts Microfilm, SCHL; LPWT to DPTM, [July 1811]; DPTM to Richard Cutts, 11 Aug. 1833; DPTM to APC, [ca. 23 July 1818], DMDE.

31. DPTM to APC, [ca. 23 July 1818], DMDE.

32. "Reminiscences of Madison Hemmings," cited in Fawn M. Brodie, *Thomas Jefferson: An Intimate History* (New York: W. W. Norton, 1974), 473; DPTM to Elizabeth Parke Custis Law, 17 Oct. 1804, DMDE.

33. David S. Shields asserts that "familiar letters" between families, neighbors, and friends were the glue that held the country together during the nineteenth century, transcending section, party, religion, and class. David S. Shields, "Questions, Suspicious, Speculations," *Journal of the Early Republic* (Summer 2004), 339.

34. DPTM to APC, 16 July, 26 April 1804, DMDE.

35. DPTM to APC, May 1812; Joshua Gilpin to DPTM, 20 Sept. 1812, DMDE.

36. DPTM to Lucy Henry Southall Cutts, 29 Aug. [1807], DMDE.

37. Holly Cowan Shulman, "Dolley (Payne Todd) Madison," in *American First Ladies: Their Lives and Their Legacy*, ed. Lewis L. Gould (New York: Garland Publishing, 1996), 51.

38. See John G. Jackson to DPTM, 20 May 1803, 20 July 1806, 8 April 1809, 11 June 1810, DMDE.

39. DPTM to APC, 28 August [1808]; John G. Jackson to DPTM, 8 Oct. 1808, DMDE.

40. JGJ to DPTM, 11 June 1810; DPTM to John G. Jackson, 10 April [18]11, DMDE.

41. JGJ to DPTM, 23 Oct. 1809; DPTM to APC, 26 Apr. 1804, DMDE.

42. DPTM to EC, 15 June 1811; DPTM to APC, May 1812, DMDE.

43. DPTM to James Taylor, 10 Nov. 1810, 13 Mar. [1811], DMDE. On the same issue, see also DPTM to APC, 22 Dec. [1811], DMDE.

44. DPTM to James Taylor, 10 Nov. 1810, DMDE.

45. DPTM to APC, [ca. 27 Mar. 1812]; [8 Apr. 1812], DMDE.

46. DPTM to APC, [ca. 15 Apr. 1812], DMDE.

47. DPTM to James Taylor, 13 Mar. [1811], DMDE.

48. On sending papers, see DPTM to APC, 15 Apr. 1812, DMDE.

49. DPTM to Samuel Poultney Todd, 16 March 1809, DMDE.

50. DPTM to Samuel Poultney Todd, 31 March 1809, DMDE.

51. DPTM to Samuel Poultney Todd, 5 May 1809, DMDE; Paul Hamilton to Samuel Todd, 21 Nov. 1809, DM Papers, DLC.

52. DPTM to Samuel Poultney Todd, 21 Nov. 1809, DM Papers, DLC.

53. Washington Irving to William Irving, 16 Feb. 1811, cited in Pierre M. Irving, *Life and Letters of Washington Irving* (New York: G. P. Putnam, 1863), 1:272.

54. "Land conferred wealth, wealth conferred power, and power in eighteenth-century terms meant access to patronage, from lucrative government sinecures down to the local parish office." Amanda Foreman, *Georgiana: Duchess of Devonshire* (New York: Modern Library, 2001), 6. On the role of manners in ameliorating this depersonalization, see Fredrika J. Teute and David S. Shields, "Jefferson in Washington: Domesticating Manners in the Republican Court," Institute of Early American History and Culture Third Annual Conference, 1997, 7.

55. Linda Colley, "The Female Elite in Unreformed Britain," Paper presented at Brown University, April 1995, 5, 8–9.

56. James Sterling Young, *The Washington Community, 1800–1828* (New York: Columbia University Press, 1966).

57. MBS to JBK, 15 Dec. 1831, MBS Papers, DLC.

58. David B. Mattern and Holly C. Shulman, *The Selected Letters of Dolley Payne Madison* (Charlottesville: University of Virginia Press, 2003), 97.

59. Josiah Quincy, *Annals of Congress*, House of Representatives, 12th Congress, 2nd Session, Jan. 1813, 550.

60. Abijah Bigelow, 10 Feb. 1811, in "Letters of Abijah Bigelow, Member of Congress to His Wife, 1810–1815," *American Antiquarian Society Proceedings* 40 (October 1930), 317; *Federal Republican*, 21 April 1813, 2, AAS.

61. See for instance: AM to DPTM, 7 Mar., 15 June 1812, DM Papers, DLC; DPTM to PPM, 10 May 1811, DMDE.

62. AM to DPTM, 20 July 1812, DM Papers, DLC.

63. AM to DPTM, 16 Apr. 1813; PPM to DPTM, 1812?, DM Papers, DLC; PPM to AM, 17 Feb. 1812, cited in Laura Haines Belman, "Dolley at Dumbarton" (exhibition catalog, Dumbarton House, 26 Mar.–2 Nov. 1996), 5.

64. DPTM to AM, 2 Mar. 1812; AM to DPTM, 24 June 1812; DPTM to PPM, 29 July 1812, DMDE.

65. Belman, "Dumbarton," 7, 8.

66. AM to DPTM, 1 Aug. 1813, March 1812, DMDE.

67. JM to Richard Cutts, 17 Aug. 1804, Cutts-Madison Papers, MHS.

68. Stephen Sayre to DPTM, 8 March 1809; David Bailie Warden to DPTM, 19 Jan. 1811, 12 Mar. 1811; John Astor to DPTM, 20 Feb. 1811; Caroline Langdon Eustis to DPTM, [ca. Jan. 1815], DMDE.

69. Allen C. Clark, *Life and Letters of Dolly Madison* (Washington, D.C.: W.F. Roberts Co., 1914), 144–45; John Astor to DPTM, 29 Nov. 1812, DMDE.

70. Many thanks to Donald R. Hickey for his expertise in interpreting and understanding this information.

12: THE REPUBLICAN QUEEN

1. Anonymous, "Hammond Memoir," n.d., n.p., *PJM*, UVA.

2. For a variation of this story, see also William Elwell, "Diary," Archibald Henderson, cited in Ethel Stephens Arnett, *Mrs. James Madison: The Incomparable Dolley* (Greensboro, N.C.: Piedmont Press, 1972), 253; DPTM, "Miscellany," DM Papers, DLC.

3. Charles J. Ingersoll, "James Madison" in *The National Portrait Gallery of Distinguished Americans,* James B. Longacre and James Herring, eds., vol. 3 (New York: Hermon Bancroft, 1836), 10.

4. CM I, 44; DPTM to Dolley P. Madison Cutts, 10 March 1830, DMDE.

5. On women's bodies in the polity, see the collection edited by Lynn Hunt: *Eroticism and the Body Politic* (Baltimore: Johns Hopkins University Press, 1991).

6. Linda Colley, "The Female Elite in Unreformed Britain," Paper presented at Brown University, April 1995, 17–18. See also: Karin Calvert, "The Function of Fashion in Eighteenth-Century America," in *Of Consuming Interests: The Style of Life in the Eighteenth Century*, ed. Cary Carson, Ronald Hoffman, and Peter J. Albert (Charlottesville: University of Virginia Press, 1994), 252–83.

7. DPTM to Ruth Baldwin Barlow, [ca. 19 Apr. 1812], DMDE.

8. Richard L. Bushman, *The Refinement of America: Persons, Houses, Cities* (New York: Knopf, 1992), 69–72.

9. Charles J. Ingersoll, *History of the Second War Between the United States and Great Britain* (Philadelphia: Lippincott, Grambo and Co., 1852), 207; Arnett, *Incomparable*, 200.

10. CM II 2; MBC to MHB, 11 Nov. 1816, *Letters of Mary Boardman Crowninshield*, ed. Frances Boardman Crowninshield (Cambridge, Mass.: Riverside Press, 1935), 16, 35.

11. MBC to MHB, 7 Dec. 1815, 2 Jan. 1816, *Letters*, 23.

12. Bushman, *Refinement*, 70–71.

13. "Black velvet trimmed with gold [and] a worked lace turban in gold, looked brilliant,—a lace and gold kind of a something over their shoulders." MBC to MHB, 24 Feb. 1816, in *Letters*, 57–58; Frances Few, "The Diary of Frances Few," ed. Noble E. Cunningham, Jr., *Journal of Southern History* 26 (Feb.–Nov. 1963), 8 Dec. 1808, 353.

14. SGS, 2 January 1814, cited in Josephine Seaton, *William Winston Seaton of the "National Intelligencer:" A Biographical Sketch* (Boston: James Osgood and Company, 1871), 113.

15. JQA, "Diary," entry for 23 November 1804, in *Memoirs of John Quincy Adams, Comprising Portions of his Diary from 1795 to 1848*, ed. Charles Francis Adams (Philadelphia: J. B. Lippincott and Co., 1874), vol. 1, 316; Phoebe Morris to Anthony Morris, 23 Feb. 1812, cited in Laura Haines Belman, "Dolley at Dumbarton," Exhibition catalog, Dumbarton House, 1996, 7.

16. Harriet Otis, journal, entry for 1 January 1812, Harrison Gray Otis Papers, MHS.

17. Linzy Brekke, "Fashioning America: Clothing and the Politics of America, 1783–1845," Diss. Harvard University (forthcoming, 2006).

18. David B. Mattern and Holly C. Shulman, *The Selected Letters of Dolley Payne Madison* (Charlottesville: University of Virginia Press, 2003), 93–94.

19. Emily Christine Burns, "Portraits of a First Lady: Images of Dolley Madison," M.A. thesis, George Washington University, 2005, 46–48, 64–66; Fredrika J. Teute, "The Spectacle of Washington: Creating Public Celebrity in the New Nation," paper presented at the Omohundro Institute of Early American History and Culture Annual Meeting, 2005.

20. Anonymous, "Hammond Memoir," n.d., n.p., *PJM*, UVA.

21. Colley, "Female Elite," 16–17.

22. Alan Lloyd, *The Scorching of Washington: The War of 1812* (W. Vancouver,

B.C.: David & Charles, n.d.), 86; Mattern and Shulman, *SL*, 93; Burns, "Portraits," 61–62.

23. William Campbell Preston, cited in Elizabeth Ellet, *Court Circles of the Republic* (Hartford: Hartford Publishing Co., 1869), 84–87; Allen C. Clark, *The Life and Letters of Dolly Madison* (Washington, D.C.: W. F. Roberts, 1914), 295.

24. Bushman, *Refinement*, 63–69; SGS, 2 Jan. 1814, in *Seaton*, 113.

25. Ralph Ketcham, *James Madison: A Biography* (Charlottesville: University of Virginia Press, 1990), 496.

26. As one scholar has observed, at court, "conduct becomes so highly structured that life approaches art," but this was art not for art's sake, but for state power. Stephen Jaeger, *The Origins of Courtliness: Civilizing Trends and the Formation of Courtly Ideals, 939–1210* (Philadelphia: University of Pennsylvania Press, 1985), 258.

27. Richard Rush, quoted in Bushman, *Refinement*, 68.

28. William Maclay, quoted in ibid., 69.

29. Ibid., xiv, 52, 55–56.

30. *Intelligencer*, 6 Nov. 1837, Cutts Family Papers, MHS.

31. In *Seaton*, 12 Nov. 1812, 85; Bushman, *Refinement*, 84; Few "Diary," 11 Oct. 1808 (Feb.–Nov. 1963): 351

32. CM I, 32; SC(S) to DPTM, 16 Oct. 1815, DMDE.

33. *Intelligencer*, 6 Nov. 1837; Cutts Family Papers, MHS; Anonymous newspaper clipping, "'Aunt' Dolley Madison," Cutts Family Papers, DLC; Sophia May Diary, entry for 13 Feb. 1807, Sophia May Papers, AAS; Lucia B. Cutts, *Memoirs and Letters of Dolly Madison* (Boston: Houghton Mifflin and Co., 1886), 26.

34. MBS, "Inaugurations," *Ladies' Magazine and Literary Gazette*, vol. 4, no. 12 (Dec. 1831): 536; Margaret Truman, *First Ladies: An Intimate Group Portrait of White House Wives* (New York: Random House, 1995), 22; Anonymous newspaper clipping, 22 May ?, Cutts Family Papers, MHS.

35. DPTM fragment, Cutts Family Papers, Miscellany, MHS.

36. Ellet, *Court*, 87–88.

37. MBC, 7 Dec. 1815, cited in MBC, *Letters* 24.

38. William Campbell Preston, cited in Ellet, *Court*, 86.

39. Ibid.

40. Ellet, *Court*, 265; George Watterston, *A Wanderer in Washington* (Washington, D.C.: Davis and Force, 1827), 62.

41. Irving Brant, *James Madison: The President, 1809–1812* (Indianapolis: Bobbs-Merrill, 1959), 89; Beckles Willson, *Friendly Relations: A Narrative*

of Britain's Ministers and Ambassadors to America (1791–1930) (London: Lovat Dickson and Thompson Limited, 1934), 69.

42. CM I, 37.

43. Ellet, *Court,* 264; Frances Few, "Diary," 11 Oct. 1808, cited in "Few," 351–52.

44. Among many mentions, SGS, cited in Josephine Seaton, *William Winston Seaton of the "National Intelligencer": A Biographical Sketch* (Boston: James Osgood and Company, 1871), 82. Martha Washington, however, had been addressed as "Lady" beginning in the Revolution. Carl Sferrazza Anthony, *First Ladies: The Saga of the President's Wives and their Power, 1789–1961* (New York: William Morrow, 1990), 36.

45. SGS, 12 Nov. 1812, cited in *Seaton,* 86; SLM to CAM, 3 Jan. 1802, cited in "Letters," 743.

46. MBS, *A Winter in Washington, or Memoirs of the Seymour Family* (New York: E. Bliss and E. White, 1824), 43–44. This is an observation that MBS remembered and included in her novel.

47. Amanda Foreman, *Georgiana: Duchess of Devonshire* (New York: Modern Library, 2001), 14; Charles Bagot, cited in Ingersoll, *Second War,* 27; Lord Francis Jeffrey, quoted in Benjamin Ogle Tayloe, *Our Neighbors on La Fayette Square* (Originally published Washington: 1872; reprint, Washington, D.C.: Junior League of Washington, 1982), 70.

48. AM to Anna Payne, 19 May 1837, cited in Laura Haines Belman, "Dolley at Dumbarton," Exhibition catalog, Dumbarton House, 1996, 10.

49. Lucia B. Cutts, *Memoirs,* 49; Joseph J. Ellis, *Founding Brothers: The Revolutionary Generation* (New York: Knopf, 2000), 186–87.

50. Anonymous, "Hammond memoir," n.d., n.p., *PJM,* UVA; Paul M. Zall, *Dolley Madison* (Huntington, NY: Nova History Publications, 2001), 54. RSC to IVH, 12 Aug. 1810, cited in *Mistress of Riversdale: The Plantation Letters of Rosalie Stier Calvert,* ed. and trans. Margaret Law Callcott (Baltimore: Johns Hopkins University Press, 1991), 224; MBC to MHB, 16 Jan. 1816, cited in *Letters,* 42. For a good discussion of Dolley's personality and politics, see: Zall, *DM,* 106.

51. Frances Few, "Diary," 11 Oct. 1808, cited in "Few," 352; Sophia May Diary, 13 Feb. 1807, Sophia May Papers, AAS; Allen C. Clark, *Life and Letters of Dolly Madison* (Washington, D.C.: W.F. Roberts Co., 1914), 143.

52. For a wonderful evocation of this side of the " 'great little Madison,' " see Ellis, *Brothers,* 53–55.

53. Alexander Dick, "Journal," 7 June 1809, cited in Barbara Carson, *Ambitious Appetites: Dining, Behavior, and Patterns of Consumption in Federal Washington* (Washington, D.C.: American Institute of Architects Press, 1990); SGS, 2 Jan. 1814, in *Seaton,* 113.

54. Washington Irving to H. Brevoort, 13 January 1811, cited in Brant, *President*, 239.

55. Truman, *First Ladies*, 23.

56. MBS, *Winter, What is Gentility?* (Washington: Pishey Thompson, 1828); George Watterston to DPTM, 10 Mar. 1809; Cornelia Hopkins to DPTM, 13 Apr. 1810; Henry C. Lewis to DPTM, 14 Jan. 1811; Elizabeth Brown Harner to DPTM, 27 Nov. 1812; Joseph Milligan to DPTM, 13 Dec. 1811, DMDE. George Watterston obviously believed that one good turn deserved another; in 1812, he asked Dolley for help in obtaining a post in the Department of the Treasury. George Watterston to DPTM, 28 Feb. 1812, DMDE. Echoes of Astor, Barker was a merchant shipper and one of the eventual financers of "Mr. Madison's War."

57. Seymour Martin Lipset, *The First New Nation: The United States in Historical and Comparative Perspective* (New York: Basic Books, 1963), 18, 30, 34. For more on women and nationalism, see Elizabeth R. Varon, *"We Mean to be Counted": White Women and Party Politics in Antebellum Virginia* (Chapel Hill: University of North Carolina Press, 1998); David Waldstreicher, *In the Midst of Perpetual Fetes: The Making of American Nationalism* (Chapel Hill: University of North Carolina Press, 1997); Rosemarie Zagarri, *Petticoat Government: Women and Politics from the American Revolution to the Age of Jackson* (forthcoming, Penguin Press).

13: AFFAIRS TO REMEMBER

1. CAM to MAM, 3 Apr. 1806, CAM Papers, DLC; *Annals of Congress,* 2 Feb. 1811, 863–64.

2. Cynthia A. Kierner, *Scandal at Bizarre: Rumor and Reputation in Jefferson's America* (New York: Palgrave Macmillan, 2004), 97, 115–16.

3. CAM to MAM, 28 Feb. 1810, CAM Papers, DLC. Louis Sérurier quoted in Ethel Stephens Arnett, *Mrs. James Madison: The Incomparable Dolley* (Greensboro, NC: Piedmont Press, 1972), 102.

4. Joanne B. Freeman, *Affairs of Honor: National Politics in the New Republic* (New Haven: Yale University Press, 2001), 178–79, 192, 195; Joseph J. Ellis, *Founding Brothers: The Revolutionary Generation* (New York: Knopf, 2000), 39.

5. Irving Brant, *James Madison: The President, 1809–1812* (Indianapolis: Bobbs-Merrill, 1959), 113–15.

6. Louis Sérurier cited in ibid., 263; Arnett, *Incomparable,* 102–103.

7. Brant, *President,* 90–92; Ralph Ketcham, *James Madison: A Biography* (Charlottesville: University of Virginia Press, 1990), 484–85.

8. For good accounts of this affair, see Ketcham, *JM,* 487–91 and J. C. A. Stagg,

Mr. Madison's War: Politics, Diplomacy, and Warfare in the Early Republic, 1783–1830 (Princeton: Princeton University Press, 1983), 71–77.

9. Robert Smith to Samuel Smith, 22 Mar. 1811, Samuel Smith Papers, DLC.

10. Robert Smith to Samuel Smith, 23 Mar. 1811, Samuel Smith Papers, DLC; DPTM to EC, 15 June [18]11; EC to DPTM, 10 June 1811, DMDE.

11. EC to DPTM, 10 June 1811, DMDE.

12. DPTM to EC, 15 June [18]11, DMDE.

13. DPTM to EC, 15 June [18]11, DMDE.

14. DPTM to APC, 20 June [1811], DMDE; Brant, *President*, 302, 309, 304.

15. DPTM to APC, 15 July 1811, DMDE; Brant, *President*, 307–308.

16. Brant, *President*, 302, 305.

17. DPTM to Ruth Baldwin Barlow, 15 Nov. 1811, DMDE.

18. Brant, *President*, 306, 307.

19. Ketcham, *JM*, 518.

20. Ibid., 517.

21. Brant, *President*, 415–16; Stagg, *War*, 93–95.

22. AJF, "Diary," 18 Mar. 1812, AJF Papers, DLC; DPTM to APC, 20 March 1812, DMDE; Brant, *President*, 419.

23. DPTM to APC, [ca. 27 March 1812], DMDE; John Harper to William Plumer, 13 Apr. 1812, Plumer Papers, DLC.

24. DPTM to APC, 15 July [1811], DMDE.

25. Stagg, *War*, 104; DPTM to RBB, 15 Nov. 1811, DMDE.

26. Ruth Baldwin Barlow to DPTM, 4 Mar. 1812, DMDE.

27. Brant, *President*, 407–408; Ketcham, *JM*, 502–503, 507–508.

28. Joel Barlow to DPTM, 14 Aug., 21 Dec. 1811, DMDE.

29. Joel Barlow to James Monroe, 19 Dec. 1811; Joel Barlow to JM, 19 Dec. 1811, *PJM-PS*, 4, 76–77, 78.

30. Ibid.

31. Ruth Baldwin Barlow to DPTM, 15 Apr. 1812, DMDE.

32. Brant, *President*, 440; Stagg, *War*, 104. Many thanks to J. C. A. Stagg for his personal clarification of the issues.

33. DMDE to Ruth Baldwin Barlow, [ca. 19 April 1812]; Brant, *President*, 521.

34. Brant, *President*, 534.

35. Bess Furman, *White House Profile* (New York: Bobbs-Merrill, 1951), 61; Brant, *President*, 379. Sixty-three of 140 members lost their seats.

36. "War Hawks" in Eric Foner and John A. Garraty, eds., *The Reader's Companion to American History* (Boston: Houghton Mifflin, 1991), 1128.

37. Arnett, *Incomparable*, 189.

38. MBS, "Mrs. Madison," in *The National Portrait Gallery of Distinguished*

Americans, James B. Longacre and James Herring, eds., vol. 3 (New York: Hermon Bancroft, 1836).

39. DPTM to Henry Clay, 8 Nov. 1836, in David B. Mattern and Holly C. Shulman, *The Selected Letters of Dolley Payne Madison* (Charlottesville: University of Virginia Press, 2003), 340.

40. Peter Field, review of Elaine K. Swift, *The Making of the American Senate: Reconstructive Change in Congress, 1781–1841, William and Mary Quarterly,* 3rd ser., vol. 55, no. 1 (Jan. 1988) 187; Judith Walker Rives, "Autobiography," William Cabell Rives Papers, DLC; Brant, *President,* 381.

41. DPTM to APC, 22 Dec. [1811], DMDE.

42. Ketcham, *JM,* 523–24; James R. Chiles, "Congress Couldn't Have Been *This* Bad, or Could It?" *Smithsonian,* 76 (Nov. 1995); DPTM to APC, May 1812, DMDE.

43. Brant, *President,* 476–77.

44. MBS to JBK, 13 Mar. 1814, MBS Papers, DLC; Charles J. Ingersoll, "James Madison," in *The National Portrait Gallery of Distinguished Americans,* James B. Longacre and James Herring, eds., vol. 3 (New York: Herman Bancroft, 1836), 10.

45. James Sterling Young, *The Washington Community, 1800–1828* (New York: Columbia University Press, 1966), 218.

46. LPWT to DPTM, [July 1811], DMDE; Bigelow, 25 Dec. 1811, cited in "Letters of Abijah Bigelow, Member of Congress to His Wife, 1810–1815," *American Antiquarian Society Proceedings* 40 (October 1930), 322.

47. RSC to IVH, [Mar. or Apr. 1812], cited in *Mistress of Riversdale: The Plantation Letters of Rosalie Stier Calvert,* ed. and trans. Margaret Law Callcott (Baltimore: Johns Hopkins University Press, 1991), 245; DeWitt Clinton ran as a "spoiler" Democrat-Republican and almost split the vote, which would have resulted in a Federalist win. Since the Federalists were pushing for New England to secede from the union, the election of DeWitt Clinton might have had disastrous consequences. Brant, *President,* 452–59.

48. Fredrika J. Teute, "Roman Matron on the Banks of Tiber Creek: Margaret Bayard Smith and the Politicization of Spheres in the Nation's Capital," in *A Republic for the Ages: The United States Capitol and the Political Culture of the Early Republic,* ed. Donald R. Kennon (Charlottesville: University of Virginia Press, 1999), 111.

14: "MR. MADISON'S WAR"

1. James R. Chiles, "Congress Couldn't Have Been *This* Bad, or Could It?" *Smithsonian,* Nov. 1995, 76. For the latest work on this understudied

conflict, see Donald R. Hickey, *Don't Give Up the Ship: Myths of the War of 1812* (forthcoming).

2. William Burwell to Letitia Burwell, 19 Jan. 1813, 20 Dec. 1812, Burwell Papers; Jeremiah Kilburn Smith to J. B. Moore, 29 Jan. 1809, Jeremiah Kilburn Smith Papers, DLC.

3. CM I, 57.

4. CM I, 53.

5. AJF, *Jeffersonian America: Notes on the United States of America,* ed. Richard Beale Davis (San Marino, Calif.: Huntingdon Library, 1954), 100; Donald R. Hickey, *The War of 1812: A Forgotten Conflict* (Urbana: University of Illinois Press, 1995), 75.

6. Hickey, *1812,* 52–53; Roger H. Brown, *The Republic in Peril: 1812* (New York: W. W. Norton, 1971), 177.

7. Hickey, *1812,* 53.

8. Ibid., 56–67; Anthony S. Pitch, *The Burning of Washington: The British Invasion of 1814* (Annapolis, MD: Naval Institute Press, 1998), 3–12.

9. Marshal Smelser, *The Democratic Republic, 1810–1815* (New York: Harper & Row, 1968), 291.

10. Hickey, *1812,* 75–77; Smelser, *DR,* 228.

11. Hickey, *1812,* 78–79.

12. Smelser, *DR,* 292; Irving Brant, *James Madison: Commander in Chief, 1812–1836* (Indianapolis: Bobbs-Merrill, 1961), 157–58.

13. Hickey, *1812,* 74; J.C.A. Stagg, *Mr. Madison's War: Politics, Diplomacy, and Warfare in the Early American Republic, 1783–1830* (Princeton: Princeton University Press, 1983), 4–7.

14. Hickey, *1812,* 72–73.

15. Ibid., 80, 127. Ultimately, the American efforts proved fruitless, and Astor had to wait until 1814 to retrieve his property. For more on the Michilimackinac campaign, see Robert Malcomson. "'Carry Michilimackinac at all hazards': How the Capture of Michilimackinac Affected American Campaign Plans in the War of 1812," *Inland Seas* (forthcoming, 2006).

16. Hickey, *1812,* 80–84. Donald R. Hickey speculates that the militiamen who cited their constitutional right to refuse to cross the border may have been inspired to do so because the use of militia in "foreign wars" was being hotly debated in the newspapers. Personal communication.

17. Ibid., 86–87.

18. Ibid., 88.

19. Ibid., 90–91.

20. Ibid., 92–93.

21. Ibid., 93–94.
22. Ibid., 94–96. Decatur originally intended to bring his prize into New London, Connecticut, but bad weather forced it into Newport, Rhode Island. Personal communication, Donald R. Hickey.
23. DPTM to PPM, [ca. 17 October 1812], DMDE; CM I, 57.
24. CM I, 57. DPTM to PPM, [ca. 17 Oct. 1812]; Seaton, Diary, 5 March 1813, cited in Josephine Seaton, *William Winston Seaton and the National Intelligencer* (Boston: James R. Osgood and Company, 1871), 98.
25. CAM to MAM, 11 Jan. 1809, CAM Papers, DLC; MBS to JBK, 1 Jan. 1814, MBS Papers, DLC.
26. DPTM to EC, 10 June 1813, DMDE.
27. DPTM to EC, 31 Aug. [1812], DMDE. Letters from this time show that Dolley's involvement with politics deepened, as reflected in the quite visible scissoring by later, solicitous relatives whenever the topic appeared.
28. Alan Lloyd, *The Scorching of Washington: The War of 1812* (West Vancouver, B.C.: David & Charles, n.d.), 86.
29. Frances Carpenter Huntingdon, "The Heiress of Washington City: Marcia Burnes Van Ness, 1782–1832," *Records of the Columbia Historical Society* 69–70 (June 1971), 92–93; Paul A. Jennings, *A Colored Man's Reminiscences of James Madison*, www.whitehousehistory.org.
30. Lucia B. Cutts, *Memoirs and Letters of Dolly Madison: Wife of James Madison, President of the United States* (Boston: Houghton, Mifflin, 1886), 141–42.
31. Samuel Taggert to John Taylor, 21 Dec. 1812, AAS; CM I, 48–50.
32. DPTM to APC, 22 December [1811]; SGS to 2 Jan. 1813, in *Seaton*, 91.
33. Rebecca Crispin Hubbs to DPTM, 13 July 1813; SC(S), 19 July [18]13, DMDE; CM I, 57.
34. William Burwell to Letitia Burwell, 19 Jan. 1813, Burwell Papers, DLC.
35. *New England Palladium*, 19 Jan. 1813, AAS; Hickey, *1812*, 126–27.
36. Present-day Toronto.
37. Hickey, *1812*, 128–30. Contemporary Canadian scholars doubt whether a scalp was ever found. Personal communication, Donald R. Hickey.
38. Ibid., 130–35.
39. Ibid., 135–39.
40. William Burwell to Letitia Burwell, 2 June 1813, Burwell Papers, DLC.
41. PPM to DPTM, 23 October 1813, DMDE.
42. Hickey, *1812*, 151–53.
43. Brant, *CC*, 155–56.
44. Ibid., 190–91; AG to John W. Nicholson, 5 May 1812, cited in Brant, *CC*, 159; DPTM to HNG, 28 July 1814.

45. Washington Irving to James Renwick, 24 Nov. 1812, cited in Raymond Walters, Jr., *Albert Gallatin: Jeffersonian Financier and Diplomat* (Pittsburgh: University of Pittsburgh Press, 1957), 214.

46. AG to HNG, 6 May 1800; HNG to AG, 7 May 1800; AG to HNG, 12 May 1800, NYHS. For the best discussion of Hannah Nicholson Gallatin and her relationship with Dolley, see Holly Cowan Shulman, "Finding Hannah: Hannah Gallatine Through the Eyes of Dolley Madison," *The New-York Journal of American History*, 46: 1 (spring–summer 2005), 22–28.

47. AG to HNG, 4 July 1807; HNG to AG, 5 July 1807, AG Papers, NYHS.

48. DPTM to HNG, 28 July [18]14, DMDE; AG to HNG, 4 July 1814, AG Papers, NYHS.

49. John Jacob Astor TO HNG, 25 July 1813, cited in Brant, *CC*, 192–93.

50. Brant, *CC*, 184–88.

51. DPTM to EC, 2, 29 July 1813; DPTM to HNG, 29 July 1813, DMDE.

52. DPTM to HNG, 29 July 1813, 15 Aug. 1813, DMDE.

53. DPTM to HNG, 30 Aug. 1813, DMDE.

54. HNG to DPTM, 15 May 1814, 21 Jan. [1814], DMDE.

55. DPTM to HNG, 22 May 1814, DMDE.

56. DPTM to JPT, 6 Aug. 1814; DPTM to HNG, 22 May 1814, DMDE.

57. DPTM to HNG, [6] Aug. [1814], DMDE.

58. HNG to DPTM, 9 Aug. 1814; DPTM to HNG, [5 March 1815], DMDE.

15: POTOMAC PHOENIX

1. DPTM to PPM, 16 Aug. 1812; DPTM to EC, 13 May [18] 13, DMDE. MBS to JBK, 20 July 1813, MBS papers, DLC; William Burwell to Letitia Burwell (wife), 21 July 1813, Burwell Papers, DLC. Many thanks to Holly C. Shulman for the preceding account (from an unpublished paper) of the British attacks on Havre de Grace and Craney Island and its implications for Dolley Madison.

2. DPTM to EC, 13 May [18]13, DMDE.

3. Donald R. Hickey, *The War of 1812: A Forgotten Conflict* (Urbana: University of Illinois Press, 1995), 221–25.

4. Ibid., 153–54.

5. Anthony S. Pitch, *The Burning of Washington: The British Invasion of 1814* (Annapolis, MD: Naval Institute Press, 1998), 17–18.

6. Ibid., 19.

7. Ibid., 21, 147.

8. Andrew Tully, *When They Burned the White House* (New York: Simon & Schuster, 1961), 108.

9. Ibid., 108; DPTM to JPT, 6 Aug. [18]14, DMDE; Michael Shiner Diary, 1814, 5, Shiner Papers, DLC.

10. DPTM to HNG, 28 July [18]14, DMDE.

11. DPTM to HNG, 28 July, [6] August [1814], DMDE.

12. Pitch, *Burning*, 32.

13. DPTM to EC, 13 May [18]13, DMDE; CM I, 53.

14. Eleanor Young Jones to DPTM, 23 August 1814, DMDE.

15. DPTM to LPWT, 23 August 1814, DMDE; Michael Shiner diary, 1814, 6, Shiner Papers, DLC. Many thanks to Holly C. Shulman.

16. DPTM to LPWT, 23 August 1814, DMDE; APC to DPTM, [ca. 23 Aug. 1814], DMDE.

17. Dolley also saved a "dimijohn of pure wine" that she presented to her friend Minerva Denison Rodgers, [Sept.–Dec. 1814], DMDE.

18. Paul A. Jennings, *A Colored Man's Reminiscences of James Madison*, www.whitehousehistory.org; Ethel Stephens Arnett, *Mrs. James Madison: The Incomparable Dolley* (Greensboro, NC: Piedmont Press, 1972), 240–42.

19. Jennings, *Reminiscences*; DPTM to Mary Hazelhurst Latrobe, 3 Dec. 1814, DMDE.

20. Now Dumbarton House at 2715 Que Street, N.W. William Jones, "Memorandum," U. C. Smith Collection, the Historical Society of Pennsylvania. Many thanks to George Boudreau.

21. DPTM to LPWT, 23 August 1814, DMDE.

22. Pitch, *Burning*, 96–97; Jennings, *Reminiscences*.

23. Pitch, *Burning*, 97; Michael Shiner Diary, 1814, 6, Shiner Papers, DLC.

24. Pitch, *Burning*, 117–19; William Seale, *The President's House: A History* (Washington, D.C.: White House Historical Association, 1986), 1: 135–37; James Scott to George Cockburn, cited in "Eyewitness Accounts of the Burning of the White House: They Were There," *White House History* 4 Fall (1998), 56–57. See also MBS to JBK, August 1814, MBS Papers, DLC.

25. MBS to JBK, 25/30 Aug. 1814, MBS Papers, DLC.

26. Jennings, *Reminiscences*; Anna Maria Brodeau Thornton Diary, Aug. 24, 25, 1814, William Thornton Papers, DLC.

27. Charles J. Ingersoll, *Historical Sketch of the Second War between the United States of American and Great Britain* (Philadelphia: Lea and Blanchard, 1849), vol. 2, 208.

28. Constance McLaughlin Green, *Washington: Village and Capital, 1800–1878* (Princeton: Princeton University Press, 1972), 62; Anna Maria Brodeau Thornton Diary, Aug. 25, 1814, William Thornton Papers, DLC; M. Peter to Thomas Pickering, 28 Aug. 1814, Tudor Place, Washington, DC.

29. Pitch, *Burning*, 138–39.

30. Michael Shiner Diary, 1814, 7, 8, Shiner Papers, DLC.

31. Pitch, *Burning*, 143–44, 219–20; Hickey, *1812*, 202–04; J. C. A. Stagg, *Mr. Madison's War: Politics, Diplomacy, and Warfare in the Early Republic, 1783–1830* (Princeton University Press, 1983), 427–28; Anna Maria Brodeau Thornton Diary, 25 August 1814, William Thornton Papers, DLC; Green, *Village*, 62; Michael Shiner Diary, 1814, 9, Shiner Papers, DLC.

32. MBS to JBK, August 1814, MBS Papers, DLC; Anna Maria Brodeau Thornton Diary, Aug. 28, 1814, William Thornton Papers, DLC; William Wirt to Elizabeth Washington Gamble Wirt, 14 October 1814, Wirt Family Papers, MDHS.

33. Anna Maria Brodeau Thornton Diary, Aug. 28, 1814, William Thornton Papers, DLC; William Wirt to Elizabeth Washington Gamble Wirt, 14 October 1814, Wirt Family Papers, MDHS.

34. Cited in Anna Maria Brodeau Thornton, "Diary," *Records of the Columbia Historical Society* 19, 178; William Wirt to Elizabeth Washington Gamble Wirt, 14 October 1814, Wirt Family Papers, MDHS.

35. MBS to JBK, August 1814, MBS Papers, DLC; DPTM to Mary Hazelhurst Latrobe, 3 Dec. 1814, DMDE.

36. Anna Maria Brodeau Thornton Diary, Aug. 30, 1814, William Thornton Papers, DLC. For national vitriol, see Tully, *Burned*, 220–21.

37. Richard Cranch Norton to Jacob Norton, 6 Nov. 1814, Jacob Norton Papers, MHS; Arnett, *Incomparable*, 423, 427–28.

38. Tully, *Burned*, 221; Charles G. Muller, *The Darkest Day: 1814, The Washington-Baltimore Campaign* (Phila.: J. B. Lippincott and Co., 1963), 170–71, 209; Robert V. Remini, "Becoming a National Symbol," in *The White House: The First Two Hundred Years*, ed. Frank Freidel and William Pencak (Boston: Northeastern University Press, 1994), 24–25.

39. For a detailed discussion, see Arnett's appendix in *Incomparable*, 422–43; *Annals of Congress*, 13th Congress (1814–1815), III, 335.

40. MBS to JBK, August [1814]. See also HNG to AG, 5 February 1801, 5 June 1804, AG Papers, NYHS.

41. Arnett, *Incomparable*, 423–25.

42. *National Intelligencer*, 2 Sept. 1814, AAS.

43. Barnabas Bidwell to Mary Bidwell, 28 Nov. 1815, Barnabas Bidwell Collection, DLC.

44. Arnett, *Incomparable*, 426–28; William Lowndes to ?, [1814], 11 October 1814, William Lowndes Papers, DLC; John Forsyth to Richard Henry Wilde, 8 October 1814, John Forsyth Papers, DLC; Thomas Law to John Law, 2 October [1814], Thomas Law Papers, DLC.

45. Green, *Village*, 67; Frances Carpenter Huntingdon, "The Heiress of Washington City: Marcia Burnes Van Ness, 1782–1832," *Records of the Columbia Historical Society* 69–70 (June 1971), 96; Susan L. Klaus, "'Some of the Smartest Folks Here': The Van Nesses and Community Building in Early Washington," *Washington History* 3: 2 (Fall/Winter 1991–1992), 24.

46. Thomas Law to HNG, 3 April 1809, AG Papers, NYHS; Thomas Law to JM, 26 Nov. 1816, cited in Allen C. Clark, *Thomas Law: A Biographical Sketch* (Washington, D.C.: W. F. Roberts Press, 1900), 18–19.

47. Fredrika J. Teute, "'A Wild, Desolate Place': Life on the Margins in Early Washington," in *Southern City, National Ambition: The Growth of Early Washington, D.C., 1800–1860*, ed. Howard Gillette, Jr. (Washington, D.C.: American Architectural Foundation, 1995), 52, 57–59; Klaus, "'Smartest,'" 33.

48. *National Intelligencer*, 10 October 1815, AAS; Green, *Village*, 70–71; Huntingdon, "Van Ness," 97. For more newspaper coverage, see *National Intelligencer*, 13 Oct., 14 Oct., 28 Nov., and 9 Dec. 1815; 3 Jan. and 30 Jan. 1816.

49. Richard Cranch Norton, 7 Oct. 1814, Jacob Norton Papers, MHS; Arnett, *Incomparable*, 426.

50. Arnett, *Incomparable*, 427.

51. Ibid., 437.

52. Ibid., 442.

53. *Washington City Gazette*, 19 Sept. 1814, cited in Arnett, *Incomparable*, 249–50. For more on the Octagon House, see George McCue, *The Octagon: Being an Account of a Famous Washington Residence: Its Great Years, Decline and Restoration* (Washington, D.C.: American Institute of Architects Foundation, 1976).

54. CM I, 54; DPTM to HNG, 14 Jan. 1815; HNG to DPTM, 18 Jan. 1815; DPTM to HNG, 5 Mar. 1815, DMDE.

55. Arnett, *Incomparable*, 199.

56. Barbara Carson, *Ambitious Appetites: Dining, Behavior, and Patterns of Consumption in Federal Washington* (Washington, D.C.: American Institute of Architects Press, 1990), 4; MBC to MHB, 11 Nov. 1815, cited in *Letters of Mary Boardman Crowninshield, 1815–1816*, ed. Frances Boardman Crowninshield (Cambridge, Mass.: Riverside Press, 1935), 16.

57. DPTM to EC, 6 March 1816, DMDE; MBS to JBK, 7 Feb. 1817, MBS Papers, DLC.

58. Paul F. Boller, Jr., *Presidential Wives: An Anecdotal History* (New York: Oxford University Press, 1988), 43.

59. Thomas Law, "Verses," Thomas Law Papers, DLC.

60. "Peace on Honorable Terms," broadside, 1815, MHS.

61. DPTM to HNG, [7 Aug. 1815], 12 August 1815, DMDE.

62. Hickey, *1812*, 204–205.

63. William Ward to Thomas Wren Ward, 10 December 1814, Thomas Wren Ward Papers, MHS. Thanks to Michael Rush.

64. "Thirty-Four Years Ago: A Reminiscence," *Intelligencer*, Cutts Family Papers, DLC. See also CM I. Though bylined as "Anonymous," this account was written by none other than the ubiquitous Margaret Bayard Smith. Interestingly, Smith used this piece as part of an obituary for Dolley in 1849. So closely linked was Dolley with the war in the public mind that Margaret spent the lion's share of the tribute detailing the war itself, only getting to Dolley and arrival of peace in the final paragraphs.

65. Jennings, *Reminiscences*; "Peace on Honorable Terms," broadside, 1815, MHS.

66. DPTM to HNG, [5 March 1815], 19 Mar. [1815], DMDE.

67. Harrison Gray Otis to SFO, 22 Feb. 1815, Harrison Gray Otis Papers, MHS.

68. Stagg, *War*, 471–83.

69. Thomas Baker Johnson to DPTM, 19 Jan. 1815, DMDE.

70. Just as surely, the losers were the native tribes who had hoped to regain their lands with a British victory. For a good assessment of the war, see Stagg, *War*, 501–17.

71. Albert Gallatin, cited in Ray Walters, Jr., *Albert Gallatin: Jeffersonian Financier and Diplomat* (Pittsburgh, PA: University of Pittsburgh Press, 1957), 288.

72. "Thirty-Four Years Ago: A Reminiscence," *Intelligencer*, Cutts Family Papers, DLC.

73. Beckles Willson, *Friendly Relations: A Narrative of Britain's Ministers and Ambassadors to America (1791–1930)* (London: Lovat Dickson and Thompson Limited, 1934), 96; RSC to IVH, 6 May 1815, cited in *Mistress of Riversdale: The Plantation Letters of Rosalie Stier Calvert*, ed. and trans. Margaret Law Callcott (Baltimore: Johns Hopkins University Press, 1991), 282.

74. Charles Hurd, *Washington Cavalcade* (New York: Dutton, 1948), 46; Carson, *Appetites*, 6; James Kirke Paulding to Henry Brevoort, Jr., 1 December 1815, Paulding Letters, NYHS.

75. *National Intelligencer*, 30 Mar. 1815, cited in Remini, "National Symbol," 26.

76. Hurd, *Cavalcade*, 50.

16: TO HOME AND HISTORY

1. Georgetown Invitation, DM Collection, Greensboro Museum; CM II, 33; David B. Mattern and Holly C. Shulman, *The Selected Letters of Dolley Payne Madison* (Charlottesville: University of Virginia Press, 2003), 105.

2. "Poem," 11 March 1817, Manuscript Collection, 47, James Madison's Montpelier, Orange, Va.; William Johnson, Jr., to DPTM, [16 March] 1817; PPM to DPTM, 22 March 1820, DMDE.

3. Benjamin Ogle Tayloe, *Our Neighbors on La Fayette Square* (Originally published Washington: 1872; reprint, Washington, D.C.: Junior League of Washington, 1982), 36; Lucia Alice von Kantzow to DPTM, 28 June 1818, DMDE.

4. "Mrs. Madison," *The Port Folio,* V, II, Feb. 1818, AAS.

5. John Rodgers to DPTM, 6 Dec. 1815; ECL to DPTM, 4 March 1817, DMDE.

6. DPTM to HNG, [5 March 1815]; DPTM to EC, 6 March 1816, DMDE.

7. Drew McCoy, *The Last of the Founders: James Madison and the Republican Legacy* (Cambridge, U.K.: Cambridge University Press, 1989), 10–11; Marshal Smelser, *The Democratic Republic, 1810–1815* (New York: Harper & Row, 1968), 318–20.

8. John Adams to Thomas Jefferson, 2 Feb. 1817, APM, MHS; McCoy, *Last,* 12–13.

9. McCoy, *Last,* 14.

10. Ibid., 18–21.

11. Ibid., 34.

12. The selection of adjectives is from ibid. For another positive assessment of James's character and its political manifestation, see J. C. A. Stagg, *Mr. Madison's War: Politics, Diplomacy, and Warfare in the Early Republic, 1783–1830* (Princeton: Princeton University Press, 1983), 436. For absorbing accounts of James's presidency and career, see: Jack N. Rakove, *James Madison and the Creation of the American Republic* (Glenview, IL: Scott, Foresman/Little, Brown, 1990); Garry Wills, *James Madison* (New York: Henry Holt and Company, 2002).

13. Joseph J. Ellis, *Founding Brothers: The Revolutionary Generation* (New York: Knopf, 2000), 78.

14. Ralph L. Ketcham, ed., "An Unpublished Sketch of James Madison by James K. Paulding," *Virginia Magazine of History and Biography* 67 (1959): 432–37.

15. ECL to DPTM, 29 June 1817; ECL to DPTM, 30 March 1819; DPTM to APC, [ca. 15 May 1832]; DPTM to APC, 5 July 1816, DMDE.

16. DPTM to ECL, 21 April [18]19, DMDE.

17. DPTM to ECL, 21 April [18]19; DPTM to Elizabeth Coles, 8 April 1831, DMDE.

18. DPTM to JGJ, 29 Nov. 1822; DPTM to SC(S), [ca. Feb. 1820], DMDE.

19. DPTM to APC, [ca. 23 July 1818], DMDE.

20. DPTM to APC, [June 1819–1821], DMDE.

21. DPTM to JPT, 20 July 1832, DMDE.

22. CM II, 87. On Payne's disappearances, see DPTM to APC?, 4 Dec. 1829; DPTM to APC, 25 Jan. [18]30, DMDE; John C. Payne to James Madison Cutts, 1 Sept. 1849, cited in *SL,* 220; JM to EC, 23 Feb. 1827, cited in *SL,* 220.

23. DPTM to JPT, 20 July 1832; DPTM to JPT, 14 June 1845; DPTM to JPT, 27 April 1828, DMDE. See JPT to DPTM, Nov. 1844, in *SL.*

24. DPTM to APC, 6 June [18]29, DMDE.

25. DPTM to JPT, 27 April 1828, DMDE.

26. DPTM to PPM, 10 May 1811, DMDE.

27. DPTM to JPT, 2 Dec. 1824, DMDE.

28. DPTM to Mary Elizabeth Payne Allen Jackson, 25 Feb. 1834, DMDE.

29. DPTM to MEEC, 13 Mar. [1833]; DPTM to Richard Cutts, 11 Aug. 1833, DMDE.

30. DPTM to MEEC, 4 Nov. 1833, DMDE.

31. DPTM to MEEC, 10 Mar. 1833, *SL,* 298.

32. DPTM to MEEC, 20 Apr. 1834, 10 Mar. 1833; DPTM to DPMC, 11 May 1835; DPTM to MEEC, 13 March [1833], *SL*; DPTM to MEEC, 2 Dec. 1834; DPTM to MEEC, 22 Jan. 1825; DMDE.

33. DPTM to MEEC, 31 Oct. 1835; DPTM to MEEC, 22 January 1825; DPTM to DPMC, 10 Mar. 1830, DMDE.

34. DPTM to DPMC, 2 Feb. 1832; DPTM to MEEC, 11 Dec. 1834; DPTM to MEEC, 22 Jan. 1825; DPTM to MEEC, 13 Mar. 1833; DPTM to MEEC, 16 Sept. 1831; DMDE.

35. DPTM to MEEC, 13 March [1833], DMDE; DPTM to MEEC, 10 March 1835, DMDE.

36. DPTM to MEEC, 16 Sept. 1831; 22 January 1825, DMDE.

37. James Madison Cutts to DPTM, 4 Sept. 1835, *SL,* 221; DPTM to MEEC, Oct. 1834, DMDE.

38. DPTM to Caroline Langdon Eustis, 22 Jan 1819; DPTM to EC, 16 April 1834; DPTM to APC, 3 April [18]18; DPTM to MEEC, 10 March 1835; DMDE.

39. CM II, 46.

40. DPTM to FDL, [March 1832]; DPTM to EC, 16 April 1834; DPTM to APC, [ca. 15 May 1832], DMDE.

41. DPTM to EC, 16 April 1834; DPTM to JPT, 27 April 1828; DMDE.

42. DPTM to MEEC, 10 March 1835, 2 December 1834, DMDE; DPTM to EC, 7 Jan. 1837; *SL,* 342–43. Dolley may have suffered from severe chronic blepharitis, an inflammation of the eyelids. None of her home remedies

or professional potions had a chance of healing it; even modern treatments cannot necessarily cure severe cases of blepharitis. The diagnosis is the best guess of the editors of DM's papers, see *SL,* 343.

43. For examples of petitions for her influence after 1816, among many, see Ann Emlen Hare to DPTM, 6 Mar. 1822; AM to DPTM, 3 June 1824; DPTM to Jane Bancker Woodside Cathcart, 20 Jan. 1827; DPTM to SC(S), [ca. February 1820]. DMDE.

44. JWR to DPTM, 26 Jan. 1829, DMDE; PPM to DPTM, 19 Jan. 1824, DMDE.

45. DPTM to DPMC, 10 Mar. 1830, DMDE.

46. For the best (and most entertaining) accounts of the Eaton Affair, see John F. Marszalek, *The Petticoat Affair: Manners, Mutiny, and Sex in Andrew Jackson's White House* (New York: The Free Press, 1997); Kirsten E. Wood, "'One Woman So Dangerous to Public Morals': Gender and Power in the Eaton Affair," *Journal of the Early Republic* 17:2 (Summer 1997): 237–75.

47. On Dolley and the Eaton Affair, see DPTM to APC, 28 Dec. [1829]; DPTM to APC, 25 Jan. [18]30; James Taylor to DPTM, 2 Jan. 1831, DMDE.

48. DPTM to APC, 6 June 1829, DMDE.

49. Ibid.

50. DPTM to Christopher Hughes, 20 March 1828, DMDE.

51. DPTM to APC, 23 Apr. 1827, DMDE.

52. DPTM to JM, [5 Dec. 1826], DMDE.

53. CM II, 33.

54. CM II, 37, 39.

55. Cutts II, 37–38, 40.

56. Ralph D. Gray, ed., "A Tour of Virginia in 1827: Letters of Henry D. Gilpin to His Father," *The Virginia Magazine of History and Biography* 76: 4 (Oct. 1968), 469; L. G. Moffatt and J. M. Carrière, "A Frenchman Visits Norfolk, Fredericksburg and Orange Country, 1816," Part II, *Virginia Historical Magazine,* 53(2), 1945: 202.

57. Gray, "Gilpin," 470. See also Mary Lucille Proctor, "After-Dinner Anecdotes of James Madison: Excerpt from Jared Sparks, Journal for 1829–331," *Virginia Magazine of History and Biography,* 60 (1952): 257.

58. Arnett, *Incomparable,* 126.

59. Betty Churchill (Jones) Lacy, "Memories of a Long Life," April 1903, Unpublished Manuscript, Fredericksburg and Spotsylvania National Military Park; "Notes by Kate K. Blattermann of Atlanta, GA," CM II, 40; JWR, "Autobiography," William Cabell Rives Papers, DLC, 56; Cutts II, 40. For a fictional account of Dolley through a child's eyes, see Anonymous ("A

Lady of 'Louise Home,' Washington"), *Dora Lee; or The Visit to Montpelier* (Baltimore: Charles Harvey & Co., 1872).

60. JWR, "Autobiography," 55, William Cabell Rives Papers, DLC.

61. Ibid., 56–57.

62. DPTM to John G. Jackson, 27 Nov. 1824; JM to DPTM, [5 Nov. 1824], DMDE.

63. Auguste Levasseur, *Lafayette in America in 1824 and 1825; or, Journal of a Voyage to the United States,* trans. John D. Goodman (Philadelphia, 1829), 222; Frances Wright Darusmont to DPTM, 26 July 1825; JM to DPTM, [5 Nov. 1824], DMDE.

64. DPTM to MEEC, 31 March 1835, DMDE.

65. Harriet Martineau, *Retrospect of Western Travel,* ed. Daniel Feller (Armonk, N.Y.: M. E. Sharpe, 2000), 75.

66. Ibid.; McCoy, *Last,* 5–6.

67. McCoy, *Last,* 22; Martineau, *Retrospect,* 76–77.

68. Martineau, *Retrospect,* 78–79; DPTM to Ann Maury, 31 March 1835, DMDE.

69. DPTM to Richard D. Cutts, [ca. 1824]; DPTM to Richard D. Cutts, [ca. 1827–1829], DMDE.

70. Martineau, *Retrospect,* 76.

71. "Reminiscences of Madison Hemmings," cited in Fawn M. Brodie, *Thomas Jefferson: An Intimate History* (New York: W. W. Norton, 1974), 473. Dolley was on intimate enough terms with Jefferson's slave mistress, Sally Hemmings, to ask her to name a son after James, though it is not clear whether she knew or assumed the child's father to be Thomas Jefferson. See also Bettye Kearse, "The Other Madisons," unpublished manuscript.

72. DPTM to MEEC, 16 Sept. 1831, DMDE.

73. Proctor, "After-Dinner," 257–64; McCoy, *Last,* 130.

74. McCoy, *Last,* 48–50, 65, 73, 107–113, 119–70, 163.

75. SCS to DPTM, 22 Nov. 1833, DMDE.

76. DPTM to SCS, [ca. Feb. 1820], DMDE.

77. DPTM to MEEC, 10 Mar. 1833, DMDE.

78. DPTM, 16 Mar. 1839, Henkels Catalogue # 1478.

17: LEGACIES

1. DPTM to JPT, 20 July 1832, DMDE.

2. DPTM to JPT, 20 July 1832; DPTM to Frances Dandridge Lear [March 1832]; DPTM to Mary Allen, 25 Feb. 1834, DMDE.

3. "He lives near us with a large family & in poor circumstances—& we have some hope of turning the land to acct. for his helpless family." DPTM to John G. Jackson, 27 Nov. 1824, DMDE.

4. DPTM to Mary E. P. Allen, 25 Feb. 1834, DMDE; DPTM to DPMC, 11 May 1835, in David B. Mattern and Holly C. Shulman, *The Selected Letters of Dolley Payne Madison* (Charlottesville, University of Virginia Press, 2003), 311.

5. DPTM to APC, [June 1820?], DMDE.

6. Ibid.; ECL to DPTM, 12 Feb. 1824; ECL to DPTM, 5 April 1824; DPTM to FDL, [March 1832], DMDE. For a sample of Dolley's letters concerning Anna's health during this time, see DPTM to APC, 28 Dec. [1829], DMDE.

7. DPTM to APC, [ca. 4 Aug. 1832], DMDE.

8. DPTM to Richard Cutts, 6 Aug. 1832, DMDE.

9. Annie Payne to MEEC, 26 July 1836, Cutts microfilm, SCHL; CM II, 69.

10. Paul A. Jennings, *A Colored Man's Reminiscences of James Madison*, www.whitehousehistory.org.

11. Andrew Jackson to DPTM, 9 July 1836, *SL*, 329; LCJA to DPTM, 2 July 1836, *SL*, 328.

12. DPTM to Richard Cutts, 5 July 1836, *SL*, 328; DPTM to ECL, 26 July 1836, *SL*, 329.

13. DPTM to Andrew Jackson, [20 Aug. 1836], *SL*, 330; CM II, 74; *Niles's Weekly Register*, 17 Dec. 1836, 51: 16: APS Online, 245; "An Act to extend the privilege of franking letters and packages to Dolly P. Madison," 2 July 1836, *U. S. Statutes at Large* 5:107.

14. DPTM to AM, 27 July 1836, DM Papers, DLC; Annie Payne to FDL, 16 July 1836, Henley-Smith Collection, DLC.

15. James Madison's will, James Madison Memorial Collection, *PJM*, UVA.

16. DPTM to ECL, 26 July 1836, *SL*, 329; DPTM to Andrew Jackson, [20 Aug. 1836], DMDE; *Niles's Weekly Register*, 17 Dec. 1836, 51, 16: APS Online, 246.

17. Annie Payne to FDL, 16 July 1836, Henley-Smith Collection, DLC.

18. EC to DPTM, 7 Nov. 1836, *SL*, 338.

19. DPTM to Richard D. Cutts, [ca. Oct. 1837], *SL*, 347.

20. DPM Papers, DLC.

21. William Kemble to William Kemble, Jr., 25 Jan. 1839, in *Letters of James Kirke Paulding*, ed. Ralph M. Aderman (Madison, WI: University of Wisconsin Press, 1962), 243, n. 1.

22. DPTM to Caroline Hite, 13 Dec. 1838, *SL*, 348.

23. JPT, "Diary," cited in Richard N. Coté, *Strength and Honor: The Life of Dolley Madison* (Mount Pleasant, S.C.: Corinthian Books, 2005), 345.

24. CM II, 71–72.

25. EC to SC(S), 12 Nov. 1836, cited in Drew McCoy, *The Last of the Founders: James Madison and the Republican Legacy* (Cambridge, U.K.: Cambridge University Press, 1989), 320.

26. George A. Waggaman to DPTM, 6 Oct. 1839, *SL,* 348; DPTM to George A. Waggaman, 10 Oct. 1839, *SL,* 349.

27. DPTM to EC, 26 Sept. 1842, *SL,* 361–62; DPTM to JPT [ca. 1 Sept. 1842], *SL,* 359–60.

28. Paul Jennings to DPTM, n.d., Sarah Steward to DPTM, 24 Apr. 1847, *SL,* 383.

29. DPTM to LPWT, 13 Nov. 1842, *SL,* 363.

30. "Deed to John Payne Todd" [16 June 1844], *SL,* 372; Sarah Steward to DPTM, 5 July 1844, *SL,* 372–73.

31. DPTM to John Jacob Astor, 12 Sept. 1842, *SL,* 361.

32. DPTM to APC, 23 April [1827], DMDE. "Poem," n.p., n.d., Autograph poem, EBay auction #2161865372, March 2003; "Poem," www.historyforsale.com.

33. "Untitled," 14 June 1848; DPTM to Saltonstall, 17 June 1848. Cutts Miscellany, probably copied by Richard Cutts, Unsigned copy dated 2 Aug. 1844. See also DPTM to Elliot Cresson, [28 Jan. 1834], DMDE.

34. DPTM to MEEC, 1 Aug. 1833, DMDE.

35. DPTM to DPMC, 10 Feb. 1835, DMDE.

36. CM I, 44; DPTM to DPMC, 10 March 1830, DMDE.

37. "Poem," 23 May 1842, DPM Papers, DLC; DPTM to Richard Cutts, 16 July 1845, *SL,* 380–81.

38. DPTM to Christopher Hughes, 20 Mar. 1828, DMDE.

39. DPTM to MBS, 31 Aug. 1834, DMDE; Mattern and Shulman, *SL,* 3–7. Many thanks to Susan H. Perdue for her help.

40. DPTM to MBS, 31 Aug. 1834, DMDE.

41. Ibid.

42. DPTM to MEEC, 10 March 1835, DMDE.

43. DPTM to APC, 6 June [18]29, DMDE. Louis McLane agreed. In 1811, while acknowledging Bayard Smith's influence, he also told his wife that she was "the most infernal gossip I ever met with. I am sure she detailed the scandal of 10 years, sparing neither friend nor foe." Some of her stories of "vice and immorality" kept him up at night. Louis McLane to Kitty McLane, 7 Feb. 1818, McLane Papers, DLC.

44. DPTM to MEEC, 2 Dec. 1834, DMDE.

45. DPTM to MBS, 17 Jan. 1835, DMDE.

46. Ibid.

47. David B. Mattern, "Dolley Madison Has the Last Word: The Famous Letter," *White House History* 4 (Fall 1998), 38. Nor has any original subsequently turned up. The only extant version is copied from the *Portrait Gallery* entry in Dolley's best hand.

48. Mattern, "Word," 39; Mattern and Shulman, *SL,* 5.

49. DPTM to Mary Elizabeth Hazelhurst Latrobe, 3 Dec. 1814, DMDE.

50. DPTM to MEEC, Oct. [1835], DMDE.

51. Ibid.

52. DPTM to MEEC, 2 Dec. 1834, DMDE.

53. DPTM to DPMC, 2 Feb. 1832, [1834–1835], DMDE.

54. MBS to MBB, 6 Feb. 1836, MBS Papers.

55. Robert G. L. De Peyster to DPTM, 11 Feb. 1848, *SL,* 387.

56. Near the end of Dolley's life, Elizabeth Fries Ellet, the first popular women's historian, contacted her about including Dolley in what would be a groundbreaking three-volume set, *The Women of the American Revolution.* Dolley unequivocally, though politely, refused, citing her young age at the time of the Revolution. It also may be that she did not want too close an examination of her pacifist family, especially her father.

57. Anonymous, *Boston Cultivator,* 4 Apr. 1846: 8, 14, 104; DPTM to the House of Representatives, 9 Jan. 1844, *SL,* 368; Henry Barrett Learned, "Some Aspects of the Cabinet Meeting," *Records of the Columbia Historical Society* 5: 18 (1913–1914), 128; "M. C.," "Wages of Labor," *Workingman's Advocate,* May 14, 1831: 2, 39, APS Online. Though Dolley was invited to the cornerstone ceremony, she begged off the day before. Notwithstanding, strong evidence exists that she did indeed join the celebration. See Fanny Lee Jones, "Walter Jones and His Times," *Records of the Columbia Historical Society* (5: 1902), 149. President John Tyler reinstated Dolley's receptions. He was quoted as saying that it was "a Virginia notion," which brought "all classes of people together . . . it Americanizes them." Paul M. Zall, *Dolley Madison* (Huntington, N.Y.: Nova History Publications, 2001), 90.

58. DPTM to JPT, 21 May [18]48, *SL,* 380, 388–89.

59. DPTM to JPT, [19 Feb. 1846], *SL,* 382; Jennings, *Reminiscences.*

60. DPTM to JPT, 24 April 1848, *SL,* 387.

61. DPTM to FDL, 17 May 1839, 30 July 1843, Henley-Smith, DLC.

62. DPTM to JPT, 10 July 1848, *SL,* 390.

63. CM II, 90; also in handwriting in Cutts Miscellany, MHS.

64. ECL to Zaccheus Collins Lee [1849], *SL,* 390–91.

65. AM to Annie Payne, 26 June 1837, cited in *Records of the Columbia Historical Society,* vols. 44–45 (1942–43): 217–20.

EPILOGUE

1. Many thanks to Catherine Corman; Betty Boyd Caroli, *First Ladies* (New York: Oxford University Press, 1987), xviii; John Milton Cooper, Jr., "Introduction," in *The White House: The First Two Hundred Years*, ed. Frank Freidel and William Pencak (Boston: Northeastern University Press, 1994), xvii; David B. Mattern and Holly C. Shulman, *The Selected Letters of Dolley Payne Madison* (Charlottesville: University of Virginia Press, 2003), 6.

2. Benedict Anderson, *Imagined Communities: Reflections on the Origin and Spread of Nationalism* (New York: Verso, 1991), 55–56. Margaret Truman, *First Ladies: An Intimate Group Portrait of White House Wives* (New York: Random House, 1995), 16, 354.

Acknowledgments

It is a cliché to say that biographers live with their subjects in a weird kind of marriage, one destined for divorce, and, if they are lucky, they like them when it is over. If they are *very* lucky, as I am with Dolley Payne Todd Madison, they can also leave their subjects having learned the larger lessons a single life can impart. Dolley shaped her world around bonds and connections with a wide circle of friends and family, demonstrating that no project, great—like establishing a government—or small—like writing a book—is possible without the cooperation and collaboration of a great many people of good heart. My luck holds on that score as well. The efforts on my behalf of the individuals and groups listed below have been enormous, and they all have tried to make this the best book ever. That it could not meet the standards they have set with their own work is my failing, not theirs.

Dolley Madison taught me a great deal about the importance of home. She and I have been supported financially and otherwise by several home institutions. This project began with my dissertation at Yale, and generous colleagues read early stages of this work and encouraged me to make it a second project, most especially my advisors and close friends, Nancy F. Cott and John Demos, along with Catherine Corman, David Brion Davis, John Mack Faragher, Glenda Gilmore, and Rachel Wheeler. The idea of a political biography was nurtured in the bosom of my first professorial home, Simmons College. Thank you to all my colleagues in the History Department—Keith Phelan Gorman, Laura Prieto, Zhigang Liu, and Marie McHugh. I was lucky enough to receive several grants from Simmons to fund my initial investigation and the memory of the institution-wide encouragement remains potent. Likewise, my present colleagues at the History Department at the University of California at Riverside have provided good cheer and valuable advice. I am particularly grateful to my chairs, Thomas Cogswell and Sharon V. Salinger, who adjusted my burdens in order to make a full-time faculty member meet the deadlines of a full-time writer. The extraordinary staff of the UCR History Department— Constance J. Young, Rosie Mamaril, Susan Komura, Christina Cuellar, and Rachael Beals Easterling—made all things possible. Many thanks to Dean Patricia O'Brien, the administration, and the Academic Senate for gifts of time and money.

For two years, my home was in Cambridge, Massachusetts, where I was the Evelyn Davis Green Fellow at the Radcliffe Institute for Advanced Study, under the watchful and wise eyes of Drew Gilpin Faust, Judith Vichniac, Paula Soares, Janice Randall, and the whole staff. Time at the institute was a rare treasure, and my fellow and sister Fellows were a steady source of encouragement and inspiration, especially Liz Canner, Lynn Festa, Beverly McIver, Stephen Kantrowitz, Linda K. Kerber, Susan Pedersen, Susan M. Reverby, Mark Robbins, Gwendolyn DuBois Shaw, James Steintrager, and Kevin Kopelson, who alerted me to the Dolley Madison-Lorelei Lee connection. As a visiting professor at Harvard, a new set of colleagues provided wisdom, laughter, and Hi-Rise muffins: Jane Kamesky, Jill Lepore, Joyce Chaplin, and the ones really in charge: Janet Hatch, Mary McConnell, Cory Paulsen, Gail Rock, and the whole staff.

As a former teacher of librarians and archivists, I worship them like gods. My work is only possible through theirs. All of my gratitude to:

Patricia Durisin, Gianna Carmel Gifford, Vivienne Brady Piroli, and Laura Lidano Saunders, at the Simmons College Library; Michael Colford and Scot Capehart at the Boston Public Library; Ellen S. Dunlap, John Hench, Caroline F. Sloat, Joanne D. Chaison, Laura E. Wasowicz, and Thomas G. Knoles, at the American Antiquarian Society; William Fowler, Conrad E. Wright, Peter Drummey, Brenda Lawson, Nicholas Graham and the Reading Room staff, Celeste Walker and the staff of the Adams Papers at the Massachusetts Historical Society; Fred W. Bauman, Ernest J. Emerich, Jeffrey M. Flannery, Joseph Jackson, Patrick Kerwin, Bruce Kirby, Michael J. Klein, Kathleen C. Mc-Donough, and most especially the late, much mourned Mary M. Wolfskill at the Library of Congress (Manuscript Division); Julie Helen Otto, reference librarian, at the New England Historic Genealogical Society; Phillip Lapansky, Library Company of Philadelphia; J. Stephen Catlett and Susan Webster, Greensboro Historical Museum; Gwen Gosney Erickson and Ann W. Upton, Friends Historical Collection, Guilford College; Kathe Chipman, Maine Historical Society; Kyle DeCicco-Carey, Harvard University Archives; Diane L. Dunkely, Daughters of the Revolution Headquarters Library; Patricia M. McDermott, U.S. Court of Appeals for the Federal Circuit; Jeanne Cross, David Mattern, Holly C. Shulman, and J. C. A. Stagg, Madison Papers; AnnaLee Pauls, Rare Books and Special Collections, Princeton University Library; Paula Kaczor Aloisio, Marilyn Dunn, Sarah Hutcheon, Kathryn Allamong Jacob, Jane Knowles, and Ellen Shea, Schlesinger Library, Radcliffe Institute for Advanced Study; Vicki Bloom, John Bloomberg-Rissman, and the staff of the Tomás Rivera Library at the University of California at Riverside; the staffs at the Widener Library at Harvard University, the Washington Historical Society, the Phillips Library of the Peabody Essex Museum, the American Philosophical Society Library; Jonathan Randolph at the Abbott Public Library and the Salem Public Library.

Like perfect guests, many patient, generous people sat through presentations and lectures that helped to develop my ideas about this project. Many thanks for the inspiration from: Susan Porter, Susan D. Ware, and the members of the Radcliffe Book Group; Laura Johnson and the students of her History and Literature seminar on biography at Harvard University; the Harvard History and Literature faculty seminar; and various audiences at Decatur House; Roger Williams Chapter, National Society Colonial Dames XVII Century; Dumbarton House, Headquarters for the National Society of the Colonial Dames of America; the Massachusetts Library Association; the American Antiquarian Society; University of Connecticut; the Radcliffe Institute for Advanced Study; James Madison's Montpelier; the Sulgrave Club; Tudor Place; the Massachusetts Historical Society; Yale Center for British Art; Winterthur Museum; Bostonian Society at the Old State House; Polly Logan Fund, Center for Women in Politics and Public Policy at the University of Massachusetts at Boston; the New England Seminar in American History at Clark University; DC Center for the Book and Washington Independent Writers; the Center for the Book, Library of Congress; the Historical Society of Washington; the Natick Indian Plantation and Needham West Militia Companies; Litchfield Historical Society; University of California Affiliates LIFE Society at the UCR Extension; Citizens' University Committee; the White House Historical Association; the U.S. Capitol Historical Society; the Society for the Preservation of New England Antiquities. The best audiences in the world are groups of alumnae and alumni, and I have been lucky enough to speak with graduates from Mount Holyoke College, Radcliffe College, Harvard University, Simmons College, and the University of California Alumni Parents Association.

Conference audiences and panelists have played a large part in the festivities. Thank you to all who participated in: the Berkshire Conference of Women Historians; "Working Out Her Destiny: Virginia Women Through Four Centuries," the Library of Virginia; "Thomas Jefferson and the Founding Fathers in Retirement," Robert H. Smith International Center for Jefferson Studies; the North American Society for Court Studies; the Western Social Science Association; and most especially, the Boston Area Early American History Seminar at the Massachusetts Historical Society, where Ellen Fitzpatrick offered some of the first public (and still the best!) comments on my work.

During this project, my respect for those who work to bring history to the public has only increased. I've had the good fortune to work with the best people in television, the documentary film makers: Catherine Allan, Ron Blumer, Ellen Hovde, Muffie Meyer, and Gerry Richman of Middlemarch Films, and Bob Uth, Glenn Marcus, Susan Schreiber of New Voyages Productions. Museum professionals were the inspiration for my first book and continue to amaze me. Many thanks to: Phyllis Silber, Goochland Historical Society; the National Park Service at the Todd House; Margaret Macon Boeker, Allison Enos, Randy Huwa, Lee Langston-Harrison, Susannah McClellan, Michael Quinn, Elizabeth Taylor, and the whole staff at James Madison's Montpelier; J. Stephen Catlett, William J. Moore, and the staff at the Greensboro Historical Museum, which houses the Dolley Madison Collection; Carrie E. Taylor at Monticello; Brian Lang, Donna Tully Dudley, and the Colonial Dames of America at Dumbarton House; Leni Preston, Wendy Kail, Judy Pratt, and everyone at Tudor Place; Cynthia Malinick, Carla Jones, Katherine Malone-France, and the staff at Decatur House; Amy Conroy and Jennifer Spencer at the Sewall-Belmont House and Museum.

As a professor, I have been blessed to associate with dedicated teaching assistants, who, in addition to relieving my pedagogical burdens, have taught me as well as our students: at Simmons College, the inspiring Tina McCusker; at Harvard, Katherine Alysia Grandjean; and at the University of California at Riverside, Jamie Mayhew Bufalino, Denise Rose Garrison, Michael Johnson, Tracy Ann Leach, Brendan Lindsay, Anne M. Longanbach, Moises Medina, Joy Rainbow Novak, Julia Nottberg, Lance Wollwage.

Many have helped along the way with the enormous task of researching Dolley's life and times. Sarah Goracke was my first researcher at Simmons College, Jennifer Cook took over the task; at UCR, Matthew Nakata helped out and the indefatigable and endlessly patient Anne M. Longanbach has brought this project to fruition. No scholar has had a more distinguished group of colleagues ready to help with questions large and small. The talented Cynthia Diane Earman tops the list; my "woman on the scene," Cynthia was my Washington connection to all things Dolley and never failed. My gratitude as well to "Dolley watchers": Rose Barquist, Doron Ben-Atar, George W. Boudreau, Kenneth R. Bowling, Susan Branson, Emily Burns, Barbara Carson, Patricia Cline Cohen, Minna Crasson, William diGiacomantonio, Dianna Diatz, Suzanne Cooper Guasco, Sarah Kristena Hagan, Donald R. Hickey, Carolyn Sung Hoover, Conover Hunt, Kathryn Allamong Jacob, Sarah Luria, Ann L. B. Miller, Kathryn Jacob, Richard Labunski, Charlene Boyer Lewis, James Lewis, Susan H. Perdue, Michael Rush, Holly C. Shulman, Woden Teachout, Fredrika J. Teute, and Rosemarie Zaggarri.

Like a White House squeeze, the crowd grows. So many people have offered their support and expertise. At the center of the crowd is "Team Dolley"—Jonathan N. Lipman (still my Favorite Ex-Husband), Lisa Cardyn (the best writer I know), Sarah Kristena Hagan (the ideal Educated General Reader), Lee Langston-Harrison, curator at James Madison's Montpelier, David B. Mattern, senior editor of the James Madison Papers, and Dolley's own editor, Holly C. Shulman—who read every word, and then some, of this manuscript. At crucial moments, J. C. A. Stagg stepped in to prevent tragic historical errors. Again, I wish that I could have fulfilled and followed through completely on all their wonderful suggestions, but in any case, I hope that my most heartfelt gratitude will compensate a bit for their time and energy.

Many others filled out the guest list with their support and feedback. Thanks to: Gail and Carley Altenburger, Joyce O. Appleby, Carol Berkin, Jacqueline Berger, Patricia Brady, Linzy Brekke, Gianna Gifford, Sylvia Frey, Richard Godbeer, James Horn, Dr. Bettye Kearse, Phyllis Karas, Barbara Healey and the Ladies of the Greystone Book Club, Donald R. Kennon, Cynthia Kierner, Robert Malcomson, Chandra Miller Manning, Tina McCusker, Jack Rakove, Carey Roberts, Frances C. Roberts, Kirk Davis Swinehart, Jeffrey Sharlet, Richard Sobel, Marjorie Spruill, Claire Ullman, Laurel Ulrich, Robert P. Watson, Priscilla S. Randolph, Myra Weatherly, Paul M. Zall. And many thanks and much love to Joseph J. Ellis, who, as James was with Dolley, has been unfailingly supportive of my efforts, always with one eye on the big picture and an attention to detail that is downright Madisonian.

Special thanks to the folks at the University of Virginia Press, who were there at the beginning and continue to be an important part of my work: Emily Grandstaff, Richard Holway, Penelope J. Kaiserlian, Mary Ann Lugo, Trish Downey Phipps, Ellen G. Satrom and, most especially, Mark H. Saunders. Nothing works without the technical folks, and my gratitude goes out to Bart Kats and Clare Johnson at UCR; Anne M. Sudbay at the Radcliffe Institute for Advanced Study; Allen Aloise, All-around Computer Guru; Michael and Elizabeth Baker and the staff at the Canyon Crest UPS.

Researching and writing is one task, turning it all into a book is another. I have been so fortunate as to be under the care of Christy Fletcher, agent extraordinaire, of Fletcher and Parry. Thank you for being my friend as well as my champion. All my gratitude to her colleagues and assistants, Emma Parry, Melissa Chinchillo, Kate Scherler, Beth Sullivan, and Liza Bolitzer, who was there when it all started. Everyone at Henry Holt has risen to the considerable task of turning an academic into a writer, most especially my editor, Jennifer Barth. "Long-suffering" is a cliché to be sure, but she has shown the patience of a saint and the good humor of the best kind of friend—one that will tell you the truth. Thank you, Jennifer—tell Abigail that we are done now.

Her assistants, Ruth Kaplan and Sam Douglas, aided by Patrick Clark, have suffered along with her, but provided me with everything I needed and more than I could ask for—sometimes even just ten more minutes. John Sterling believed in this project; I hope the final product justifies that faith and that I do the Alma Mater proud. Special thanks to Vanessa Mobley, and fervent blessings upon the head of Kenn Russell, managing editor, and Jolanta Benal, the best copy editor in the world—I am so grateful for their eyes and ears. Thank you, Raquel Jaramillo and Meryl Levavi for making this book a thing of beauty; you know that Dolley would appreciate *that*. I am so grateful to Claire McKinney, Kurt Miller, Annsley Rosner, and Angela Hayes for getting me ready to meet the world, and to Denise Cronin, Tom Nau, Janice O'Quinn, Lucille Rettino, Richard Rhorer, and Maggie Richards for getting the world ready for Dolley. Thank you, too, to Michael L. Kaplan, who always looks out for me.

As I ended Dolley's story with love, so I must end here with what some might call the "schmoopy" part. Dolley knew that love manifested itself only partly in words and mostly in practical care. Love and thanks to the "Ladies of Riverside," who fed me, listened to me, and laughed right on cue—Sharon Salinger, Juliette Levy, Lisa Geering Tomoff (and Lilia Dennison Geering Tomoff, in utero), Dale Kent, and Ann Goldberg. Just to show that such care is not limited by sex—Andrew Jacobs (the source of peace and gin), Kiril Tomoff, and Randolph Head were also perfect "Ladies." Some things never change—Jonathan Lipman still takes care of me, though I don't know what I did to deserve it. Cheryl Ann Burke from Java Sun, George Shubie and the staff of Shubie's, and Cheryl Duffy and staff at Jammin' Bread provided nourishment of all kinds. Cheryl Ostrander took care of my precious girls, Lydia and Teasel, when work took me away.

Kin—real and fictive—was the heart of Dolley's life, and so love to my "hearts"—my parents, Clifford and Mary Allgor, my big sister, Elizabeth, my brothers, Patrick and Christian, and my little sister, Corrie. Special love to my nieces and nephews, Danielle, Casey, Kiley, Jackson, and the Little Stranger. "Aunt" Dolley is pleased to make their future brighter. Dr. Mark Steinberg taught me some about the human mind and much about the human heart. Jacques, Nick, Peggy, Emily, Budd— all friends from another life, but who live in my heart, "fresh and full of sweetness." Finally, my two best teachers—the women to whom this book is dedicated—Gianna Carmel Gifford and Sarah Kristena Hagan. Their love for each other, and for me, demonstrates on a daily basis the power of the heart.

Illustration Credits

Index

About the Author

A professor of history at the University of California–Riverside, Catherine Allgor has received the George Washington Egleston Prize from Yale, the Lerner-Scott Prize from the Organization of American Historians, and the James H. Broussard First Book Prize from the Society for Historians of the Early American Republic. She was awarded a Bunting Fellowship from the Radcliffe Institute for Advanced Study for her work on Dolley Madison. Allgor lives in Riverside, California.